Lords of Cuzco

A HISTORY AND DESCRIPTION OF THE
INCA PEOPLE IN THEIR FINAL DAYS

CIVDAD
LA GRÃ CIVDAD ICAVE

sa ycorte real delos 30.71 reyns ynagas gñago del cuzco enmedio delleyn

circaenço pucara suchona

yobospa go

S. blas

ui roy pae gña

S. cristobal

pingo llonopam

curicancha

carmña

yawcaypata

uatanay mayo uno

uas picancha

uaca pucco

cui pata

S. sebas tian cachi

san cay uaú

yllapa cancha

pinasuau

cuci cancha

belen

cantoc uno ya

pomap chupa

cantoc uno egntol

corte del ynga

la gña

Lords of Cuzco

A HISTORY AND DESCRIPTION OF THE INCA PEOPLE IN THEIR FINAL DAYS

By Burr Cartwright Brundage

WITH DRAWINGS FROM HUAMAN POMA

UNIVERSITY OF OKLAHOMA PRESS

NORMAN

By Burr Cartwright Brundage

The Juniper Palace (New York, 1951)
Empire of the Inca (Norman, 1963)
*Lords of Cuzco: A History and Description of the Inca People in
Their Final Days* (Norman, 1967)

*The paper on which this book is printed bears the watermark of the
University of Oklahoma Press and is designed for an effective life of
at least three hundred years.*

Library of Congress Catalog Card Number: 67–15576

Copyright 1967 by the University of Oklahoma Press, Publishing Division of
the University. Composed and printed at Norman, Oklahoma, U.S.A., by
the University of Oklahoma Press. First edition.

This book
is for the rest of my small *ayllu*,
Christina and Anya, my daughter and hers

Preface

In 1963 my book entitled *Empire of the Inca* was published. That work was an attempt to give a connected account of the rise, maturity, and collapse of a state. All material, therefore, which did not necessarily forward or clarify the political story was rigorously omitted. It was the empire as an institution in which I was interested.

But the story of Tahuantinsuyo was more than that of an imperial office and more than that of the *sapa* or "only" Inca who filled that position. It was additionally the story of a caste. This caste surrounded the emperor, gave him its blood and its authenticity, provided him with many of his captains and administrators, and advised him with the wisdom of its old men. Nevertheless, it also lived a life apart from him, and profound dislocations were to arise from this polarity. This separation was only sketched in as background in the first volume. Here it is presented fully.

The Incas were not a true family, nor a clan, nor a tribe, nor even a nation. They were a caste built up out of a mixture of cultic households called *panacas* and traditional Peruvian *ayllus* reworked to fit into the system. Even this statement does not contain the whole of their secret. The Incas as a people are totally inexplicable if Cuzco, their capital, is not understood also for what it really was.

Cuzco today is what we mean when we employ the word "city." Under the Incas it was not a city in any sense of the word. It was an inner community of the households of sacred kings—all but one of them deceased—surrounded by a heavy outer shell of less sacred *ayllus*. It was not so much an area of residence, for Incas could and did on many occasions reside elsewhere, as it was a theater for an auto-intoxicated people, a stage most richly provided with props on which this people attempted to arrest history by reiteration. Like the two sides of a coin, this city and this people were inseparable. Therefore every alley, every terrace, every stone where possible, and every suburb of the ancient city has been searched in detail.

But this book is neither a sociology nor a guidebook. It is a history, for only in the chronology of change and repulsion to change—that is, in action—can the spirit of a people be felt profoundly. I have selected for investigation the period that begins roughly with the inception of Huayna Capac's rule, witnesses the coming of the Spaniards in 1532, and displays the confrontation between conquerors and conquered up to the year 1572. Only the first part of this period was covered in the previous volume which ended with the year 1533. Here the emphasis is on the deterioration of a people as they struggled on to their ultimate extinction which occurred, for all intents and purposes, in 1572.

I wish finally to draw attention to the lavish use of Quechua words and phrases in this exposition. No people can be reborn between the covers of a book if the most richly symbolic and creative part of their culture, namely their language, is neglected. I look to one of the most exceptional books in the English language as a model for this, Charles Doughty's *Arabia Deserta*. Dictionary citations for all words and phrases are given (an arrangement which should please the expert) since no particular system of transcription of Quechua sounds is used here. I myself am not as learned in the language as I would wish, and my purpose has been first and foremost to make the reader feel the integrity of the people being described rather than to impose on him a difficult or cumbersome orthography. To this end, and not for reasons of pedantry, their own words are here displayed.

Burr Cartwright Brundage

St. Petersburg, Florida
February 16, 1967

Contents

Part III: The Beliefs of the Last Reign

Part IV: War Enters the Great City

Contents

Part V: The Lords Perish

Maps and Table

I
The Lords Described

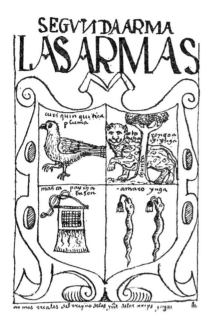

SECTION I.

The Hummingbird

IN THE SIERRA or *sallca* of southern Peru there is a pleasant valley not exceptional from the point of view of its situation—there are many Andean valleys more impressive— but certainly none more distinguished in its history. Through it runs the Huatanay River. At its lower end and at the point where the river turns suddenly through a gorge to join the Vilcañota, it widens out into a spacious bowl. In this hollow is situated Lake Lucre, anciently known as Lake Muina, on whose shores in hard battle was finally achieved that power which pointed the way to Tahuantinsuyo, the Inca empire. And here also in the year 1493, an adolescent Inca prince named Huayna Capac resided while awaiting both the death of his father the emperor and the birth of a son.

Once year later in the traditional ceremony of the first haircutting, the child who had been born was given his boyhood name Huascar, called thus after the brilliant red hummingbird whose feathers were used in the adornment of Inca princes. The father of "Hummingbird" was now legitimately the emperor; the mother was the emperor's sister Rahua Ocllo. The terraces and private apartments which were the scene and occasion of the fateful birth and naming were appropriately called Huascar Pata, "Hummingbird Terraces."

3

EL PRIMERO MES ✚ ENERO.
CAPACRAIMICAMAI
quilla

ponetencia yayunos del ynga
papac

The Hummingbird's People

IT IS USEFUL to sketch in some background here, for the child so born was to preside over the Inca people during the final days of their empire. He would in fact be counted as their twelfth and last independent ruler. He it was who would erode away their traditions, insult their mummies, and, removing himself from their midst, leave them without a protector. In his madness he was to carry them over the lip of disaster, and he was destined to slip with them into the abyss.

In the annals of humanity few people as noble as the Incas have so abruptly ceased to be, leaving only stones and the rubble of a cheapened culture behind them. *They* are the subject of this book, and whatever pertains to them, as they moved about in the eerie twilight of Tahuantinsuyo's demise, is a proper subject for our investigation. This then is a history of a people in the last days of their greatness.

In the early days, before Cuzco became their capital, they had been scattered bits of peoples. Some lived in small places in the warmer valley bottoms; some went about on the *puna*, shivering in the bleak air of that untillable part of the world and tending their llamas. They wove for themselves coarse woolen capes and kilts; their lank-haired women wore the blanketlike *lliclla*, pinned in front with a silver *tupu*, their only adornment. They were neither an elegant nor indeed a thoughtful people. When they were not expelled from their steadings by a stronger people and forced apart to live the mean lives of wanderers, they inhabited family yards called *canchas* wherein the gabled stone-and-mud houses were as drab as the fieldstone wall ringing them in. They struggled desperately for their harvests of potatoes, quinoa, and maize, and they stored the seed and the *chuño*, or desiccated potato flour, in bins made holy by their need. The earth was their mother, a slumberous being of many shapes, flat under their feet but cusped and white with snows on the horizon. Whether they walked in the valleys, their shoulders brushing the *cantut* bushes with dangling crimson flowers, or whether they carried their loads along the edge of the glacier, they perceived no heretical distinctions which would destroy the oneness of this great Earth Mother. They viewed the earth and all things in it mostly with that tired and unquestioning wonder that the easy and the affluent do not know.

But a ferocious power lurked in the bones and sinews of this people, a power which was ultimately to be harnessed by their leaders to the remodeling of the vast Peruvian world. As desperate and often hostile groups they had pretended to little, for merely staying alive had been enough. Once welded together in one tribal structure, however, their arrogance grew disproportionately. They stumbled as it by accident upon a new art of war, and for this mighty Moloch they gave up much. Their rise to greatness was accompanied by almost suicidal strife, but in the process their hardness was only intensified and their sharpness made more cutting. Their great captains climaxed this rise by giving them a well-defined and sacred mission, clad in which blazing light the Incas—a mere handful of people—stormed and seized the Andean world.

And so it came about that Incas no longer had to stoop to the *taclla*, the digging stick, or spread out their stores of potatoes in the sun and frost to dry—others did these things for them. They no longer shivered, for others wove for them and brought up fire logs from the deep *huaycos* in the montaña. Where once the hands of their women were gnarled and grimy, they were now soft and used for stroking and teasing downy birds from the jungles or feeding fish in the clear palace tanks. Their *ñustas* were the loveliest of young women, graceful because their mothers had been selected for grace, with cheeks as red as apples and teeth as white as snow. Their young men went about richly sandaled; they were alert, boastful, and confident on the field of battle. The melee, *aucanacuy*, was their constant theme; the *huaminca*, the thoroughly skilled and veteran warrior, was really the high priest of their culture.

But this too began to change; the interest of the Incas began insensibly to gravitate toward a stately kind of play acting, a posture of cult, as it were. They did not forsake their vocation of war, but that superb concentration on it which had brought them the empire in the first instance gradually eroded. By the early part of the reign of Huayna Capac, which is the period in which we begin, the Inca folk were performing a ritual ballet of ceremonies in the streets of Cuzco to the detriment of their solidarity and toughness as a people—for the very flesh and bone of their historic life had been, and could only be, war. Nor were the Incas to regain their former identity when the prince Huascar became emperor. This failure, added to the fewness of their numbers, inevitably paved the way for their downfall.

Certain traits of the Incas underlay their world view: the simplicity or single-mindedness of their character, their aggressiveness, their genius for organization and for ceremonialism, and lastly their grandiosity. Here, by way of introduction, however, it is perhaps single-mindedness which best unlocks the secret of Inca power.

Most peoples in history as they grow in numbers and importance tend to proliferate their interests, and while thus enriching their culture, they dilute the intense concentration of their early days. To this concept the Incas, in a way, are an exception. As already implied, they had grown out of a minor confederation of hamlets which, after many agonies, flowered into that single sacred site known as Cuzco. As this was happening, they created a matching legend about themselves: they were, so they told, *one* homogeneous people who, under *one* great chieftain, entered the area in times past and founded the city at *one* unique point in time. Underscoring the simplicity and austerity of this tale, they also told that the sun-god was their father and that he had commanded them to found Cuzco and subdue the whole earth to its empire. They had proceeded industriously to do this.

The singleness of this picture of their past and its lack of detail reveal to us a people who were not tempted to understand too many things. Their art was crude, symmetrical, and unimaginative, often abstract, almost, in fact, nonexistent. Their architecture was simplicity itself, the great blank walls of the *canchas* slightly inclining inward, entrances few

6

and narrow, heavy crowns of thatch and decoration at a minimum. At a time when Aztecs and other Mexican Indian groups far to the north of them were in full possession of the world's most complicated calendars, the Incas evinced no interest in astronomy. They evolved no real intellectual caste, as did the Mexican groups. They were undistracted by the knowledge of writing, and the imperial economy was simplicity itself. When the Aztecs of Mexico had merchants organized into recognized guilds, the Incas had none. The Aztecs had a highly sophisticated and spiritualized culture, enshrined in poetry of amazing beauty and enriched by a vast array of plastic symbols. The few relics of Inca poetry and prayer we have are more moving in their simplicity than in their elaboration. Cuzco was the universal point, the single radiant center of holiness whose aura lighted the whole empire.

Administratively there were, of course, numerous and significant urban communities in Tahuantinsuyo, but there was only one *Inca* city, one capital or *capac llacta;* thus it can be said there was only one true city. The empire itself the Incas carefully arranged into its simplest directions or four component parts, Cuzco being that place where all four regions of the world joined at the corners. A state of singleness was thus thought to exist geographically, defining outwardly the inner perfection of the Inca people.

DEPOCITODELIИGA
COLL CA

topa ynga
yupan qui.

Depocitos del ynga

Cuzcoquiti

THE SANCTION supporting the Incas lay in the fact that they alone of all people resided by right in the city of Cuzco. "That city," said the Jesuit Father Cobo, "was the richest found in the whole of the New World." The keenest of the *conquistadores*, Cieza de León, remarked that "Cuzco evinced a manner and a quality of greatness; it must have been founded by a people of exceptional presence." The Incas themselves called it "royal Cuzco," Topa Cuzco.

Careful descriptions of the city as it existed in its prime are rare. The following from the pen of Pedro Sancho de la Hoz is perhaps the best in short compass; it is also the official version of the first sighting of the city by the Spaniards, for Pedro Sancho was Pizarro's personal secretary.

Cuzco, because it is the capital city and the residence of the Inca nobles, is large enough and handsome enough to compare with any Spanish city. It is full of the palaces of the magnates, for in it reside no poor folk. Each one of these Inca magnates, as well as all the *curacas*, erect there their dwellings, although they do not permanently occupy them. Most of the houses are of stone; others have stonework only half way up; many are of adobe and all are very regularly built. The streets, all stone-paved and straight, cross each other at right angles and have each a stone-lined water channel running down the middle. The only fault the streets have is in being too narrow, for only one horseman can pass on either side of the gutter. The city is placed on high ground and many houses cling to the slopes above and many can be seen on the flat lands below.

The city lay along the spine of a narrow ridge between two fairly deep gullies, the whole shaped like a triangle pointed to the southeast. Within this triangle were the great palatial *canchas* or compounds of the dead and living kings and the town residences of the true or Capac Incas. Square or rectangular, each *cancha* was a separate walled ward in itself, separated from its neighbors by the darkened slitlike streets and by its own formidable blankness; entries were narrow and exceedingly few. The lower parts of some of those walls were essentially terraces, made of vast, roughly rusticated boulders; on top of these were the smaller, finely laid stones which the Incas called *checosca* or "worked," each one of which in its own intricate setting was a masterpiece. Over-hanging those sections of the stone walls which were the back walls of the gabled stone houses were ornate thatches, impermeable and neatly cropped mats often three or more feet thick. By walking up either one of Cuzco's two steeply pitched streets leading northwest, one soon could gain a vantage point for looking back on the city below. From the ter-races of this upper part of the city one could look down into the interiors of the *canchas* and note that they were cut up by means of a multitude of inner walls into complicated labyrinths. Here were the stone houses, some of them two and even three stories high, all pitched steeply and gabled. Their thatches made pleasing cubes, rectangles, squares, and other geometric patterns, and their weathered earth colors were in con-trast to the painted outer walls that could be occasionally seen. These *canchas* were worlds within worlds, crushed up against each other but sternly apart and, in this exclusiveness, almost belying the well-advertised cohesion of the Incas as a group.

Beyond the gullies, but still nearby, were the villas mentioned by Pedro Sancho, half-stone, half-adobe. These suburban clusters were generally on the higher ground and usually perched on one or other of the innumerable terraces round about. They offered overall a comfort-able yet busy effect. The wonderful patterns of the fieldstone faces of the terraces, the penciled green line of the maize growing on some of them, the softer precision of the house thatches, and the irregular, angled lines of the watercourses dropping in stages off the hillsides, all gave variety to the scene.

Beyond these wealthy suburban clusters and down the Huatanay

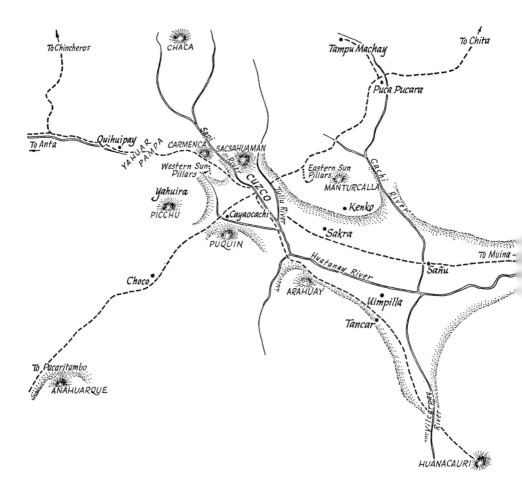

MAP OF CUZCOQUITI

Valley were the gabled mud huts or *chucllas* of the workers, arranged occasionally within low *cancha* walls. These walls were not, however, of the beautifully labored masonry or finely plastered adobes used in the city. They were, instead, of *pirca*, a rough mixture of mud and broken stone. The more pretentious of these mud dwellings were smeared with a rough plaster mixed with the sap of one of the local plants, a coating which settled firmly and gave a somewhat lacquered effect. Isolated *chucllas* often had fences of cactus planted around for protection and definition. Twenty-five thousand is a likely figure for the population of Cuzco between the rivers and such suburbs and clusters of houses as one could see close in to the city.

For some twenty-five miles around Cuzco in several directions such habitations housed the servants and minor officials of the Incas. Within this vast population a busy life went on. Here herds of llamas were penned in stone corrals or kept in the *canchas*, herds which belonged not only to the various religious establishments or royal estates but also to individual Inca magnates, just as many of the workers so belonged. Here also lived in organized squalor the people who tilled the soil, as well as those of the yearly *corvées* brought in from distant provinces to work in the quarries, to clean the streets and squares of Cuzco, to labor on new buildings, in the rope sheds, and at all the other menial tasks necessary to a metropolis. These were the *yanca ayllu*, "the worthless people." Interspersed among all these tiny but frequent settlements were the terraces and fields where the maize or quinoa ripened in elongated checkers of dark green or russet. Everywhere on the slopes enclosing the Huatanay were the country villas of Incas, of ambassadors resident at the court, or wealthy and respected *curacas* who had to reside among the Incas a part of every year. All of these last were "men of good blood," *alliyahuarcay*, "upper-class," and knowledgeable in the control and exploitation of their people.

Wherever one looked up or down this amazing valley, it was a land of garnered plenty. Here were the long strings of state warehouses, their many thatched and rounded domes a common sight on the hillsides, each cluster jammed with the specialized tribute of some one of the empire's subject people. Cuzco normally drew on harvests and goods from 150 miles around, and so into these capacious warehouses came a wide variety of goods: maize, beans, *uchu* or dried hot peppers, various dried fruits, *chuño*, salt, *charqui* or dried meat, salted or sun-dried fish. Other warehouses contained raw cotton and various grades of raw wool, as well as piles of roughly made garments already woven. Others were stocked with rope of various dimensions, all properly stored away in coils; some had containers of powdered dyes ready for use, sandals, or bronze crowbars for the quarrymen. There were even storehouses reserved solely for the feathers of hummingbirds and the scarlet *pillco*, as well as for the stuffed skins of conquered enemy chieftains of earlier days, now turned into *runatinya* or burlesque "man-drums." Only the implements of war were lacking in these depositories, the slings and slingstones, camp tents, halberds and battle-stars of bronze, stone-headed war hammers and the deadly *macana*, wooden sword-clubs of heavy *chonta*-wood, war paint, shields, and reed helmets; these were stored in the great fortress above the city.

The warehouses were slightly separated from each other or strung along in files with common walls. They were of rough *pirca* masonry and their tight thatches easily turned the summer rains. Their contents were accurately known, down to the last item, and the records of revenue and disbursements kept on *quipus* or knotted strings. From every hillside around Cuzco and lining the great road down the valley these warehouses stared out with their blank doors and windowless walls, mute testifiers to the abounding plenty of the Incas. It is of interest that the word which the Incas used to mean "wealth" also meant "empire."

Each day saw this peripheral landscape, mountain and riverside, come wonderfully to life as if Cuzco were the center of a vortex drawing all folk into its center. Long before the morning star had paled, the roads and tracks leading in from the lesser districts and pueblos were crowded with menials and servants mixed in with lesser noblemen and officers with their reports, all trotting with various degrees of haste through the half-darkness, coming to light the fires, prepare the food, or honor the levees of their Inca masters. The soft slapping of rope sandals, the grunting sounds of the trotting carriers bent almost double under their loads, the explosive spitting of some irritated llama pushed too rapidly, and the rough challenge of the soldiers zealously guarding the approaches to the city—these sounds were the morning melody of Inca history, imperial, organized, heartless, common, and magnificent.

Great numbers of the lesser people of this circumferential world were *mitmacs*, the so-called "newcomers," who represented almost every highland province in the far-flung Inca empire. The Incas had roughly divided this upper end of the Huatanay Valley into four administrative areas, corresponding to the four mammoth quarters of Tahuantinsuyo, the empire. At propitious times, but almost always after a conquered people had just been chained to the empire, *mitmacs* were brought in to Cuzco, each group organized into its traditional *ayllu* or lineage and each under its native *curaca* or headman. They were then settled in that area of the environs reserved for the particular quarter of the empire from which they came; here they were assigned fields and huts which theoretically were placed a distance from Cuzco relative to the distance of their homeland from the heart of the empire. This neatness, however, was more of a theory than an actuality.

Greater Cuzco was thus a model of Tahuantinsuyo in miniature. The nations represented here were all governed under a harsh code drawn up by their Inca masters and covering matters of cult, of work obligation, and of dress. For instance, it meant death if one wore the headgear typical of another nation. Thus in a short walk over one of the four main roads out of Cuzco one could see dumpy Collas from Lake Chucuito wearing over their long hair the high hats of their people, black wool cylinders narrowing to the top, or in another direction handsome Cañars from the equatorial north with their locks wound round their brows and the whole surmounted by a wickerwork coronet which looked like the rim of a fine sieve. On the hillsides back and above their *chucllas* were the tombs of their dead, each buried according to the ancestral custom and served by imported rites. Nowhere in history, perhaps, has the wide world been so small, yet nowhere has it been so divided, for, by imperial fiat, no one could wander from his assigned hamlet nor could anyone weave a cloth patterned differently from his nation's custom. The forces which bound this well-domesticated Andean world together were one language spoken and understood in common, one nobility over all, and one imperial master.

This world was Cuzcoquiti, "the Region of Cuzco," a great central province surrounding the capital city, containing at least twenty thousand families or approximately two hundred thousand persons and extending about thirty-five miles in all directions, to Vilcaconga on the west and Urcos on the southeast. Beyond Cuzcoquiti were the many provinces of the empire.

But everything centered in the *capac llacta*, "the rich city" of Cuzco, whose intimate and holy few acres of earth mothered the Inca people. The meaning of the word "Cuzco" is unknown. Possibly it is from a language other than Quechua, the official Inca tongue. If so, it is probably a pre-Inca name for the first settlement on the interfluvial ridge. Sarmiento, who had access to some early traditions, says that in an ancient tongue Cuzco meant "the stone which marks possession." This stone is what in Quechua is commonly called a *huanca* and acts as the guardian spirit of a place. In Inca lore the stone called "Cuzco Huanca" had originally been set up on a flat shelf of the lower part of the ridge. Here at any rate dwelled the local soul, identified in legend with one of the founders of the city.

This then was the land of whom it was said, "The Incas at first made themselves lords more by cunning than by force, for they were few and possessed few fields."

Down the Valley to Huanacauri

CUZCO was most regally placed. It was situated at the head of the Hautanay Valley in a capacious hollow affording satisfying sights, room enough for rich fields, and some protection from inclement weather. Two streams joined at the point of the city triangle to become the Hautanay. This river then flowed in a southeasterly direction some twenty-five miles down to Lake Muina, at which point it turned abruptly north, as we have noted, to join the Vilcañota through a narrow gap.

Standing today in Cuzco's central square, one can look down the valley and out east beyond the hills to the white patch on the horizon today called Apu Ausangate but then known as the mountain Vilcañota. This was the only snow-clad peak visible from Cuzco, so it is not to be wondered at that it was a *huaca*, a sacred object, of great importance in the life of the city. The community called Urcos, which we have seen marked the limit of the extension of Cuzcoquiti in this direction, lay on the far skirts of this vast white giant. Let us trace again this ancient path to Urcos, the so-called Collasuyo road, and see it as it was on that day when Huascar was born.

Leaving the city proper via Rimac Pampa or "the Field of the Oracles," one soon came to a small community much looked down on, as it was called Sakra, "Shantytown," no doubt the place where resided those domestic menials whose presence close to the city was desired. Across the river and parallel to it could be seen a smooth natural platform at the foot of the hills. This was Tancaray, "the Bramble Patch," where the dead were supposed to gather. Here, on All Souls' Day in

15

November, the mummies and bones of the ancestors were assembled and regaled during a three-day *taqui* or fiesta. The mummies were set up in positions of honor, censed, and given food to eat and *akha* to drink. Those few who had been killed by lightning were treated to exceptional honors, the clothes they had worn in life and the staves of authority they had borne being displayed with special ceremony. At this time the mummies were also provided with new garments. When the *taqui* was over, the dead were escorted back to their clefts in the rocks or to their tombs, the great ones being carried in litters on the shoulders of their descendants. In Tancaray one could be shown the corpse house, Acoyhuasi, where the mummy of the second Inca ruler was later to be secreted from the Spaniards, for he had been intimately connected with this area in the far-off days.

Nearby was Uimpilla, where could be seen an infamous Inca prison used for the detention and generally the demise of state criminals. This place was intimately associated with Arahua, the Gallows, which is still the name of the mountain on whose skirts it was situated and from whose rocks criminals were hanged by the hair or the heels. The lower slopes of Mount Arahua today show no trace of any structure. Within the stone walls of Uimpilla, at the foot of the rock, dampness, cold, starvation, filth, and impenetrable night had claimed during many reigns the lives and sanity of notable Incas who had offended majesty or who had unsuccessfully reached for power. The last reign of all was to see Arahua claim a veritable surfeit of Inca lives, some guilty, many innocent. The area today is quite barren; it lies due south of the airport. All that it has bequeathed to the present is a collection of meager huts called Tancarpata and an obsolete word in the language, *uimpillay,* "to hang."

Crossing the river back to the Collasuyo road again, neatly paved, walled on both sides, and lined with ferny *molle*-trees, we continue our journey.

We pass a fertile piece of land well grown with maize, green and lovely. This is Huanaypata, Correction Field, very famous in Inca history. Here had been the *chacras* of the Hualla Indians which the first Inca in his advance upon Cuzco had seized. Here he died and here he

16

passed on to his successor the mission of taking Cuzco, still only a mile or so away. A short stroll down the road beyond this point brings us to Sañu. There is said to have been here a zoological garden wherein the Incas kept specimens of the three-toed rhea, the South American ostrich, brought in from districts farther south. Here also were salt springs and the elaborate evaporation pans from which the Incas drew quantities of this precious commodity. Today Sañu is called San Sebastián and possesses a lovely decrepit church and a well-known image of the Virgin. Nor have the people of San Sebastián forgotten those days when the Inca lords ruled them; they still flip drops of *akha*, before drinking, to the pagan gods whom they call the *machu* or "grandfathers," they still invoke the river, the mountains Ausangate, Senca, and Pachatusan, and they give the care of their flocks to the Earth Mother. In this area the river could be glimpsed off to the right where it ran straight, contained within sloping masonry walls, a gigantic masonry flume elaborately engineered to prevent erosion and flood. The Incas had walled it thus all the way to Muina.

Sañu originally had been a rival of Cuzco. As the earliest Inca bands moved up the Huatanay Valley, Sañu had stood as a roadblock barring their further progress. It was the marriage of the second Inca *sinchi* to a princess of Sañu which created that first partnership of peoples which would ultimately result in the creation of the Inca caste. Thus closely confederated, the men of Manco and the men of Sañu had stormed the head of the valley together in the first push on Cuzco. So close was this alliance that the men of Manco even took over as their own the special *huaca* of Sañu, a mountain called Huanacauri on the south side of the river.

Of this *huaca* chilling stories were told. It was believed by the people of Sañu that they had emerged from this bleak mountain after the great world Flood. As their *pacarina*, or place of origination, this mountain and its associated sites possessed therefore a singular holiness. This holiness had been made manifest in a sky-god who in the mists of early time had gouged ravines out of the surrounding massif with giant boulders hurled from his sling. Even more concretely, it had been manifested in a sorcerer or shaman whose name was Rainbow, Huanacauri, and who therefore was a most dire portent. He sat alone up in the un-cultivated pasture land, the sloping meadows of *ichu* grass. He was not only the iridescent spirit of the place but also contained within himself the fertilizing power of a father of his people. It had been he with his burning red eyes who had magically turned into stone two legendary creatures, later to be identified as two brothers of Manco Capac, the first of the Inca rulers. A crude and curiously shaped stone, rather small and roughly comparable to one human form crouched upon another, was all that was left to tell of this miracle. It was, of course, oracular as befitted the spirit of the rainbow and the place. That stone was indeed the congealed history of the Inca folk, for it was the locus within which was to reside most intimately the warlike soul of the Inca people. Following the absorption of Sañu into the growing federation which was to become the Inca caste, this fetish became one of the two central *huacas* in the lives of the Incas as a people, the other being Inti.

The Huanacauri idol was kept in a special masonry sanctuary up on a windy and stony ridge. Only the most casual relics of these buildings exist today, the whole area having been heavily mined for buried treasures by both Spaniards and Peruvians. The sanctuary was called either Chimpu, a word for "halo" (with reference to the appearance of the rainbow), or Kahua, meaning "the Lookout," for it was from here that Manco Capac had his first sight of his holy city. It stood in an open field two thousand feet above Cuzco, which can be glimpsed far in the valley below. But more than that can be seen from this splendid eminence, for with the white teeth of Salcantay and Ausangate equidistant on the horizon at opposite points of the compass, a significant portion of the *sallca* of southern Peru is enclosed within the sweep of one's view. The processional way up to this height had been paved, leading out of Sañu to cross the river. It passed close to a community of Chachapoya *mitmacs* who had been settled up the gully of the Huilcarpay. This stream it crossed via three stone bridges placed almost side by side, at a place in the ravine called Huarmichaca, Bridge of the Women. At an open place on the ascent, not as steep as the surrounding area, was the site of Matahua, a field in which, according to lore, the Men of Manco halted to make their hardscrabble potato plots and to endow the second Inca ruler with the regalia. No place today is archaeologically recognizable as Matahua but it was a singularly holy station in Inca history. Several crude rocks outcropping on the dull slopes nearby were said to be Huanacauri's sons, so one blew them kisses in passing. They had been turned to stone for their crimes.

Here on Huanacauri, Inca boys took new names and became men in the initiation rites which opened the Inca year.

SECTION 5. *Huanacauri to Muina*

IN THE DAYS before the Incas had formed themselves into a caste, the folk of Sañu had been a community of Ayamarca Indians. Beginning with Sañu and spotted down both sides of the Huatanay Valley as far as Muina were other *ayllus* of this tough people. The fact that the Men of Manco had weaned Sañu away from its independence and into alliance with them did not prevent frequent and violent passages between Inca and Ayamarca in the course of the years. The Ayamarcas were vigorous farmers and aggressive warriors, and they were led by daring *sinchis*. At one point in Inca history they even abducted the young son of one of the Inca rulers, thus forcing on Cuzco an accommodation favorable to them. But those wild days had long since faded into the mists of history, and the *curacas* of the eighteen Ayamarca pueblos were now confederate Incas of the Tocay Capac *ayllu*. They no longer felt any particular tribal cohesion; like the various *mitmac* pueblos spotted among them, they were only a part of Cuzcoquiti, albeit from their militant tradition, not an insignificant part.

We noted previously a community of Chachapoya *mitmacs* across from Sañu. A people formidable in battle themselves, they had been introduced among the Ayamarcas as a kind of rural police to warn them against any memories of past greatness that might lead to discontent or insurrection. These people were a thousand miles from their montaña homes across the deep canyon of the Marañón, a road they could never hope to tread again without the permission of their masters. The Chachapoya men who were not in the valley on garrison duty (their main form of tribute) worked their plots at the foot of Mount

Huanacauri or on the slopes of Carmenca or dug under skilled supervision to keep their irrigation ditches clear. They were easily distinguished from the Ayamarcas in their headgear; they wore narrow *llautos* or stringlike turbans wound tightly around their brows. Of these interesting people, the great traveler Cieza de León said:

> These Chachapoya natives are the least dark and the most graceful of all the Indians I have seen in the New World, and their women are so lovely that it is small wonder that the Incas prized them and carried them off to their temples.

Four miles beyond Sañu was another Ayamarca community called Oma (today San Jerónimo). The people of this *ayllu* originally had been notorious enemies of Cuzco. After coming under the dominion of the Incas, they had been granted the privilege of wearing the earplugs, but were at the same time not allowed to cut their hair short. They were thus confederate Incas and therefore noblemen, but they were not lords. In the dry months just before the coming of the December rains their women had been accustomed to spin thread for the fine breechclouts which their youths would assume as signs of their manhood. This pleasant family spinning had been taken up by the Incas into their calendar of festivities, just preceding the *akha*-brewing and it sometimes gave its name to the month of October. This whole section of the valley had once been hostile Ayamarca territory; now the smokes of their many fires rose peacefully from the valley floor or wavered up the steep slopes on either hand. There were no towns as we know them but only scattered small clusters of houses and *canchas,* each with a name. Oma (Head) itself was in no sense a town such as San Jerónimo is today.

Two miles beyond Oma one came to the Narrows. Here the mountains became steep, shouldering their way in on both sides of the river and creating the Acoya Puncu, Sand Gate, the possession of which in that middle stretch of the valley had once made the Ayamarcas such a redoutable people. Here at a place called Huanacancha (possibly to be identified with Sailla today) the Men of Manco were reputed to have made their first stop on the historic trek to Cuzco. Here also the greatest of Inca conquerors, Pachacuti, once and for all destroyed the Ayamarca power in a last terrible battle, after which contest the Huatanay Valley was incontestably an Inca appanage. Today's tourist, glancing up at the mulberry-colored dirt slopes around Sailla, with difficulty reconstructs the events of those days when the Incas were forcing the Narrows, and he strains to hear the dry clatter of their battle and the hoarse shouts of the attack—"haycha! haycha!"—almost swallowed in the valley's silence. He looks upward and wonders which one of the heights was Llulpac Turo (Pure Clay) on the summit of which the Inca people gravely offered to the Creator young children gaily dressed, regaled with *akha,* and then strangled to the approving murmurs of the beholders.

Emerging from the Narrows—only about three miles of the valley's total length—terraces and villas of the Cuzco magnates again came into evidence, especially in the area around Quispicancha, Crystal Enclosure, on the north side of the river. Many handsome apartments and thatched villas here attested to the attraction of these purlieus. It was in Quispicancha on the hillside facing south where the emperor, Huascar's father, underwent a thrillingly close escape from death in his youth. His uncle, who had been ruling for him during his minority, had conspired to have him assassinated at a drinking fiesta, the plot almost succeeding. It was the steadfast loyalty of another uncle which saved the adolescent emperor. In the melee the prince had been pushed through a high window in the drinking hall by members of his bodyguard who then swung back to die in his behalf. Fortunately, loyal troops who had been dispatched from Cuzco arrived just in time. Little is left today of these ruins.

Five miles beyond Quispicancha, continuing down the beautifully paved Collasuyo road, the traveler suddenly debouched into a spacious bowl marking the lower end of the Huatanay Valley. In those days it was filled with marsh and lake. Thickets of *totora*-reeds lined the shores and filled the shallower parts of the lake. The road which was elevated drove straight into and through this marsh as though it were an aviary, for it was full of flamingos and ducks of many varieties. In those days this region was by far the most beautifully appointed part of the Hua-

][Panticalla Pass

MT. SAUASIRAY

MT. VERONICA

MT. PITUSIRAY

Machu Picchu

Ollantaytambo

Yucay

Calca

Pampacahuana River

Pachar

Anta River

Huchuy
Cuzco

ANDES MTS.

Urquillos River

LAKE
CORICO

LAKE HUAYPU

Chincheros

Huarocondo

LAKE PIURAY

CUZCO

MT. SALLCANTAY

Sillapampa

BASIN OF ANTA

MT. ANAHUARQUE

MT. SORAY

CHINCHAYSUYO ROAD

Anta

MT. HUANA

Ichupampa

Villaconga
Pass

)[[

Yaurisque

Chinchaypucyo

CONTISUYO ROAD

Tantar

Sumaro

TILLCA
(MOLLEPATA)

Pacaritambo

Limatambo

Marcahuasi

Cusipampa River

Bridge
To Northern Peru

Cotapampa

To the Coast

Apurimac River

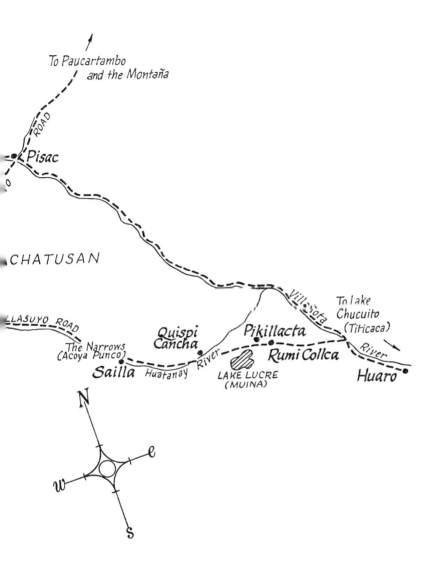

To Paucartambo
and the Montaña

ROAD

Pisac

CHATUSAN

To Lake
Chucuito
(Titicaca)

Vilcanota

LLASUYO ROAD

Quispi
Cancha

Pikillacta

River

The Narrows
(Acoya Punco)

Rumi Collca

River

Sailla

Huatanay River

Huaro

LAKE LUCRE
(MUINA)

N

e

w

s

NEAR ENVIRONS OF CUZCO

tanay Valley—its emptiness and bleakness today present an unhappy contrast.

Here stood once the city of Muina surrounded by a multitude of outflung dwellings. Muina was in the early days to the lower end of the valley what Cuzco was to become to the upper. But a long series of desperate encounters had marked the relationships between Muina and the arrogant young Cuzco. Muina was the greater and the older city and had fought the upstart people from the other end of the valley with determination. Her power rested on her command of the routes leading out of the valley; she had exercised this power in conjunction with Pinahua, a sister settlement of which modern Oropesa is perhaps the successor. This compact little world over which Muina presided—before the Incas finally broke it—was a separate culture.

Customarily in those days a community depended for its security on a *pucara*, a fortified height nearby which could be stocked quickly for siege. Muina did not have such a *pucara*; she must therefore have felt singularly in command of her destinies. She was able not only to involve Pinahua in her battles but also to summon up the forces of Antahuaylillas, Huaro, and Urcos behind her. Indeed, all of these communities must have formed an early state, no doubt confederate, under the presidency of Muina.

The history of the stirring events as the two deadly antagonists, Cuzco and Muina, anciently sparred can be briefly told. Little indeed is known, and not all of that is certain.

The Ayamarca confederation which controlled the center valley had been able for a considerable time to contain Cuzco, backed up as it was by at least the neutrality of the state of Muina, and undoubtedly at times by her actual aid. In the days of the third Inca ruler, Cuzco was too weak to conceive an aggressive foreign policy, so the loose Ayamarca *ayllus* felt no pressure from that side. Rather it was Muina which decided to funnel its armies up through the Narrows and attack the Incas, who were at that time under a mediocre leader, Lloque Yupanqui, "Honorable Javelin."

This encounter was the first recorded meeting between the two states. It carried in it the germs of all later Inca history, for the leader of the Muina forces knew of a god far greater than any the Incas at that time had. This god was not just a common Peruvian *huaca*; he was a *viracocha* and was specifically referred to as the "Only Lord in the Universe." So wonderful were his oracular powers that he was able to indicate to the aged and impotent Lloque Yupanqui a wife who would provide him with a son. The correct historical interpretation of this reputed miracle is probably the temporary subjugation of Cuzco and the Ayamarcas to Muina. At any rate, the prestige of Viracocha was solidly established in Cuzco at this time. Later on, in a most remarkable development, the cult of another Viracocha, called Hatun, "the Great," situated in nearby Urcos, was to become the foundation of the imperial religion supporting Tahuantinsuyo.

By the time of the sixth Inca ruler, Cuzco had consolidated its own end of the valley, strengthened and integrated its water supply, and had produced its first crop of able fighting captains. Muina was raided by Cuzco, but the effect was not lasting. A more successful raid was that undertaken by her seventh ruler. By the reign of the eighth ruler of Cuzco, the state of Muina was fully alert to its danger, and a frontal attack launched by the Incas was repulsed. The strategic problem involved in Muina's basic inaccessibility was finally resolved for the Incas when they crossed the divide over into the Vilcañota Valley and were thus enabled to take the state of Muina in the rear, in this way also avoiding having to fight their way again through the Narrows held by the Ayamarcas.

We know nothing about the details of this all-out effort, but when the campaign was ended, the *curaca* of Muina had been destroyed, the Ayamarca people crippled, and their leader, the Tocay Capac, removed. The state of Muina, which included Pinahua, Huaro, and Urcos, was now for the first time garrisoned and a formidable Inca captain assigned as its first resident governor.

At this point the course of Andean history was deflected. The Inca emperor who had mastered this important state and its satellites was deeply impressed by the power of Viracocha, the god of the region, as we have seen above, and adopted him as his own, even taking his name. Thus the eighth Inca ruler became for history the emperor Viracocha

Inca. When Muina and the Vilcañota communities lost this potentially imperial god to the deeply religious Incas, the doom of that city and its satellites had been sealed, for Viracocha would be used to provide the sanction for that empire in which Muina was to be submerged.

But Muina, under the stern eye of Huallpa Rimachi the governor, filled the role of a vassal with reluctance. So it came about, in those dark and turbulent days when the Chancas from the far north almost hammered Cuzco into submission, that Muina arose and along with the Ayamarcas attempted to bring Cuzco down from behind. When miraculously the Chanca danger had passed, Pachacuti, the ninth Inca ruler, whose name means "Cataclysm," turned upon Muina and her confederates and wreaked savage vengeance upon them. The great battle was fought at the Narrows near the place called Huanacancha mentioned above. The *curaca* of the Ayamarcas succumbed and disappeared into the frozen night of an Inca dungeon. Ordered up as a holocaust by Pachacuti, Muina's walls were breached and tumbled down and its people scattered. As a functioning city, it almost certainly was destroyed at this time, to become overnight a *purun llacta*, "a ruined city," haunted by apparitions of blood and the unsuccessful ghosts of its once hopeful past.

Around the year 1550, Cieza de León described the general site as follows:

> In Muina there is a marsh full of sloughs across which carries the great embankment and its paved road. In Muina are large edifices, all today ruined and undone. It is said that at the time when Francisco Pizarro first entered Cuzco with his Spaniards, there were found in and around this settlement vast quantities of gold and silver and even more of the finest weaves of cloth. Some Spaniards told me that there had been a stone statue here, the size of a man, clad in a long garment and holding a string of beads in his hand, as well as other forms and figures. These were a part of the pomp of the Incas, for they wished the images to last. Some were idols they themselves adored.

The whole basin, over which brooded the smoking and looted ruins of the city, was soon parceled out to the great Inca families and the *curacas* who had remained loyal during the war with the Chancas. Gangs were brought in, new and extensive terracing undertaken, new water channels dug, and luxurious villas built. It soon became a rural paradise for the ruling Inca caste, who now hunted in the *puna* round about, fished in the reedy lake, ate from gold and silver plates cast from Muina's wealth, watched the drenching summer rains from under safe thatches, and enjoyed the winter sunshine on their terraces. The great earthworks mentioned above pushed across the swamp to carry the new extension of the Collasuyo road southward, a route which ultimately would take Inca conquest far beyond the Lucre Basin.

In the near vicinity of the wreckage—perhaps on the razed site itself —there would shortly arise a new kind of community, a *churana llacta* or "warehouse city" symbolizing the Incas and all their works. The ruins of this site are known to the traveler today by the modern name of Pikillacta, Flea Town. Very likely the Incas at that time called it Rumi Collca, "Stone Bin," which name is now applied only to its spectacular southeastern entryway half a mile away. Into the large walled area of this unusual storage city on the high knoll overlooking the end of the Huatanay Valley poured over the years the tribute of much of the southern part of the empire. Here in open corrals and bins, thatched cubicles, or cofferlike rooms the tribute was stored, having first been checked in and then recorded on string *quipus,* themselves packed away in archives. Great numbers of workers must have been employed in this labyrinth, moving sacks, sorting bales, measuring piles, and feeding and caring for the livestock. Here also was quartered a permanent garrison to guard this accumulated wealth, and here lived the Inca commissioner and his secretaries.

Inside it there was a maze of walls, a veritable checkerboard of containers. *Pirca* walls twenty feet high enclosed the whole and there were only two gates, one the southern entrance already mentioned, the other the exit leading down the hill to the highroad to Cuzco. The southern entrance lay in a saddle of the hills easy to guard and blocked by a rampart. All traffic had to siphon through a double portal in this wall, which was at this point topped by an observation tower. All those having their business directly with Cuzco were shunted through one gate, while the tribute from the south moved through the other into a walled runway funneling into the depot area proper.

The visitor today stands among these weedy walls and wonders at those who conceived so cunningly the conservation and piling up of man's surpluses. Why did not such a people last forever?

Somewhere in this lovely basin, in some stone apartment long since demolished by the Spaniards, had been born the prince Huascar, the events of whose reign form the scaffold of this book. His youthful father, Huayna Capac, had been sojourning here, and here it was that the news of the death of his father had reached him.

A few miles beyond Rumi Collca one entered the fertile embayment of Antahuaylillas, Huaro, and Urcos, formerly the other half of the state of Muina. One was now in the Vilcañota Valley. With Urcos and its sacred hill of Viracocha, its *pacarina*, one reached the end of Cuzco-quiti in this direction.

SECTION 6.

The Three Roots of the Inca Stock

As Huascar was growing up, the Inca people were at the peak of their grandeur. The shadow of one *pakuyoc*, one Inca who wore the earplugs, seen stretched out on the most distant hillside of the great empire, was enough to throw terror into a whole community. Nevertheless, the frightful excesses of the Incas as warriors, their ubiquity as administrators, the monopoly of communications which they held so stringently over the whole Andean world, were as nothing compared to the splendor of their descent. Wherever they went they moved with the ease and arrogance of a true aristocracy. The knowledgeable

28

Polo de Ondegardo said of them, "From what I have learned, the real aspiration of the Incas was the subjugation of all men—a thing I have never heard imputed to any other people."

The fact that their claims of descent would seem to us today confused and illogical had no bearing on the matter. Every Inca was a "Sun child," an *Intip churin*. Inti, that fetish they had early identified with Punchao, God of the Day, was their father whenever they wished to look back for validation of their aristocratic mission. He was their father as he was, of course, the father of every highborn woman of the caste, *palla* or *iñaca*. He was also the father of every Inca girl or *ñusta* and of every Inca youth or *auqui*. These were then the lords and dames, the princes and princesses—never more than a handful in number—of Tahuantinsuyo. No caste in history was ever more aware of its apartness from the common herd of mankind.

Every Inca was also a lineal descendant of Manco Capac, the legendary first Inca who wandered over from the Apurimac watershed toward Cuzco. They were *Mancop churin*, "Manco's children," and this title defined for them their *ayllu* or house. In this sense they were thus all members of the august line of the Capac Ayllu, that extended family whose founder had been Manco, the man to whom Inti had conceded his great mission.

Manco's consort had been Mama Ocllo, and Incas were accustomed to swear by her holy womb. In the legends she sometimes appears under the name Mama Huaco, "the Lady of Fangs," for she had a bloodthirsty, Medusa-like side to her nature. No one can doubt that the name Mama Ocllo, "Pure Lady," is that of the great and universal Earth Mother, here in her avatar as a corn goddess. Sauscro, the holy *chacra* just outside the eastern entrance to Cuzco, belonged to her, and *akha* made from the maize grown there was offered to her image. Thus on their mother's side all Incas and *pallas* came from the sacred earth.

Inca men had another father, Huanacauri, that curious *huaca* already described which had been the *pacarina*-spirit of the Sañu people. As we have seen, Huanacauri was the embodiment of a tabooed mountain, as well as the petrified remains of two of the legendary three brothers of Manco Capac, to say nothing of being the oracular power of the

29

Rainbow. In the knighting ceremony, the *huarachicoy*, the young Inca braves received the symbols of their manhood and their warrior's vocation from Huanacauri whom they addressed as "our father." And when the Inca armies trooped out to the frontiers of conquest, they carried Huanacauri with them as the *huaca* of their indomitability. Huanacauri thus defined their common dedication to war as the most select and aristocratic activity of mankind.

Thus Inti gave them their prerogatives, Manco gave them their *ayllu*, and Huanacauri gave them their ideal. Caste, family, and war therefore are the three touchstones by which one undertakes to delineate this people.

SECTION 7. *The Incas as a Caste*

THE WORD "INCA" is untranslatable. Or perhaps we should rather say that we do not have an etymology for it. "Lord" is as good a rendering of its meaning as any. A man of this caste was addressed simply as "Inca," which therefore carried the sense of "sir" or "excellency" or "lordship," and his son—once initiated—became an *auqui*, which word also did duty for "noblemen" in general.

The visible signs of the Inca man were three in particular. He wore around his forehead the *llauto*, a narrow band in the front of which were generally fastened two small feathers and a *canipu*, which was a small silver plate. Depending on its shape, the *canipu* identified him as belonging to either Upper or Lower Cuzco. But these items stressed his affiliation, not his caste. The latter was denoted by the earplugs, gold, silver, or worked wood, depending on his status within the caste. The lobes of his ears had been slit during the *huarachicoy* and larger and larger plugs inserted until the size required was attained. An ear torn in the wars was a tragedy for an Inca inasmuch as he could not properly display his caste after such a mishap. The Incas were always and foremost *pakuyoc*, "earplug men," or *cori rincri*, "golden ears." Thirdly, they were identifiable by their closely trimmed hair.

All other races and groups, with the occasional exception of their *curacas* individually, were of "worthless blood," *yanca ayllu*, and the contempt with which the Inca viewed such beings was rich and unmitigated, his own unmatched creations in war and statecraft proving to him, if proof were needed, the abyss that separated him from all other nations. He had the privilege of secret confession of sins, while for all other groups in the empire, confession was a public matter and a part of state control. The basis for all of his arrogant claims to privilege was the fact that his ancestors were the first of all men to appear after the Flood and lay claim to the land.

But there were, of course, gradations in his own ranks. Of these we can discern at least three.

The *Capac Incas* were the true Incas, being incontestably descendants of Manco Capac, of absolutely pure blood on the paternal side and of at least high birth in all levels of the maternal side. Besides being legitimate, some were also *curac*, "the senior one" of their brothers, thereby possessing exceptional prestige. All of them were related to the emperor. Of right they and only they resided within the sacred triangle of Cuzco. In the days of which we are speaking there were probably not more than three or four hundred of these adult Incas. All of them can be considered to have been great earls or true "Cuzcos"; they alone staffed the Inca armies at the top and sat in the royal council. Cuzcoquiti and the empire belonged to them; indeed, by charter from the Sun, the whole world belonged to them. This was the reason for that special gravity of deportment found in them and evidenced in the proud personal name so many of them bore, Yupanqui. Only their wives were the true *pallas*. Counting the legitimate members of their families, there were probably no more than eighteen hundred Capac Incas, men and women, and children, at any one time—an astounding concentration of the world's best people.

Recruitment into this upper class, however, was possible. Foreign princesses of exceptionally high caste in their native lands could be equated with *ñustas*, that is with fullblood Inca girls, but with the patronymic of their origin added. If such a girl came from the tribe of Huancas, she was a Huanca *ñusta*, if from the tribe on the shores of Lake Chucuito she was a Lupaca *ñusta*. Such girls, when given in marriage to Capac Incas, immediately became *pallas*, and their issue were thenceforth considered to be legitimate Incas.

The *Hahua Incas*, "Outer Incas," imitated the Capac Incas in almost all respects. They wore the earplugs, claimed Inca privileges, and lived in the environs of Cuzco. They could not claim such purity of blood as the magnates, and as a rule they were not concerned with policy. Some of the groups wore their hair long. Many of them were related by blood or marriage to the Capac Incas. In this class there were two levels, the confederate Incas and the sons of the royal concubines.

Many of the ancestors of the confederate Incas had been granted Incahood as a favor in the days of Pachacuti, since which time, of course, many of their descendants had been freely mingling their blood with the true Incas, and these confederates were classed as *caylla ayllu*, or "close relatives." The founders of their houses had all come from Cuzcoquiti, having been members of such tribes as the Papris, the Mayos, Quihuars, etc. It had been the historical trauma of the Chanca war which had created for Cuzco in A.D. 1438 the need for more fighting men than it had available at that time. In return for their services in those dark days, Pachacuti had extended to the few groups loyal to him the privilege of the earplugs and had given them *ñustas* to be their wives and *chacras* and llama herds for their livelihood. Of course, only the *curacas* and a few of the important men in these tribes received the earplugs. The commoners remained, naturally of "worthless blood."

Since that time, extension of Inca privileges had continued, although on a reduced scale, for not only had those original marriages early begun to produce numbers of new Hahua Incas, but succeeding emperors created additional patentees. These Outer Incas had the honor of living in the neighborhood of Cuzco, although they also retained their privileged domiciles more distantly in the *ayllus* to which they belonged, and back to which they could be sent if some singular effort were demanded of that community. One might guess that their numbers never exceeded fifteen thousand. Gifted captains of far distant people who fought in the Inca armies or lordly *curacas* of kingdoms which adopted a pro-Inca policy were also admitted to the caste and given each a *takya huarmi*, an "unchangeable woman" of Inca blood, who immediately assumed the place of the first or legitimate wife, displacing her who had previously held that honor. Her progeny were, of course, Incas by birth.

The second group of Hahua Incas were the sons of the emperors by their ordinary concubines, presumably a very numerous group. It can be inferred that the status of these Incas varied greatly, ranging from moderately influential to negligible, depending on the emperor's interest in the mother. These Incas, although they lived on lands near Cuzco granted by the state, wore their hair long. They served as junior officers in the armies, but were denied important provincial posts. They were looked upon as a potentially troublesome group, for they seem to have had no *ayllus* to which they belonged, whereas the first class of Hahua Incas did. By the time of Huascar, they had probably become a truly professional group of army officers. They were free knights with immunities, and in return for this status they fought for the empire.

While the Capac Incas' policy, guidance, and social definition centered in Cuzco, it was the Hahua Inca living in the environs who performed the chores of the empire, officering the armies, bringing in and dispensing the vast revenues of Tahuantinsuyo, gathering information and representing the emperor in many ways and in many distant provinces. Under the earls, they were the knights. Their prerogatives in certain areas were hereditary. Incas from the Anta people, for instance, by charter right provided the empire with its overseers of the royal roads. The administration, upkeep, and toll collection of all bridges, an equally significant office, were the prerogatives of the Acos Incas. Mayo Incas were the imperial executioners. Papris and Chillquis were the provincial inspectors. Confidential informers for the government were chosen from the Quilliscachis, an unsavory prerogative. The Huaro Incas specialized as confessing priests for their caste.

The careers of these Hahua Incas, when young, reveal how the caste educated its members. A Capac Inca would have of course, besides his legitimate children, others by secondary wives and concubines. Some of the secondary wives themselves carried social caste in their own right so that their children by the magnate, both male and female, would become Hahua Incas or the equivalent. When quite young, these children were assigned by their fathers to serve as pages and maids-in-waiting either in the emperor's retinue or the *coya's*, in one of the *panacas*, or in the establishment of one of the magnates or *pallas*. When they came of age, the boys assuming the earplugs in the *huarachicoy*, the girls combing out their hair in the *quicuchicoy* (the menstruation rite), they were released from their apprenticeship and considered to be adults. In the above ceremonies they had been sponsored by older men or women of the pure Inca blood. Thus it often happened that, when they then took their permanent adult names, they adopted those of their sponsors, thereby allying themselves with great Inca families in a system half-clientage, half-*padrinazgo*. This system must have had the effect of vastly increasing the prestige of the few great houses, although we have no other details about it. It may even have created what were family buccellarians, although the evidence for this is inferential at best. We do know that each one of the principal *pallas* of Cuzco always had fifteen to twenty younger women in her household over whom she presided as a duchess over her ladies-in-waiting. How marriage affected this clientage we do not know. Though they could never hope to be counted as Capac Incas, after two or three generations as Hahua Incas, the members of a family could almost always claim some distant connection with the royal house, so multiple were the emperor's sexual alliances.

There was another melancholy caste, the *huaccha concha*, or "poor relatives." Many of them formed an unplaced and floating class. They were children of Inca men, even of the emperor himself, by women outside the Inca caste who were not their wives or concubines; such women were naturally of "worthless blood." These offspring were despised by the Incas and possessed no wealth in Cuzcoquiti. Only in their mothers' communities, presuming that they were far removed from Cuzco, could these individuals parade any prestige at all. The young men of this caste did not, as far as we know, wear the earplugs; the young women of this caste immediately sank into obscurity.

SECTION 8. *The Ayllu*

THE PERUVIAN *ayllu* was a social form far older than the Incas. It always looked upon itself as having descent from a *ccallaric machu*, a "first grandfather," as its progenitor. It was a vague and extended family by common agreement, if not actually by blood, and could—because it considered itself derived from that common grandparent—refer to itself as *villca*, "the grandchildren." It was probably given cohesion by a tillable locale, concretely symbolized by its *huanca*, the stone which in their sight contained the spirit of the land. It reverenced the mummy or the skull of the supposed ancestor, was generally exogamous, held all lands under *ayllu* ownership (just as Tahuantinsuyo was the patrimony common to all the Incas), and possessed elective leadership for war. It was highly competitive with other *ayllus* for water and arable land, and probably it only rarely confederated with success. It might absorb other less virile *ayllus*, but it could not find a common ground with them. In short, it acted the part of a miniature nation.

Each *ayllu* possessed numerous family fetishes over and beyond the founder's bones. The ancestors collectively were important and could appear as sparks in the fire complaining of hunger, and they would then be appeased by the throwing of a bit of maize or red pepper on the fire. But perhaps more in evidence were those who were present in certain pebbles, dried roots, *ayayllas* or "bezoars," or other small objects; taken together, these were referred to as *conopas*. At the hour of death these objects, perhaps as many as four, were handed over to the *pihui*, "the eldest son." Each one had its own name, and they were worshiped only in the family. These items represented the staunch, narrow, and ingrown quality of the *ayllu*, and while each *ayllu* was very much aware of the larger world of the *huacas* around it and, more dimly, of the Creator's universe, the care of its founder's mummy and of its *conopas* was the very foundation of its own prosperity.

Our first data on the *ayllus* of Cuzco appear in the tales told by the Incas concerning their origins.

There were two of these tales. The first was a *pacarina* story and identified the original invading groups as Sutic and Maras Indians who together in later times were probably designated as the Tambos. These were supposed to have emerged out of two or three caves of origination. In order to create an impression of original harmony, the legend refers to these three conjointly as Pacaritambo, "the First Campsite," or as Tamputoco, "the Holes of the Tambos." These groups probably had little or no connection with each other and were probably not true *ayllus* but abbreviated plundering bands which broke off from originally larger groups.

The second of these tales relates to the founding of Cuzco. It identifies the three *ayllus* indigenous to the area round about as the Huallas, the Antasayas, and the Sañus. In the legend they become, respectively, Ayar Auca, Ayar Ucho, and Ayar Cachi, the three brothers of Manco Capac.

The injection of the war bands and their belligerent captains into the bucolic valley is the beginning of Inca history. Manco Capac and his successors assumed leadership of the Sañus and then precipitated hostilities against the Huallas, who were finally defeated. Some of the Hualla group fled, abandoning the remainder of the *ayllu*, which was forced into a state midway between that of subject and confederate. In the reign of the third ruler the Sañus were able to settle in the city. The Antasayas held out under a tough *sinchi* called Alcaviza. It was not until the fourth ruler that the Incas—if we may identify them at this point—were able to subject these groups and force them into alliance. The Mascas were apparently brought in by the sixth ruler. Thus was the Inca state of Cuzco manufactured, piecemeal and with a sporadic and uncertain chronology. A formal canon of ten *ayllus* was artificially established by Pachacuti, the ninth ruler and reformer of the state.

As with most Peruvian communities, Cuzco was divided into two moieties, Upper and Lower. To Upper, or Hanan Cuzco, belonged the following five *ayllus*: Chavin Cuzco, Arayraca (or Cuzco Callan), Tarpuntay, Huacaytaqui (or Quisco), and Sañu. The second of these was a reformulation of the original Antasaya *ayllu*, the bulk of which Pachacuti had expelled from the new city of Cuzco which he was building. Because of their superior status these five *ayllus* as a group were referred to simply as "Cuzcos." The first two claimed descent from two of the four founding brothers, and we have already identified the Sañus with the third brother.

The Lower or Hurin Cuzco moiety were collectively called the

"Tambos." The five *ayllus* included in this moiety were the Sutic (or Tambos specifically), the Maras, the Cuycussa, the Masca, and the Uru.

Whatever the origins of the moiety system in Peru—and it may have been very ancient—it served to organize hostility, prerogative, and competition in the community. It still does. San Sebastián today, the ancient Sañu of the Incas, is divided by the main highway into Upper and Lower moieties, each composed of two *ayllus*. The men of the first make tiles, and those of the second grow onions. They view each other with permanent suspicion and enmity.

It is probable that the Capac Ayllu, or "King's Family" (the king here being the first of all the rulers, Manco Capac), was separate and distinct from the two halves of Inca Cuzco; in fact, it was probably a third *saya* or moiety. This separation is hinted at in that part of the founding legend which relates that a twofold division of the people, coming from Sutictocco and Marastocco, was capped by an even more important group from a third cave of origination, the Capactocco. This third and regal group is undoubtedly a late construct. It appears then that when Pachacuti restructured the city, he squeezed the two former Cuzco moieties that had before existed into a new Hurin Cuzco, and then artificially created a new Hanan Cuzco of complex social groupings. He left the Capac Ayllu hanging unattached and exalted above this customary Peruvian dualism, and to this third *saya* he gave the prestige of descent from Manco Capac. We can see why this was so when we come to understand the role of the ten *panacas* which together formed the Capac Ayllu and worshiped Manco Capac as their direct ancestor. In one sense, only these men and women of the Capac Ayllu were true Incas.

SECTION 9. *The Panaca*

THE *panaca* is one of mankind's most curious social inventions. The word itself is a formation from *"pana,"* which means a man's sisters, female cousins, or indeed, by extension, any women of his *ayllu*. The word *panaca* thus presumably means literally the grouping or household of the sisters and female cousins of a certain man. Our words

37

"sisterhood" and "womenfolk" both approximate the meaning. The man who provided the definition was in theory always the second son, or the descendant of a second son, of a dead Inca emperor. The *panaca* is mentioned in the sources as an establishment of the sixth Inca ruler, Inca Roca. It was he at least who first defined it.

It was based on the twin concepts of the deathlessness of the departed Inca ruler and of his eventual return. As a consequence of this dual expectation, the ruler therefore passed on to his legitimate heir only the exercise of his office, not his wealth. The wealth he retained inalienably locked away in this exotic kind of an *ayllu* which was called the *panaca*. To this end the institution is also once referred to as a *pachaca*, which would carry a collective connotation of "those acting in the capacity of major-domos for the goods of the dead emperor."

The *panaca* began to function immediately upon the demise of a ruler. His mummy was promptly installed in his palace or in some chosen villa on one of his estates where it became the object of the continuous solicitude, veneration, and filial care of his second son and the loosely designated sisterhood. This second son specifically filled the office of *pachaca* or "major-domo" of the estate. The *panaca* perpetuated itself from within through his legitimate issue. Whether or not the unmarried sisters and female cousins in the *panaca* became the secondary wives of this Inca, we do not know. There is some presumption that it was so. The heir apparent who became the new emperor, of course, would found his own *panaca* in similar fashion, designating his second son as the prospective headman of the eventual estate. But in addition to this legitimate and nuclear bloodline in the *panaca*, it engrossed also many others, Incas and non-Inca retainers who had freely chosen to enroll in it. While the included Incas and *pallas* were classed as members of the *panaca*, their issue, unlike the first-born male descendants of the *pachaca*, were not thereby bound, for they might select a different *panaca* to enter. Each *panaca* venerated only one of the dead emperors, but all of them venerated Manco Capac, the peculiar possession of the first *panaca*. Taken all together, they formed the Capac Ayllu and looked back to their common ancestor.

Inca Roca's second son had been named Vicaquirau, and Inca Roca's *panaca* was known therefore by the name of that son. The succeeding five *panacas* were, as they came into existence: the Auccayhaylli or Victory Shout; the Sucso, the name of the appropriate son; the Iñaca, a word denoting a highborn lady; the Capac Ayllu *panaca* (not to be confused with the Capac Ayllu or the moiety of *all* the *panacas*); and the Tumibamba, the name of an Inca city in Ecuador frequented by the eleventh ruler and the scene of particularly splendid festivities which he ordained.

It was Pachacuti who artificially completed the system by creating *panacas* for the five Inca rulers who had preceded Inca Roca. He began by assigning to the *panaca* a male descendant of the second son of the ruler in question who became thereby its *pachaca*; in addition, he designated to the several *panacas* whatever women seemed suitable. In this group of five *panacas* all were named after the designated *panaca* headman and the group as a whole designated as Lower Cuzco. From the Vicaquirau *panaca* on down, the group belonged to Upper Cuzco. The relationship of these *panacas* (all forming together the Capac Ayllu) to the rest of Cuzco may be grasped in the diagram found among the notes.

In pre-Inca Peru there had existed an institution which throws some light on the *panaca*. If a man killed another householder, he could take away from that man's *ayllu* as much of his *chacra* or tilled land as was defined by a slingstone's flight. What completed the deceased party's alienation from his *ayllu* was the custom whereby the victor would keep his dried body as a highly valued possession in his own house. This mummy was dutifully fed and in fact treated with great tenderness. In this way the murderer exercised a hold over the dead man's family which of course could not exist apart from the paternal mummy; in some curious way the mummy was still thought to possess both house and *chacra*. The institution is described in an anonymous and difficult source as follows:

> He preserved the mummy in his house in order that it would allow him to feed it and reverence it (one of the superstitions which they held to). He and his family were subject to it, just as the dead man's own family had formerly been to him. Hence it came about that it was more

desirable to marry that woman who had the greatest number of relatives, rather than the merely rich woman, for the former brought with her the support of many people.

It was also the custom in the sierra for a family to entertain the corpse of the newly deceased paterfamilias for a month before burial; the mummy was set up and prominently displayed in the house while feasts were offered to all who came. What emerges from this information and the statement quoted above is the supremely close connection between a man and his household, the household being conceived as both a lineage and an estate. These factors are also the basic ingredients of the Inca *panaca.*

Panaca property was held in different tenure from *ayllu* property. The former was vested in perpetuity in the sole person of the dead emperor. In the latter case, members of the *ayllu* theoretically had only usufruct rights, for at certain seasons the *ayllu* redivided its holdings among all its members to take into account the year's changes in the circumstances and size of families. How far this normal periodic reallotment of *chacras* and llama herds was observed by the Inca *ayllus* of Cuzco, however, we do not know. At any rate it did not affect the *panacas.*

Thus *ayllu* wealth was, within its own confines, transferable and therefore potentially productive, whereas *panaca* wealth was inalienable and stagnant. The mere presence of the *panacas* created an unhealthy and torrid dynamic in the state, for a newly proclaimed emperor possessed only that wealth he brought with him from his own holdings as prince and that additional wealth which he could demand in the form of investiture gifts. Until he could send his armies out and receive them back fat with loot, he was outranked as *capac* by all of his dead and unburied ancestors. With them, therefore, he was inevitably in violent competition. Nothing that had been theirs—except the nonparturient women of a predecessor's harem—could ever be his. Inca Roca, as we pointed out above, is the one who is said to have institutionalized this unique form of property holding.

The effects of this impounded wealth upon the Capac Incas was deleterious as there was no responsibility in connection with it, whereas with *ayllu* wealth there was periodic reassignment and public scrutiny. In the latter days of which this history speaks, there was a rapid increase in the number of retainers and other hangers-on in those dead and sacrosanct households. Upon coming of age, any Inca could choose to enter a royal *panaca*, such an act being considered a demonstration of devotion which in return would secure for the person all the blessings and protections which an all-powerful dead emperor could provide, both here and in the afterlife. This action effectively divorced an individual from the *ayllu* into which he had been born. In other words, dual citizenship in both *panaca* and *ayllu* seems to have been impossible or at least meaningless. After the great reorganization of the *panaca* system by Pachacuti, it became increasingly common for natives of Cuzco to enter the *panacas* so that, by the time of Huascar's princehood, many of the Incas were serving the dead kings. The *panacas*, being miniature courts, also served as training grounds for young Inca pages and ladies-in-waiting before coming of age. This system eroded the effectiveness of the older *ayllus* that were still functioning, without at the same time adding to the strength of the city. When Pachacuti created his own *panaca* to care for his mummy when he should die, he placed in it one hundred of his bastard sons and fifty of his bastard daughters. His successor's *panaca* claimed about one thousand members at the time of the entry of the Spaniards, not including the thousand or so menials and domestics assigned thereto.

Organized under the *pachaca*, the major-domo, these establishments meant for the women enrolled in them far greater freedom than for the women in the establishments of the gods. Sexual license seems to have been prevalent within the close walls of the great stone *canchas* which housed the *panacas*, and much of the time was spent in the convivialities of *akha* and feasting.

That vice should have become one of the distinguishing features of the late *panaca* is not to be wondered at, for a dead man is in any case an easy master, and any conception of his eventual return in the flesh for a reckoning must have been in all cases minimal. The pitchy blackness of the Cuzco night was often disturbed by the sounds of women drumming and by the carousing, quarreling, and singing of men—

these sounds coming as blantantly from the palaces of the dead as from that of the living ruler. We must beware, however, of thinking of the *panaca* as a hypocritical institution. It was not. The members of these *panacas*, both men and women, were to suffer formidable burnings, rackings, and tortures as Spaniards often fruitlessly tried to extract from them information on the whereabouts of the mummies and the wealth hidden with them. The *panaca* remained as pious as it was to become vicious.

The center of the cult was the mummy bundle of the dead emperor. He was attended throughout the day, served his meals, whisked for flies, entertained, relieved, and retired, the normal daily ritual of the living great. His *chacras* annually poured their produce into his bins out in the countryside, his coca plantations in the montaña baled the finest leaves for his use, his pastors regularly sent to him their tallies of the newborn llamas in his herds. It is probable that the actual administration of the *panaca* estates was in the hands of capable *yanaconas* who were owned in the family and who could and did wield power in the institution, even though they were not Incas. If he owned some all-important water channels, as did the dead Inca Roca, his permission had to be sought for the use or diversion of those waters. A story is told of a young Inca brave's falling in love with a girl of his own ancestral *ayllu*. The girl had left the *ayllu* to enter one of the important *panacas*, whereupon—and not withstanding their real consanguinity—the young man had to appear before the dead emperor in question to ask for the girl in marriage.

In his mummified and abeyant state the dead emperor was not an *aya*, a common corpse, but an *illapa*, a word whose basic meaning is "an electrical discharge, a spark, lightning." *Illapa* personified was the god of storm, of thunder, of rain, of floods, and of lightning. Applied to great figures of the past, the term *illapa cari* designated an "illustrious man," one known for his outstanding exploits. Through this fact of language we can better appreciate the awe in which these royal mummy bundles were held. Depending on the degree of spiritual power he had evidenced while alive, the emperor's mummy was able to dispense that same amount after death. His mummy was primarily

a *huaca* of fertility expressing itself in the multiplication of his descendants, but it could also dispense other benefits as well—the mummy of
Inca Roca for instance, because of his well-known connection with water
during his reign, could be used to persuade the gods to send rain.

But there was always confusion about the real presence. By some
the vital part of the deceased ancestor was thought to be with his
refulgent father in the heavens, at whose side he made constant intercession for his living descendants in the *panaca*. Others held that he continued to live on earth in his mummy.

The fact that the *illapa* represented concretely—indeed *was*—the
spirit of the family helps to explain the growth and popularity of the
Inca *panaca*. Responsibility to the *ayllu* was defined in a rigid and iron-
bound code, known to all and, if infringed, punished by ostracism or
universal contempt. The *ayllu* was rigid, but it was tied to the earth
and it was a proved way of life. The cult of the *illapa* imposed no difficult patterns of reciprocity on its members; its affluence did not each
year have to be carefully redivided, scrambled for, and sweated for.
Panaca wealth was in theory as eternal as the life of the surcharged
mummy who owned it. To serve an *illapa* was to bet on a sure thing.
We cannot doubt that this release from the tyranny of the *ayllu* meant
the beginning of a more imaginative social and intellectual exploration,
but no records of such have come down to us, and, in any case, the *panaca*
was in existence for too short a time.

The mummies lived where they wished. The mummy of Pachacuti's
grandfather was venerated in an Ayamarca community where his ancestral *chacras* were and where many stirring events had happened to
him before he came to the rule. The mummy of Pachacuti's father
lived over the watershed to the north in a high mountain eyrie to which
he had retired in his old age. This particular dead emperor came in his
litter to Cuzco only for the greatest state festivals. Because of this fact
and because of the stigma which historically attached to his retirement,
his *panaca* was perhaps the most ingrown of them all. Nevertheless,
it was large and important and survived well into the colonial period.

The dead Pachacuti normally inhabited his Patallacta villa which
was only a short stroll from the center of Cuzco. He had constructed

43

Patallacta for this very purpose and that was why he had chosen to die there as a very old man. His son and successor had died in a lovely country estate near Lake Piuray, but his mummy seems to have been kept at least part of the time in his palace on the great square. His successor was Huascar's father, and this emperor, who was to die in far-away Ecuador, would be kept also in his palace fronting the square.

As for the lower five *panacas*, having been brought into being by fiat, they were smaller and less important than the upper five. Their palaces were located in the constricted area of the ridge near the confluence of the rivers, for geographically that was Hurin Cuzco.

SECTION 10. *The Purucaya*

THE SPLENDOR of these dead kings and the long tale of their deeds could be seen concentrated in the *purucaya*, a ceremony which belonged specifically to the *panacas*. In this remarkable fiesta, which was partly a historical drama and partly a lament for the dead, the Capac Incas had a chance to display those qualities which had made them great. The *purucaya* was *their* statement of identity distinct from the cultus which centered about the living emperor, and as such it displayed them as a society of free knights under the protection of immortal rulers.

The *purucaya* was an integral part of most of the great state occasions, for it was the way in which the royal mummies participated in those festivities. It was both a procession and a play-acting, and songs of heroic deeds out of the past accompanied it. We may imagine its moving out from the narrow Street of the Sun (now Loreto) which led from Coricancha into the great square. The *panacas* proceeded in their chronological order, the ruler most lately dead heading the procession, with Manco Capac, the *ccallaric machu* or founder of the line, coming last. Each mummy and each *huaoqui* was borne in a palanquin. In the case of the Upper Cuzco mummies, the conveyances were those which they used while alive. These stately carrying chairs were trimmed with gold leaf and canopied under awnings of iridescent feathers. The mummy itself was tightly crouched into a shape easily bundled and was wrapped with beautifully textured garments and mantles, the dead face meanwhile staring out from the top and adorned with a masklike appurtenance of gold. The *pachaca* or headman of the *panaca* attended the mummy personally, holding over its head the brilliantly colored *achihua* or feathered umbrella. Preceding the *rampa*, or litter, selected members of the *panaca* bore the various parts of the dead ruler's regalia, while at the very head of the group came his *capac unancha* or royal coat of arms. This latter item was a square flaglike standard with a distinctive device painted on it. The standard carried by the Chima *panaca* was particularly distinguished, for it was the *pacarina capac unancha*, and it depicted the three traditional caves of origination with two trees flanking the center cave, one displaying golden, the other silver, roots. These trees represented the father and the mother of all the Incas, the two glorious ancestral stocks, while the gold and silver fruits depicted on their boughs were the Incas and *pallas* respectively of the current day.

Among the other elements of the regalia there came the *suntur paucar*, a staff topped with a mound of closely set and variously colored feathers and sprouting three plumes at the top. This the emperor had used during his lifetime, and it was therefore still charged with all his great personal power. There was the *mascapaycha*, the red fringe that hung down from the *llauto* and covered the royal eyes and the bridge of the nose—in every way the equivalent of the crown in European history. There was the *champi*, the mace, here done in gold or silver, and the *topa yauri* or "royal halberd" equaling the sword carried in the processions of European kings. Affixed to poles carried by selected servitors in the *panaca* came the sandals, the coca bag and the "king's robe," the *capac uncu*, that rich tunic with its singular and unrepeatable pattern woven solely for that ruler. Each ruler could be recognized by this state garb alone. The tunic of Manco Capac, for instance, was a rich red around the shoulders, a belt of three bands of *tocapu* (abstract squared designs) around the middle, and a skirt of plain blue. Pachacuti's *uncu* was of solid color with a band of *tocapu* lining the collar and running down the front of the skirt as a double band. Huayna Capac's tunic was richly checkered and squared all over but with green squares in the upper field alternating with orange, while below they were blue and white. This profusion of color and detail on the garments and banners of the dead was intimately known to all Incas, for their family loyalties were thus visually centered and their minds implicated. Add a common livery worn by all the members of each individual *panaca*, and their separateness can be understood. The men of the Chima *panaca*, for example, wore the *purupuru*, a feathered headband; it was reserved for them alone.

The courtly duties of the *panaca*, whether the members were acting as jesters, as keepers of the *champi*, as litter bearers, as concubines, or as female domestics, sealed them tightly within the little world of that *panaca* while still allowing them, in the *purucaya*, a view of the totality of their history as a whole people. The pomp of these occasions was exceptional. As the procession wanderingly moved along around the four sides of the great square, finally to settle down, each individual in his appropriate place, a mood described by the Quechua word *yuyaycucuy* was established. This verb states a thoughtfulness and a desire to dwell on faraway and past events; it summarizes the romantic historicism of a people who thus in the *purucaya* were miming their frozen past.

From our sources, here quite explicit, we can recover the scene taking place in Haucaypata. The *panacas* of Upper Cuzco were ranged in chronological order in front of Pachacuti's palace, those of Lower Cuzco across from them on the other side of the square. After the public meal, in which the mummies and *huaoquis* were honorably served first, the women began to pour the *akha* out of slender-necked vessels which they brought in on their backs.

In this mood now, both benevolent and nostalgic, was sung the *haravi*,

46

a chant describing the ancient rule. Each *panaca* had its own group of *haravis*; no *panaca* could sing the *haravis* of another *panaca*, for they had been the personal possession of the rulers when alive and a part of their glory now that they were dead. Among the Incas there was a special class of the nobility who memorized these *haravis*, passing them down to their eldest sons with great accuracy. In each *panaca* there were four or five of these *haravicos*, custodians of these verse histories, whose services were indispensable at such celebrations. It was they who intoned the words which recounted the deeds of the beloved *machu*. As the drinking continued, the members of the *panacas* in turn rose and danced in chorus, men and women, hand in hand and responding in unison to the chorus leader. At intervals the deeds of the rulers were acted out as well as sung by the dancers. The victories of the dead kings were again celebrated with the *haylli*, the shout of triumph, and their cruel deaths were proclaimed with shrieks of sorrow and cries of *caymi suminchic!* and *caymi marcanchic!*—"behold! our talisman, our protector!" Pachacuti's *panaca* in its *haravis* memorialized particularly the appearance of Viracocha, the god who had given him victory over the Chancas; it boasted of the emperor's successful siege of the Sora Indians and his mighty crushing of that people. But most graphically of all it depicted in a little play how the great emperor had once entered the green world of the montaña, there to do combat with the *llactayoc* or guardian spirit of the land, a huge dragon which was represented by a masked dancer. Pachacuti himself was mimed by a member of the *panaca* bearing a parrying shield with the device of a jaguar on it. Huayna Capac's *panaca* sang, among other things, of the loss of many noble Inca warriors in the waters of the Gulf of Guayaquil, treacherously slain and ever lamented.

As the shouted *hayllis* and the intoned *haravis* continued, the *akha* flowed more copiously. Through their proxies the dead emperors toasted each other continuously, as did the other members of these miniature courts. Passions soon became violently aroused, and a dangerous combativeness would flare up between certain *panacas*. Excesses of sorrow for the dead and all that belonged to the past rose to the heights of deliberate incoherence, for only in such a dramatic abandonment of reason could the dead kings revel in the devotion and bereavement of their families. Sexual indulgence, expected and allowable under the circumstances, plus general inebriation ended the *purucaya*. Drunkenly the mummies made their ways home as the night filled the cold streets of Cuzco with darkness.

In few other places on earth could a people re-enact the *huayma pacha*, "the ancient times," in such loving detail and in the very presence of the actors in that past. A powerful and a splendid sense of history animated the Incas; in the institution of the *purucaya* they formally and repetitiously recovered the pieces of the past. It was one of the cornerstones of their greatness.

SECTION 11. *The Cult of the Panaca*

WE HAVE MENTIONED that a Peruvian custom long antedating the Incas was to maintain an honored corpse a whole month before burying it. In this prolonged wake, friends and family brought gifts and placed them conspicuously near the mummy, which was thought to be involved that very moment in the giving of an extended feast. In other words, for a month before being relegated to his cleft in the rock, the dead man continued a joyous and magnanimous existence in his own house. It was this custom of the sierra which suggested to the Inca emperors that their own wakes be indefinitely carried on so that burial, with all of its finality, need form no part of their obsequies. Thus we cannot really describe the cult of the *panaca* as a cult of the dead. Its insistence was upon the aliveness of its hero.

Life in the *panacas* could not, of course, go on wholly in the pattern of a living emperor's family, but there were important elements in common. Both the differences and the similarities should be described if we are to understand the functioning of the *panaca*.

In the *panaca* the *ayllu*-master was in theory the mummy but in practice the *pachaca*. A newly created *panaca* was, of course, in a different situation than one established over the years, because it included some brothers and a number of the sister-wives of the recently reigning monarch. The incumbent monarch possessed his father's legiti-

48

macy and powers, but the members of the *panaca* possessed his father's wealth. As explained before, it was a dangerous dichotomy which was only eased as the new monarch won wealth and prestige on his own. Until that time the new ruler and the *pachaca* of his father's estate represented potentially hostile forces. To the sibilant whispers of intrigue and maneuver, never absent from the Cuzco scene, the mummies out of the Inca past added their own ghostly voices.

All the mummies had assigned niches in the thick stone walls of Coricancha, the cathedral site, and here they sat flanking Inti, their heavenly father, for certain important state ceremonials. On such occasions they were arranged under the headship of their earthly progenitor, Manco Capac—a vivid display of the stitching together of heaven and earth. Manco Capac had no mummy, but a stone substituted for him. Its presence was especially required in any festival honoring the magic mountain Huanacauri, the scene of Manco's earthly deeds. From that small fetish of his flashed ineffable strokes of victory, and for that reason it almost always accompanied the Inca armies on the march— as even at this moment it was with Huayna Capac in the north.

The mummies had voices, for they spoke through the oracular lips of two persons, a man to represent the emperor and a woman to represent his *coya*. Through them the mummy carried on his conversation with the world of the living, calling for *akha*, for food, or for coca to chew, toasting other dead kings or living magnates at the fiestas or inviting them to visit him in his palace and regale themselves. It is probable that it was the *pachaca* who was the male oracle in all such cases. *Mamaconas*, or religious women, were assigned to each *panaca*, for it was as much a cult as it was a functioning family. One of these *mama conas*, wearing a mask of beaten gold, flanked the mummy, whisking away the flies that settled on its face with a brightly colored fan. *Yana-conas*, or domestics, selected from among the more intelligent and handsome of the subject peoples, were assigned to duties in the *panaca* too menial for Incas but requiring skill and judgment; and it was they who carried on the actual administration connected with the ruler's estate and festivities. In general, there seems to have been a far greater number of women than of men in the *panacas*.

49

During the annual All Souls celebration the *panaca* left its residence to wander out among the hills, bearing the beloved mummy, his clothing, and his weapons to certain spots which he had enjoyed while alive, the scenes of his hunting, carousing, reception of embassies, or viewings of the progress of important constructions. In these visits it was the role of the women of the *panaca* to wail for the emperor and his lost pleasures, drumming feverishly on their little tambourines and calling out his name in the deep gorges, impatient to hear the hot distance giving back the empty whisper of his name. Echoes coming from the *yachapayak caca* or "imitating rocks" seemed to intensify for them the mystique of his presence.

Along with the mummy, the *huaoqui* was an integral part of the *panaca* cult. The *huaoqui* generally possessed its own palanquin and service of assigned people, and in the case of the greatest of the dead emperors, it possessed and inhabited its own villa as well, to which it would retire when ceremony did not demand its presence beside the mummy. Every new moon a fire was kindled before it into which was cast the choicest of foods. The fire represented the idol's soul which through this means consumed its needed nourishment.

The *huaoqui*, "brother," received equal veneration with the mummy, as it had with the ruler while he lived. From the Creator himself down to rulers, all eminent beings had *huaoquis*. The Capac Incas had them, but common people did not. Each person while alive selected his own *huaoqui* with appropriately solemn ceremonies. It was a way of extending and insuring personal immortality, for if the mummy should be destroyed, the departed spirit would still possess a locus in this world. In the case of emperors the *huaoqui* was of singular importance, for through it he could reside among his people and receive their veneration even while away on extended campaigns. The *huaoqui* possessed the power of extracorporality, for with its councils it guided the living person or the mummy by dispensing useful or occult information. Because of this clairvoyance, it was often taken by an Inca to the wars.

Manco Capac's *huaoqui* was the Inti-bird, a small dried bird kept in a cane basket. His son's *huaoqui* was a stone fish called Huanachiri Amaru. That of Lloque Yupanqui was called Apu Mayta which was the name of a great Alcaviza chief. Capac Yupanqui's was called simply Ayllu, "Family." Inca Roca's bore the same name as his *panaca* (as his second son, in other words). That of Viracocha Inca was Inca Amaru, "Dragon Lord." Pachacuti's *huaoqui* was the solid gold image of a two-headed serpent called Inti Illapa; once in a distant and lonesome spot the god of the lightning had met him and had given this talisman to him as an earnest of divine protection. Topa Inca's was Cusi Churi, "the Fortunate Son," and that of Huayna Capac was Huaraqui Inca. There is no record of Huascar's *huaoqui*.

The royal mummy could have other fetishes besides its *huaoqui*. Huayna Capac's mummy had five or six protective idols in attendance, probably those of the peoples he had conquered, as well as the mummy of his mother whom he had especially deified after her death. Pachacuti's mummy possessed a great charm of power in the *huaca* of the Chancas, that nation whose defeat at his hands had raised the Incas to empire. This *huaca* was named Usco Villca, Cat Fetish, and wherever the ferocious mummy went, there went also in its train the servile god of that formidable people he had conquered. The *panaca*, in other words, was not simply an ancestor cult. It had become a little pantheon, a constellation of divine powers which was to some extent self-sufficient and disconnected from the great world of the spirit over which the Creator presided.

It can easily be seen how the *panaca* as a cult was saying something quite different from the great state festivals. This insistence upon ceremonializing the dead emperor's retinue, instead of burying him, inevitably built into the structure of Inca society the germs of extreme faction; the life of the Inca people was thus to be riven with division as its past was progressively put into grotesque compartments neither dead nor alive but in any case untouchable. In the days of Huascar, who found himself unable to control these *panacas*, the dissolution of the Inca fabric was to be complete.

SECTION 12. *Time and the Inca Calendar*

OUR DISCUSSION of the *panaca* hinted at the fact that the Incas did not conceive of time as we do. Time to them was not horological, for no ticking clocks nor dripping clepsydra partitioned off their hours and days. Time, rather, was a function of a singular divine event in the past, the *paccarik pacha*, "dawn time" or the beginning of the world. Beginnings and prime movers always loomed large in the thought of the Incas. They described Viracocha as *Paccarichik*, the One Who Causes to Begin. Time was thought not to flow past one, but to display continuously the result of this original creative activity. The value of time thus lay not in its present potentialities nor in its trend, but in its mingling of past with present.

The Incas had no system of dating the years; they had no one imagined point among the years to serve as a beacon in time as did the Mayas, nor did they date by regnal years. As the established aspect of the world order, Tahuantinsuyo the empire was to them the happy congelation of all years and all eras of the past. The empire *was* time, and their responsibilities as a ruling caste were ordained by that pristine act when Inti, the sun god and surrogate for Viracocha, had revealed to them their imperial mission. Time was not supposed to progress from one state to another so much as simply to unfold its inevitable flower. As a logic of this idea, time in a real sense belonged to the Incas and was a part of their patrimony.

Their calendar expressed therefore not a sequence as our calendar does, but aspects of the relationships between the Incas and the Creator on the one hand and between the Incas and all other peoples on the other, or, to put it geographically, between Cuzco and the provinces of the Empire. This state calendar did not, however, suppress the agricultural one which spoke of plowing, sowing, irrigating, reaping, and harvesting. The two sets of rites, political and agricultural, the new and the old, were allowed to exist side by side in the twelve-month calendar created by Pachacuti. This calendar can be logically subdivided into the following clusters:

(1) The year began (our November and December) with the *huara-chicoy*, the rite whereby the Incas renewed their vigor. This ceremony tested the craft, strength, and swiftness of their young men and then formally endowed them with the breechclout or *huara* as the sign of their manhood and the earplugs as the sign of their exalted caste. In this rite, or rather series of rites, the young knights were pledged to strict loyalty to the emperor, the keystone in their political structure. Thus at the opening of the year the Incas renewed their muster of fighting men on whom all else depended. At the same time the girls become *ñustas* or young women in the associated rite of the first menstruation.

(2, 3, 4, 5) During these four months of the rainy season (January, February, March, and April) the rites were traditionally bucolic and pertained to the ripening crops. These necessary and functional rites concerning food, fundamental in the early history of the city, were by imperial times consigned to a ritual undertone, for Cuzco itself no longer greatly feared dearth and starvation, so well had it organized its economy. The second month opened with the *purapucyo* or "confluent rivers," a ceremony of gratitude to water, essential to an agricultural state. With great splendor this celebration took place at the holy spot where Cuzco's two rivers joined, Pumapchupan, or the Lion's Tail. The *arihua*, when the standing maize was cut, ended this basic agricultural statement in the fifth month.

(6, 7) With the summer rains now over, there followed in May and June two rites closely bound together, in fact inseparable, the *aymoray* ("harvest") and the *Inti Raymi* ("sun festival"). The first was the harvest-home ending the agricultural year, and the second combined the thanksgiving to the sun god and the breaking of ground for the coming planting year. Foisted on these purely local celebrations was, however, a vast imperial pastiche. The new knights from the previous December now came to the end of their period of fasting and took a prominent part in the celebrations. Not only was the grain garnered out of the fields of Cuzco, but all the provinces of the empire sent in tribute to be counted into the many warehouses of Cuzcoquiti. All the leading *curacas* and governors of Tahuantinsuyo assembled in Cuzco to offer their homage, and auguries were held for the coming prosperous year. In this rite the Incas identified their own prosperity with the world's good fortune. The corollary was that a contented Inca people brought about a joyous world. These two rites will be more fully described.

(8, 9) Two festivals (in July and August) again celebrated the agricultural basis of the Andean year. The first had to do with Cuzco's water supply, the repair of the irrigation ditches, and the reassignment of the *chacras* by the *ayllu* leaders; the second was the early sowing of the maize crop. Placatory prayers were offered to the earth, frost, hail, storm, and sun that the good year coming might not be altered.

(10) In September, the month that ended with the general sowing, the weather changed. This was the month when the pent-up fears of the Inca people against pestilence and all other unseen ills were codified in the Situa festival. It had no connection either with the agricultural or with the solar year. It was a *suspira de profundis*. All evils, ailments, diseases, weaknesses or misfortunes, seizures or premature deaths—all these were expelled from Cuzcoquiti. Thus fumigated, Cuzco with relief mimed its coming immunity and joy with exaggerated dances, drinking, and general abandon. But if these rites were a confession of the common humanity of the Incas, their superiority over all other people had once again to be emphasized in appended ceremonies. Here the magnates of the empire assembled to eat the communion bread which fortified their loyalty. Because of its relative isolation from the rest of the ritual calendar of the Incas, the Situa has a peculiar intensity and will be described in detail later.

(11, 12) These last two months were signalized by preparations for the *huarachicoy*. In October the women spun the thread from which the boys' ceremonial breechclouts were to be woven. This was the *puchcay*, "the spinning"; it was followed in November by the *cantaray*, the special brewing of the *akha* to be drunk on the occasion, and an *itu* when the boys petitioned Huanacauri for success in the approaching rites of manhood.

Often the expected rains needed in October did not come and the new sprouts, not planted on *carpana allpa* or "irrigated land," would die in the furrows. At such times the *huacayllicuy* was organized, a singing of agonized songs appealing to the Creator to relent. These nocturnal processions ranged over the hills round about and through the stricken streets of Cuzco. The shouts, screams, and sobs of a desperate people were punctuated by the uproar of dogs and llamas being beaten so that they might add their voices to the general appeal, "Lord, maker of men, send us your rain!"

November was All Souls, when one remembered the dead ancestors and heroic warriors of the past who, when thus honored, added their blessings to the young knights preparing to assume the arms which they themselves had anciently carried. The various Inca families went out among the crags and clefts of Cuzcoquiti where their dead were buried, took them out from under their rock ledges, carried them through the streets of Cuzco on litters and then, after feasting and dancing, returned them to their *pucullos* or tombs until another year's fiesta should come around.

The above description is a very sketchy picture of the Inca calendar. The splendor, color, and detail of most of these ceremonies were in themselves powerful statements adding to the meaning of the series as a whole. The Inca talent for making visible in rites and festivals the power of their manhood, the plenty of their fields, their affiliation with the sun, the purity of their lives, and the homage which the whole world rightfully owed them was indeed extraordinary. These rites were the books in their holy canon, to be read as one progressed through the year. Without this aptitude for the language of ceremony, Tahuantinsuyo could not have beheld its own features nor have known its own majesty.

The foregoing account presents an outline of the calendar of festivals. There existed also a lunar calendar of named months into which the above fiestas were not always skillfully fitted. These were as follows:

December	Capac Raymi	Emperor's Feast
January	Samay	Relaxing
February	Hatun Pocoy	Common Ripening
March	Pacha Pocoy	Complete Ripening
April	Arihuay	Field Guarding?
May	Hatun Cuzqui	Common Plowing
June	Aucay Cuzqui	Plowing of the New Shoots
July	Chahuahuar	?
August	Yapa	Growing
September	Coya Raymi	Queen's Feast

| October | Oma Raymi | Feast of Oma (the town, today San Jerónimo) |
| November | Ayamarcay | Carrying the Dead |

These feasts represented the elaboration of the Inca year on a lunar basis. Underneath remained the primitive year of only two seasons, *pocoy pacha*, the "ripening season," which was the period of rainfall, and the contrasting "season of sunlight," *chirau pacha*, colder and almost devoid of rain.

Cuzco possessed a rough solar clock in the *sucancas*, moderately sized stone towers erected on the city's high sky line, four on the east to mark the path of the rising sun and four on the west where the sun went down. Designated *amautas*, or learned men, took observations from the stepped *usno* in the center of the main square, and when the sun rose squarely between the first two towers, they proclaimed the time for the first sowing. Harvesttime was read in the western markers. These towers were important *huacas* in themselves and received adoration. They were there, however, simply to standardize the festival year and not to explain the mysterious permutations of time, for the Incas thought they already knew what the depths of time contained, and they were incurious about the rest.

LAONZENACOIA
RAVAOCLLO

Reyno quito chyanbi quensabilca canori chashapoyo
yaua

The Lessening Power of the Inca People

AT THE TIME of the birth of Prince Huascar, unprecedented changes which bore upon the status and the traditions of the Inca people were taking place in Tahuantinsuyo.

Most destructive of the privileges of the Incas was the accelerating drift toward full divinization of the emperor. Huayna Capac had been consciously moving in this direction. He had declared his deceased mother a goddess and merged her with the divine mother of the Inca line whose name she bore. Additionally, he was to have one of his court favorites, Manco the Younger, probably his son, converted into a powerful *huaca* upon his early demise. Huayna Capac certainly viewed himself as in peculiarly close converse with the heavens and, to that extent, was moving farther from his people.

Strains and stresses could be found within the royal family as well. Huayna Capac, who had many sons by the women in his harem, became convinced that his first *coya* would not give him a male heir, and his desires fixed upon another sister, Mama Coca, whom he greatly wished to add to his female entourage. In the past she had consistently rebuffed him. When she again refused, he turned to the mummies of his father and mother in whose *panaca* she was enrolled, to ask that they provide their consent and deliver her up to him. The royal dead were unresponsive to this request from their living son; as if to make manifest their displeasure, portents signifying blood began to appear in the skies over Cuzco, and the god of storm even smote Cuzco's impregnable *pucara* with lightning. Resigned, Huayna Capac then tried to give Mama Coca in marriage to a notable magnate, old and loath-

57

some, so says the tale, but Mama Coca escaped by fleeing incontinently into the *acllahuasi*, the house from which all men were excluded. There, in time, she became the mother superior, sacrosanct in her person and eminent, it is to be supposed, in her virginity. In this incident we can realize the great strength of the *panaca* when it was negatively exerted.

As a boy Huayna Capac had come to power amidst treasonable tumults and ructions raised by his close kin. He had survived these assaults and had demoted or extinguished the conspirators. Some of that opposition had undoubtedly come from the high priesthood of Inti; consequently, Huayna Capac had taken the remarkable step of adding the prerogatives of that office to his own *capaccay*, or "dominion." Thus he was now not only *capac apu*, "emperor," and *sapa Inca*, "sole Inca," but the *Intip michi* "shepherd of the Sun," as well. This assumption of priestly power was a severe blow at one of the *ayllus* of Upper Cuzco, the Tarpuntay, for its members had regularly filled the Inti priesthood under an old patent. The ramifications went even further, for Inti had been the god by whom the Incas as a caste had been first empowered to rule. Inti was now in a sense subjected to the emperor, and to just that extent were the Inca *ayllus* weakened.

According to the old state dogma, Inti was the god who had first appeared out of the rock of Titicaca in the distant land of Collao. As long as this dogma was maintained, the Incas as a people did not feel their immunities seriously invaded. But now the adolescent Huayna Capac in another epochal action changed even this state of affairs. He took an army of inspection down with him into that vast basin on the roof of the world and ordained that, thenceforth, Viracocha the Creator should be supreme in the area. By the Aymara-speaking Indians round about, this high god was to be called Yatiri, a translation from Viracocha's Quechua title, Pachayachachic, He Who Knows, or Disposes of, the Earth.

Viracocha was not a god to whom the Inca people could easily give their first allegiance, for he represented a centralizing power above Inti—a god, in short, who might easily prove hostile to their traditional honors. Huayna Capac, most magnificent of all the Inca emperors, was ultimately unsuccessful in his effort to unseat Inti in his Titicaca house, but in the attempt the Inca people had been put on notice that their divine father might some day cease to provide them with sufficient sanction for their being.

The prince Huascar was born and reared while Inca religion was thus undergoing these basic reformulations at the hands of his father. His father, who was not only a Child of the Sun, as indeed were all Incas, but his Shepherd as well, was therefore by definition one of the great heavenly functionaries. Huascar was not to forget this lesson in the statecraft of heaven when it should come his time to preside over the empire.

Rahua Ocllo, who was very young herself, looked down in her arms at the child she was suckling and then out across Lake Chucuito, where, with her lord and the other women of the harem, she was sojourning. In the blue and windy depths of the vast lake was the island called Paapiti which her imperial husband, over the sullen objections of his people and hers, had just designated as a spot holier by far than Inti's island home. Although the heavens were thus patently cleft in twain and shaken at the whim of an emperor, how was she to know that the babe she carried in her arms, all other issue of her body, and she herself would one day be bloodily swept away in the wake of a division in part caused by such a remodeling of the gods?

ANDAS DEL INGA PILLCORAMPA

guayna capac

ynga, ua ala conquista
de los cayanbis guanccbis
ca cañaricic cho chacha
po ya quito Cataioga

Ilcuan los ynis an sasmar cas y
soras lucanas parina cccha
alaguerray batalla separico
sa toliuan

batalla del ynga   como

ONLY A FEW YEARS later the emperor began the most extended military campaign in Inca history. Tahuantinsuyo had just been shaken by the news of widespread revolt in the far northern provinces, and it was into those equatorial regions that Huayna Capac proposed now to lead his armies, promising them magnificent victories, abundance of loot, and the joy of chastising the wicked. This campaign was to have the effect of driving deeper the wedge already inserted into the stout timber of the Inca community.

Huayna Capac left his brother Auqui Topa Inca, a most distinguished member of Upper Cuzco, to govern the capital in his absence. A vicarial council of five was formed under Auqui Topa's presidency to administer the empire in the emperor's absence and to keep sedition far off.

The emperor made another important disposition before moving into the north. He invested Huascar, his oldest son, with the yellow *mascapaycha* of coregency. While this move was intelligent and designed to prevent any future mishap to the empire should sudden death carry him off, nevertheless it created a serious political anomaly in Cuzco after Huayna Capac's departure. An administrative machinery responsible only to an absentee emperor existed in the city of Cuzco alongside a coemperor who was not the president of the *camachinacuy*, or council. Huascar reigned in Cuzco but he did not rule, and we may suspect that this situation produced conflict and probably mighty designs of revenge. It must have been particularly galling to Huascar to behold the appearance in Cuzco of the special officials sent by his father from faraway Ecuador to investigate the manner in which his vicars were carrying on the government, to punish infractions, and to administer an empire-wide census. Such acts must have openly demeaned the prestige of the young coemperor.

As generalissimos of the huge army which he took north with him, Huayna Capac nominated Auqui Toma to lead the Incas of the Upper Cuzco regiment and Misi to lead that of Lower Cuzco. This division of command was customary, for both moieties of the Inca nation had to be represented in any division of honors or responsibilities. What was unusual and indeed ominous to the Incas, however, was the emperor's decision, in preparing this formidable undertaking, to elevate many hitherto unknown *curacas* from Collao and elsewhere to high dignity, allowing some of them to use golden drinking vessels and to ride in litters instead of the customary hammock. Such honors, indiscriminately passed out, threatened the standing of all members of the Inca caste.

Another imperial action pointed in the same direction. Huayna Capac decided against forming the army around Huanacauri, the traditional war-*huaca* and victory-bringer of the Inca pantheon. Every Inca boy had received his warrior's sling from this great *huaca* and had learned that only through it could victory come on the field of battle. But the emperor seemed to be leaning instead upon the Creator to assure his success. Viracocha lived nowhere and anywhere and possessed no real and ponderable *huaca*. But Huanacauri was concrete, he could be carried into the melee, and he was of proved efficacy. Furthermore he was of Inca blood. So deeply and forebodingly ran the doubts of the *pakuyoc* concerning the emperor's wisdom in this matter that while the army was still at Vilcas, on the way north, the emperor felt obliged to appease his knights by sending back for their traditional mascot.

This division between a warlike people and their semidivine leader was to become open mutiny in the days that followed the Inca disaster at the siege of the Carangui fortress. For a real or fancied defection from duty which he attributed to his Inca regiments in this unusual defeat, the emperor decided to break their spirit of independence. As at Lake Chucuito, he was again forced to concede failure, but only after a dramatic confrontation and full revelation of the division which by this time existed in the Inca community.

News of this famous incident enacted in the far north could not be kept long from Cuzco. It became known that Misi, the leader of the lower moiety, had reacted violently with the full support of his *ayllus* against what he felt to be a humiliating discrimination against his moiety and the favoring of Upper Cuzco as well as of certain powerful non-Inca provincials. For a short while he had held Huanacauri captive and threatened to return with him to Cuzco. In Cuzco the news sharpened the normal competitiveness between the two Inca wards. The Lower Cuzco moiety was not in any case the weaker one, for it possessed two of the important *ayllus* and, in addition, included the Chima Panaca, the keystone of the whole *panaca* system.

Still the situation in the Inca capital was radically different from the state of affairs in the peripatetic and warring court in the north. In Cuzcoquiti dissidence and division had probably been reduced after most of the aggressive Incas had gone north with their regiments and after the fire-eating Huanacauri had decamped from his mountain outside Cuzco. The period must have seemed like an extended holiday for the *panacas*. With the virility of the city thus weakened, with all heroism, boasting, and excitement in the north, and with the council under Auqui Topa Inca at home always balancing between doing too much and doing too little, the ceremonial aspects of life took on a vastly increased importance in the city. Even the bustle attendant upon the imperial census ordered by Huayna Capac from his second capital in the north did little to break in upon the heavy pleasures of life in Cuzco. Cuzco throbbed with the comings and goings of the *quipucamayocs*, the "accountants," bringing in their loads of *quipus* or knotted strings. Stern secretaries sent down by Huayna Capac to oversee the task worked night and day sorting, tabulating, dispatching runners asking for additional information, or holding trial of delinquent *curacas* called in from the provinces. A whole world of administration was centered in this Andean city; yet the Incas and *pallas* in it knew that all decisions were made in the far-off valleys of Ecuador—and they seem not to have cared.

It was in this world which was losing its centrality—and with it its sense of reality—that Huascar grew up.

SECTION 15. *The Events of Huascar's Youth*

WHEN HUASCAR, or Hummingbird, had completed the rites which brought him full membership in his caste, he had been given as the prerogative of his manhood the name Topa Cusi Huallpa, which meant Royal and Fortunate Turkey Cock, because the male turkey with its arrogant strutting and the intensity of its display represented in the Inca mind manliness and rich vesture. Because he was now an Inca, his family situation became of the highest importance.

In his harem his father had taken north with him not only the *coya* or legitimate queen but Huascar's mother as well. Although Huayna Capac had appointed Huascar as his coemperor and therefore heir, in reality the future of the succession was confused and dangerous, for a *coya* without male issue was permitted to adopt one of the many sons of the emperor whose social status was acceptable. Even though Huascar was Huayna Capac's "first-born son," the *curac churi* in other words, his mother was still not the *coya*—an anomalous situation. The *coya* in fact appears to have taken an adopted son after some years with her royal husband up in Ecuador—this just before she died. This young man, Ninan Cuyochic, Fire Flaunter, was to be for a time a serious threat to Huascar's future. He was with the armies in the north, and it was certainly no secret that the emperor was becoming increasingly fond of him. When shortly thereafter the *coya* died and the emperor raised Huascar's mother to the queenly rank, the difficulty was only in part resolved, for Ninan Cuyochic, a warrior already of some renown, was still one of his father's favorites. Huascar, on the other hand, reigning in an uncertain half-splendor in Cuzco, was unable to gain similar laurels for himself either in exploits of war or in wise advices given in the *camachinacuy*.

63

Those distant northern battlefields had created for Huascar another anxiety in the person of that brother called Atauhuallpa, Heroic Turkey, who was accruing considerable renown under the proud direction of his father. The erosion in Huascar's position became apparent to all in fact when a sudden whim of the emperor brought forth the imperial decree that thenceforth the land of Quito should be a special marquisate, separate from Tahuantinsuyo but owing it homage. The person selected to fill the viceregal post was Atauhuallpa. By this action the emperor was depriving Huascar, whenever he should come to sole rule, of full dominion over this land won by Inca valor. To validate this arbitrary act and to impress it firmly upon future history, Huayna Capac summoned Huascar to Quito for a great love feast wherein this division would be agreed to by all interested parties. At a lavish *taqui* or entertainment Huascar and Atauhuallpa met as brothers and pledged themselves to uphold their father's action. At the time Huascar had little choice but to agree as graciously as he could. And it did at least confirm his future possession of Cuzcoquiti, the bastion and heart of the empire. The agreement also reconfirmed him as the *pihui churi,* thus specifying his legitimacy.

Huascar's youth witnessed other signal events. In the year 1523, while his father was still occupied in the intractable north, cannibals, called the Chiriguana, from Amazonia broke open the gates of the empire to the south. From Ecuador the emperor dispatched the tough captain Yasca with a mandate to muster in Cuzco a sufficient force to deal with the situation.

Cuzco stirred with the greatness and glamour of the occasion as various levies poured into the valley, each contingent under its own captain and bearing in its midst its own national *huaca.* The attendant fiestas were presided over by the royal council and attended by all the *panacas* and *ayllus.* As perhaps the most eminent of all the Inca magnates there, Huascar took a prominent part in the proceedings, but it was the royal council under Auqui Topa which ordered all arrangements. The foreign warriors gaped at the magnificence of this greatest of all cities, at its splendors and running waters, and above all at the sacredness of its people as they so knowingly sacrificed to the *huacas*

64

and with familiar ease blew kisses in the air to Inti and the Creator.

When the contingents finally moved off down the Huatanay Valley, with Yasca's litter carried in the midst of a small group of Inca fighting men, their faces painted red and adorned with many feathers, with the provincial *ayllus* in the van and bringing up the rear, the dust from that concourse of marching men hung over the valley for hours. Some time later this army, after dire fighting on the high lip of the Bolivian montaña, returned victoriously and its *ayllus* were discharged. Rewards were meted out, the most prized being round medals called *purapura*, made of gold or silver and worn dangling from the neck, and each subject *ayllus* then took the road back to its native valley.

About this time the *runatinya* or "man-drum" of the defeated enemy chieftain from the north, having been jocundly sent down to Cuzco, was even more jocundly received. This dried human skin of a brave man whose name had been Pinto with its grass-stuffed belly and skinny hanging arms was deposited in the trophy house in Cuzco where other dried and defeated chieftains, great *sinchis* and great *capacs* out of the Inca past, were stacked away in musty corners awaiting those boastful fiestas where they would be introduced among the participants along with buffoons, dwarfs, harelips, and hunchbacks. This particular relic would be kept in the charnel house of war until the next Inti Raymi when the Incas would enjoy the humor of having the gruesome object pounding out on its belly not its native songs and boasts of victory but theirs.

But if such successes were in the air, so also were certain disquieting rumors. One persistent and haunting report that afflicted Cuzco was that of the coming end of the world. The distant "edges of the world," the *pachap caylla caylla*, seemed to be stirring and festering with antique memories that now insistently presented themselves for re-examination. It was remembered that in the misty past the god Viracocha had disappeared into the wandering waves of Mamacocha, the great sea, along with his attendant spirits. It had also been said that he would return. Rumor was that the Viracochas (a people) had recently been in those equatorial waters across which their Creator had fled. What did this news presage? Fearfully and with fascinated uncertainty the Incas

65

of Cuzco contemplated some of the possible meanings. Perhaps it was the "end of the world," the *pacha puchucay*. And would the universe dissolve in a catastrophic flood such as that with which it had begun, or an inferno of fire, a *nina pachacuti*? And what of Cuzco, the footstool of holiness? And what stature would an Inca have as time came to an end? But as yet these rumors formed an undercurrent, nothing more.

Cuzco could throw off such portents of trouble and drown itself in the joint festivities it was holding with the northern court in Quito upon the occasion of Huayna Capac's marriage to Rahua Ocllo. Cuzco welcomed Huascar now as the son of the *coya*, and there followed a series of *taquis* designed to drive this fact home and at the same time to bury the memory that, when born, he had not been the legitimate heir. *Curacas* and provincial Inca governors came with rich gifts, glowing words of congratulation, and servile acts of homage. One Inca governor in particular was remembered for the great splendor of his gift to the prince, a beautiful girl named Cumpi Illya, Tapestry Treasure, a princess from the royal house of Icá on the coast. Accepting her with transports of delight as his favorite concubine, Huascar changed her name to Cori Cuillor or Golden Star. So smitten was he that from then on the other women in his harem—some of them *pallas* and thus well above the new acquisition in caste—were systematically and rudely neglected. A few years later, after she had borne a daughter to her husband, the harem cabal which had formed against her succeeded in effecting her destruction. She was found dead one day, presumably of poisoning. Her name was thereupon given to her daughter, who, for the sake of her personal safety and further nurture, was removed to the country estate of one of Huascar's sisters. Huascar had the mummified remains of the mother returned to her parents in Icá as a mark of great favor.

Not too many years after, a pestilence broke in upon Peru, wreaking havoc such as none of the *amautas* could match from their tales of antiquity.

PROCICION·AIVNOS·IPENITECIA·
VACAILLISA3ICVLLAOVI
cvi

SECTION 16.

The Pahuac Oncoy

THE QUECHUA PHRASE for a fulminating and excessively contagious disease was *pahuac oncoy*, "swift-running sickness." One of the most dire phrases in the vocabulary of the Incas, it was always spoken soberly, for no visitation was more greatly dreaded. What appalled them was its fleetness, for it seemed to fly like an invisible swallow or gallop like an unseen *huanaco* over the land. The heart-chilling roar of the earthquake was no more dreaded than the awful silence of these contagions.

No sooner had the news arrived in Cuzco by runners that the epidemic was raging down the coast, no sooner had faces turned toward each other in mute terror at the news, than the first stricken persons began to slump down in Cuzco and the first women to wail their dead. This enemy the Incas could not face. They huddled together in their *canchas*, wishing they could flee to safety but not knowing where. The humble working folk laboring in the *chacras* outside of Cuzco continued to perform their tasks, plowing, planting, irrigating, hoeing, and reaping, but they too were frozen with terror and slowed by their abjectness. Their fellows were caught in the fields or on the roadsides with the fevers and sometimes died so suddenly they almost seemed to sink into the ground. The spouting summer rains soaked their ragged *yacollas* or capes for the last time as they trembled and died at the feet of the pale green cactus lining the roads. Those squatting under dripping *molle*-trees in their *cancha* yards blew frantic kisses to Ausangate, the snowy mountain seen at intervals through sheets of warm rain, but they kept looking back into each other's faces, waiting for the one who would first suddenly clutch his throat and scream out in terror as he

67

felt, or thought he felt, the mealy fingers of the disease searching his insides. Everywhere in the streets of Cuzco, on the terraces above, and in the streamsides below, Incas and lesser folk squatted, biting their mantles and tearing at their garments with their teeth, for to do this, *pachacta canillipuy*, was to show the rage, the fear, and the frustration which overpowered them. This all took place in the year 1524.

It was to be a disaster of almost unheard-of magnitude. The government of Cuzco was almost entirely swept away. That strong man and patient president of the council, Auqui Topa, Huascar's uncle, was carried off. Apu Hilaquita, his counterpart from Lower Cuzco, died also, as did others on the governing body. Numbers of the young virgins impounded in the *acllahuasi* were stricken, and it finally came time for Mama Coca, the abbess of the establishment, to bite her garments and die too.

For the sake of the city Huascar ordered an *itu*, the ultimate abasement by the Incas of themselves as a people and a cry from their smitten hearts for mercy. For two preliminary days the city fasted, abstaining from all but the most unpalatable foods, from all sexual intercourse, or from any expression of individuality or desire. A morbid quiet descended on the city except for such inevitable sounds as were connected with attendance upon the dying and the disposal of the dead. All dogs and other animals were chased from the streets of Cuzco, and all folk who were not Incas were for these few days also expelled. Nothing was allowed to detract from the wholeness, the selfishness, and the uniqueness of this people's profound plea.

With the sunrise of the third day the Capac Incas, the city's highest expression of arrogance and self-confidence, donned special livery. These costumes were of the finest weave, red in color and with long fringes. They wore feathered headdresses and shell necklaces; they carried dried birds of startling green plumage and very small white drums. All of these appurtenances were stored away in one particular room in Cuzco and were brought out only on such occasions. No arms were carried by these great warriors, the flower of Inca soldiery, for they came before their gods with pleading and not with any display of power. And for twenty-four hours not a single word was to be spoken in Cuzco.

Austerely arranged in the center of the square were the Inca gods. On the far edges of the spacious square sat huddled the remaining Incas with their women and children, all with their mantles covering their heads and all perfectly still. Two flawless and beautiful young children, a boy and a girl, had been that day taken up on the hill to Chuquicancha and there, first being made drunk with *akha*, were strangled and offered to Viracocha. Their richly adorned bodies were buried on the spot, and their fresh spirits, supreme and valued gifts from the Inca people, were wafted away to their heavenly *apu*.

Now in Haucaypata began the monotonous petition. In single file and widely spaced the knights proceeded slowly around the square, each beating his drum spasmodically and without rhythm, each one twisting his face in mute and piteous grimaces and awkwardly swinging his feet. Behind each one walked his *palla* carrying in her hands his club, his javelin, and his sling. When one round was completed, they sank down each where they were and one of their number alone circled the square strewing coca leaves in his path. Then again the painful and eerie circle by the full company was retraced. This alternation continued throughout the day, eight times in all and without rest, and eight times between sunset and the next dawn. The *ayllus* sat bowed and covered throughout the cold night listening to the shuffling feet, the senseless drumming, and the great silence beyond.

Thus did a noble people ritually organize their anguish and admit their dependence. They were appealing to Viracocha, creator and sustainer of the world, through his archangel, Inti the Sun, who was the most splendid of all the Inca gods. Inti would hear his people and would favorably intercede for them with Viracocha.

As the sun rose on the following day bringing some warmth to the people stiff with the damps of night or the fatigue of the dance, it was assumed that he brought with him Viracocha's compassionate acceptance of their pleading. Thereupon followed feasting, drinking, and abandon, symbolizing their release from the prisons of fear.

It was not long after this that over the northern rim of Carmenca the flying feet of a *chasqui* were seen; he was risking his neck leaping down the steep and muddy slopes and not trotting down the paved Royal

Road as was usual. The Incas assembled to hear the panting message from the dark lips and to receive the unbelievable sign he carried in his hand.

The *pahuac oncoy* was in the north, and Huayna Capac the emperor was dead.

II
The Last Reign Opens

PALACIOSREALES
INCAP,VACICVIVSM
casas del ynga   corte

SECTION I. *The Center of Cuzco*

HERE, as we stand in the heart of Cuzco at such a crucial moment in her history, let us pause to look about us, for this is Haucaypata, Recreation Square, the capacious center of the city. Today it is the Plaza de Armas. At that time it measured about four hundred feet along the riverside and about three hundred feet on the other axis. Its southern side was defined by the Sapi River which then as now was covered with huge stone slabs and, thus buried, produced the contiguity of Haucaypata with Cusipata, the square on the other bank. The conjoined squares in effect produced a single cleared area seamed across only by a subterranean gully. Each, however, was terraced back from this gully with stone steps in certain places leading up from the lower levels. The flat part of the area of Haucaypata was surfaced with clean sand.

Handsome as this square was, its remarkable quality would not have been apparent to the casual stranger. Outwardly it was very spacious and impressive indeed, but inwardly it was far more; it was a symbol, a lesson in universal geography. Into the area at roughly the four corners came the four main roads of the empire. At each entry was the *huaca* of that particular highway, the Ecuador road, for instance, coming in at the northwest corner where it was worshiped as the Capac Ñan, the Royal Road—here one made sacrifice for the road's solidity and for ease of traveling. At the opposite corner, the spirit in the road to Bolivia was venerated in a *huaca* called the Cold Land, Chiripacha. This arrangement was a statement that the four quarters into which the empire was divided here merged into the Inca heartland. Better

73

still one could read it reversed—that out of Haucaypata had licked four long tongues of empire.

The verb *haucacuy* means "to cease work and enjoy oneself." In this broad and irregularly terraced square it could be visually grasped that the Inca people neither digged, nor toiled, nor spun; others did these things for them while they here enjoyed the ripe fruits of the empire which their boldness had over the years acquired. The name Cusipata meant Happy Square.

The center of the square was by definition the very *omphalos* of empire, the ultimate spot. Here was placed the *capac usno*, the irregularly stepped stone dais and *huaca* of the city which ordinarily only the emperor or the gods might ascend. It was at once a tribunal, an altar, and a talisman. When seated on this stone reviewing troops or presiding over the great festivals, the emperor most especially deserved his patronymic of "Cuzco." At the base of the *usno* was the famous worked stone basin worshiped by lesser folk as a substitute for the image of Inti—for that image was generally visible only to Incas and only in Coricancha. Shaped like a sugar loaf, sheathed in gold and hollowed out, this stone was the gullet of the sun. When any of the great Inca magnates wished to toast their solar father, the contents of the cup offered to him were poured into this receptacle which drained away underground, thus forming an allegory of the sun's potation. On this spot and sitting as it were in the center of their cosmic web, the sun-god and his earthly heirs could be seen in the warm fellowship of father and sons.

The three enclosing sides of Haucaypata were royal residences and their attached buildings.

On the west side was Condorcancha, the palace of the greatest of all the emperors, Pachacuti. He had chosen this site because it adjoined that of Coracora, or Weedfield, his great-grandfather's palace. That former ruler, whose name was Inca Roca, was the ancestor from whom Pachacuti was most pleased to derive his dignity, for he had been a ruler amply displaying the bellicose posture which was finally to gain for the Incas an empire. He had been the planner of Cuzco's splendid irrigation system; he was the first to settle beside the site of Haucaypata, up to then an overgrown and somewhat marshy slope. So closely did Pachacuti identify himself with this ancestor and his "voice of thunder" that he joined their two palaces with a common façade. More than this, he joined both of them in the rear to the House of Learning, the Yachahuasi. This whole huge complex, separated into its component parts only by common interior walls, was termed Casana, "the Admirable," from its uniqueness, its extent, and the skill of its construction.

On the north side of the square was another ward of the city called the Great Yard, Hatuncancha. This area occupied what had formerly been the site of two royal residences, that of Yahuar Huacac (today the site of the Church of the Holy Family) and that of Viracocha Inca (roughly the site of the present Cathedral and the Church of the Triunfo). Both of these areas were enclosed by the same wall when Pachacuti rebuilt Cuzco; the site faced south onto the square. Attached to it on the east side was a section called Quishuarcancha wherein Viracocha Inca had enshrined the god after whom he had named himself. It was later averred that the Spanish altar of the Triunfo marks the spot where the solid gold statue of that creator-god stood in Inca days. Hatuncancha had formidably high walls and only a single narrow entrance. Besides the two *panacas* which possessed the site, it contained a bewildering array of apartments, cells, and houses, mainly for *mamaconas* serving in various cults.

Out in the square directly in front of Quishuarcancha but detached from it stood the imposing Suntur Huasi, a circular tower of peerless masonry, about twenty-five feet high and capped with a thick rounded dome of thatch from the peak of which protruded a supporting pole. Suntur Huasi means "elegant house" which seems to give us a derived meaning like our "kiosk" which implies casual use and an associated leisure. Windows high up under the eaves and one simple entry at ground level varied the effect of the plain masonry walls.

To the east of the Hatuncancha block and across a small adjunct square was Calispucyo Huasi, the palace of Huascar's grandfather Topa Inca. It was part of an impressively large complex called Pucamarca. Only one corner of Pucamarca appeared on Haucaypata; the rest stood out on a terraced area overlooking the Tullu gully in back. The north-

75

I am here appending a glossary of the Quechua names found on the chart of Cuzco in the belief that it will serve the purpose of greater clarity. The usual difficulties in the translation out of Quechua occur here—for instance, *casana* could also mean "the cynosure" (place of astonishment), *Choqque Chaca* could mean "Lance Dam," *Huatanay* could mean place of untying. *Puma curco* may be a reference to a lion's backbone, and *tica tica* could mean "a field of flowers."

Aclla Huasi: House of the Selected Ones (females in this case)
Allpa Suntu: Earth Mound
Amaru Cancha: Dragon Enclosure
Amaru Cata: Dragon Slope
Calis Pucyo: the Spring of the *Calis*-jars
Cantut Moya: Garden of *Cantut*-flowers
Capac Ñan: Royal Road
Chaquil Chaca: Water Cress Bridge
Choqque Chaca: the Golden Dam
Chunchul Mayo: River of Entrails
Chuqui Pampa: the Field of the Spear
Collcampata: Storehouse Terrace
Condor Cancha: the Condor's Enclosure
Cora Cora: Weed Field
Cori Cancha: the Enclosure of Delights
Cusi Pata: Joy Square
Hatun Cancha: the Great Enclosure
Haucay Pata: Leisure Square
Haylli Pampa: Victory Field
Huaca Punco: Sacred Gate
Huatanay Mayo: River of the Place of Tying
Illapa Cancha: Thunder Cancha
Inti Huasi: House of the Sun-God
Llimpi Pata: the Terrace of Many Colors

Mana Huañunca Huasi: the House of the One Who Will Never Die
Muyo Marca: Round Villa (i.e., storied building)
Pata Llacta: Terrace Town
Piñas Huasi: the House of Prisoners
Puma Curco: Lion Beam (i.e., ridge-pole?)
Quillipata: the Terraces (lit., terraces in series)
Rimac Pampa: the Field of the Speaker
Sacsahuaman: Speckled Hawk
Sanka Huasi: the House of the Pit
Sapantiana: the Unique Seat (?)
Sapi Mayo: Root River
Sausero: ?
Suchona: Sliding Place
Suntur Huasi: the Kiosk (lit., house with a mounded roof)
Tampu Cancha: the Cancha of the Tampu Men
Ticatica: the Plumes
Tullu Mayo: River of Bones
Usno: Altar, Tribunal, Throne
Yacha Huasi: House of Knowledge

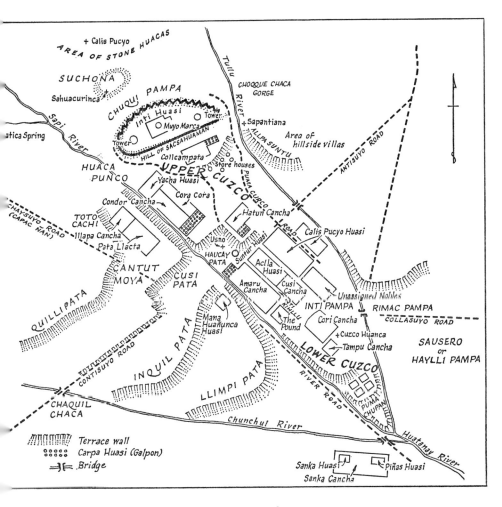

+ Calis Pucyo
AREA OF STONE HUACAS
SUCHONA
Sahuacurinca
CHUQUI PAMPA
Tullu River
CHOQQUE CHACA GORGE
Sapi River
atica Spring
Inti Huasi
Tower
Muyo Marca
Tower
HILL OF SACSAHUAMAN
Collcampata
+ Sapantiana
Area of hillside villas
ALLPA SUNTU
PUMA CUZCO
ANTISUYO ROAD
HUACA PUNCO
UPPER CUZCO
Yacha Huasi
store houses
Cora Cora
Condor Cancha
TOTO CACHI
CHAYSUYO ROAD (CAPAC NAN)
Illapa Cancha
Pata Llacta
CANTUT MOYA
CUSI PATA
Hatun Cancha
Calis Pucyo Huasi
ROAD
Usno
HAUCAY PATA
Suntur Huasi
Acla Huasi
Amaru Cancha
Cusi Cancha
QUILLIPATA
Mana Huanunca Huasi
TULLU
The Pound
INTI PAMPA
RIMAC PAMPA
COLLASUYO ROAD
Cori Cancha
INQUIL PATA
CONTISUYO ROAD
+ Cuzco Huanca
Tampu Cancha
SAUSERO or HAYLLI PAMPA
LLIMPI PATA
RIVER ROAD
LOWER CUZCO
Unassigned Nobles
PUMA
CHUPAN
CHAQUIL CHACA
Chunchul River
Huatanay River

Terrace wall
Carpa Huasi (Galpon)
Bridge

Sanka Huasi
Piñas Huasi
Sanka Cancha

GROUND PLAN OF CUZCO

77

ern retaining wall which supported this massive terrace probably still exists as the south side of the street Hatun Rumiyoc today. The southern wall of Topa's sprawling palace faced on a dark narrow street which separated it from the Acllahuasi, the House of the Selected Women.

Somewhere in the mazy interior of Pucamarca there was a compact, thatched house which enshrined the statue of Chuqui Illa, "Golden Flash," one of the forms of the Inca thunder-god Illapa. Just as the great Pachacuti had monopolized the presence and sustained the cult of Inti Illapa, "Sun Thunder," in his suburban house across the river, so did his son Topa Inca in his palace here jealously guard another avatar of that same god. Such secluded palace shrines lent prestige to the *panaca* of each ruler, for in a sense the god was the family's private possession.

The Acllahuasi was also a part of Pucamarca and was the longest of all the edifices known to us in Cuzco, for it ran all the way down to Coricancha. The street presently called Maruri was driven through the building by the Spaniards soon after the conquest and does not represent the Inca plan. The end that emerged into the great square (what is today the Portal Carrizos) is still extant, an authentic piece of masonry from the days of the Incas. In the Acllahuasi were kept the women of the emperor's own harem as well as those he retained under seal to be granted as gifts or rewards to his favorites. It is probable that the Acllahuasi was built by Topa Inca as a harem adjunct to his palace. Certainly it was used after him by the last two emperors for the same purpose.

South in turn and completing the roster of edifices on the east side of the plaza was Amarucancha, Dragon Yard, the palace of Huayna Capac. It was separated from the Acllahuasi by the Street of the Sun, the Inti Kihllu. One may still walk down this alleylike and shadowy way, today called Loreto. It was Cuzco's most sacred street because all processions between Coricancha and the square had to move along it.

Amarucancha was something of a miracle of construction, for the ground upon which it was built was unstable because of seepage from a spring. On the side running along the Sapi it had been terraced up with *callanca rumi*, a masonry style using great semiworked poly-

78

gonal blocks, examples of which can be seen by the modern tourist along Santa Clara. Amarucancha has long since vanished, and the Church of La Compañía and the old University today take up the site. In its day Amarucancha had a façade on Haucaypata more imposing than any of the others, for the severe and regal front was pierced by a wide entrance flanked on either side by two low turrets. These were not designed for defense because they were topped with thatches which overhung them like the brims of wide hats.

Thus all of the palaces of the emperors of Upper Cuzco were present on Haucaypata. Only that of Huascar was yet to be built.

These palatial complexes must now be described in detail beginning with those curious vestibules which the Incas called *carpa huasi*, "awning houses," which we can liken to sheds open on the inner face and running around three sides of an enclosed rectangular court or patio. They were in all cases built up against the façade of the palace *cancha*, the wall of which thus enclosed and completed the rectangle. The outer plank wall of the *carpa huasi*, unlike the jealous and exclusive palace to which it was attached, had a number of doors scattered along its three sides, thus permitting free and easy access. Numbers of wooden posts on the inside supported great beams heavily thatched over to turn off the storm. The width of the shed area could be as much as fifty feet and the length of a side any distance desired. There were three of these *carpa huasi* on Haucaypata, one for Casana, one for Quishuarcancha, and one for Amarucancha. The purpose of these sheds was to provide protection to the *panacas* during the fiestas of the rainy season. In winter when the season was clement, the *panacas* carried out their ceremonials in the open square outside. The Casana *carpa huasi*, which was the largest of them all could seat among its wooden columns three thousand people of the Iñaca and Vicaquirau *panacas* and all their guests and retainers. This side of Haucaypata was faced with a terrace-wall, because of the steep pitch of the ridge at this point, and on this terrace the great hall stood. The shed attached to Quishuarcancha apparently filled a part of that indented corner of Haucaypata where the street of the Triunfo now enters and served to shelter the *panacas* of Yahuar Huacac, Viracocha Inca, and Topa Inca.

The palace proper generally resembled on an exaggerated scale its model, the traditional stone-walled Peruvian farm enclosure called the *cancha*. In such rural family steadings llamas could be corralled, produce stored away in covered bins, protection offered from beasts or the terrors of the night, and the houses of the family head and his sons' families erected. The gable-ended stone houses generally used a part of the yard wall in their construction. Thus is explained the labyrinthine ground plan of the *canchas* in Machu Picchu and in what is visible of the interior walls in the center of Cuzco. Each *cancha* wall thus outlined a small and very resistant Peruvian world.

Expanding greatly on its rustic model, the royal *cancha* in Cuzco was divided into an irregular series of apartment complexes. These were the *pitita*, the areas and rooms separated from each other by partition walls thinner than the heavy and protective walls enclosing the whole. Access from one of these areas to another was generally restricted to one narrow entry only—with a winding staircase between walls if a terraced slope was the case. What seems unusual to us is that the small darkened, often windowless quarters were really not apartments in one large edifice, but many small individual thatched houses, sometimes separate, often in files with common walls. There could easily be a hundred of these separate habitations in a royal *cancha*, some with a second floor or steeply pitched garret room reached by a ladder. Only the outer *cancha* entries had timber doors that could be effectively barred with heavy wooden bolts; the apartment areas within possessed only hangings over the doorways. Privacy was gained by porters stationed at these inner gates. The office of *puncu camayok* or "doorman" was a well-known and a heavy responsibility in Inca life. Interior patios on an intimate scale served the inner areas of the palace. Sometimes there were four or five of them in a single *cancha*. The *coya*'s quarter had, of course, its own patio.

From its intricate arrangements and many cul-de-sacs, the harem was a *kenko huasi*, "a house of winding passages." The *coya*'s apartments took up a significant portion of this area, her women being domiciled in files of adjoining cell-like rooms. In the patios well-watered gardens and arbors had been so platted that one could enjoy there the blue *siclla* flower, trimmed bushes of crimson *cantut* flowers hanging their clusters in profusion, beds of brilliant salvia, *ñuhchu*, or the pink *mayhua*, the lily of love. Tanks of clear water constantly replenished from stone spouts provided drinking facilities and fishponds for entertainment, while in little pots beside them grew the slender stems of the prized *hamancay*, the yellow narcissus. There were aviaries for green parrots, doves from the Yucay country, and gaudy or sweet-singing birds of the upper montaña. On rope leashes the small yellow monkey called *paucar cussillu* huddled down in this foliage, never to live long in this high world so remote from his warm aerial world of the great *hacha hacha*. Some of the walls within the women's quarter displayed on their plaster surfaces near-abstract friezes of butterflies, snakes, or flowers laid on in strong, flat colors. There were rougher areas for work and privys for each of the sections, *acana huasi*.

One entered the palace through the *carpa huasi* courtyard, in the outer area of which was stationed, in the case of the living emperor, a regiment of Chachapoya Indians or of Cañars, each carrying an ornate tufted lance. Crossing this vestibule, one came to the single entry of the *cancha* proper, guarded this time by Inca knights, their war slings wound around their foreheads and their battle maces in their hands. Immediately inside this main entry was the guard room or armory, for the palatial *cancha* was designed to withstand a minor siege if necessary. Beyond was an antechamber where ambassadors and great *curacas* waited for audience, and upon this room opened the quarters for the many young squires, all of them highborn, attached as pages to the household.

In this general area was one of the largest buildings of all, a thatched, gable-ended, and commodious building open to the air all along one of the long sides and leading on to a kind of patio. This structure was the *cuyos manco* and housed all important gatherings of the Capac Incas and meetings of the royal council whenever extended deliberation was necessary. All important administrative and judicial decisions issued from this heavy-beamed council chamber with the open side. In a sense it was also the throne room, for here sat the emperor on his low stool of state when he received ambassadors and other dignitaries.

In raw weather fires of special aromatic wood warmed and lighted the capacious interior. Farther back in the recesses of the palace was a quarter housing the *churacona huasi*, the "storage area," in which was the treasury, the *capac marca huasi*, a large two-story building in which were kept precious mantles, jewels, regalia, gold utensils, and feathered work used by the emperor. This building possessed strong doors and a dry and lofty garret and was under the particular supervision of a treasurer and his assistants. The livery of the corps of pages was changed frequently, and those pieces of clothing were stored in designated wardrooms where they were readily accessible. Mementos of the emperor's victories and the stuffed and dried bodies of conquered enemy chiefs were kept in another chamber called the house of spoils, *llasa huasi*.

In the harem quarter, the one most sequestered of all, the making of *akha* by the lesser women went on constantly, and special storage space was allotted for heavy jars of this fermented maize beer, the staple for any celebration. The emperor's private quarters were back in the harem, and here his servitors were selected young women, no men being allowed in these precincts. Within this area the living emperor ate, slept, and played. If the emperor were a mummy, about the only building in his palace for which he had little use was the *cuyos manco*, for with policy a mummy did not concern himself.

Section 2. *Coricancha and the Lion's Tail*

LARGEST OF ALL the households in Cuzco, except that of the living emperor, was Coricancha, that majestic family yard wherein each of the Inca gods possessed his own rectangular *huasi* or thatched house, all arranged around a central patio. Only Huanacauri on his windy ridge some miles southeast of the city was domiciled outside the shrine area. All of Cuzco to the northwest of Coricancha was Upper Cuzco; that part below it and toward the joining of the rivers was Lower Cuzco.

There were probably more than four thousand people attached to the divine households in Coricancha of whom some two hundred were *mamaconas* serving as Inti's wives, preparing his food and *akha*, clothing him, coaxing favors for the ruling emperor from him, drumming for him at the fiestas, and offering him sexual satisfaction. That one chosen to be his consort for the night ascended a high stone bench in his house. This marital couch was placed next to his statue and beautifully decorated with blankets of the iridescent feathers of rare Amazonian birds. Of these consorts of Inti only one, however, was the sungod's true vicarious wife; she was always elected from the imperial house and was either a sister or daughter of the ruling emperor. Her office was that of Coya Pacsa, literally "Queen Moon," for as the sun's female consort in the heavens was the moon, so was there a priestess who represented her in Coricancha. Others of the hierodules of Coricancha belonged to the household of Illapa, the threefold god of the storm, and possibly some belonged to Viracocha, although the latter is doubtful in view of the highly spiritualized conception which the Incas had of the Creator.

Mama Quilla, Moon Mother, had her own house and retinue headed by the Coya Pacsa. On ceremonial occasions the *panacas* brought to this house-shrine the mummies of their *coyas* and ranged them on both sides of the great silver disc placed conspicuously against the façade of her house. In a spot singled out for divine honors there was a special niche for that one of the dead *coyas* who had been most splendidly deified. This was Huayna Capac's mother, Mama Ocllo, who in life had been a most decided person, in stature small and plump and with a pretty face but much feared by all. Her shriveled mummy sat in this chapel now as a goddess identical with the consort of Manco Capac, who as the progenitress of the Inca people had borne that same name, Mama Ocllo.

Besides these abodes of the great gods there was a chapel to Chasca Cuillor, the Radiant Star, who was the morning star or Venus. This beautiful god was considered to be the sun's page, and his house sheltered all the others of the starry host, including importantly the Pleiades who were the ladies-in-waiting of the moon. Lastly there was the chapel of the rainbow. In all there were thus five active households miming the lives of their divine masters or mistresses.

83

In a corner under a shed sumptuously thatched danced the ever-burning *nina villca,* "the fire god." Only from this sacred stone hearth could there be taken the brands to light the fires of sacrifice in Cuzco's many festivals. Into this fire were thrown the fine foods daily desired by Inti and the gods. The ashes of this fire were themselves so sacred that they were collected and stored for a year until they could be ceremonially disposed of in the Huatanay River.

Coricancha was an impressive quarter and seems to have included a larger area than just the enclosed patio of the gods. There was a small place where the priests kept the woolen cable called the *moroy urco* or "spotted male" used in Inca dances. Here also was a small shrine where were kept the sanctified weapons and regalia used by the great emperor Pachacuti when he fought and won the memorable battle of Yahuar Pampa. Also adjoining Coricancha was the supposed residence of Manco Capac, appropriately called Tambo Cancha, as well as another very small dwelling, Inticancha, which legend said had been the home of his four sister-wives. Both of these were venerable *huacas.* The former was probably where the Chima *panaca* kept an effigy of the First Ancestor and therefore may well have been the residence of that *panaca.* In this area also was one of Cuzco's most cherished *huacas,* an isolated stone which was the petrified relict of Ayar Auca, one of the Four Brothers who first settled on the site of Cuzco. In this *Cuzco Huanca,* as it was called, lurked the dangerous and ghostly powers of the old and autochthonous Hualla *ayllu* which had been uprooted from its home in the lurid days of the founding.

The open area in front of Coricancha was called the Field of Pure Gold, Choqquepampa. Opening on it was a large pound or corral, a part of which was kept constantly filled with llamas of specified colors for sacrifice; the remainder of the pound was a separate area with shed-like constructions and huts within which were huddled those young boys and girls, ranging in age up to about twelve, who were awaiting sacrifice on the hills round about. The whinnying and spitting of the llamas crowding together, shaking their tasseled ears and stamping, contrasted with the awful silence from under the children's thatches. Customarily the priests came to inspect certain of the children three times a year for the absolute purity and soundness of their bodies, and to take away designated ones that they might be richly clothed, made drunk, and then strangled. How the children were fed and tended in the pound, what the sanitary arrangements were, or whether there were any provisions for recreation and exercise before their time arrived—of these matters we have no knowledge. They were children of many tongues and different races and were therefore unable to communicate with each other. All they had in common were their beauty and their destiny. The visitor today who stands on the public corner where the Pampa del Castillo opens onto San Domingo may strain his ears to catch again that uneasy shifting of animals muffling the heavy silence of the motherless children in an effort to grasp the terrible intensity with which the Incas lived.

The walls of Coricancha and the precipitous terraces upon which it rested marked the oldest area of the city, called originally *Cuzco Caca* or "the Rock of Cuzco." This eminence of clay and gravel cliffs was ingeniously engineered with massive terraces carefully stepped back. It overlooked the point where the Sapi and the Tullu came together. Four *canchas* of the Lower Cuzco moiety occupied the lower terraces. These were the palaces of the remaining *panacas*, those of Sinchi Roca, Lloque Yupanqui, Mayta Capac, and Capac Yupanqui. They were, of course, far less pretentious than those of the group around the great square. From this low point one could look back up to the terraces of Coricancha, the verdure of which made an emerald circlet just under the blank walls during the ripening season, for these were gardens of the gods and the plots for their sacred maize. The lower terraces probably supported some of the detached outbuildings of Coricancha as well as a high walkway looking far down into the neat gully of the Sapi and across to the wide valley beyond. Today one can stroll down the busy Avenida del Sol, probably representing the lowest of those old terraces, and by looking up on the left to Santo Domingo, which has inherited the site of Coricancha, still take in the pronounced steepness of ridge, although the undisciplined mass of ugly dwellings today gives little hint of the beauty and gravity that was once there.

This whole narrow triangle of land below Coricancha was called the

Lion's Tail, Pumapchupan. The walled point of land jutting out into the waters of the two streams was a park area happily planted with a grove of trees. This was the *mayu tincu*, "the meeting place of the rivers," exceedingly holy. In a small edifice on the esplanade were kept all the ashes from the meals offered to the gods during the year, refuse that no one dared touch without proper safeguards. Annually, therefore, and with all proper precautions, these ashes were cast over the wall into the running waters to be ceremonially removed from Cuzcoquiti.

Now, much shrunken in size, the site of this point of land is a bare triangular plaza appropriately dedicated to the Spanish discoverers of the Amazon, for here was one of that vast river's most remote of headwaters. The dusty and unlovely scene of today looking into the railroad yards hides the muddy trickle of the Sapi and the Tullu from view, for they are buried under the street, giving one no sense of the antique geometry once created here.

SECTION 3.

The Waters of Cuzco

IN DESCRIBING this city as it was before the Spaniards entered, we must keep in mind that we are describing, not a city at all in our sense of the word, but a shrine housing a sacred people and their gods. Springs and rivers in the area were thus far more than mere functional watercourses. They were living waters filled with a superior *huaca*. They were the visible signs of the ichor that flowed in the veins of the Incas.

Two streams, the Sapi and the Tullu, fell out of the steep heights against which the city was set. In converging, they formed the triangle which defined the city's limits. The base of that triangle was marked by the headland of Sacsahuaman. Thus as one moved up the axial streets of Cuzco from the point of the triangle to its base, the way became increasingly precipitous and the view down into the city more imposing.

The river that was formed by the juncture was the famous Huatanay, a word meaning "place of tying," suggested perhaps by the nearness of the famous Inca dungeons. Confluences of rivers were known as *mayo tincu* and by the Andean Indian were thought to be peculiarly august *huacas*. This one was perhaps the most sacred in all the Peruvian *sallca*. Here was annually performed the festival, common to all Peru, of the *purapucyo*. Flowers of many kinds were thrown into the river, and in a great bonfire lighted at the terraced point of land many llamas and other animals were burned that the river might eat and be fat. Rich and lovely garments were also added to the flames so that the water-spirit might not lack clothing. Finally the Incas here toasted the special *huaca* of their waters, throwing into the tumbling stream cups of *akha* while themselves drinking from others.

This ceremony was performed with somber pageantry. It opened as the sun was setting, and a great rush of water poured down the two gullies, released at a preconcerted time from impounded reservoirs above. This rite was the symbol of the hunger of the waters. The tabooed ashes of the sacrifices, the burnt meats, and other debris from this and previous festivals were escorted downstream by men with long poles and flambeaux. They saw to it that the river rejected none of this matter, for as they moved along the banks, they pushed the flotsam back into the channel wherever it was cast up. The black night of the Andes sparkled with these pinpoints of light moving downriver and with the leaping light of the great bonfire at the point of the *mayo tincu*. With this beautiful homage to the waters of Cuzco, the Incas helped to assure a fertile year ahead.

But *mayo tincu* were more than meeting places between man and water. They were also holy lavatories where sin and illness, the latter the result of sin, could be washed away. As such these select areas were *upacuna*, literally "face-washing places." Therefore to Pumapchupan

87

came the Incas when they were ill to state their sins in private prayer: "I have told my sins to Inti. You, O river, receive them. Carry them down to the sea where they will never be heard of again." Dangerous sins could be disposed of in three ways at the *upacuna*, depending on the seriousness of the disease or misfortune in question. An Inca could simply wash them away by throwing water on his face so that the residue fell into the river and was borne away. Or, if one were less than a great nobleman, he could confess to a special priest called an *ichuri*. A bundle of grass or *ichu* would be spit into and then this object, to which the contamination had been transferred was thrown into the river and disposed of. Or if the case were very serious, one employed sin-eaters who were hunchbacks, dwarfs, mutilated people, and monsters residing in a special ward close by, probably in Sakra, and who were always available, clustering here day after day on the riverbank. These unfortunates were considered to be already so hated and damaged by the gods that one could rightly pass off on them one's own vice or sin; this goal was achieved at the *upacuna* by having them beat or stroke one, so that the evil flowed off to them by physical contact.

As hydraulic engineers the Incas were among the world's greatest, although it is not to be denied that in the possession of this great skill they stood on the shoulders of the rich civilization of the Peruvian past. Their control of headwaters was as exemplary as their canalization of flooding rivers. In the case of the Sapi, which rose some three miles behind the city on the slopes of Mount Chaca (today Mount Corcor), a series of dams impounded its waters and gave complete control. One of the largest of these dammed areas was the Sapipakchan, or "the spillway of the Sapi." In the *purapucyo* ceremony, as we have noted, when a great abundance of freshet water was desired to scour out the Huatanay, all of the dams could be unlocked at once. This annual man-made flood was one of the impressive sights of Inca Cuzco. The tumbling waters came down through the locks and out the mouth of the romantic Huacapunco gorge to plunge foaming into the buried passageway under the squares of Cuzco. They emerged well above the *mayo tincu*. Below the point of land the Huatanay had been artificially straightened and ran between sloping and slabbed banks of heavy masonry almost to its end, thus carrying the swollen waters smoothly and easily out into the valley.

The Tullu comes down a far smaller but even more sylvan glen, so steeply pitched as to form more a series of cascades than a stream bed. Its course was everywhere interrupted by rock cutouts and artificially deepened pools and caves. Anywhere along the upper course of this ravine, which is today called Choqquechaca, one could look up and see the magnificent outer walls of the fortress of Sacsahuaman lowering over one's head. At the point where the Tullu emerged into the upper city it flowed into a large and intricate masonry tank from which its waters could be distributed. The ruins of this magnificent reservoir are still well preserved. The deep cleft made by the Tullu is secluded and protected from violent winds. It was for these reasons chosen by some of the great *curacas* of Cuzcoquiti as a preferred site for their many pleasure and suburban villas, built up one above the other on narrow *patas*. Each of these *patas* presented to the city below high vertical walls with flat stones jutting out like pegs and echeloned up to form projecting stairs, most frightening for those who need the support of a balustrade. A commodious but steep road followed the course of the stream down into Cuzco from the fortress; in places this roadbed was stepped. Hardly any of this descent remains, and of the rich villas and multiple terracing hanging over the little ravine there is nothing at all. The slopes are bare.

The waters of Cuzco brought in via open aqueducts or *rarca* were twofold. They were divided into Hananchacan and Hurinchacan, the Upper and Lower water systems. A splendid piece of engineering was responsible for at least one of these, a great drainage ditch drawing on the water of Lake Piuray near Chinchero on the other side of the mountain and coming into the Huatanay Valley down the side of Carmenca. Probably this trench served mainly to water Cuzco's high *carpana allpa*, or irrigable land, both flat and terraced. For this water Cuzco was indebted to Inca Roca, first of the rulers of Upper Cuzco, and it was permanently in the possession of his *panaca*, for the ownership of water was always an *ayllu* or family affair.

Besides these two major supplies, fine drinking water was brought in either in underground pipes or in masonry runnels leading into spouted basins or fountains called *pakcha*. There were several of these quality systems and it is difficult for us now to disentangle them, for the many fountains through which the water successively passed were each given names. The original source of the water, the *pucyo*, also had its special magical properties, as did each of the basins. One of these systems of sweet drinking water was that which supplied the Uiroy Pakcha, "Sweet Cornstalk Fountain." This water was on the south side of the Sapi and came from the hillside reservoirs of Ticatica, less than a mile from the city in the Sapi gorge. Pachacuti had some of this water led into a large tank called Pillcopucyo in the palace of his *huaoqui*. Here Inca rulers were accustomed to cleanse themselves ceremonially, and to the *huaca* of these impounded waters one also prayed for the repose and well-being of the ruler. That part of this clear stream which ran through the beautiful gardens nearby was referred to as the *cantut* waters, the reference being to the red-flowered *cantut*-bush.

Then there was the spring which was brought down from just under Sacsahuaman's walls. The topmost fountain of all, on the wide and lovely terrace of Collcampata, was the famous Ticcicocha or "Foundation Pool." Its waters fell in a series of stepped basins and were finally taken into Casana. The route of its ancient channel is today commemorated in the street called Teccecocha. Another channel apparently came down the Pumacurco road, passed by or through Topa Inca's palace, and emerged through spouts into the famous basin called the Spring of the *Calis*-jars. From this source the noble Inca families in the near neighborhood drew their water. It is probable that the small open area today called the Limac Pampa Chico marks this spot from which serving-girls once drew up the sanctified water for their masters.

Probably unconnected with either of these two channels was the fountain called Haucaypata in the northwest corner of the square of the same name. This spring was probably the origin of that seepage which had from early times turned the whole area into a bog and a weed field until it was finally filled in by Pachacuti who, probably at the same time, tamed the source. The old name of the piece of land on which existed the spring that fed the fountain was Skunk Corner, and it was situated just to the rear of the present Church of the Holy Family. This spring was an exceedingly powerful rain *huaca*, for in it the priests of Illapa were accustomed to bathe their god of storms whenever drought threatened.

This discussion by no means exhausts the tally of fountains and basins in the city. In the famous garden attached to Coricancha there was a source called the Spring of the *Pillco*-bird from which water was piped in underground (so ran the reports) from a distance. This running water was later lost by the friars of San Domingo and never recovered. The Spring of the Mortar served the area of Limacpampa just below, refreshing travelers from the far Collao as they entered the city. A famous water system was the Silver Serpents or Collque Machacuay. This was a dual set of underground pipes carrying the waters of a spring on Mount Puquin and running in toward the city from the south. It is possible that it was the Silver Serpents which supplied the water for Coricancha's garden.

Water was indeed the life of this high city in the Andes, and to its distribution, its uses, and its worship the Incas applied their notable talents. Each basin, as explained, had its own name and its own *huaca*. Running cleanly and swiftly along well-made stone channels, whether irrigating the terrace gardens around or contributing to the city's pleasure or taken into the *canchas* for the intimate uses of great families, each became a little center of life and lore for the inhabitants. During the festival of the girls' first menstruation, the *quicuchicoy*, which took place as an adjunct of the breechcloth ceremony of the young knights, each girl received from a near kinsman a new name. She put on the beautiful red and white *acsu* marking her as a young woman and nubile, and she threw away the headband of girlhood. This activity was all associated with the *huarmihapiy pacha*, or "wife-taking time." But before these events had all happened and in preparation for the event, the girls ceremonially bathed, purifying themselves in the Sapi. While they clustered together, naked in the cold mountain water, on the terraces just above them the young men—undergoing their own initiation—came to watch them publicly and to play on their flutes. The thin sounds of that annual fluting, the shrieks of the bathing girls, and the splashing and low rumble of the water no longer sound from the cleft of Ticatica, Place of Flowers, but sometimes a hot noon sun and the ability to dream can bring it back.

Thus were the waters of Cuzco wedded to the life of the city.

DELOS IÑGAS IDESVCOИЗЕ
PIИAS CARЗELES

Section 4.

Cuzco South of the Sapi

INASMUCH as the sacred triangle is pressed up against a steep slope on the north, little room for expansion of living quarters could be had there. But across the Sapi, to the south, at least a square mile of upward rolling land was available. Most of it now is inhabited Cuzco, but at that time it was open country with only a few small clusters of habitations, the whole geometrically though irregularly terraced with great facing walls stepping back and up to the heights of Carmenca with increasingly narrow *patas* on top, many of them planted to crops but some serving as basements for isolated villas or groves of trees.

All of this setting could be seen from Haucaypata. If one had stood here in those days on the line of the buried Sapi, sweeping one's gaze from left to right and then back into the center, one could have identified a series of important sites.

Looking left and straight downriver to the *mayo tinku*, one would have seen on the opposite or south bank an isolated group of buildings that bore an infamous name, Sankacancha "the Place of the Pit." The site today is about where the railroad tracks and the Avenida Centenario meet. Within the closely guarded outer walls were two separate dungeons. One was for the Inca criminal, the *iscaysoncco auca* or "double-hearted traitor"; the other, called the Piñas Huasi, "the House of War Prisoners," was for captive enemies or other non-Incas.

Each was an elaborate underground construction of pits and galleries strewn with heavy jagged flints that afforded no place of rest or momentary relief. Within the area also was a nightmarish zoo where were kept such poisonous snakes as the bushmaster and the deadly fer-de-lance, scorpions, half-starved pumas, and other beasts; these creatures were introduced at will into dens where prisoners to be tortured were kept. Because of its terrifying reputation and its site on the *mayo tinku*, Sankacancha was a *huaca* which was profoundly reverenced by all the folk around. Whereas today the spot is one of the crowded but less desirable parts of the modern city, at that time the Sankacancha stood isolated among rich fields and winding irrigation ditches. Back from it and over toward the first hill was a settlement, older than Cuzco itself, called Cayaocachi, today the parish of Belén.

Cayaocachi was in part inhabited by the Ayar Ucho *ayllu*, a group which had once lived within the sacred triangle itself but which had been broken up and later expelled by Pachacuti. Earlier they had had strong *sinchis* but had lost the leadership of Cuzco to the Men of Manco led by the fourth ruler, Mayta Capac. It had been this latter who had built the Sankacancha and had cast the defeated *sinchi* of the Ayar Ucho group into its freshly dug pits to meet there a horrible death. This *ayllu*, because of its power and prestige, remained in the Inca canon, but it seems always to have been under some suspicion. It was in fact to greet the Spaniards on their entry with a welcome made savagely exultant by the long decades of semideprivation and discourtesy it had suffered; the Ayar Ucho *ayllu* could not forget that once it had been the possessor of the ground of Haucaypata before the Men of Manco ever came into the valley.

Directly in front of one, and in an air line about three miles back, could be seen the bare top of Mount Puquin. One of the four imperial roads, the Contisuyo road, came in past this hill. On Puquin important ceremonies were performed in a shrine referred to as the House of the Sun. Here was one of Inti's country villas, as it were, and to this place for recreation his priests brought from Coricancha that image which represented him as the rising sun. But what made Puquin unique were its archival treasures; stored here were sacred legends of the Incas: the flood sent by Viracocha, the election of Manco Capac, the deeds of all the Inca rulers, the blazon of each emperor—all painted in pictures on wooden tablets. Nothing of the remains of this wonderful ancient library can be positively identified. The contents were probably ransacked and destroyed by Atauhuallpa before the Spaniards came.

From the grim walls of Sankacancha a tree-lined road led up along the riverbank to enter Cusipata at a point opposite where we are now standing. This Via Dolorosa ran up onto a broad terrace called Intipata bearing *chacras* green with young maize or flowering potato plants; from here, crossing the Contisuyo road, it ascended the broad-faced terrace upon which Cusipata was situated. At this point, exactly where La Merced is today, one could see "the House of Her Who Shall Not Die," the *Manahuañunca Huasi*. This small *cancha* belonged to one of the departed *coyas*, probably Mama Ocllo, the mother of Huayna Capac, for the terrace on which it stood—called Llimpipata—is directly across the river from that ruler's palace. This *coya* had been deified by her son who had early in his youth owed his throne to her courage and resourcefulness. It was in this curious shrine that her mummy was undoubtedly kept, surrounded by a small court of *pallas*. Our Lady of Mercies had arrived on the exact same site by the year 1536, the year of the Siege, and just as Mama Ocllo had been Tahuantinsuyo's greatest *coya* and had once protected it from a deadly conspiracy, so Our Lady of Mercies was to become the patroness of the Arms of Peru.

Cusipata, facing us, has disappeared, buried under one of the busiest and most crowded parts of modern Cuzco. Standing on this spot over the Sapi which runs underground, we are today looking up the steep street of Medio crowded on both sides with shops and dank living quarters, and we can see at the end the corner of the Government Hotel. In the days of the Incas we would have seen stairs ascending from Haucaypata up through the face of a notable terrace of *ccallanca rumi* and out onto the surface of Cusipata. If we had ascended those steps, we would have been on the edge of a great open area capable of holding more than one hundred thousand people, dusty in the dry winter but well drained in the summer. The only edifice opening onto it was the afore-mentioned Manahuañunca Huasi. Only two remnants of this vast open area remain today, the Plaza de Regocijos, a literal translation of the Quechua name, and the Plaza de San Francisco behind it.

Because Cusipata was outside the pomerium of Cuzco and therefore less sacred than Haucaypata, it was used by those non-Incas who participated in the great state festivals, *curacas*, visiting dignitaries, ambassadors from subject states, and priests of foreign *huacas*. The presence of these people adjoining Haucaypata could thus properly complete the festivities, but their feet would not thereby profane the soil sacred to the Children of the Sun. When Cusipata was not in use for such celebrations, it served as the *catu* or "market" where those few goods not swallowed up by the Inca warehouses could be freely exchanged. This market was in no sense as colorful or enterprising as the great fairs of contemporary Mexico because of the nature of Inca monopoly and the rigid social structure of the city of Cuzco.

At the far end of Cusipata was the curving face of another gigantic backing wall supporting in turn another terrace on which crops were cultivated. Today the Church of San Francisco occupies the edge of this elevated face. Beyond this point, the slope becoming measurably steeper, another terrace wall faced one, after which the Chinchaysuyo road, cutting up through both walls, moved gracefully and windingly up the pitch of Carmenca, occasionally carried along for a distance on higher and much narrower terrace tops. So steep is the pitch that even the natives today stop a time or two to rest on their way up to Santa Ana.

On the terrace close to where the Chinchaysuyo road entered Cusipata was Patallacta, one of the most unusual sites outside the sacred triangle.

Patallacta—or Terrace Town as it is translated—was inappropriately named, for it was a complex of houses and not a large community. As explained, it stood on one of the terraces of the steeply tilted southwest bank of the Sapi. Pachacuti had many years before usurped this site for

95

his own purposes, improving the situation with those gigantic retaining walls which were the wonder of their day. Directly across the Sapi was Condorcancha, his own palace. It was therefore fitting that on this opposite bank and on a corresponding site he should have erected this shrine to himself—for that is what he designed it to be. Here his successors came to sacrifice children to his charismatic spirit, and here with retirement and fasting they requested his powerful intercession with the gods. In this house also, by prearrangement, he had died, a very old, silver-haired man, shrunken and senile. Everything about that ghostly palace was magical and exuded wisps of the frightful presence that had once been his.

In addition he had erected nearby for his *huaoqui* a small palace which he called Illapa Cancha. This *huaoqui* was a form of the thunder-god which he had commanded to be formed as a solid gold image and which he called Inti Illapa. He had it taken with him on all of those campaigns of his later years, and it had been invariably the bringer of superb victories. Like his mummy, therefore, it was provided with a palanquin covered with gold leaf and it was constantly served by members of his *panaca* who resided on the spot.

Some of the terrace tops here were not only *purina* or "walkways" but were landscaped as gardens. The area had been planted as a park with *chachacoma* trees and elaborate rows of those bushes which bore the cherry-red flowers so beloved by the Incas, bushes which gave their name to these famous gardens, *Cantut Moya*, "the Garden of *Cantut*-flowers." The Chinchaysuyo road came down the hill just back of these gardens, one of the most agreeable spots in Cuzco. A branch of the road turned down past the site to cross the Sapi where Santa Teresa is today and thence to clamber up to Collcampata. Exact locations cannot of course be made, but it is very tempting to see Cuzco's Prefectura of today as occupying the site of Illapa Cancha, while in the ruined or remodeled Inca fountain at the rear of the Plazuela de Silva it is easy for us to imagine that we behold again one of the famous basins in the house of Pachacuti—perhaps Pillcopucyo itself.

From the place where we have been standing, on the south side of Haucaypata, it was easy to follow with the eye the Chinchaysuyo road up to where it began to carry over the top of Carmenca. Carmenca is today the parish of Santa Ana. As a community, Carmenca, perched up on the nearest spur, was at least as old as Cuzco below it. Its *ayllu* had only with the long passage of time fitted into the Inca pattern, for it insisted on carrying on an aboriginal feud with Cayaocachi below. It was the most strategically placed of all Cuzco's suburban hamlets, for it controlled the entrance into the Huatanay Valley from the northwest. Therefore the Incas had planted it with Cañar *mitmacs* from Ecuador, for the Cañars had become the mercenaries of the later Inca emperors. By Huascar's time Carmenca was a true community of *Incapmichuscan runa*, "people brought in by the Inca," with a resultant mixture of natives and newcomers eternally suspicious of each other, the ideal imperial community. The spur on which Carmenca is situated looks across the ravine of the Sapi to the heavy outworks of Sacsahuaman, Cuzco's fortress. At the top of the road one came to that most sacred spot, Urcos Calla, where the traveler from the north received his first view of Cuzco. Urcos Calla was a check point as well as a *tambo* or inn. On the way up to this point from Cuzco one passed the sun pillars or *sucanca* and just beyond them a small shrine within which certain outcropping stones were venerated as the wives of the Creator who, because of their night-wandering and their sexual irregularities, had there been metamorphosed into stone.

On its opposite side, Carmenca looks over the ravine of Aya Huaycco, "Dead Man's Gulch," to the hill of Picchu. At the spot where Aya Huaycco opened out into the bowl of Cuzco, the eye might have perceived two thatched edifices, called Huaman Cancha, "Hawk Enclosure," where the prospective Inca youths fasted during the culmination of the knighting ceremonies. Upon the completion of this fast, they were required to ascend to the top of Picchu to worship Yahuira from whom they received their loincloths, symbols of their manhood. Apu Yahuira was the ancestral *huaca* of the Maras *ayllu*, one of the most well-knit clans of Lower Cuzco. The *huaca* itself was a stone which had once been one of Huanacauri's brothers and was therefore one of the ancestral four who had emerged from Pacaritambo, although which of the four is somewhat uncertain.

97

The Contisuyo road had a higher importance in Cuzco's religious life than in her economy; this was the road to Pacaritambo, the rock of origination out of which the Incas had emerged following the Flood. The area penetrated by the road was excessively rough and broken and lacking in broad fertile valleys. The road left Cuzco making its initial ascent between Puquin and Picchu. About two miles out the traveler came to the community of Choco, a well-known hamlet suburban to Cuzco. The ancestral *huaca* of these people, Mount Anahuarque, had the power of conferring fleetness of foot; thus, the young Inca candidates for knighthood here staged their breath-takingly dangerous race down that particular mountainside to display their agility. Magical preparations for this test were taken in a meadow called Raurana, the Place of Burning, near the base of the mountain; here both the young men and the *ñustas* slept in tents before the race, and here took place the *machachicuy* or carousal which followed.

The Contisuyo road had a strategic importance also. In the darkest days of Cuzco's past, the black whirlwind of the Chanca invasion had threatened from that quarter as well as from the north, at which time the people of Choco, led by a legendary woman called Cori Coca, halted and finally helped to crumple the attack. Therefore, Pachacuti had taken as his *coya* a woman from that community—perhaps Cori Coca herself—and had given her the throne name of her people's *huaca*, Mama Anahuarque.

The road ran over the divide, past the community of Yaurisque where there were *mitmacs*, and down the deep and narrow Cusibamba River to a great headland called Old City or Maucallacta. Here the road left the river to ascend the mountain, for among those serried and savage clefts was one huge cone-shaped rock, today called Poma Urco, "Lion Mount," which the Incas claimed as their *pacarina*. This was Pacaritambo, "the Inn of First Appearances."

Speckled hawks float across the face of the sky here, and on warmer days rains rush down today exactly as they did then, but very few visitors go to this site any more, for the way is difficult and lonely. It was a site artificially selected by Pachacuti to stand for that crag out of which the eight ancestors of the Incas crawled after the Flood had receded. A dead rock to us, pitted and tumbled about, it was to the Inca who stood worshipfully at its base, the very home of glory.

SECTION 5. *Huascar's Assumption of Power*

WITH THE CONTINUING deaths of so many of her great men, the demoralization that attended the plague in Cuzco had deepened the tides of intrigue that were common among the *panacas*. They rose again in flood. Then when the news of the emperor's death was received, the last barriers to restraint were swept away. At stake now was the incredible wealth of the empire of the world, if only one could be swift enough to gather it up.

The two Upper Cuzco *panacas* with the greatest prestige seem to have been Iñaca and Vicaquirao. They controlled the joint palaces of Casana, Coracora, and the Yachahuasi, as well as Patallacta across the river, a most formidable concentration of social and ceremonial power. We do not know where the Auccayhaylli *panaca* stood in this alignment. The other two, Sucso and Capac Ayllu, may have been allied if we can argue from the fact that they shared the same *carpa huasi*. Huayna Capac's *panaca* had not been formally activated, as his mummy was not even in Cuzco, but whoever was to be put at its head, it would not be Huascar, for he had for several years been designated as the heir. A part of the struggle would thus shape up over how this new *panaca*, which was to be named Tumibamba, would be structured. The control of Huayna Capac's mummy would be vital to any of the brothers who may have dreamed of forestalling Huascar in a seizure of power.

For reasons unknown to us, Huascar's power was concentrated in the Capac Ayllu *panaca*. With the help of this group he was able to move with dispatch. The small bodyguard of Inca knights which had been recently assigned to his father's deputies in the city was quickly disbanded, and in their place Huascar appointed a personal bodyguard of twelve hundred Cañars and Chachapoyas. Hastily assembled, these subject warriors were taken to Coricancha to keep watch outside the walls while Huascar was being invested inside with the *mascapaycha* by one of the magnates of the Sucso *panaca*, Challco Yupanqui. This man was officiating as Inti's high priest, and in effect this action of his deposed the one who had long held that office under Huayna Capac and who was still in the north helping to prepare the royal mummy.

For his council Huascar appointed five of his half brothers who were to form from that time on his most trusted confidants: Titu Atauchi, Topa Atau, Inca Roca, Urco Huaranka, and Titu Conti Mayta. Thus equipped with the skeleton of a government, his first move was now to enlist the wary loyalties of as many kinsmen as possible by opening up the *acllahuasi*, hitherto inaccessible even to him, and distributing a large number of the loveliest girls from it as immediate largess. This vast sexual holiday was made possible because, for some years before, the "selected girls" or *acllas* had been accumulating there under the rigorous seal of his father in the north. These desirable girls made regal gifts, and Huascar was able to blunt temporarily the ill dispositions of some of his male relatives in this fashion. Warehouses full of the choicest garments and featherwork were tapped also, as were some of the state llama herds. These gifts completed the delight and disarray of most of his closer kinsmen; for a short time they were quiet, their designs temporarily drowned in this calculated spate of generosity.

Satisfied for the nonce, Huascar proclaimed an imperial mourning in honor of the deceased god who had been his father. He himself retired to Muina to lament his lost father, as was the custom, for Muina had been one of the pleasure spots in which Huayna Capac had taken the most delight and where he had been at Huascar's birth. Huascar left orders with his masons and engineers to begin the expansion of the living quarters in Amarucancha preparatory to an increased occupancy. He was able thus to invade the sanctity of his father's estate, probably because he had already installed as head of the new *panaca* a brother pliant to his will.

All seemed to be well in the north also, for news had just come that the plague there had carried off Ninan Cuyochi as well, the only serious contender to the throne.

SECTION 6. *The Slaughter of the Brothers*

HUASCAR HAD FREQUENT reports as to the progress southward of his father's mummy. About the time it arrived in Vilcas, he dispatched a brusque command that his mother Rahua Ocllo leave the cortege which she was accompanying and come on ahead. Whether this unexpected order was issued as part of a hidden but conscious design on Huascar's part, we will never know. Suffice it to say that it was the occasion for the first of the many tragedies to afflict this reign. The reason given for this command was that Rahua Ocllo might wish to sacrifice in Cuzco to Viracocha for his many mercies to her!

The *coya's* retinue broke off from the solemn procession and with all decent speed pushed ahead over the Apurimac bridge and up past Limatambo into the Anta Basin. Meanwhile, back in Cuzco, a group of Huascar's brothers who had long been disaffected and filled with hatred for Huascar concerted somewhat loosely to make a move before it was too late. Their problem was to contrive a meeting that would not invite suspicion. Representing this group was a brother whose name was Chuqui Huaman, "Swift Hawk." It was he who requested of the young emperor permission to go with some of the others out on the north road to meet the *coya's* party and thus show it honor.

Permission granted, this evilly assorted group left Cuzco. At their first night's stop they conspired to seize power after unseating or killing Huascar and then to elevate in his place a brother called Cusi Atauchi. This latter, who was in Cuzco at the time, was not involved in the plot but was selected because of his innocuousness and popularity. The brothers felt they could best begin their undertaking by first assassinating Rahua Ocllo and her daughter whom she was bringing home with her.

They were not aware that Chuqui Huaman was feathering a nest even more devious than theirs. Under cover of a believable pretext he slipped away and returned to Cuzco. He immediately sought out Titu Atauchi with the full tale of the conspiracy but exculpated himself. With Chuqui Huaman in tow, Titu Atauchi, the most important member of Huascar's new council and the man through whom were made all communications to and from the emperor, gained instant admittance to Huascar.

This unsavory tale, common in so many corners of mankind's history, had the expected ending. Out through the night sped a picked squad of Cañars with orders to enjoy themselves at the awful sport. The cabal of brothers was destroyed, and when the innocent Cusi Atauchi presented himself in the next dawn at Amarucancha to attend the emperor's levee, he fell in a pool of blood at the gate.

Rahua Ocllo's train swept into Cuzco with public rejoicing but inner panic. At Huascar's command the *coya* performed sacrifices to the gods for her son's welfare and the prosperity of his rule just beginning. She had brought with her a number of lovely girls from the warm coast lands of the north. Treated more carefully than was usual, most of them had survived the cold and the high altitude to add glamor and beauty to her court. But a few had a different destiny, for they were to be handed over to the priestly strangler on that solemn occasion of sacrifice for the contentment and ease of her dead husband.

Chuqui Huaman quickly rose to royal favor as a reward for his successful espionage. Whether he was also behind the event which was next to transpire, history does not record. But there went out another swift and ominous order from the secret conclaves of the capital, this time to the commander of the troops stationed at Limatambo, to halt the cortege approaching before it crossed the Apurimac and to bring the mummy's executors on to Limatambo for questioning and torture.

CONZEJO ALCALDEDECORTE
HAVIAVICVSCOINGA
CAPAC APO·VATAC·

capac

THE AFFAIR of the brothers had brought into lurid prominence an incident connected with the departure of the royal mummy from Ecuador.

A brother well-known as a capable captain, Atauhuallpa, had refused to accompany the cortege back to Cuzco and do homage to Huascar in person. The excuses he gave were specious. He commanded veteran troops in Quito and had been confirmed by Huayna Capac's executors as the marcher lord of that region which was always so liable to insurrection and only so recently subdued. All brothers with troops under their command, all brothers not under the surveillance of the court in Cuzco, all brothers who had not offered instant homage by setting out posthaste on the road to Cuzco —all such brothers were in the eyes of the government insurrectionary. At the very least they were under suspicion. There would obviously be no more trouble from the brothers remaining in Cuzco, but Atauhuallpa was neither in Cuzco nor on his way to Cuzco. The great men of Huayna Capac's court, now with the mummy on its way south, had not insisted that Atauhuallpa accompany them—indeed he had been left by them in Quito in a position of trust.

It followed in Huascar's mind that the mummy's executors were in league with Atauhuallpa and that the vast concourse of _huacas_, prisoners, loot, and military contingents moving slowly south with the mummy was really not a funeral party at all but a hostile army led by a ghost and directed from a distance by a scheming brother. Huascar moved promptly to circumvent the approaching threat.

Swift bearers sped north up the Chinchaysuyo road carrying in a

103

litter that most dreaded of officials, the *huatac* bearing at the end of his staff the *mascapaycha* as his credentials. He was one of Huascar's confidants and had the power to make arrests. The mere sight of this official anywhere in Tahuantinsuyo was enough to dim the eyes and make the heart stand still.

SECTION 8. *Limatambo*

IN THE FAR NORTH of his empire a great ruler had died, cut off in the midst of mighty actions. His mummy had been lavishly prepared, and he was thus at last to return to his holy city, not in the common indignity of death but surrounded by the able ministers of his will, men whose reverence for him had in no wise abated because he was now an egg-shaped bundle. In his state litter he had been borne without a stumble, without a jolt, down the terrible highland road and across many deep gorges; the last one of these gorges lay just ahead, the deep and windy Apurimac. Here he was halted.

Limatambo was a well-known and strategically located station on the Chinchaysuyo road. The few ruins of Limatambo left are modernly known as Tarahuasi, "the House of the Tara-tree." Here, and not on the exact line of the Apurimac, as one might have thought, was the effective northern limit of Cuzcoquiti. It was at this point that—for the traveler going to Cuzco—the king's road turned up the steeply pitched valley of the Sunturmayo, a spot easy to defend. The valley was one of the loveliest and possibly the most salubrious in all of Peru. The Inca lords had established their military power there in the shape of a formidable holding-wall running up from the stream bed to the heights on both sides of the valley. They had also made the valley, as was their wont, into an agricultural paradise with the steep declivities all handsomely terraced and green with multiple harvests of maize, quinoa, squash, beans, *oca*, and chili peppers. This abundance was purely owing to the skills of the Inca engineer who here tamed the cold waters that tumbled down out of the snow fields of Soray and Salcantay.

The effect which this valley makes upon the visitor today, with its bits and pieces out of the past, is distinctly archaic. It should be. No stretch of road in all of South America has witnessed so much history. One cannot move from north to south in the highlands of Peru without passing through this blue and sleepy valley. It is the essential valve through which all commerce and communications passed and still pass. In the days of the Incas it was the artery of their empire.

Here, therefore, they had planned carefully, building among other things a garrison, a *chasqui* or "post" station, and a customhouse where highly placed and inevitably suspicious officials performed their inspectorial duties. Here also were quarters for officers of Tahuantinsuyo in transit or on special assignments, and here too were splendid masonry apartments reserved for the emperor and his harem whenever they should pass through, with thermal baths and gardens to match. The produce of this narrow land was stored in many stone warehouses linked in series up on the higher ground and carefully guarded. Here also were posted an Inca governor over the people of the valley and, as an ineluctable sanction for his power, a shrine wherein dwelt the Inca gods. The only remnants of this temple today are some severely beautiful masonry and a most elegant porch. It is in fact difficult for us to reconstruct in our mind's eye those many edifices and to sense the urgency of the place as well as its deliberateness, the unrelenting harshness of the Inca taskmaster, and the dull and faultless busyness of the valley people. It is difficult to envision the shambling gangs from distant provinces, heavy sacks on their backs, brought up to the gates by their *curacas*, or files of unburdened men checked through by the guards, hastening to perform in some part of the empire one of the many duties so lightly assigned by the lords of Cuzco.

Left to us today are only the blue haze and the wonderful silence of this benign valley; the past that we are concerned with is like that condor which floats over the valley occasionally, unattached and distant, not a real being but the spirit of a being.

To Cuzco on the Chinchaysuyo Road

A COLUMN of sweating hammock bearers pressed up against the fortified gate at Tarawasi and came to an uneasy and jostling halt. In those hammocks were the legally appointed executors of Huayna Capac's will. Colla Topa (Royal Scion) was the first of them all, an esteemed member of the Susco *panaca*. He was the empire's greatest living captain, and was that one of the late emperor's entourage singled out to counsel Huascar with his wisdom. This great veteran of the northern wars, carrying on a pole in his right hand the *mascapaycha* of his dead lord, now strode up to the head of the column to meet the summons that had brought them on so unexpectedly ahead of the cortege. Behind him came the other notables who were his coexecutors, among them the highborn Cusi Topa Yupanqui, priest of the sun. They were men in their middle age and older; most of them belonged to the esteemed and powerful Iñaca *panaca*. They moved with dignity but their faces showed concern, for they had news of Huascar's indecent haste in the establishment of a government, and they may even have heard rumors of the slaughter of the brothers.

There was now to occur one of the appalling chapters in the history of the great empire.

When the terrible deed was over, and the smashed and torn bodies of the executors had been hurled out onto the roadside in derision, the commander of the guardpost herded the distraught and disorganized remainder through the gate detailing a squad to escort it past the bodies and up to the Plain of Anta. Finally, when it was deemed safe to do so, *chasquis* were sent racing back down the road to bring on the funeral party so that it might be reorganized in Limatambo. The executors had died under the most excruciating torture, but the information from them had been meager and disappointing. Apparently they had no real knowledge of the plans of Atauhuallpa, the prince who had so dangerously elected not to accompany his father's mummy home. Appearances indubitably were that he was remaining in the region of Quito so that he might prepare it as a base for future treachery against Cuzco, but no such proof was elicited. Thus when the cortege, back on the line of the Apurimac, took up its route again, the dead emperor had been effectively shorn of all real power. No supporters of the mummy could now make trouble for the new emperor; the old emperor's stalwart and respected brothers, wise uncles, and eminent cousins—in short, the greatest men in the empire—had been ignominiously destroyed.

Rumors of the slaughter had raced more swiftly back to the funeral party than the *chasquis* and had broken it into splinters; many of the *curacas* who had accompanied it had already fled back in utter fear to their distant provinces, and even some of the Inca captains of the contingents turned and moved with forced marches back to Quito intent only on immediate safety. But at last the cortege was reorganized and again put on the road.

The files of men and women that were climbing from the Apurimac bridge up to Limatambo, bearing their deceased lord, cannot be accurately described, for they were two things at once, to us quite incompatible. On the one hand they formed a funeral procession escorting a dead emperor back to his native soil. Accordingly he was accompanied en route by women keening and shrieking in the approved fashion: *"anay! ananay!"* Certain of these women, concubines of the dead man, had exposed their breasts and smeared themselves with soot and grease. In the more extreme cases they had sawed their long tresses off, and thus dishevelled, stumbled along in the road beside the dead demigod, rapping on their tambourines, shrieking, calling on him, and praising him immoderately, forlorn creatures of cultic sorrow. Several had already hanged themselves en route or rushed off narrow ledges to die on the rocks below that they might more quickly find themselves back in the august presence. Yet this funeral was at the same time a return in triumph from a hard-fought and successful series of campaigns. As such the train was a military display, exultant and fiery in its ardor, boastful of the loot and women it was returning with, the captured Ecuadoran gods, and the chieftains led by ropes threaded through their shoulders. Mourning and triumph walked side by side in this strangest of processions.

The litter in which the mummy had been carefully set up was surrounded by the usual bodyguard of Inca knights, the toughest fighting men of their day, imperturbable and dark-faced, proud of their reputation as slingers, masters of siegecraft, soldiers unwearied in pursuit. In front of the imperial palanquin came the litter in which Huanacauri, the war idol, was ensconced. An almost shapeless piece of stone, it was richly adorned with many mantles of *cumpi* and a feathered headdress. Huanacauri's own priesthood walked beside it. Next in importance, also in a litter, came the emperor's *huaoqui*, a small idol of solid gold. Then came the captured *huacas*, the idols of those nations across which the Inca juggernaut had so ponderously but so inevitably crawled, each one also accompanied by its native priesthood. These gods and *huacas* were Huanacauri's prisoners and would be kept in Cuzco until such time as they had demonstrated their willingness to keep their people quiet and properly bent to the Inca yoke. In this concourse of dead, living, and divine beings, came, of course, the famous regiments of warriors and auxiliaries who had earned the great victories; but these contingents were now officered by Incas sent out by Huascar. There was to be no treachery from that direction. The veteran captains who had previously led them and who had not escaped back to Quito were demoted or cashiered or worse.

From Tarawasi the Royal Road climbs steeply. Cleverly and neatly engineered all the way up the rounded slopes, it finally came out over the dry saddle to emerge onto the high basin today called the Pampa de Anta. The air was much thinner and cooler as one passed over the watershed called Villcacunca and began to move down a shallow valley. Here at Villcacunca one could look back for a farewell glance at the hollow vistas of the Sunturmayo Valley with the stupendous wall of the Apurimac gorge as a magnificent curtain behind it. The contrasting view of the mild and level meadows ahead was far less awesome and perhaps for that reason more inviting.

As the Royal Road twisted out onto this broadening *pampa*, it passed on the near left a detached and mammoth rock, its rough surface worked by the hand of man and nature into innumerable shelves and cavernous overhangs. Earth Mother had cast up this thing of power on the saddle between the Apurimac and the Urubamba drainages; it was itself the congelation of the spirit of the locale, a *huaca* which contained in its frozen bulk the life of the Royal Road. Under its idle shadow the procession halted to perform the *mocha* of worship; from here on, the way to Cuzco was easy.

As the road took up again, one could see on the right a flat table of land against the dun-colored hills. Here was Ichupampa, a name famous in Inca history. Some ninety years previously the Chancas from across the Apurimac had vainly fortified themselves there against the ferocious onslaught of the renascent Incas. The fate of all Peru, of the entire chain of the Andes in fact, had on that day been decided by the fortune of the greatest of all the Inca emperors, Pachacuti. But the royal mummy now being borne past did not turn his eyes of inlaid stone to behold that scene of his grandfather's feat of arms, once so tumultuous and splendid in all its effects.

In those days the Plain of Anta was a green miracle of cultivation, the surrounding slopes being extensively terraced and parts of the level plain in the center utilized as pasture for uncounted herds of llamas. Much of this flatland, however, was bog and salt marsh even as it is today. Across this the Royal Road ran, straight as an arrow, carried on an embankment provided with raised parapets on each side. Thirty-six well-engineered culverts made any excessive flooding of the contiguous areas in the wintertime impossible.

This well-stocked land had been one of the first provinces acquired by the Incas, and for decades now its history had been intertwined with that of Cuzco. It was an essential part of Cuzcoquiti. Just over the ridge on the left of the road, in a pleasant bay in the surrounding hills, was Sillapampa, "Rubblefield." It was a quiet and restful place close to the Royal Road yet secluded from it. Placed here and there among its terraces were the country villas of Incas and *pallas*. One belonged to Carua Ticlla who was a half sister of Huascar; it was a thatched house of good design set among masses of white and purple lupines. Around this house in a few years were to swirl currents of intrigue and espionage, for Carua Ticlla was finally to adhere to the party hostile to her brother and emperor, Huascar, but now it was merely typical of any one of those lesser manors which the lords and ladies of Cuzco owned in the territory surrounding. Today Sillapampa is called Surite.

At the base of the mountains on the south side of the plain was a community called Conchacalla from which a zigzag road led off across a *puna* where thousands of llamas grazed. This pitched and broken watershed country was sprinkled with small ponds that bore names like Grassy Pond, Red Lake, and Earth-Mouth. Their waters were cold and their margins, boggy with a kind of thin alpine peat, were crowded with the llamas come to drink. Below these ponds were the deep *huaycos* through which their spill-off and seepage ran down into the Apurimac. In these trenches were sequestered Inca villas and terraced areas worked by *mitmacs*. Rahua Ocllo owned property here in pleasant Chinchaypuquio.

Passing on along the Royal Road, one came next to the important community of Anta (or Sacsahuana) situated on a bench of hills overlooking the spot where the Cachimayo or "Salt Creek" flowed into the expanse of the plain. From this point a famous branch road went north to Lake Huaypu, crossed the downs to Maras, and then dropped down into the deep trench of the Vilcamayo. Round about Anta were other elegantly thatched villas belonging to the magnates of Cuzco, and in the community itself a rest station, almost as well provided as Limatambo, for traveling dignitaries. Two related *ayllus* lived here, Equeco and Quilliscachi; they had very early earned Inca gratitude and the right to wear the earplugs. To the men of these *ayllus* were reserved the permanent and unsavory prerogatives of being the eyes and ears of the emperor, official informers in short. So assiduously did they fill these crucial offices that the word *equeco* came in time to mean the same thing as "spy" or "ensnarer."

In the environing *chacras* the subject peoples labored with plow-stick and clod-hammer. Many of them had been brought in as *mitmacs* from far-off regions, although some few were depressed remnants of the original possessors of the land. As the dead emperor, surrounded by the expert slingers and mace-wielders of his son, was now borne past these lowly people, they fell on their faces in the meadows where they were, awe-struck and sullen.

The Cachimayo ascent was gradual and pleasant to the eye. The potato fields were green, and the sun was faintly warm as the cortege neared the watershed, with Cuzco just beyond. At the top of the saddle, where gullies and bare hills closed in to narrow the approach to Cuzco, the cortege passed Quiachilli, a sloping meadow by the roadside which was the site of the historic repulse of the Chancas; from this battle it was also known as the Field of Blood. In all their history the Incas had lived through no more desperate day than that one, and their reverence for the spot was correspondingly profound. The modern traveler who is just coming up to El Arco on the back of Carmenca, is probably very close to that historic piece of ground, if he is not actually passing over it.

Finally, one caught one's first sight of Cuzco tucked down in the deep basin below. This spot was, of course, named, being called Urcos-calla, and was very sacred, for here all travelers coming in from the north stopped to worship Cuzco, that miracle of miracles and the empire's greatest *huaca*. This site was also, as we have mentioned, the first *tambo* or way station on the way out of Cuzco offering luxurious apartments to the official traveler, although for the one in a hurry it represented only the smallest part of a day's journey northward.

SECTION 10. *The Turning Point*

TAHUANTINSUYO was an empire built by a people of outstanding energy and dedication. It had, of course, suffered many shocks and in its short past contemplated many horrors. Its people had continued to be great because to them a holocaust, a blood bath, was a cheap price to pay for their exalted positions as the lords of the earth. But the shock attendant upon the extermination of Huayna Capac's magnates, the men charged with putting into effect the last wishes of this god-emperor—this was a different matter.

The Incas of Cuzco had been struck in a vulnerable spot, and they were never again to be quite the same. The secret of their unswerving dignity as a people had been, first, the mission of conquest and acculturation given to them by Inti and, second, their belief that the difference between "barbarians," or *purun runa*, and a civilized people was the latter's capacity to raise up an *apu* to give them laws and command. Their own *apus* had been not only elected—in the sense of agreed on—by the Capac Incas, but they had also been historically justified. Divine mission and the justification of their leaders by their works, like the two pillars of a porch, supported the edifice of their lives.

Huascar cut down one of these pillars when he smashed his predecessor's infallibility. By wiping out the human instruments left behind by his father, he destroyed a continuity with the history of his people which otherwise he might have had. By putting to question his own father's divinity and infallibility, he injured his own. The silver cord that led back to Manco Capac had been frayed, indeed almost severed.

Accustomed as the Capac Incas were to bloodshed as a way by which an *apu* demonstrated his will, they were not accustomed to the assassination of their history. They cowered.

SECTION 11. *The Intellectual Life of the Incas*

HISTORY to the Incas was not a speculative subject leading to chronological or spiritual inquiry. Their very real feeling for the importance of history did not impel them to produce a true calendar, a body of moral questions, or an area of intellectual doubt. Here the contrast with the cultures of Middle America is most vivid. The Mayan calendar was a model of complexity and accuracy, and the Toltec and Aztec feeling for the moral tension in history was profound, as can be seen in the Quetzalcoatl story. Speculative intensity, spiritual pessimism, and an exuberant symbolism were hallmarks of these Mexican cultures. Not so with their contemporaries, the Men of Manco.

Our direct knowledge of the Inca mind is practically nil, but what we do perceive leads us to believe that they held single-mindedly to the revelatory character of the world, and that to them this understanding was sufficient. All things, stones, trees, people, storms, and ears of corn kept revealing themselves, announcing and reiterating their identity and respective powers. When seen this way, they were called *huaca*. We might class them altogether as defining a general revelation of the quality of the world. But the rock upon which the Incas as a caste stood was that of a very special revelation.

They believed that their *pacarina* and the story of their emergence as a people were of a different order than those of other peoples in Peru, for theirs was not only pristine in time but was also accompanied by a moral command. This precept meant that while the divine powers of other nations were classed as *huacas*, Inti and Viracocha were truly gods with unalterable wills insofar as Tahuantinsuyo was concerned. Mission, not identity, was the supreme good.

In pursuance of this conception they cast Viracocha not only as the creator of man and the molder of the world but as that being who had created all the *huacas* of all nations everywhere. Potentially therefore any *huaca*, because of its essentially low and derivative character, could become a *llullay supay*, "a lying demon," liable to offend Viracocha's divine plan as evidenced in the Inca empire.

To explain why their empire was tantamount to all of mankind's history they pointed to *apucay*, the majesty and jurisdiction that by nature belonged to a superior person. A barbarian was a *mana apuyoc*, one who lived in the anarchy of having no visible decision-making apparatus in his political life, literally "one who has no leader." The vilest man was he who acknowledged no chief. The best man, the world's aristocrat, was he who supported the rule of a chief ordained by Viracocha.

This in turn defined "truth" for the pragmatic Inca. Truth was "orderliness." It was not beauty, freedom, humility, change, or any such later concepts. Rather it was the very garment the Inca wore as an imperial administrator. It was sheer—or mere—"establishment."

The beginning of things was of serious import in any study or explanation of the world. The Inca was always obsessed by the *pacarichisca pacha*, the time when and the place where something was first invented. In origins he found all historical explanation. Of process he was totally ignorant. His view therefore was powerful, severe, and rigid. Time to him did not so much move forward in a rectilinear fashion and towards a consummation as it seemed to surround the ancient rock of Creation in an aura of rightness. The pristine quality of that early time had been evidenced in an aboriginal aristocracy called the *allicac* or "the good ones." All virtue was in their descendants, such as the Incas. Basely born, all other peoples were destined to be ruled by the *allicac*.

Only in one area was the Inca forced to believe something different; there did exist throughout Peru a monstrous conception which threatened him intellectually—perhaps the only one which did—the hoary concept of the *pachatikray*, the end of the world, a vague dogma held by all Peruvian peoples and therefore an inescapable one for the Incas.

The last *pachatikray* which had occurred was that one called the *uno pachacuti*, or "flood cataclysm," a disaster which had necessitated a wholly new creation. It was thought that another universal calamity would bring the present dispensation to an end, but no one knew whether it would come by fire, flood, pestilence, or earthquake. In any case, it would come as an act of the Creator's will, and in its nebulous and terrifying lineaments it held the only real menace in which the Incas could believe. It stayed in their minds as an unlovely, though probably intermittent, doubt. The greatest of their emperors, a man of the most ferocious will and brilliance of mind, had taken as his own name one of the words for cataclysm, Pachacuti, "Aeon-overthrow," as if he had been the Creator's own archangel in the making of a new age. So skillfully had he associated himself with the concept that his name became for the tough *ayllus* along the shores of Lake Chucuito far to the south the very synonym for a time of war, the final judgment and Armageddon. It was only this *pachatikray* which threatened the supreme arrogance of the Inca and brought him down to the ordinary level of anxious humanity. In any case, the Creator would be the prime mover in that dreadful event to come, some even holding that the new creation to follow would involve his raising up all the dead of the past age in a general renovation. But even the mitigation of this last concept did not really smooth over the horror of contemplating the aeonic disaster ahead.

Besides explaining beginnings as pure essences of time, the Incas also explained present things as emanations of models. All things, they said, had a "mother" which the Creator had provided. Water for instance had a mother; so did fire, maize, llama herds. But the "mother" principle itself had to have a locus, a *huaca*, which generally would be a rock or a star. Thus, in the end, their principle of explanation clarified nothing, for it too inhabited a concrete object or was that object. It did, however, help to systematize their knowledge.

We can be sure that the above concepts were not taught in this fashion to the young in the Yachahuasi, the House of Learning. Nevertheless in the Yachahuasi there apparently did exist something like a curriculum which helped to produce the *amauta* or "sage."

Amauta was a descriptive and not wholly a professional term. Specifically, there were only four or five of the most venerable and learned of these individuals whose memories could contain all Inca lore of importance. They formed, as it were, an elite and informal faculty, while under them were others, many of them priests, charged with the innumerable data of cult, augury, oracles, calendar, and *ayllu* histories. These men assembled their knowledge in *harauis*, short historical verses or bardic lays which became set pieces and were thus more easily learned by the young. That these men were in fact the censors of Inca culture is evident, for their *harauis* exalted the warlike among the ancestors and either slighted or totally neglected those who had spent their days in unmanly dalliance. In their hands was the maintenance of the masculine structure of Inca society. But under Huascar their role was to suffer erosion as the ancient traditions were jolted and the structure of the true order cast in doubt.

The Yachahuasi seems to have been unsophisticated and rather more

practical than the Aztec *calmecac* where the subject matter of the curriculum rose in the order of abstruseness and intellectual content as
one advanced through the grades. High-ranking boys of the Capac
Ayllu were trained in the Yachahuasi along with the sons of the most
important *curacas* in the empire. The Yachahuasi specifically and early
taught them facility in the Quechua tongue, for the ability to speak
elegantly was that accomplishment which most plainly put the stamp
of caste and privilege on one. Next came knowledge of the Inca cults,
then countings on the *quipu*. The essential details of the Inca legend
and the deeds of the Inca rulers in their correct order according to a
canon were learned, as were the powers of each of the *pururaucas* scattered about in the city and the environs, the names of great captains, the
duties of sons to their fathers, and the reliance of all upon the emperor.
Thus the course was completed. That there was conflict between official
tales and the family traditions held in the various *ayllus* is certain, but
we do not know how these were harmonized. Only after this early
schooling did the boys serve as pages at court, learning under the patron
assigned to them such pragmatic work as court protocol, administration,
the duties connected with roads and posts, engineering, water control,
command of work gangs, etc.

A highly specialized branch of learning and one of basic importance
revolved around the *quipus*, those knotted and variously colored strings
upon which numerical records were kept. The Inca *quipucamayoc*, or
"secretary" as we would translate it today, was a key figure in the
government; it was he who had to check the accounts that were filed
in his office by lesser officials, many of them non-Incas who might be
in a position to mulct the empire of its due. So clever did the Incas
become in the use of the *quipu* that they could use it as a partial substitute for a written script, aiding them in remembering histories, laws,
treaties, etc.

Loyalty to the *apu* and the standards of manliness, as we have stated,
were strongly inculcated, and inasmuch as the boy entered the Yachahuasi probably as early as the age of seven or eight, by the end of his
curriculum he was ready for a few years of page duty before he grad-
uated through the rites of the *huarachicoy* into full Incahood. And an

Inca preferably was not one who contemplated the mysteries of the Creator but one who above all acted. His schooling was designed to make him a hero, not a priest.

Yet in this respect the lords of Cuzco were to fail, if we may judge by the events of the reign that was about to begin. It was the bastard Incas in the distant city of Quito who would produce the only heroes.

SECTION 12.

Coronation, Marriage, and Mourning

THE TRIUMPHAL ENTRY of the mummy with its reconstituted retinue, memorable as it was, was only a prelude to the splendor of Huascar's formal investiture as the Sapa Capac Inca, "the Magnificent and Unique Inca," or more freely, the Emperor. The year was 1525.

In the nature of things a coronation could not be complete without the simultaneous investiture of a *coya*. Pachacuti had been the last ruler to take a girl from the outside as his *coya*; since that time the tradition had been established for the new emperor to marry his full sister. One of the reasons Huascar had demanded the presence of his mother in Cuzco ahead of the mummy was to assure himself of the presence of the daughter whom she had with her, Chuqui Huipa, his full sister. This young woman was to become one of the tragic queens in history, little valued then and unsung today. Her name, which means Golden Ecstatic Joy, was a masterpiece in irony, for the historian knows of her life only as a succession of humiliations, terrors, shocks, and, finally, a violent and undeserved end.

For marriage among the Incas to be a fully legal transaction, the

117

mother of the girl had always to grant her consent. Accordingly Huascar sent emissaries to his mother for her formal agreement. In a reign that was to be iridescent with novelties and scandals, what now transpired was no doubt the most unexpected of all possibilities. Rahua Ocllo refused.

The virulent hatred which possessed this woman toward her son can be apprehended in this action, for it flouted all imperial usage. The slighting of her husband's testament, the precipitate massacre of the brothers, the torture and death of the most respected men in the empire, her own brothers and uncles, and the cruel arrogance with which Huascar had already treated his own lickspittle court—these events had almost destroyed Rahua Ocllo's sanity. Until the plague had come to Quito, the world under her royal husband and his favorite god Viracocha had seemed perfectly fixed, stable, and dependable. Yet in the space of a few months the tides of disaster had flowed with such fury as to undermine all things, including the Inca sense of rightness. And in her eyes the author of some of these shattering events was her own son.

She refused not only the emissaries he sent, she refused him in person, obdurately and long, thus suddenly presenting him with the frightening possibility that the legitimacy of his rule might be put in question should he have to marry a girl not his full sister. Bitterly, Rahua Ocllo held her ground until Huascar, distraught, ordered all the Inca gods out of Coricancha to come begging at her dwelling. Thus overwhelmed by thunders from heaven, her will was subdued, though not her hatred. The *piui ñusta,* "the legitimate princess," was handed over to her brother, and the coronation could begin.

The coronation ceremony began with the customary purificatory four-day fast and retirement of the emperor-elect. For this period Huascar sat in a bare darkened chamber, without sexual solace and with little to eat. He had previously selected one of the Capac Incas belonging to his party to carry on the imperial duties during his obliteration. This custom was fraught with danger, for the interim emperor always took over the full regalia and bodyguard.

This essential prologue successfully passed, the ceremonies which included the royal wedding could begin. To assure the continual favor of the heavens two hundred young children were singled out for their health and beauty, and in a vast *capac hucha* performed throughout the empire they were destroyed. They were messengers to the Inca gods and the major provincial *huacas* who in turn petitioned the Creator for the well-being of the new emperor; it was thought that their innocence would beguile the affections of those supernatural beings. These selected children were led in a drunken state twice around the *huacas*, and they were then strangled and sent on their glorious errands sumptuously dressed and jangling with gold ornaments. If strangling were not employed as the method of execution, the young people were decapitated or, in some cases, had their hearts torn out and held up to the *huaca* to whom the offerings were intended. The blood of the sacrifice was then smeared in a line across the face of the *huaca*. The officiants, meanwhile, had dug shallow holes in the soil round about with sharpened stakes, for metal was tabooed, and the broken bodies were tumbled in helter-skelter with their gold, their silver, and their gay little bags of coca. Thus solemnly were these children done away with. Certain Inca fathers in Cuzco voluntarily gave their own daughters as sacrificial victims, convinced of the outstanding excellence of the deed. Inti, Illapa, and Huanacauri received these young spirits, as did Viracocha, on those various hilltops sacred to them in Cuzcoquiti. Never had the Incas beheld such an extravaganza of sacrificial blood.

The ceremony of homage and fealty revealed clearly the reliance which the Incas placed upon their *apu*. Unsandaled, they approached him as he sat on the sacred *usno*. First they adored him, plucking out hairs from their eyebrows and blowing them with kisses toward him. Then they each approached him holding a small white feather which they waved slowly back and forth in front of his face and then returned to an attendant. At the completion of the rite all the feathers were gathered together and carefully burned. Symbolically, each Inca and every magnate of the empire thus announced his person and spirit as openly adhering to the *capac apu,* and that there might be no possible retraction of this dedication, the object in which the unison of ruler and ruled resided, the feather, was forever destroyed.

There followed weeks of merrymaking in the plazas, along the esplanades, and in the *cantut* gardens of the park above Patallacta where Huascar had ordered the placing of animals and birds fashioned in gold and silver.

For us, the most significant thing about the ceremonies in which Huascar formally received the *mascapaycha* was the coronation name which he took. To the name Topa Cusi Huallpa, Royal and Fortunate Turkey Cock, he appended Inti Illapa, a fusion of the sun-god's name with that of the thunder, the first such use of the name in Inca history. His father, Huayna Capac, had decreed divine honors for himself and had even made for himself a peculiarly exalted position under Inti. But he had not gone so far as to identify himself with a high god, as Huascar now did. By elevating himself to the heavens, he correspondingly abandoned his position in the peerage of the Incas, thus by implication demoting his own people. But self-divinization could have been effective here only if Huascar had had the personality and the charisma to go with it; and these qualities he did not have.

Because of the dogma of his divinity while alive and because of the mourning ceremonies so extravagantly carried out for him when deceased, Huayna Capac overnight had become a greatly revered *huaca* in Cuzco. Huascar certainly had something to say about the arrangement of his *panaca*, and it is likely, as already stated, that he installed his own appointee as *pachaca*. Having taken over and enlarged a part of Amarucancha as his own palace, Huascar to an extent controlled the *panaca*, for the mummy would be kept near him and thus under his oversight. It is a fair guess that many of the bastard brothers who remained in Cuzco were assigned to the Tumibamba *panaca* as a kind of immunization procedure.

SECTION 13. *A Tale of Brothers and Sisters*

As MANY AS forty half brothers remained to Huascar after the execution of those who had conspired against him. Many were to play important roles in the events to come. If we wish to understand the power of those divisive forces which had come among the Incas, a summary of the names and subsequent doings of these people is therefore in order.

Most prominent of all, because far away in the north, was the well-known Topa Atauhuallpa (commonly and erroneously called Atahuallpa), a man at the time almost the same age as the emperor, perhaps a few years older. His mother's name had been Tocto Coca, Tender Coca. She had been a pure-blooded *ñusta*, a cousin of Huayna Capac, and had belonged to the powerful Iñaca *panaca*. She had died early and, therefore, her son had been taken north by his father to acquire glory in war. Ninan Cuyochic had also been taken on that campaign, but this brother, as we have seen, died there in the same plague that carried off his father. As for Atauhuallpa, he was already one of the empire's great fighting captains, having learned his trade as well on the chilly *páramos* as in the sultry lowlands of Ecuador. Although the contingents under his control on the Carangui frontier were not especially numerous, his situation there as military governor at the very end of the northern line of communications greatly increased his potential power and certainly his personal security. In addition, his troops and subalterns were all veterans. His refusal to return with the other *auquis* to do homage to the new emperor was certainly seen by everybody to be a declaration of distrust if not of treason. His name, Royal and Victorious Turkey Cock, seemed to be a standing challenge to Huascar, the new emperor. Their names were ominously the same except that *Cusi* occurred in the name of Huascar, meaning a fortunate outcome in general, whereas the corresponding element in this prince's name was *Atau*, specifically good fortune in war.

With him was an adolescent brother, Topa Huallpa Inca, whose sole distinction would come when Francisco Pizarro designated him to be the first puppet emperor under the Spaniards; he would die, probably poisoned by one of Atauhuallpa's former generals, before he ever reached Cuzco.

Chuqui Huaman we have already met as the first delator of Huascar's reign. As a reward for this unsavory service, Huascar was soon to give him the highest of the dual commands in the Pomacocha campaign, the first martial exploit of the reign. The irresponsibility of Huascar in this choice of commanders for a tough border war in the wilds of the northern montaña becomes evident from the sequel. The Pomacochas, pre-tending submission, indicated that they desired to have a meeting under truce; they stated that they wished to discuss the terms of a formal treaty. Chuqui Huaman incontinently rushed ahead to the spot desig-nated and, in so doing, placed himself in the trap. He and about two thousand of those under him were cut down in the drunken aftermath of a convivial *taqui*. Treachery was not an Inca monopoly in Peru. The other of the Inca generals on this campaign was Titu Atauchi, a loyal but not particularly able brother who carried on as best he could, al-though he was initially forced to abandon the area with all his troops because of the disaster. Titu Atauchi was to be with the emperor his brother at the very end of life. On news of the Pomacocha disaster, Huascar decided to go into the field himself, but the augurs reported unfavorable omens, so the late Chuqui Huaman's post went to another brother, Mayta Yupanqui. The two brothers, Titu Atauchi and Mayta Yupanqui, performed more creditably and were finally able to report a degree of success. In the modest triumph which followed, Huascar went out to lead the victorious army back into Cuzco, and the two generals therefore played relatively subordinate roles in the procession and the festivities which followed. Being in a sense the very person of his archangelic god, Huascar could not logically allow any person to eclipse his splendor. Yet the meagerness of the loot and the inability of the Incas to impose full provincial administration on the Poma-cochas must have contrasted poorly with that triumph so recently per-formed for a dead emperor.

Atoc, Huanca Auqui, and Mayca Yupanqui were three of Huascar's brothers destined for some prominence in the last days of the reign. All were sent by Huascar against the forces of rebellion in the north, and all were flung back in that terrible human hurricane. Huaminca Atoc belied both elements of his name, "Veteran Fox"; through over-confidence he failed in the opening skirmishes of the War of the Two Brothers, was captured, tortured to death, flayed, and made into a drum for festivities for his brother, Atauhuallpa. His skull was fashioned into a vessel from which his brother drank victory draughts while boasting of the exploit. Huanca Auqui replaced Atoc, losing one battle after another with dreary persistence, until he too was replaced at a crucial point by Mayca Yupanqui, a brother with a fighting record, who, however, broke in the tremendous battle of Yanamarca and subsequently lost the line of the Ancayaco. Both of these unfortunate generals were to be tortured and later killed by order of Atauhuallpa along with their brother Huascar.

Three other brothers, loyal to Huascar, were to end in the same shambles: Inca Roca, one of Huascar's confidants and a member of his council; Titu Atauchi, already mentioned, a man in his middle thirties but still younger than Huascar; and Topa Atau, to become a miserable captive in the hands of Atauhuallpa's two most ferocious captains.

A number of the brothers would be remembered as partisans or puppets of the Spaniards: Huallpa Roca, Cayo Topa, Inguil Topa, and Inca Pascac. The third and fourth were killed by their brother Manco Inca while they were on an embassy of peace to him in the montaña of Vilcabamba. Another brother, Tisoc, fought valorously against the Spaniards for a number of years under his brother Manco Inca, achieving renown and restoring Inca arms to some vestige of their former glory. When the cause became hopeless in his eyes, he left his mountain lairs and surrendered to the invaders, lending his name from then on to the party of conciliation.

Manco Inca was about fifteen years younger than Huascar and thus relatively innocuous as a threat to him. In the short but sanguinary occupation of Cuzco by Atauhuallpa's troops, Manco Inca was to escape by fleeing over the Andes to the region around Paucartambo. With Huascar, Atauhuallpa, and the young puppet emperor, Topa Huallpa Inca, all dead, the youthful Manco was that son of Huayna Capac legitimately entitled to inherit the *capaccay*. Thus for a short time, insulted and scorned by the Spaniards, Manco reigned in Cuzco without ruling. In 1536, he finally rebelled against his Hispanic masters, as shall be related more fully below, and besieged them in Cuzco. This attempt failed, and he fled into the difficult Vilcabamba montaña where he became either the first Inca chieftain of the rump state of Vilcabamba or, if one wishes, the pathetic thirteenth Inca emperor, exiled

123

from his city. With him was associated his brother, Vilauma (whose name in Aymara meant "Blood Drinker"), acting as captain-general of the Inca forces. He was an implacable enemy of the Spaniards. It was this brother who was to engineer so astutely the great rebellion of 1536. The Spaniards were not to forget Vilauma, and when they finally captured him in 1539, bringing the rebellion to an end, his demise was, as can well be imagined, unenviable.

Just as well known to the Spaniards as Manco Inca, and far better liked, was Paullo Topa. Because of their youth both of these brothers had been left in Cuzco while their father was campaigning on the equator. Like Manco, Paullo also had managed to escape Atauhuallpa's terror in Cuzco and had fled south to Lake Chucuito. Here he acted as an efficient and well-liked Inca governor over the whole province of Collao. When Almagro, a Spanish conquistador, went exploring into the Chilean desert, Paullo accompanied him with other important remaining Incas. He then returned to live in Cuzco while Manco Inca was establishing his independent *capaccay* in the province of Vilcabamba. In this tragic period of rapine and readjustment, the young Paullo carried himself well, earned the respect of the Spaniards, and ruled the few remaining Incas in Cuzco. He eventually was baptized Don Cristóbal Paullo Topa Inca. His eldest son, a fullblood Inca, was to marry a white woman from Spain.

Other brothers bore reputations as fighting men: Huari Titu, Conono, Quiso Yupanqui. Almost all of them are mentioned in connection with great violence in the period of the dismantling of the Inca state. The last fought valiantly and well against the Spaniards on the coast and was there killed in battle. Huaman Titu, along with another brother, was killed by order of the captured Atauhuallpa out of jealousy and hatred. Illescas Inca was skinned and made into a drum by one of Atauhuallpa's sadistic captains. Huayna Pallca had the dubious honor of impaling one of Atauhuallpa's two great men of blood on the point of his javelin. While on one of his more feverish treasure hunts, Almagro the Spaniard had Atoc Sopa most cruelly dispatched. Cusi Rimachi became a focus of intrigue and Spanish suspicion until he threw in his lot finally with his brother Manco Inca. He would be burned to death by the Spaniards in the beautiful Yucay Valley.

As for Huascar's many sisters, the names of a few only are recorded. His *coya*, Chuqui Huipa, would share with him his end at Andamarca. Two of his favorite sisters and concubines, Coya Miro and Chimpu Cisa, would be torn apart in his presence because they had issue by him. Other sisters were Mama Huarcay, Carua Ticlla (she who befriended Golden Star's daughter), Huayllas Ñusta, and Cori Ocllo. The latter was to become the *coya* of Manco Inca and to die a captive of the Spaniards who, irritated at her fortitude, her chastity, and her pride, dispatched her with arrows in Ollantaytambo. Another sister, unnamed in our sources but considered to be one of the noblest of the *pallas* (possibly, therefore, a full sister of Huascar), had, before the coming of the Spaniards, been the *asarpay*, the high priestess of the Apurimac. She had apparently fled from her sacred office in the path of Atauhuallpa's juggernaut but had turned up after his death in company with her brother Topa Huallpa. During the terrible year 1536, she was with the Spaniards in Lima while the Inca army was besieging the city on the hills around. Her own sister, Doña Inez Huayllas Ñusta, who had become Francisco Pizarro's concubine and the mother of his child, had this sister garroted because she was envious of her high caste. Another full sister Tocto Oxica, of the Vicaquirau *panaca*, under the Incas had held a position equally exalted, for she was the high priestess of the moon in Lake Chucuito. With Huascar's fall and Atauhuallpa's execution, Paullo Topa, her half brother who was governing the area, married her as the only *palla* available to keep his lineage pure. She also would become a Christian, Doña Catalina.

This compilation of fraternal and sororal data, uncertain in some of its details and by no means complete, gives an idea of the temptations, the incitations, and the dangers that lurked behind the handsome façade of the Inca caste. The above-mentioned individuals were among those holding the highest rank in Inca society during the last reign. Contrary to their own myth therefore, the Men of Manco did not form a pious and self-dedicated greater Peruvian *ayllu*. The bright light of empire had blinded them.

TRAVAXOS
PAPAALLAIMITAPA
que punto haucay cusqui quilla

labrador
pacyaca

junio — yauca cascqui   junio

Cuzco Harvest—the Aymoray

THE LORDS OF CUZCO showed themselves off most elegantly in the round of festivities that began with the harvest-home in May and ended with the new year's ground-breaking at the end of June. This concourse of related celebrations is known as the Aymoray and the Inti Raymi. These names are really catchalls, for there is subsumed under them a multitude of activities and diverse rites. Their very richness invites research. Their importance in displaying to us the underlying gravity and formality of the Inca character is unquestioned.

Aymoray as a verb means "to bring in the threshed grain and put it down in bins." *Aymoray* can mean that act, the month in which it customarily took place, or the ritual celebrations of that event. We would translate it as "harvest-home." So central was this act in the lives of those people speaking Quechua that there were at least five words in the language for the precious repository in which grain was stored and four for the act of storage.

The action centered about the *pirua*, the wicker grain bin made of large *sunchu* canes, the single most indispensable appurtenance in any Peruvian *cancha*. It could be made in other fashions. *Collca* was a bin or edifice or storage space of adobes, *taqque* one of woven mats, and *collona* a storage hole excavated in the house floor and carefully plastered within. *Chahuay* was a garner which was mud-plastered on the outside. The *pirua*—for this was also a generic word for all grain bins —contained the seed corn called *marca moho* or "reserved seed," that which would be treasured even through a starving time against the next year's planting, for it was tragically often in the life of the Peru-

126

vian that a harvest did not provide a fifth part of what was needed to sustain life.

The *pirua* had a superior power to carry over the strength and vitality of the grain. If it failed, if rot or must or animals or thieves invaded or depleted the *pirua's* contents, then the people themselves died. Its special *huaca* was thus preservative, abounding, hopeful of coming plenty, kindly but full of whims and tantrums and, sometimes, death.

This *huaca* in the *pirua* had an abstracted location. The Pleiades was that constellation in the night sky most in the minds of the Incas and foremost in their stellar pantheon. It was called *Capac Collca Coyllur* (or simply Collca), "the Star of the Overflowing Grain Bins," and possessed the power of bringing things into being. It was an invisible womb, as it were, and it was thus worshiped as a power of motherhood. The constellation was also referred to, therefore, as Mama or "Mother." Every *ayllu* worshiped Collca for the increase in its own members, just as the state worshiped Collca for abundance in general. *Pirua* was thus a localized fragment on earth of that universal power resident in the constellation Collca.

Just across the bridge on the Collasuyo road leading east out of Cuzco was a commons called Rimac Pampa, Oracle Field. On its far side and along the road was an old tilled and terraced area called Huanaypata, and there was planted the most sacred corn field in all of Tahuantinsuyo. Its name was Sausero, and it belonged to Mama Huaco, a form of the Inca Earth Mother. It was possibly included in those blocks today bounded by Avenida Garcilaso and the Avenida de la Cultura.

Mama Huaco, so ran the story, was the first *coya* of Cuzco, for she was Manco Capac's mother, sister, and wife combined. She is alternately referred to as Mama Ocllo, and she carried a golden *taclla*, or digging stick, the foot plow of the Incas. The founding legend had it that the Incas, led by Manco Capac and Mama Huaco, came up the valley from Sañu to invade the *chacras* of the Hualla Indians, Cuzco's first inhabitants. They made two heavy raids, if we may thus interpret the legend, each time moving in closer toward the Hualla settlement. The third push was successful, Huanaypata was taken, and the

Huallas forever dispossessed. The legend added that Mama Huaco tried her golden *taclla* in this soil where it easily sank in, thus fulfilling the prophecy that here the Men of Manco would found their city. Here, then, the first maize was planted, and thus it was holy ground for the Incas. Sausero was thought to be the very body of Mama Huaco, as indeed it was, for she was the Earth Mother.

The corn grown in this sacred *chacra*, especially well-tended and vigorous, was in a sense an allegory of the young Incas who had been knighted some six months before. Their apprenticeship had not been quite completed by the assumption of the earplugs and the donning of the breechclouts, and they had continued their fasting and continence. But now, even as the Mother's corn was at last mature full manhood also came upon these young Incas. Thus the new harvest of knights was brought into mystic conjunction with the first fruits of Sausero. Only these fresh young men, clad in their special short kilts hung with medals, and with gay feathers thrust in their *llautos*, could shuck and bag this corn, bringing it in on their backs with the same war cry they would later use when victorious on the field of battle, "*Haylli! Haylli!*" This marriage of youth and the first corn from Mother Earth was to act as an earnest of the Inca future.

The whole of that first day the knights, singing and merrymaking, worked to carry this ceremonial corn into the *pirua* specially designated for it. The refrain of their song was: "Give us only our share of the precious corn; we will not take all from you, Precious Fallow Mother." The procession was finally led back into the city by the *napa*, the spotless white llama which symbolized Cuzco.

During this festival every household in Cuzco made a rough figure from cornstalks taken from its own family *chacra*; this figure was intended to represent Mama Sara, the Corn Mother. They clothed the figure and laid it away in a small *pirua* in the house. In this dry little doll there would reside for another year the spirit of that corn which grew in their fields. Every family had its own Mama Sara asleep in its own toy *pirua*. These were *ayllu huacas*, and they loved only their own.

Conjoined with this event was a rite which should interest every tourist, for it was held on that much-visited site today called Kenko

128

but then known as Chuquimarca. The probable meaning of the name Chuquimarca is Lance Precinct. This theatral area is a most dramatic site, situated as it is on the lip of one of the hills overlooking Cuzco. This hill, which was then called Manturcalla, Red Slope, today is rather vaguely called Senca, the Ridge. On the spot we are describing, a semicircle of fine Inca masonry with niches facing in to the center surrounds two bulky rocks which the Incas apparently called Unu Huallpa, "Water Maker."

According to legend, the sun occasionally used to sleep here. Commemorating this vast and mystic performance, the Incas used to sacrifice children on the spot. The impressive phallic-appearing rock that stands on its low platform was probably vaguely conceived to contain the masculine creativity of Inti, boldly, crudely, and splendidly designed. The massive rock which serves as a backdrop is most curiously and baroquely sculptured both within and without. In the passages enlarged through this rock by human hands the visitor can sense, as perhaps nowhere else, the abstract quality of "rock" itself, a feature of their environment which the Incas intimately understood and one which they felt to be included in the very essence of *huaca*.

The Capac Incas alone could invade these holy precincts. Not even their wives, the *pallas*, were allowed within the spacious masonry circle, and only the *mamaconas* who were the religiously sanctified women of the sun could here serve the Inca magnates with ceremonial *akha*. Whether orgiastic or not, the rites carried on here were probably symbolic of the generative power of the sun, for in the procession that solemnly entered this place there figured two richly cloaked images called Inca Ayllu and Palla Ayllu. This ceremony pointed to the widely distributed Peruvian tenet that noble men and women were of different orders of creation; they belonged, in other words, to different species or *ayllus* and were often represented by gold and silver. Thus all Incas were sons of Inti, and all *pallas* were his daughters. Behind these individuals followed images of the aboriginal llamas which issued from the bowels of the earth after the Flood along with the Incas. Again, these noble llamas were two of gold and two of silver, possibly to be interpreted here either as the two sexes or as the rich

129

herds of Upper and Lower moieties, respectively. In the procession the magnates of the two moieties entered the theatral area bearing on their shoulders litters containing all of these figures. At the head of the procession came the living *napa* with tassels and gold ornaments in his ears, followed by the emperor's standard. Wooden dolls of men and women decked with flowers and wooden ears of corn were cast into great bonfires, a special dance was performed, banqueting and drinking ensued, and games of chance, including dice, were played. This festival goes back to an age-old harvest ritual, but the Incas had made it into something more.

When it was all over, the *ayllus* came forward and redistributed the lands possessed by them, for in the year's interval families had increased or decreased, and it was each *ayllu*'s responsibility to see that all of its component families received their proper share. This ritual was called the *chacra ricuy*, or "field inspection," and it formalized the beginning of a new agricultural year.

SECTION 15.

Imperial Harvest—the Inti Raymi

PERHAPS BECAUSE OF the intense particularism in the aforesaid harvest rites, which celebrated only the harvests of Cuzco and her *ayllus*, there was felt a need for a wider application of the harvest-home, a rejoicing in brief over the plenty and tribute of the whole empire, a thanksgiving to Inti and the other gods for harvests out of the fields of polity. From this need came the appended rites of the Inti Raymi.

There were two parts to the Inti Raymi, a holy pilgrimage to Inti's distant home in the east and the *yahuarincha aymoray* or "Blood-smearing Aymoray." In the first part, the men of the Tarpuntay *ayllu*, a priestly family concerned especially with crops and herds, moved down the Huatanay Valley, over past Huaro, and up the Vilcañota Valley to Viracocha's temple near Mount Ausangate. From this point they passed on to the great watershed of the upper Vilcañota. En route they sacrificed at various holy mountains and on their return at others. This meritorious pilgrimage was brought to an end at Chuquimarca where the Capac Incas were performing the ceremonies which have already been described.

The *yahuarincha aymoray* was held in Rimac Pampa, today called Limac Pampa. It is now the site of a small Indian market as well as being a singularly busy truck and bus thoroughfare as one goes out to the new university or the airport. Here, as in the previous Aymoray, took place over a ten-day period the harvest-home for the whole empire, and here the emperor officiated as his own high priest.

Rimac Pampa was the eastern portal of the city. It was therefore as if Inti were to come walking down the Collasuyo road, fresh from his heroic rising, here entering his beloved city and here greeting his children the Incas, who had congregated to welcome and praise him and usher him in. It was in all respects a splendid and moving conception.

Red was the predominant color in these festivities, the red cloud rack of morning, the steaming scarlet of the sacrificial blood poured out, and the artfully designed ankle-length robes of deep red dye worn by the magnates, quite unlike their usual short tunics. In the long, cold dawning of the first designated day, well before the sun rose, the ceremonies began. The ancestral mummies, all of them gorgeously appareled and each tended by some twelve or fifteen *mamaconas*, were brought out and carefully ensconced in pavilions of bird feathers. These pavilions or tents were ranged in a broad avenue with Upper and Lower Cuzco on opposite sides. The reigning emperor was then borne sedately down this avenue, his golden *rampa* or covered litter already glinting dully in the growing light, its coat of arms featuring the sun, moon, and two serpents, its liveried Rucana carriers moving with measured ease.

The *unancha* was carried in the van of the procession, followed by

131

the *napa*, gleaming white and pacing with that precise, disdainful movement characteristic of the mature llama. In his ears were gold ornaments and beside him came the two *mamaconas* who made his *akha*
and carried it in jars on their backs, for this beast was trained both to
drink the maize beer favored by the Incas and to munch coca leaves.
As already alluded to, he was the living *huaca* of the first llama to appear after the Flood and was thus the race-soul of all llamas; he represented the goodness of their wool, their uses as carriers and acceptable
sacrifices, as spreaders of dung on the land, and as companions to the
lonely pastor. The *napa* was never himself sacrificed but allowed to live
out his natural life and in the end to be buried honorably.

Behind the litter walked the Capac Incas, clad only a little less richly
than their emperor. They, too, were arranged in two files, Upper and
Lower Cuzco. When the procession reached the end of the avenue,
the emperor was deposited on a dais under an especially sumptuous
canopy and took his seat surrounded by his magnates. Near him was
an *usno* with the Inca gods carefully arranged on its several irregular
setbacks.

In all this ritual, not a word had been spoken. The hush was to
honor Inti who was even now at the gates of dawn. One always knew
when to expect him because of the gold and rosy scud of clouds, the
acapana, swiftly fleeing away out of the sky before his muscular advance. Precisely at the moment when he appeared, the emperor arose
and walked down the avenue of mummies to its end, greeting his
father with the *mocha* of worship, blowing kisses to him, and initiating
a quiet chant of adoration and supplication. The hymn was then taken
up by both the dead and the living Incas. Beginning thus mutedly as
befitted the dawn, when awakening seemed a hard thing, the song
would rise more sonorously at midday and die away again at dusk,
lessening in intensity until it ended in soft, sad cries like those of birds
flying home.

Periodically during the day the emperor returned to his pavilion
at the head of the avenue and attended to the business of state. The
most colorful part of each day's events, however, was the entry of the
sun-women. By fives they came walking down out of Cuzco into Rimac

Pampa, pausing occasionally before proceeding. Each one bore on her back a golden jug of sacred *akha*, and each carried beautifully woven little bags of coca leaves for chewing. This prepared drink and the mild narcotic of the leaf were offered to Inti at the end of each day's banqueting. A fire of carved logs was lighted in the square near a sacred tree, and in its flame were sacrificed llamas, coca, feathered garments, etc. The emperor then advanced, holding two golden cups of *akha* full to the brim. He was always the first to toast his shining father, drinking from his own cup and holding the other aloft. While the lords followed suit, the *pallas* and *mamaconas* beat their tambourines to increase the joy of the fiesta. At the end of each day, all the tents were struck and the emperor, magnates, and mummies turned back for their rest in the holy city, to return for nine dawns in succession to greet the day.

The business transacted by the emperor during this time was the culmination of the whole imperial experience of the Incas. For weeks before, the roads of the empire had been filled with *curacas* from all the provinces, or sons and representatives of these *curacas*, leading files of llamas and of porters bent low under the weight of the year's tribute due from them. Years earlier the seed of this harvest had been sowed in battle in the blood of Inca men of war, and only here did this sowing come to its stern and splendid reaping.

First the Incas themselves brought gifts to their emperor, hailing him as "Sun-child, Merciful to the Wretched." Next the *curacas* were ushered into the presence, barefooted and trembling, with shoulders hunched and crouching almost to the ground. They deposited in front of the *usno* the sacks, bundles, sheaves, or rolls of whatever tribute they had brought, whereupon it was counted and checked against the figure originally imposed upon them. Afterward they were all searchingly questioned by the emperor, through the mouth of his *capacpa rantin rimac* or "the delegate who speaks for the emperor," concerning the affairs of their people and their life under Inca rule. Complaints concerning imperial injustice or inequities could here, by especially courageous *curacas*, be brought to the emperor's attention. If all the tribute was there and if that particular *curaca* appeared to be able and willing to continue contributing to the general prosperity, then he was rewarded by portions of the tribute from other parts of the empire.

Along with this reception and distribution of the annual tribute from the provinces went a largess to all the Incas. It was dispensed either for reasons of favoritism or as a reward for services on the field of battle, in engineering projects, or in the administration of difficult provinces. As a prelude, a certain number of nubile *acllas* were brought in. They were first allowed to present to the emperor the lovely garments or cloths they had spent months and even years in planning and weaving; these were tapestries, gauzes, twills, brocades and embroideries, all of them miracles of invention, and some of them sumptuous beyond words. Out of the virginal stalls wherein they had been so long penned, these items alone the *acllas* brought—these and their beauty. Then began the inspection and division. Some of these girls were taken by the emperor and sent to his own quarters. The rest he parceled out to his captains and favorites as wives or concubines.

With the *ñustas* the matter was differently arranged. *Ñustas* were the daughters of the Capac Incas, and the ones here in question were those who had come to their womanhood in the *quicuchicoy* and were ready now for marriage. Being of Inca blood, they were not handed out as gifts, but were assigned by the emperor to the new young knights, the matter having no doubt been prearranged by the parents. Through such marriages these young girls became *pallas* and legitimate wives.

With this pairing off of fullblood Incas and *ñustas* went the year's assignment and reassignment of the *chacras*, the water rights, and the herds possessed by the various Inca *ayllus,* for the young Inca couples needed lands for their livelihood, and these lands and rights had to come to them generally from their family *ayllus* in which alone true possession was vested. A young Inca of whatever *ayllu* who now received a legitimate wife would be assigned by his *ayllu* as much in the way of *chacras* or llamas as was appropriate to his dignity and necessary to the sustenance of his new ménage. This property was granted by the *ayllu* out of those lands or herds which had recently reverted to it from the deaths or aging of others of its members. This distribution was done under the imperial sanction.

Before the Inti Raymi closed, there took place the *villcacona*, the annual convocation of *huacas*, an event awaited always with trepidation. Here on a small eminence in Rimac Pampa called Raquiancalla were assembled the greatest *huacas* of the empire. They might be wooden posts, shriveled roots, figured idols of precious metal, small pebbles, or large and uncouth rocks, but all were assembled in a tight, closed circle on this spot whose holiness belied its common appearance. With each of the *huacas* was its own oracular priest, thoroughly drunken for the performance of his office, as well as the acolyte who interpreted his shrieks and moanings. Like the *curacas*, these holy objects and their priestly escort had been journeying down the highways of the empire, all converging upon this unwilling conclave. While resident in Cuzco they had been domiciled in Coricancha, but for this crucial moment they had come out to Rimac Pampa to meet—and to prophesy to— their masters, the Incas and the Inca gods.

What each one of these *huacas* had prophesied at the previous year's convocation was at this time reviewed and matched with what had in effect taken place—disasters, deaths, full or meager harvests, starvation or abundance, insurrection, victories or setbacks in war, and the good or ill health of the emperor. Any outstanding discrepancy was naturally pointed out, and if the outcome had worked an injury to Tahuantinsuyo, the *huaca* was held responsible. The emperor who, being the sun's very own child and heir, was this world's greatest priest ordered either rewards or punishments as seemed appropriate to him. Those *huacas* which had spoken in enigmas, *huatunacta rimay*, or had prophesied falsely or blindly were sentenced to exposure up in the high snow fields of the Andes for certain stated periods. In cases of a flagrantly mendacious oracle, the *huaca* was punished by the death or mutilation of his priest. The *huaca* itself could be exterminated if the offense were truly serious.

After this terrible inquisition the *huacas* were called upon to portray what the coming year would be like. A desired oracle took the form of a clear assurance to the Inca emperor that he would live and that a *callallallak huata* was in prospect, a year of green and abundant fields, the maize waving briskly in soft winds and under right skies, all the lands verdant and the grave *punas* sprinkled with flocks and alpine flowers. Each *huaca* was asked separately for its response which would then be compared with the oracles of the other *huacas*.

Once the proper assurances were given, the *taqui* could begin. The banqueting was introduced by a communion meal of the *yahuar sanco*, or "blood pudding." This raw corn meal mixed with the fat and blood of sacrificed llamas was served in small pellets to each Inca, one to each *curaca* and one to each of the foreign *huacas*. By this means each person and power incorporated into his own being Inti's holy demands, his constant surveillance, and the certainty of his wrath if treachery occurred.

The *taqui* itself consisted of dancing, gambling, the drinking of great quantities of *akha*, and now, for the first time, the participation of that year's selection of knights as full Incas, all of their fasting and initiatory penances completed. The heroisms of the Inca past were extravagantly displayed in mock fights, the most lavish being the dramatic contest with the Chancas out of which had emerged the Pachacutean state. A large group of Canas, who had been Inca allies in that crisis, for this occasion came down from their valley homes to fight a squadron of four hundred Cañars representing the Chancas, while the Inca braves dominated the whole scene dressed in jaguar skins and adorned with iridescent feathers and bangles of gold and silver. It was a very sumptuous scene and lurid with the passions of this caste of warriors who had mastered all others in the Peruvian *sallca*.

The conclusion of the great round of festivities came only after the *curacas* and their *huacas* had disappeared out along the four roads of the empire, each back to his separate province and each with his separate charge for the amount of the coming year's tribute to be called for at the next Inti Raymi. Once again the emperor and his magnates went out to the nearby field sacred to Mother Earth. Four young llamas were turned loose in the field and all the young knights pursued them with knives. It was good fortune to be able to catch one. When caught the beast was immediately cut into small pieces by the youths, its blood and the bits of flesh fertilizing the ground for the coming year. Then the older Incas advanced into the field and with golden *tacllas* broke the ground for the new year. There followed the *aucay cuzqui*, or plowing of the new shoots, and it began nature's new year with a good omen.

SECTION 16. *A Wall on Collcampata*

YOUNG AS THE REIGN was, it was already old in terror and insult. Huascar had become that most frightening of beings in high position, a person wholly contemptuous of others, weak and at the same time sadistic. In his smoky mind the most remote possibilities became present certainties. He became suspicious even of his own informers, the Incas of the Equeco and Quilliscachi *ayllus*, for we hear that he ordered the massacre of the men of those two communities in the Anta Basin and the butchery of all their pregnant women. His world had become kaleidoscopic, changing every moment—the only unchanging thing being the fear that could be seen on every face. The order which his predecessors had achieved, the neatness of things, the impeccable Inca superiority—all were now being put to question. A fierce and sullen caprice ruled Tahuantinsuyo, unwarlike, unrespected, and unaccountable. To the men and women of the Capac Ayllu and to the Hahua Incas as well, this emperor who stood before them in his blue mantle, in his iridescent tunic with its ornate triple band of *tocapu*, had become a *huacmansayak*, "he who stands over against," in other words, a stranger.

Huascar seldom showed himself to his people. He did not often appear in Haucaypata for the great festivals. He did not publicly banquet with the ancestors or toast them in the convivial *machachicuy* or "drinking bouts." His anger at the royal mummies was all too easily aroused, and he possessed a blind envy of their heroic qualities and their wealth. He had come to fear the *panacas* for their secrecy and the sovereignty with which they could carry on their affairs inside the *canchas*. His open threats to bury the mummies once and for all and to seize their possessions, however, did not dent the established traditions.

When it became apparent that he could not intimidate the dead, he broke with them. He whose greatest boast it should have been to have belonged to Upper Cuzco now publicly broke with the *ayllus* of that moiety. What this meant to the members of Upper Cuzco may easily be deduced, for Hanan Cuzco was the most noble of the families of earth and contained the proudest of living men and the greatest of the dead emperors. No one could hold Hanan Cuzco up to scorn without in effect undermining the structure of the Inca state.

Atauhuallpa belonged to Upper Cuzco, and this fact may have occasioned the break. The Iñaca *panaca*, once the strongest of the Upper Cuzco families, had become the inevitable center of resistance to Huascar after his slaughter of their great men at Limatambo. The Sucso *panaca*, to which Colla Topa, the first of the executors, had belonged, could not forget the brutal extermination of their greatest man. Huascar was in part able to seduce the Capac Ayllu *panaca* to his cause, although he could not effectively demolish it. He showed some favors toward the Lower Cuzco *ayllus*, while further advertising his repudiation of Upper Cuzco by moving his residence out of Amarucancha.

This move had the most radical implications. Before him every emperor from Inca Roca on down had established his palace around Haucaypata; residence in this neighborhood in fact had become one of the sanctions which supported a ruler. Huascar abandoned the area completely, choosing instead a spot well above Haucaypata on the back slope and just under the grim security of the fortress. This terraced area of Collcampata was a shelf of land cleanly leveled and spacious. The Antasaya *ayllu* claimed this high area of Cuzco, and in support of this claim the members could point out on the terrace a sacred stone which had once been their *machu* or "ancestor." Here also on the terrace was the famous Founders' Fountain, Ticcicocha, a pleasant basin of running water, and beside it the house of a *palla* who for a short time in the days of old Pachacuti had been a coempress. Her husband had been much beloved, and her former residence here was thus a *huaca*.

On this high shelf Huascar's builders provided for him apartments carefully sequestered from the life of Cuzco below. So well isolated was this palace from the life of the city just below it and so carefully protected that it was soon known as Huascar's Fortress. One of the interior walls, of superb masonry, survives today, an archaeological treasure which the visitor being driven up to Sacsahuaman passes and views but does not comprehend. This remarkable wall, backed now with eucalyptus trees which did not exist then, limns forth the peculiar serenity and timelessness which the Incas strove for and often achieved in their stonework. It does not give one the slightest hint of the phantasmagoria that for a very brief space reigned there like the dark succubus of an empire. The wall speaks of Inca confidence and Inca orderliness, but in this case it lies.

III
The Beliefs of the Last Reign

THE YOUNG EMPEROR—he who had taken Inti's name as his own—now made a pilgrimage to that rock in Lake Chucuito out of which Inti had been born. His father had followed this sacred way before him.

We have seen that his father's pilgrimage had eventuated in an imperial edict establishing the cultic pre-eminence of Viracocha over Inti in that mystic god's-land of Lake Chucuito. In a sense this action had been consistent with the policy of all the late emperors who had sensed that the fullness of their own power was associated with corresponding claims for the Creator. Viracocha had to be presented in as monotheistic a light as possible if the primacy of his vicar on earth, the Inca emperor, was to be evident.

The history of this interest in Viracocha had begun as early as the reign of the eighth ruler who had taken the Creator's name as his own, Viracocha Inca, "the Lord Inca." The succeeding ruler had announced himself as the beginning of a new era when he took the name Pachacuti and daringly proclaimed the dogma of the hierarchical ascendancy of the Creator over Inti. The next ruler, Topa Inca, was perhaps not as powerfully oriented toward religious solutions to imperial problems, but he moved in the same direction when he kept up an unrelenting pressure upon every provincial *huaca* claiming greatness. Huayna Capac, the eleventh emperor, as we have earlier seen, created for himself a special pastoral office in the religion of Inti while at the same time continuing the aggrandizement of the cult of Viracocha. Huascar, our twelfth and present ruler, had in his coronation name identified himself with Inti as a first step; now he was to move logically to further the inchoate monotheism of the royal house. This goal was, in fact, the purpose of his visit to the island of Titicaca.

While there he ordered the fashioning of a new god in gold. He named this god Viracocha-Inti, a conflation of the names, powers, and activities of the Creator with those of the ancestral Inca fetish. The idol was then installed in sacred precincts in the area. The meaning of this move is clear. It was to be another step in the swallowing up of Inca particularity into the abyss of ecumenicality; the Capac Incas who had begun as a conquering people were to become even more like subjects. Probably Huascar had as little real success with this creedal innovation as his father had had with his, but it displayed clearly the logic that increasingly united the fortunes of the empire with Viracocha.

The cause of the deepening split between the emperor and his people we have identified on the one hand as the emergence of the concept of an omnipotent god, primarily a vision of the royal house, and on the other hand the persistence of the older and pluralistic concepts of *huaca* still tenaciously held by the Incas. The Incas were not hostile to the cult of Viracocha; they clearly saw the need of it, for it immeasurably supported their prerogative. They objected to it only when it threatened to snuff out their tribal and family *huacas* which alone gave them the strength to oppose the growing authority of the imperial office.

In Coricancha, Huascar ordered changes appropriate to his designs. New idols were cast in solid gold, and grave ceremonies of installation were performed for them.

Section 2. *Huaca*

In any decipherment of Inca culture the most significant concept to explain is that of *huaca*.

It is probable that the word is a nominal formation from *huac*, meaning "elsewhere, apart, other, distinct, aside" and always carrying connotations of detachment, foreignness, or even hostility. *Huac suyu*, for instance is the enemy army, literally "the other group." As a noun then, *huaca* must mean "that which is strange or over there." This reading of the meaning of the word is backed up by a review of its secondary or derived meaning, for *huaca* means anything

144

that is untoward or out of the ordinary, such as a strangely appearing rock formation, a grotesquely ugly person, an eerily formed potato taken out of the ground, or a great and unusual city. Again, it can mean that which is terrifying, such as a bogeyman, an anaconda, a demonic emperor. It is one of man's basic religious concepts, for it englobes his sense of the inscrutability and intractability of the world beyond. Both fear and awe are included in it. It is permissible to translate it as "holy."

To the people who spoke Quechua, *huaca* seemingly never meant "power" in general. It was always to be found in a very specific concrete presence that was thought of as "apart" from all other presences, no matter how much alike such presences might on the surface seem to be. Almost every Peruvian need was propitiated as a *huaca*. When interpreted thus in terms of *huaca*, the Inca's world was at bottom pluralistic. There was, for instance, no such thing as "luck" in general. But there existed luck in war, *atau*, luck in games and transactions, *sami*, luck in the events of one's daily life, *cusi*, and luck in great undertakings, *quillpu*. A person who possessed any one of these qualities was himself a *huaca* to the extent of that possession. The intensity with which the Peruvian people lived, their awareness of themselves and of their place in the world could be measured by the number of *huacas* in their culture. On this showing the lords of Cuzco surpassed all other peoples in Peru.

Because of this particularity, *huacas* could be moved, stolen, or even destroyed. An *ayllu*, for instance, might attack the settlement of another *ayllu* and make away with its central *huaca*. This loss was always most serious and radically weakened the *ayllu* thus deprived. But while they had concrete habitations, *huacas* also possessed the power of proliferation and substitution and even some degree of movement away from their original locus. Thus it might come about that the people of the injured *ayllu* would set up an imitation of their lost *huaca* in straw; to this image they could then make petition for relief from its condign anger, sacrificing to it in surrogate as it were. A *huaca* could, if smashed into many pieces, reproduce itself in the resultant pieces which were then considered to be its sons. Or a man on a long journey might pluck some grass or pick up a stick or stone from the vicinity of his home *huaca* and, in that vicarious baggage, carry his *huaca* with him—at least to the extent of being able to address it directly. In the legends of the aboriginal wanderings of peoples the places where they stopped with their *huacas* became holy, and they were thenceforth known as *samana*, "halting places." A *huaca* always left a spoor of "apartness" wherever it went.

Almost all *huacas* possessed the powers of speech, that is to say, they were oracular. A pervasive spirit-gabbling filled the Inca's world, for on every hand, out of the ground at his feet, out of the tree beside the road, and out of the rainbow that shone in the washed sky, came voices, all weighty and all sententious. This characteristic further identifies *huaca* as a personality. It was the *villcas* or the fashioned idols, however, which were listened to most raptly, for speech seemed more natural to *huacas* made by the hand of man. They were *huacas* in the way of becoming gods, for the power to answer a man's question was the power to become something more to him than a personality experienced wordlessly. Indeed, we might even artificially separate *huacas* into two classes, those which, like the *villcas*, existed primarily to communicate with men, and those which, like the *apachitas*, did not. The former revealed themselves through priests or shamans, while the latter impinged upon men mutely and directly.

There was nevertheless one *huaca* in the life of all Peruvian Indians and among the Incas which escapes any such classification. This *huaca* was *supay*, a word which in one of its meanings can with justification be translated as "devil." There was as much knowledge of him and of his doings in Cuzco as there was of the Creator. Supay was in fact a kind of opposite to Viracocha. He was malevolence pure and simple. Where Viracocha was divine, he was demonic. As the spirit of disorder and the father of disaster, he actively pursued evil as an end. In this sense he was almost godlike, for he took advantage of any situation, however novel, to engineer his plots. He often spoke to men and rewarded those who served him. He was endowed with both wiles and will, and, being a personality, would never be destroyed.

But he was not only an eternal demiurge; he was also and generally

146

a specific *huaca* which could be destroyed in a catastrophe. In this meaning *supay* could be either good or bad, thus conforming to the diverse meanings of *huaca*. But again there was a tendency to view him as a creature of harm. He was a well-known and specific phantom that roamed the night often doing evil; in such a manifestation he was probably related to the shadow, *supa*, of a person or animal. Here he was not the Prince of Evil but rather an evil or baleful thing concretely imagined. The Incas—as might be imagined—had a pronounced tendency to see the *huacas* of all other people as *llullay supay*, "deceitful devils," thus categorizing them in moral terms.

A *huaca* when conceived as a *supay* could actually enter a person to produce the classic phenomenon of "possession." No other type of *huaca* or god seemingly did so. The possessed person thereby became a *supaypa yuucuscuun*, "one entered by a devil." Or on a less drastic scale a person might be a *supayniyok*, "one who has a devil" as his familiar, in other words, a sorcerer or worker of black magic. It is certain that the dead could on occasions be converted into *supay*.

There were other classes of *huacas* common to the world of the Incas. *Purun huacas* were those frightening presences which haunted desolate places, remote trails, far crossroads, and unpeopled places. As such they had no necessary ties to any particular *ayllu*, but the people of an *ayllu* that discovered one considered themselves fortunate and acquired, if not a proprietary right over the *huaca*, at least a knowledge of its existence more acute than others, and thus a kind of responsibility which elevated their status. But even if, for instance, an *ayllu* counted among its relationships a *huaccap ñan*, "a *huaca*-road," meaning a particularly terrifying passage along a mountainside, this association still gave it no claim to adroitness in negotiating dangerous mountain trails in general. The *ayllu* claimed only that the fear afflicting one at that particular juncture in that particular road was of great relevance to it and its members. The *huaca* focused itself through some particularity at the spot; it might be a jutting crag, the roadside cairn of a fallen traveler, or a leaning tree. It was able to adopt such a specific residence because while it was a *huaca*, it was never *huaca* in general.

The *apachita* was a type of *purun huaca*. Travelers in the *sallca*, the "highlands," customarily moved through those savage landscapes with a minimum of conversation lest they offend the winds. At the summit of all high passes when one's load became almost unendurably heavy in the rarified air, when tempests threatened to bring on the sudden white death of a snowstorm, or when the fall of night attempted to destroy one with insane terrors—at such junctures the traveler spoke directly to the *apachic*, "that which gives one the strength to carry." This type of *huaca* could be found of course anywhere where loads became heavy, in the steaming *huaycos* of the montaña or the burning deserts along the coast, but in the *sallca* he demanded special placation and recognition of his power. Anything could be offered to him, a cud of chewed coca leaves, a raveling from one's garment, a handful of sparse grass, or, most often, a stone from the ground round about along with a hushed invocation. This *huaca* was simply the "daemon" of the place, dangerous, uneasy, difficult, and touchy. Whatever gift was offered was placed on that pile of stones and human debris which had grown there by similar donations of generations of mountaineers, after which act of reverence one might count on escaping the dangers of the trail, the terrible *soroche* or mountain sickness, the snow flurries, the frostbitten feet, and the load too heavy to bear. Such a *huaca* was compounded of the spirit of the locale, of men's needs, and of their fears—one could almost refer to this type of *huaca* as being "the traveler's experience of pass country at such and such a spot."

The most significant variation on the *apachita* type of *huaca* was the *usno*. That *usno* which served as the Incas' tribunal in the center of the great square has already been mentioned. An *usno* was essentially a place of divine appearances and, in consequence, a place of sacrifices. Being a *huaca* itself, it further sanctified whatever was placed on it. Generally it was carved directly out of some rock outcrop and was thus fixed in place. An irregular series of seatlike steps or setbacks marked its form, and on these niches and levels were placed the fetishes and gods of the Incas and their offerings. The summit was sometimes hewn out as a stump or truncated pier of stone which could be sheathed in gold leaf. The *usno* always signalized in stone a special locus of the divine. In Haucaypata the *usno* served as the imperial dais. Elsewhere, as in Pisac or Machu Picchu, it enthroned more invisible powers.

Another type of *huaca* was the *marcayoc*, "the holder of the reserved [field]," which, when it was in the form of a standing stone or post set up in the community, was also called a *huanca*. So close was the union between the physical elements of a settlement (*chacras*, *canchas*, and *ayllu* members) with the traditional life lived in that community or its spirit that the latter was conceived of as a *huaca* and named; this name then served the physical community as well. Such was the case with Cuzco. One of the four founding Ayar brothers was transformed into a stone in Cuzco called Cuzco Huanca, probably the original stone revered there by the first inhabitants of the site, the Hualla Indians. There was no distinction, therefore, between the *marcayoc* of a sierra settlement and the settlement itself. The *marcayoc* was the fortune and prosperity of the community, and it stood as a visible stone or rough column in the middle of a field set aside and sacred to it.

A specialized version of the *marcayoc* was the *ayllu* progenitor, the *ccallaric machu*, the heroic person who had escaped the cataclysmic Flood in the past and had then emerged from a cave, a lake, or a tree to found the line of true men. After such an epiphany he had usually then commemorated himself for all time by changing into a stone thenceforth sacred. Manco Capac, when he was confused with Huana cauri, was such a being. These *huacas* could be reverenced in their mummies, if such existed, or as the stone into which they had been transformed. This type of *huaca* was of signal importance to the men of the *ayllu*, for only by means of its continued benevolence could they multiply as a nation and gain victories over their enemies. It was in a sense the genius or virility of the people.

Closely allied to this was the *pacarina*, or the place from which the ancestor had emerged into the postdiluvial world. The *pacarina* of the Inca people was a spectacular rock out on the Contisuyo road. In the Peruvian mind any place became a *huaca* if it was the scene of a significant event. This memorability sanctified it and gave it power and a dim personality. Here So-and-So had rested, here he had sat, here he or it was when a mighty decision was taken. There were many of such *samanas* in Cuzco identifying as holy the ground where the various *apus* had for a while remained.

Another type of *huaca* was the *simulacrum*, the *huaca* that created, categorized, and sustained a class of beings. Generally, but not always, this presence found its home in a star or constellation in the night sky. The Southern Cross was Urcochillay and was thought to be a many-colored llama spirit upon which the increase of llama herds everywhere depended. *Choqque Chinchay* or "Golden Star" (Sirius) was similarly a jaguar and controlled all jaguars and bears to be found in the mon-taña. Machacuay presided over the destinies of all poisonous serpents. Collca we have already described as residing in the Pleiades and as being the spirit of food containers and storage bins everywhere. A more baleful *huaca* of this order was the Mama Mirccuc Coyllur, "the Star of Those who Eat Their Mothers," its jurisdiction being obvious from the name. War, disaster, and the things of commerce each had a separate guardian star. There was no star, however, that contained within itself the ideal presence of all mankind, able to sustain and multiply him, for this power was seen by the Incas to be no longer strictly a power of *huaca* but one of a totally different order, that of godhead, or, as they had learned to call it, of Viracocha.

SECTION 3. *Cuzco as a Huaca*

IT IS DIFFICULT for us today to understand the physical world in which the Incas knew themselves to be living. Our own peripatetic existences have given to places only a sentimental value at best. The Incas of the Capac Ayllu inhabited Cuzco, not because it was a convenient or de-sirable site, or even because it was traditional to do so, but just because they were Incas and Cuzco was in a real sense their whole existence. The people and the place were indissolubly wedded into one being, and it was this being that they worshiped as a *huaca*. Cuzco was thus not only the greatest of the Inca *huacas*; it was the only one which con-tained the fullness of their history, their present lives, and their des-tiny. True, the city had its *marcayoc*, the stone called Cuzco Huanca;

it had its *ccallaric machu*, the stone images of Manco Capac and Huana-cauri; it had its *pacarina* in Pacaritambo; and on the island of Titicaca in distant Lake Chucuito it even possessed the *samana* of the ancestral sun which there had given to the Incas the original mission to found Cuzco and make it great. All of these were *huacas*, but none were as vital to the Incas as Cuzco itself, the immediate, the tangible, and the superior *huaca* of them all.

Garcilaso de la Vega said that "the Incas held the whole city as itself a sacred thing. It was one of their paramount idols." Juan de Acosta observed, "As if it were a holy land there were in Cuzco more than four hundred shrines. Every place in it was full of mysteries." On each of the four roads leading in toward Cuzco, as we have seen, there was a place marked where the traveler could have his first glimpse of the city and where he might offer to it his reverence. Simply for this reason these four spots became themselves *huacas*.

Cuzco was thus not a city in our modern understanding of the term. Nor was it a shrine-city like the stone and stucco communities of the Mayas. It did not create an urban way of life as did Tenochtitlan, casting forth on all sides an intellectual sophistication. It was officially Viracocha's city, a true *civitas dei*. It was the pedestal upon which he displayed his designated people who called themselves Incas and *pallas*. No others could be citizens of that city, yet such was its aura that if a visiting provincial *curaca* chanced to have a son born to him in Cuzco, though that child were the youngest son of many, the emperor would command that he inherit as the sole heir the powers and emoluments of his father.

For the Incas this complex *huaca,* of which they in their own persons were a part, was curiously divided up into a system of *ceques*, "lines" or rays, emanating like the spokes of a wheel from a central spot, prob-ably the house of Inti located in Coricancha. This system must be de-scribed in some detail if the reader is to appreciate the genius of the Incas in organizing the unseen world.

There were forty-one of these imagined *ceques*, and along them were roughly sited most of the four hundred *huacas* in and around Cuzco. The proper observance of the sacrifices due the *huacas* along a *ceque* was the responsibility in each case of a designated Inca *ayllu*, *panaca*, or other family group. Thus the holiness of Cuzco and the maintenance of this holiness were parceled out among all the Incas.

This invisible wheel of rays was divided into four sections corresponding to the four quarters of the empire. In reckoning, one began with the primary quarter, that in the north (actually northwest), Chinchaysuyo so called, which had nine *ceques*. Coming then clockwise, Antisuyo had nine, as did Collasuyo. Contisuyo had fourteen. It is certain that none of the *huacas* on these *ceques* was more than twelve miles out, and most were within a five-mile radius. A day's journey out from and back to the city was thus the factor which limited the radius of the *ceques*.

On this wheel Upper and Lower Cuzco were logically defined. The three *panacas* of the northern section were those most closely connected with the formulator of the system, Pachacuti. They were his own, the Iñaca *panaca*, and those of his son and of his great-grandfather. Those of Pachacuti's father and grandfather were in the second quarter—thus completing the semicircle which defined Upper Cuzco, for all these five *panacas* were of that moiety. Collasuyo and Contisuyo were served by the Lower Cuzco *panacas*. The Tumibamba *panaca* was missing from the system inasmuch as it had been founded after the system started to function; and Huascar seems not to have devised a way to insert it. The *ayllus* were also a part of this system, and, as far as we can ascertain, were placed also in those half-circles corresponding to their status as Upper and Lower Cuzco.

The implications are at once obvious. The Inca people were their own priests in the service of their greatest *huaca*. It would certainly be wrong to call them a nation of priests as their overmastering orientation toward war and administration makes evident, but they allowed no professional intermediaries to stand between them and the holiness of their special environment. Few people have ever felt themselves as close to the sacred.

The example of the Chima *panaca* will suffice as an example of the involvement of the Incas in this system. This *panaca* had charge of the fifth *ceque* of the fourth, or Contisuyo, quarter. The first *huaca* which it was their duty to serve on its appointed days and with its appropriate rites was called Cari Tambo Cancha, the "Enclosure of the Tambo Man." It was a *samana*, probably on the southwest side of Coricancha, commemorating the first spot of ground claimed by Manco Capac, the founder of the city. As a matter of fact, it was probably also the palace inhabited by that *panaca*. Continuing sacrifices were made here to the founder, while on great occasions young children also were offered up.

The second *huaca* on the *ceque* was called Tincalla. This was a group of ten stones, all of them *pururaucas*, gathered together in the old village of Cayaocachi only half a mile away. It will be recalled that the *pururaucas* had been those invisible heavenly soldiers sent by Viracocha to aid Pachacuti in his historic confrontation with the Chancas. With victory achieved, these had then been turned to stone each where he stood. The third *huaca* was Caya Llacta or Dried-Oca Town; this point was still farther out and was an unusual rock formation on a hill near Choco. A basin of water above that community was the fourth *huaca* which demanded sacrifices; it was called Churu Puquiu or Snail Fountain. In the hills nearby was a group of rocks thought to have been tossed there from Mount Huanacauri several miles away. No doubt in legend they had been hurled from the sling of the most violent one of the four founding brothers, Ayar Auca, whose depredations were to be seen elsewhere around Cuzco in the deep valleys plowed up by his slingstones and in the many tumbled crags and peaks which he had knocked down.

This listing of the *huacas* along just one of the forty-one *ceques* is fairly representative of the intense mingling in the Inca mind of man and nature, of history and landscape, into one conglomerate known to them as Topa Cuzco, Illustrious Cuzco.

Any *ayllu* which had not partaken of that ineluctable historical process which culminated in Cuzco could not be considered truly Inca. A person who did not live by prescriptive right within the sacred triangle was not a Capac Inca. A Capac Inca not crowned in Coricancha was not an emperor, however correct otherwise his legitimacy might be. It was in this way that the centrality of Cuzco in Inca life promoted the rise of a mystique of overpowering proportions.

This mystique was naturally vulnerable. Should an emperor ever appear who contemned or misprized the city, a dagger would be driven into the very bowels of his people. And such indeed had already happened. For more than twelve years Huayna Capac had been absent from this holy ground, and he had died in a distant place. Huascar had already publicly abjured Upper Cuzco and had allowed his father's *panaca* no part in the *ceque* system. As a *huaca* of unquestioned power, Cuzco was waning. The center and the parts of Tahuantinsuyo were tearing asunder, emperor from his people, Viracocha from the *huacas*. Huascar had the prescriptive right of being referred to simply as "Cuzco," but to many Incas and *pallas* this salutation must have seemed sadly ironic.

SECTION 4. *Gods and Huacas*

CORICANCHA was the home of the only true gods, Viracocha and Inti. Illapa, Mama Quilla, Cuychic perhaps were on a footing close to godhead but should preferably be classified as superior or intercessor *huacas*. To the Inca a god was a being who instituted and supported a moral order and who made this known through self-revelation directly to a charismatic leader.

The above should be understood as an emphasis only. The morality commanded by the Inca god was generalized only; the sketching in of the details was left up to the Incas themselves. The moral "must" turned out to be quite simply the maintenance of the order manifested in Tahuantinsuyo along with constant and pious recognition of the godhead from which the law came.

Of the two gods, Viracocha and Inti, the former really pre-empted the total meaning of godhead, for he was Creator as well as sustainer. Inti, on the contrary, is not indisputably known to have created anything. He had grown from a small fetish, a dried bird in a cane basket, to an importance which allowed him to be identified with Punchao, the sun, and to be classed as the divine father of both the Capac Incas and the Hahua Incas. In view of such an origin, he still trailed after him the telltale garments of a common *huaca*.

Viracocha was indeed no such god as we see revealed in the canonical books of the Old Testament but he was universal and he was almost wholly divorced from the limitations of *huaca*. It was known that he had created all things and held under him in hierarchical subjugation first Inti and the other Inca intercessor gods, and then under them all the *huacas* in the world. We see a line of religious ascent with *huaca* and plurality at the lower pole leading majestically up to the singular godhead of Viracocha at the other.

Viracocha was monopolized and worshiped as a right by the royal house. The Incas as a people continued however to live with equal fervor in a world of *huaca*, as evidenced especially in the *panaca* in which the family pivoted upon the ancestral mummy who was clearly a *huaca*. The heavy responsibility which each *panaca* had in the *ceque* system also bears out this assertion. Nevertheless, this statement should not be taken as an infallible test for understanding the increasing distance between the Incas and their rulers. To a real degree all the Incas had absorbed the dogma of Viracocha's suzerainty. They believed in it without any question; it was only that the enduring parochialism of the *panacas*, based in the world of *huacas*, could not be gainsaid, and it continued to form as ever the bedrock of their beliefs.

ivLIO·
CHACRARICVICHAC
(RACVMACVI·CHAVAVAROVMagguilla
vallaziza-pontifize
sacrificio
chacra

Priests and Sorcerers

THE STATEMENT previously made that the Incas were their own priests needs some further explanation. A fact of importance in understanding this people is that, while there were words in their language for sorcerers and shamans, there was no word for priest.

The word *umu* was the common word for a sorcerer; the *yanapac* was his apprentice. The concept of a sorcerer is that of a person whose calling is not specifically integrated into the community picture—in other words, the sorcerer could be removed as a rule without anything more than the inconvenience or continuing illness or enchantment of certain individuals. A priest on the contrary is in every instance a prime necessity to the society which has created his office. Priesthood implies the state. Without a priest the anger of the powers against the people cannot be placated, nor can their further needs be known or fulfilled. Magic importantly characterizes the shaman; prayer and sacrifice, the priest. Or, to put it now in Inca terms, the sorcerer serves or interprets a *huaca*; but only the priest can appeal to Viracocha. This distinction is, of course, not black and white, for the line leading from one to the other is blurred.

The fact that there was no word expressing the above conception of priesthood in the language of the Incas is simply another way of saying that the only true priestly power in their society was subsumed in the office of the emperor. He alone could be the first to invoke Inti or Viracocha, for he was the bodily son of the former. Nevertheless, he was only the first among peers, for all the Capac Incas were brothers in this office with him.

There was, however, a levitical group in Cuzco which our sources refer to as the Tarpuntay *ayllu* of the Upper Cuzco moiety. These were families of Capac Incas and they carried on certain priestly duties. Specifically they were priests of Inti alone. The verb *tarpuy* means "to sow seed," so we may guess that the original duties of the men of this *ayllu* were connected with the planting of the maize crop. We know that in this regard they were surrogates for the whole Inca community, for they and their wives and children fasted and exercised strict continence from the time the seed was planted until the young sprouts were well out of the ground. During this crucial month in the Inca calendar they carried out their ritual duties by attempting to persuade Inti to bring the crop finally to a lush harvest. In this endeavor they were abetted by the priesthoods of Viracocha and of the storm-god.

They had other priestly duties as well; they were present during the *huarachicoy*, and it was they who made the pious pilgrimage to the birthplace of the sun during the Inti Raymi festival. They were as close to a true priesthood as the Incas were to know, with duties that involved prayer, cult leadership, and vicarious suffering for the people. While they were a true professional class, they were no more than normally in evidence, at least insofar as the imperial religion was concerned, owing to the outstanding powers of the emperor's office in this regard. They were cult officiants and administrators of the imperial religion throughout Tahuantinsuyo, but they never became more than a religious arm of the state. Their power was never political.

One of the signs pointing in this direction is the title of their superior, the *villac umu*, or "the sorcerer who informs." It has been customary in secondary works on the Incas to translate this term as "high priest," but this rendering is somewhat misleading. As the title implies, his office was primarily concerned with learning the dispositions and intentions of that particular power to which he was accredited, in this case Inti, and passing on this information to those concerned. These duties, primarily, were the ones performed by a sorcerer. His office was that of "servant of the sun," and as such he administered the divine household in Coricancha, besides presiding over those Incas who were sent out to administer the Inca cults in the provincial capitals. He fasted vicariously for the emperor when necessary, especially after battles when the bloodguilt of those destroyed oppressed the state. At such times he would be allowed only as many kernels of raw maize each day as enemy killed. He was a very great personage; he always belonged to the Tarpuntay *ayllu*, and he was always either a brother or an uncle of the emperor, selected by him and serving for life. Nevertheless, he did not have the prerogative of the first approach to Inti or Viracocha, for this privilege was the emperor's alone. The latter, who was the "son of the sun," outranked him as a mediator between god and man. If for any reason the *villac umu* was removed, nothing of importance had happened to the nexus between man and god, but if the emperor ceased his ministrations, then the priestly cord between heaven and earth was severed and nothing but evil for the Incas could result. And we arrive back at the argument, for to the extent that the Capac Incas were of the emperor's blood and worshiped with him the same heavenly father, they, too, were all of them priests.

Besides the *villac umu* there existed another administrative office called the *villca camayoc*, "the one in charge of (provincial) idols." This person was called upon to apportion properly the sacrifices and honors to the provincial *huacas* in Tahuantinsuyo, to license their priesthoods, and to organize them when they were brought into Cuzco. Undoubtedly, he exercised police duties over their acolytes as well. There may have been four of these comptrollers of local cults, one for each of the quarters of the empire.

We cannot suppose, however, from what has been said, that the Incas were at all skeptical of the power of sorcery, for they employed its practitioners as avidly as did any of the peoples of Peru. The most notable example was the constant presence in the royal court of a special class of sorcerers called *yacarcas*. These soothsayers came from Huaro, an especially holy community. They were used only in great matters of state when a conspiracy at home or a revolt in the provinces was suspected. At such a time they would consult their special *huaca*, fire, using long metal tubes to blow up the flames in perforated braziers. From the low and uneasy roaring of the fire then would come the voices of suspected persons, perhaps at great distances, magically compelled to divulge the truth about their secret plottings or cabals. These voices were translated by the *yacarcas,* who alone could understand them, for the benefit of the emperor and his followers. Such supernatural inquisitions were serious and terrible; they were never undertaken lightly; children were immolated and much wealth burned to the fire *huaca* for his co-operation at such times.

Among the Incas the sorcerers from Contisuyo had high reputations, as did also those from among the almost forgotten Huallas, those people whom the Incas had once dispossessed of the site of Cuzco. But there were many others, each with their special skills. There were love-compellers, herbalists of all kinds, including of course poisoners, diviners of dreams by means of spiders, by the entrails of animals, or by the throwing of lots. There were curers, ecstatics of many kinds, and those who communicated with the dead. There were excommunicators who discovered those men hated by the heavens and then cursed them outside the pale of human society.

The Incas were one of the world's most devout people, and this fact accounted for their morbid fear of the world of *huacas.* Their persecution of these *huacas* in the persons of sorcerers and oracle-readers was one of the consistent themes in their history. They knew that, even though it was the will of the Creator that they should have universal dominion, the *huacas* of the conquered folk resented it and would do what they could to subvert it. They were left in a black and anxious state as they scrutinized every oracle and tested every *huaca camayoc* or *huaca*-priest for hidden rebellion, glozing prognostications, and lies.

The tremors which were beginning to be felt in this the twelfth reign of an Inca sovereign had their source, however, not among the *huacas,* but in the sovereign himself, Inti's elect. It was a vague apprehension of this situation which would finally paralyze the Inca folk. They could understand evil on the tongues of the sorcerers and covert attacks from them upon their empire, but how could they confess that Viracocha himself would become a *supay?*

The Sacred River

THE INCA *ayllus* in their early march to empire had especially coveted that river valley which lay parallel to their own over the northern ridge. It was greater not only in extent and richness than their own valley but greater in its *huaca*. Through this valley from its head to many unknown confluences in Amazonia ran the Sacred River, the Vilcamayo. The story of the Incas' conquest of this valley and the imposition of their dominion over it is one of the important chapters in their history. In its upper reaches the sacred river is called the Vilcañota; in its middle portion, nearest to Cuzco, it is called today the Urubamba or Spider Valley River, and farther down, below the area of Inca influence, the Ucayali. If the many-branched Amazon has any identifiable single mother-stream, it is surely the Vilcañota.

Vilcañota means in Aymara "the House of the Sun." It was the name of the watershed which separates the basin of Lake Chucuito from the valley of the Sacred River. On his return from the island of Titicaca, Huascar, accompanied by a brilliant court, passed this way, moving through the immense herds of llamas and *huanacos* that were always found pasturing there.

It is the easiest of the world's important passes to surmount, for the ascent to the watershed is broad and level and is less than fifteen thousand feet in altitude. It is certainly not spectacular; as one looks about, at the barren and marshy savanna gently bowed over between the eroded highlands to the right and left, at the smoking hot springs set among the coarse grass clumps, at the snow patches up in the clean draws against the infinite serenity of the sky which here seems very close

160

—a presence is indeed felt. This presence was one of Tahuantinsuyo's greatest *huacas*. To it in its celebrated shrine Huascar offered children whose bones have long since washed out of their flinty graves to melt down into the meadows at the summit of the pass. Then he passed on, descending the Vilcañota which here was a rushing, gravelly stream.

A shocking thing was now to occur. At the provincial capital of Pomacanchi, which was situated on the shores of a small lake, Huascar had taken the homage of the *curacas* of the area, most of whom still held their offices from the preceding reign. These Pomacanchi magnates had arrived in hammocks and open litters which attested to the various grades of prestige granted to them in the previous reign. During the festivities Huascar had mocked them for being puffed up with such puny dignities. Next he contemptuously informed them that he would allow them to retain such baubles of authority. Thus publicly disprized, the Pomacanchi magnates were at a loss as to what to do. Their consternation was compounded when the emperor, in a sudden access of sadism and irresponsibility, ordered all the virgins to be brought out of the provincial *acllahuasi* and into the open square where they were openly subjected to the unlimited sexual license of his court buffoons. Such a display, unheard of and undreamed of before and as destructive of the imperial dignity as of provincial sensibilities, certainly must have gone far in completing the divorce between the Incas and their emperor. Yet none of their *ayllus* moved to recover prestige by unseating him, for divisiveness had already entered their ranks and delation crouched behind every curtain. As accomplices thus evilly imprisoned in the weird world of their emperor, the Incas acquiesced to this horror in silence.

With the snail-like pace of a traditional imperial progress the emperor and his people now continued their way down the Vilcamayo, a great host of people. Three or four miles marked the stage of the usual journey, a *samay*, or a "breathing," while the full day itself was a "journey," *purina*.

Huascar's palanquin and the curtained hammocks of his harem close to him were thickly surrounded by his personal guard of Cañars. Walking in the rear of the royal litter came the minions and behind them the lesser courtiers. The men were clad in their *uncus*, checkered tunics or ones with variegated trim, over which was thrown the *yacolla*, that mantle which could be draped to flow off the back, tied at either shoulder or over the chest or, most elegantly of all, held in place by hand. The *uncu* was the garment which displayed an Inca's standing by its fineness of weave, *cumpi*, or its *tocapu* trim; under it he wore the narrow breechclout or *huara*. Around his brows was wound the *pillaca llautu*, the black and purple headband or string turban, and pinned on it over the forehead was the glittering silver bangle called the *canipu* which was a nobleman's special adornment. Slung over the shoulder and hanging at the side was his *runcu* or coca bag, an all-purpose wallet but always found to contain at least coca leaves and lime for chewing. Scattered among these splendidly beseen Incas came the foreign ambassadors resident at the court and the stocky sons of many great provincial *curacas*, all of them clad in their native costumes thus adding variety and color to the scene. Pages respectfully accompanied the greater nobles while *yanaconas* or domestic servants in small clusters moved along close by bearing the necessaries of the day. The procession wound in this dignified fashion down the Sacred Valley raising much dust in the cool winter air between the royal *tambos* where they halted. Royal lackeys, all dressed alike, ran ahead sweeping the route of all uncleanness and blowing on their mellow conch shells to inform the world of the sun-child's approach.

After they had passed the point at which the Huatanay joined the Vilcamayo, they were entering that part of the Sacred Valley referred to as the Yucay and famous then as now for its charm and equable climate. Here the river is shallow with many pebble beds and riffles of sand. In the eddies under the willow trees rode the *ñuñuma*, the large domesticated duck of the Andes, or else they stood in solemn clusters along the wide-wandering waters dipping their beaks and wagging their tails. In the bush behind them little girls were quietly gathering the leaves, roots, and flowers of a variety of plants. These they would take back to their mothers in sacks for drying and storing or for the making of dyes and medicines.

On a steepened gradient the river becomes a torrent and here the waters are a glaucous color, clear and very lovely, overhung in places by the giant *pisonay* tree with its red flowers. Branching cactus lined the well-paved Inca road, while cultivated terraces ran crowding upward on both sides of the river. The black and yellow bunting, which was called *tuya*, perched cunningly on the tasseled tops of the maize plants on the lower terraces and sang a sweet song in recompense for his depredations.

The first significant site below the point at which the Huatanay entered was Pisac, "Partridge." It lay at the entrance of a *huayco* or "gorge" whose crevices and rock overhangs were filled with an infinity of burial sites. Up this valley ran a vital Inca road which crossed the Andes into the half-world of Paucartambo, that imperial frontier city where came the bow-bearing savages of Amazonia to trade or, if luck were with them, to destroy. The importance of Pisac to the Inca people was manifested by the engineering miracles which they had worked here, straightening the river and enclosing it in still-existing masonry banks and, above all, building a splendid *pucara* city almost vertically above the canyon. The road up to this high city, excessively steep, passes first through a cool Arcadian glen. Nicotine plants and the orange *chinchircoma* hang over the many cascades, and several varieties of hummingbirds and raucous flights of green parrots add the interest of movement to the quietness of the scene. At the top of a dizzy series of terraces one manages finally to attain the fortress-city, magnificently defensible yet not the *pucara* itself which lay beyond over more perilous trails.

Here in Pisac, Huascar halted the imperial progress to attend to certain matters affecting lands and terraces which he owned there. Probably these had come to him by gift from his father. Besides these *chacras*, the fruits of which were deposited in his own bins and warehouses, he possessed certain *moyas* or "gardens" which in actuality were preserves of wild pasture land or game country, generally up on the *puna*, and which supported flocks of alpacas and llamas. These extensive lands, both agricultural and pastoral, which were owned not by communities but by individual Incas, were worked in general by *yanaconas*, men and women whose service belonged permanently to a specified master. These *yanaconas* or "servants" were endowed with small plots of their own, and they were considered always a part of the enlarged household of their master. It is probable that Huascar had a *pachaca* or major-domo in the area, himself a *yana*, whose responsibility it was to oversee the work on the imperial estates and who now appeared before him to report on his charge.

Below Pisac the Inca road was bordered with *capuli*-trees which bear for the traveler a sweet, dull-red fruit, as well as with ferny *molle*-trees whose berries were used in making *akha*. Down this well-paved road beside the tumbling waters of the Sacred River the royal party now proceeded after leaving Pisac.

In the center of the Yucay Valley lay Calca, "Stony Place," an old and important settlement which had been remade by a succession of Inca emperors into a favored spot. It was a place of wonderful fertility, had hot medicinal springs, and with Pisac and Ollantaytambo was one of the three jewels in the lower Vilcañota Valley. In the plaza today some Inca walls can still be seen. It lay at the mouth of a steep gorge directly under the hanging glaciers of the holy mountain Sahuasiray.

Clinging high up on the bare mountainside across the valley from Calca, on a site called Pomamarca or "the Lion's Lair," could be seen an Inca settlement arranged in a series of breath-taking terraces and setbacks, the whole area walled in for defense. This place was one of the most curious in the world and already by Huascar's time famous in Inca annals. When Viracocha Inca, the eighth emperor and Huascar's great-great-grandfather, had conquered the people of Calca after prolonged warfare, thus adding the Yucay Valley to the empire, he had exacted from them as indemnity levies of workmen to build him two palaces, one in Cuzco and one here just across the Vilcañota River which would be a pleasure retreat for him and for them an ever-present reminder of their subjugation. This palace is called in the sources Saqui Sahuana. But this same emperor, so great in his youth, fell away from his people in his age, for in the face of the Chanca enemy he abandoned the city of Cuzco, taking with him his harem, most of his court, and his beloved sons Urcon and Sucso. He had come and hidden himself away in Pomamarca, not indeed like a lion but like a fox. As everyone knew, this unworthy desertion had left for the defense of the city a few dauntless Inca warriors under the leadership of a son called Cusi. This son saved Cuzco and ushered in a new era for the Inca people, in recognition of which he took the name Pachacuti, "the Renovator." His father, the emperor who had fled, was still allowed to wear the red *mascapaycha* of supremacy, but he was forced to stay in Pomamarca for the rest of his weary and defeated years. This splendid king in exile, surrounded by the aging men and women of his court, had little to do but gaze down each day on the city of Calca, now the patrimony of another ruling emperor, his son. After his death at the age of eighty, Pomamarca became the possession of his *panaca*, and here the royal mummy was kept except when it was carried in a litter to Cuzco to take part in the great festivals.

Because of the majesty which had been present there, however discredited this majesty might be, the site was referred to from that time on as Little Cuzco, and today it is still so known even in its weeds and ruins. The people of the environs today refer with respect to a great ancestral *machu* or "grandfather" who haunts the site and who could easily destroy them for any fancied slight on their part. For the visitor who has the hardihood to seek out this place of an ancient exile, an unparalleled view of the Andes is offered and of the wonderful valley below, along with some thoughts on the strange reversals of fortune.

Seven miles downriver from Calca, Huascar's slow cavalcade was approaching a narrow throat in the valley beyond which was the most delicious part of route. A short but deeply riven valley joined the Sacred River at this point. It was the Urquillos and still today boasts the finest maize and fruits in the whole *sallca*. In those days its terraces and *moyas* were the possessions of the *panacas* of Huascar's father and his grandfather Topa Inca, and it provided their banqueting with the finest of grains, hot peppers, root crops, beans, coca for chewing, and cotton for weaving. If one cared to make the steep climb up onto the *puna* by way of this valley, one came out at Chinchero, the sedate and elegant country estate of Topa Inca, one of the homes of the Capac Ayllu *panaca*. Just below the lowest terrace of the palace area in Chinchero, where one can gaze down into the upper reaches of the

165

Urquillos, there is a blue rock deeply pitted and carved, an extraordinary *huaca*. A gallery is hewn through it and there is a royal seat where the mummy of Topa Inca was undoubtedly placed on days of pleasure so that he might look out of his quiet eyes to distant Salcantay or survey his llamas grazing on the grasses of the *moya* which faced him across the airy space, which today is called Choqque Huayco, "Golden Valley." From Chinchero three paved Inca roads radiated outward. One led to Cuzco, one skirted the massif of Tantaquilca back to Pomamarca, and the other led to the edge of the *puna*, past the potatolands and warehouses of Rakchi and then dropped in a dizzy descent through the busy terraces above Yucay back into the Sacred Valley. Many of these terraces down which one passed here were named after the *mitmac* groups assigned to work them, peoples from far parts of the empire; most of them were the possessions of Huascar's dead father and of his many wives. Great was the opulence and rich the verdancy of these slopes artificially stepped up to amazing altitudes by the power and command of the Incas. Today they are barren, dry, and devoid of any life.

Below Yucay a pleasant stretch of the river ended with the spectacular rock at Pachar, an awe-inspiring mountainside hewn cleanly in half; at this point the Vilcañota fairly entered the Andes through a series of gorges, each more profound than the preceding. Just around the corner from Pachar was the imposing Inca city of Ollantaytambo. Here was the ancestral seat of that Tambo family which had formed an important element in the ethnic make-up of the Inca people. Manco Capac had been a Tambo Indian, so it is to be presumed that he and his followers in those early days broke off from a Tambo *ayllu* here in the Urubamba Valley, seeking their fortunes in the bleaker Huatanay country to the southeast.

The visitor to Ollantaytambo is always greatly impressed by the site. Besides its role as the last city in the Sacred Valley, it also guards the entrance to the formidable Panticalla Pass to the north which in turn led into the back country of the Lucumayo and the Vilcabamba. Ollantaytambo was in fact the most accessible door to the montaña. Beyond the province of Vilcabamba were the far-out Inca frontiers marked by veteran garrisons and ruled by stern commissars. Out there was the sullen *hacha hacha* where the mettle of young Inca officers was tried; troublesome labor gangs were sent there for rapid extermination and lesser political criminals kept in exile. Those were purlieus that produced jaguar skins, rare woods, dried hummingbirds and live parrots, monkeys, strange poisons, and, above all, gold dust and coca. A vast sweating, half-forgotten, merciless, revenue-producing area would be lost to the Incas if they ever lost their hold on Ollantaytambo.

Ollantaytambo had been brought into the Inca empire by Pachacuti following a severe struggle. After its near destruction it had been thoroughly replanned as an Inca city set on an apron of thick terraces. On the almost vertical sides of the mountain out of which the tributary gorge emerged, vast works were instituted by successive emperors, the most frequently visited today being the remarkable *pucara*, the only Inca fortress in all of Tahuantinsuyo ever to repulse a determined Spanish attack. Here also was one of the empire's most splendid sun temples within which reputedly were interred the viscera taken from the mummies of the Inca emperors. This city of the Tambos, who had formed so important an element in the making of the Capac Incas, was a holy site in the understanding of the Incas. Its stonework today, the curious and famous pink wall, the staircases, the great pier in the river which supported Pachacuti's bridge, the geometrically precise streets, and the double *canchas*—still lived in today—are among the world's great ruins. They have been described by a succession of well-known travelers. What the present-day tourist sees here is far more authentically Inca than the stones of Cuzco itself, which, with several notable exceptions, as we have noted are post-Conquest.

Once past Ollantaytambo the valley bottom becomes almost tropical, and the river, a thing now of terrible danger, plunges and bucks among boulders as big as houses. One was now on the floor of a gorge sawed out by the river between the snowy peaks of Veronica and Salcantay. A tangled mass of wild tobacco bushes, begonias, and other shrubby plants lining the banks finally could no longer find a footing, for the rock walls in places rose vertically out of the water. Only orchids and air plants and some Spanish moss festooned those otherwise naked walls. Here, where Torontoy is today, access ended and the river route into the great montaña beyond was effectively blocked.

Two miles above this point a stream fed by the snows of Salcantay entered the Vilcañota from the south, its name today being the Pampa-cahuana. Up this difficult route an Inca branch road four feet wide ascended out of the heat of the gorge and into a lonesome and savage world ruled by the bear, the serpent, and the condor. The trail passed scattered garrisons, lookout hamlets, fire signal stations, and small but elaborate cities hanging on the sides of abysses, the dry ruins of which today are utterly quiet and uncommunicative in this so mammoth world. Occasionally tunneled through the face of the granite cliff where rounding a headland would have been too perilous, surrounded on every side by some of the world's most splendid mountain scenery, this *via sacra* led out, at the road's end, to one of Tahuantinsuyo's most sacred shrines, called today—in ignorance of its original name—Machu Picchu.

Having detached the greater part of his entourage at Ollantaytambo, Huascar now ordered his reduced and select party up the Pampa-cahuana. Solemnly this party then defiled into the sacred wilderness.

IDOLOS IVACAS
DELOS ANDISVIOS

IN QUECHUA there is an interjection for which we in English have no adequate translation. *Ch'in!* is the amazed word of awe with which one recognizes and greets a condition or place or situation which has been deprived of all life and all movement. It is the word of a people sensitive to the *huaca* in loneness and desertion.

Thus a deserted and silent town, with all of its secrets closed up and its ancient tumults pacified, was described by the Incas in the term *chinnic llacta*, "a city which keeps silent forever." Today Machu Picchu is such a place. Unspeakable time seems to inhabit this wilderness; it is indeed the only meaningful resident of this *chinnic llacta*. The dizzy slopes upon which the city is perched spill down two thousand feet into a canyon out of which ceaselessly sounds the miraculous *mayup ccaunrynnn*, "the rumble of the river." The city rests on the buttress of one mountain and faces another which is called Huayna Picchu, a rock mass so alive, so eerie in shape, so isolated in its immensity that no observer can doubt that the settlement looked to it as the pristine congelation of the *huaca* of the place.

Here in Machu Picchu the Incas worshiped the Earth Mother in her personification as the beautiful and terrible peaks of the Andes. As Coricancha was the cathedral wherein men worshiped specifically the Inca gods, so Machu Picchu was probably the primate church wherein was revered the colossal *huaca* of the mother of stone, the Andes. Here beat the unhurried heart of all the earth's mountains, audible most clearly to those priestesses of the cult whom we know inhabited the site.

A certain chronicler, Martín de Morúa, has left us a confused tale

169

which refers, if not to Machu Picchu specifically, at least to a garbled memory of it. It is the story of Chuqui Llantu or "Fleeting Shadow" and takes place in the wildest part of the ranges surrounding the Vilcañota. This young woman was one of the priestesses of a remote city, and in the course of her excursions into the *puna* above the city she met and fell in love with a young llama herder who, unbeknownst to himself, was a nobleman. Aided by a wild bird, a magical staff, and four enchanted springs representing the sweet waters of the four parts of the world, she deceived the keen-eyed porters of the wonderful city, who were posted at the gates to ensure the chastity of the sacred girls, and enjoyed the embraces of her lover. But fate overtook them both, and they were changed into two crags on Mount Sahuasiray.

This is a typical folktale that could have come from any part of the world; its import to us here is the memory of a sacred mountain retreat in the Urubamba country where worship was carried on by *mamaconas*. In the burials excavated at Machu Picchu only about one of five skeletons was found to be male, and these males were not of robust type and were, in addition, rather shabbily buried, whereas several of the females obviously had been important personages. The burials indicate an occupancy of several generations but are still few in number.

The remote location of Machu Picchu and the preponderance of female skeletons would indicate something about the deity in question there. It was the Earth, conceived here not as the giver of grain but as the Artemisian mother of the wilderness, of precious metals which could be mined out of her massive bowels, of great waters falling in distant thunders, of exotic dangers, and of the inconsequence of man. What is called in the guidebooks the Hitching Post of the Sun, the Intihuatana, is not that at all. It is rather the living rock of the Coya rudely manipulated into an *usno* to symbolize her abstract quality, her "rockness." Indeed this carved stone was the Mother's "word" delineating her spaciousness, as in the gorges below, her wild liberality, as in the waters and cascades beneath, her frightfulness, as in the lightnings which torment the place from September to May, and her implacable indifference and remoteness, as shown in the blank walls of granite dropping sheer for so many hundreds of feet.

But the Incas, as we have seen, were not strict unitarians in their religious understanding. They knew that one could distinguish many manifestations of one essence. The priestesses of Machu Picchu as a whole probably worshiped the Coya, but a swarm of other *huacas* also had their cults within the city walls and in the vast environs outside. First and greatest of these *huacas* was the colossal rock called today Huayna Picchu, "Young Mountain," which we have mentioned. Its hindquarters resting in the encircling river far below, it rears itself erect as if arising from a crouching position, a gigantic lion, faceless but completely identifiable. What this sculptured mountain was called then we shall never know, but it is evident that leonine power and slow ferocity were what especially characterized it. No doubt it was worshiped specifically from the Intihuatana Hill within the city.

One can reconstruct the story of Machu Picchu with a certain degree of probability. It is likely that the great Pachacuti in his retirement conceived the idea of a holy place, unique in the grandeur and inaccessibility of its setting, and that he selected a site already long revered by the Indians of the Vilcabamba Andes for just those reasons. Into this area he then drove the first engineered road, ordaining *tambos* and minor cities en route. This then was the terrible master, utilizing gangs of subjected Collas, who with his son and coemperor, Topa Inca, first called Machu Picchu into being. Pachacuti we know to have been the first Inca ruler to take a conquering army through the peaks into the gold country beyond; his was therefore a hero's proprietary interest in the forbidding land, and only his grandiose mind really answers to the choice of the site in the first instance.

That part of the settlement which we may attribute to him seems clearly indicated. It is the area just within the city gate and extending north to the Intihuatana Hill. The Stairway of the Fountains leads down to the joined and smaller area, probably to be assigned to Topa Inca. It was undoubtedly the memorable Inca architect and builder Sinchi Roca, bastard brother of the emperor Huayna Capac, who built for that eleventh ruler the central plaza at the foot of the Intihuatana Hill and the large living areas on its east side. Huascar's additions— if he continued building here, as seems most probable—would then be the extension north of his father's area, the least extensive of them all. Because of their limited resources, it is doubtful that any of the Neo-Inca rulers could have built here—except in the most cursory way. Open areas or small plazas were provided everywhere.

Each one of these four major wards possessed its own tutelary *huaca*; each was a rock of unusual shape. The best known is the one in Pachacuti's sector, a fissured rock crowned with a beautiful masonry circumvallation. The crevice underneath was artificially widened, being given that abstract modeling by the Inca sculptor which so aptly states the presence of man without at the same time imposing his visage upon the rock. When Pachacuti's mummy or his *huaoqui* wished to visit the scenes of his exploits, hither he would be carried and in this sacred fissure his fierce soul would bathe again in the wash of divine power.

Another obliquely poised rock, also fissured underneath and capped by ornamental masonry, was the *huaca* of Topa Inca's ward. The most unusual one perhaps was that in Huascar's sector, a thin slice of rock balanced on its edge like a standing leaf with a neat curb or pedestal built around it. This *huaca* was faced by open-walled shrines of the *carpahuasi* type and a small theatral area.

There is no doubt that the western side of Machu Picchu was reserved for the central cult. A jumbled field of rocks upended and splintered in huge, fantastic chips provided one of the chief burial grounds for the priestesses, their thin bodies being tucked away in the clefts and under the tilted roofs like hiding children. Adjoining was the temple area, an open court with an esplanade hanging over the abyss and facing west. In that direction could be seen the serried green teeth of the montaña backed with the snows of Soray and Salcantay. On the remaining three sides of the open court were spacious buildings, the southernmost being probably the residence of the high priestess, while the other two were heavily thatched and open-faced shrines of impeccable stonework. Leading up from this major complex of shrines to the peak of the small cusp called by the excavators the Intihuatana Hill, there ran a steep processional stairway with a vertiginous fall on the left hand into the Urubamba far below.

From analogy with the Inca shrine at the Apurimac, one can identify with some degree of probability the function of this eminence with its masonry shaman's hut at the top, its modeled rock *usno* open to the eye of heaven, and its stone balcony hanging over the world's lip. And if the analogy stands, the high priestess here in Machu Picchu must have been a sister or daughter of the ruling Inca. Here was carried on the worship of the Coya, here the oracular priestess stood over the gorge and read the divine will from the unending sonorities of the Sacred River below, and here were offered appropriate sacrifices, some of them burned on the *usno* and others hurled out into the void.

Huascar's retinue moved with exceedingly deliberate pace into this wilderness of the Salcantay. He had ordered his dead colleagues, father, grandfather, and great-grandfather to join him, each bundled mummy born in the sumptuous litter he had used while alive and each accompanied by important members of his *panaca* bearing the items of his regalia. Only in a few of the more dangerous turns of the road or while passing through the granite tunnels were the emperors dead and living forced to dismount and walk or be carried a few paces through.

Like a wavering ribbon of brightly colored ants the procession passed from one terraced cloud-city to another along the route. The splendid and daring road leading from one to another carried in places across the faces of sheer precipices. The cities along here are, of course, nameless. There were at least four of them hanging on the green slopes over the Sacred River and two more down by the waters. All of them were unwalled. This area, today so dangerous and totally uninhabited, was then a miraculously populated province called into existence by the Inca people.

Relays of Rucana Indians clad in livery were available to spell Huascar's sweating and panting bearers; the strain on bearers in such country was severe, and the horror of a misstep may well be imagined. Fire signals blinked in the night across the vast spaces, and smoke signals went up among the tumbled mountains by day, each message passing along to the oracular city at the end of the road the news of the day's arrival and the planned departure. When mists and rain enveloped the caravan, sometimes for days, then messages were sent ahead by *chasquis*.

Although the distance to Machu Picchu was not too great, the imperial dignity demanded a monotonous schedule. The day finally came, however, when the head of the column appeared at the guardhouse situated on the razoredge of Machu Picchu, "Old Mountain." Here the highly charged holiness of the site was first encountered. Purification rites were undergone by the entire party, those walking discarding their sandals as the proper sign of humility. As the procession came to the second purification lodge just above the settlement, mellow conch-shell trumpets began to blow lugubriously from within the *pirca* walls, and the log gate of the city was moved aside so that the highpriestess of the city with her retinue might proceed out to greet her resplendent kinsmen both living and dead. On entering the city, Huascar at last descended from his litter and, himself barefooted and without the *mascapaycha*, prepared to honor the mighty presence.

This city that now welcomed its emperor was an assemblage of women whose lives were lived out on a pedunculate crag. Except on such rare occasions as this visit, they never left the city. The dry fosse, the wall, and the city gate were in fact designed not for war but to ward off profane intrusions and impurities as well as to prevent such erring and sexual adventures on the part of the holy women as were related of the tragic Chuqui Llantu. As young girls these women had been taken from the Cuzco *acllahuasi* and assigned as *mamaconas* to this remote cult center which thereafter they never left. Just outside the wall were the agricultural terraces which supported the city, staffed with workers and their wives who themselves never entered the city but merely looked wonderingly down at its plazas and narrow ways from a distance; back on the more accessible slopes of Machu Picchu there were also pastors of the sacred flocks, men like Chuqui Llantu's llama boy whose love affair had ended so disastrously. Within the city proper a few trusted males, old or possibly eunuchs, performed chores, acted as porters, and carried out certain menial cult requirements.

Each of the mummified emperors on entering the sacred precinct took up his residence in that quarter which he had had built while alive, the *mamaconas* living in those areas providing the culinary and other services necessary. Only at such times did the inhabitants of the city have occasion to participate in things of common humanity, and we may envisage the sudden swelling of its population as providing conversation for many years afterward to the deprived women. The service of the Queen, the Mountain Mother, and her husband, the river, demanded just this negation of the ordinary human joys and sorrows. A devout way of life had been forged behind the thin *pirca* battlements of Machu Picchu, but so stringent was it that it reduced the *mamaconas* to mere simulacra of living women; young and lovely, aged and crabbed, like ghastly dolls they moved about over the terraces and across the plazas and up the stairways of the city, people living in the heart of earth but drowned in its limitless spaces. For the Incas the grandeur of the place could only be realized in the almost total dehumanization of its inhabitants. Here, then, Huascar lived for a short time, ordering the building of new terraces and apartments as suited his fancy. Here he recognized new *huacas* in the stones around and established their names and cult requirements and assigned to them virgins in the proper numbers. Here, in the company of his sister-priestess, he sacrificed to the mighty *huaca* of the place and put to her the severe questions that vexed his reign. Here, too, after conversing with the *apu* of the river coughing and grumbling below, or listening to the breathless song of the *checollo*-bird in the lupines, she brought him back his answers.

One of Huascar's questions surely concerned the *atitapia* or "evil augury" that had been so ominously read by that other sister of his, the oracle of the Apurimac, just a short time before. Whether this sister of the Urubamba country contrived to allay his fears will be forever unknown, for although the river and the *checollo*-bird have not changed the burden of their saying since then, the one in the gorge below and the other in the lupines near at hand, the reading is still obscure.

Thus locked away in this green park of the Salcantay, Huascar seemed to have taken leave of the great empire forever. In the abeyant stillness that seemed thus to have settled down on the empire, the Incas back in Cuzco whiled away the time telling tales to each other of the *huacas*, of their own greatness as a people, of the world they had conquered and of that which still remained to be discovered and subdued, and of other fateful things.

Hahua Ricuy Simi: Tales of Far Things Seen

THE ROCOCO SPLENDORS and darknesses of the Mexican imagination which are easily perceived by even the most casual traveler are far cries from the limited patterns of Inca thought and fancy. Whether we could go so far as to denominate the Inca mind as unseeking, stolid, even opaque, is uncertain in view of the paucity of our evidence, but what we do have shows that in no sense did the Incas stand out from the ordinary run of highland Peruvian people. In fact, if it is permissible to argue from visible artifacts, their literary, oratorical, and intellectual achievements were probably of a lesser order than those of the Peruvian civilizations down on the coast. They were an unfermented people, a part of whose undeniable powers came from the very immediacy and simplicity of their vision. As empire builders they could conceive of the stars; as aesthetes they were children. The brevity of their appearance upon the stage of history probably explains this naïveté.

Their folklore seems to have been much what one might expect of an unpolished people. They told tales about the antique heroes whom they likened to the *acapana*, the swift flying cloud rack preceding the storm. The formidable bandit or *pomaranra*, making his lair along with the mountain lion among rocks and caves and setting upon the unsuspecting traveler, was a well-known figure. Outlaws, in fact, figured more largely in popular tales than the Incas, who assumed the invulnerability of their highways, ever cared to admit. A shuddery kind of respect was always accorded to such anarchists of society, for they were the living antithesis of Inca skill in binding the parts of the world together and the tortures that awaited them when captured were well known. Although they horrified, they also fascinated.

And it was almost the same with the famous lion stalkers of the lands to the south. Here among the Aymara-speaking peoples around Lake

Chucuito lived the *poma camayoc*, a class of half-savage men designated to acquire for their Inca overlords the pelts, heads, claws, and tails
of the great mountain cats. They were specialists in the habits and
hunting of these cunning and formidable beasts. Their sons of necessity inherited their office, for they led dangerous and despised lives
and other men would not and could not do these things. They knew
caves and rocks better than homes, and the screams of their prey
were the voices they liked best. To the farmers around them they were
the same as outlaws. Their daughters were called *titi* or "cats," and
only a hardy man would take one as a wife.

Inca tales concerning their own prowess were naturally many, but
the ones most avidly told and retold were those which had as their
locale Hahua Anti, "the Land Beyond the Andes." To the Incas who
had been reared on the vast grassy *punas* and the long vistas of the
sallca, the thickets of the montaña were in the last degree dreadful,
however exotic they might be as well. This type of terrain they called
huchu huchu, "the jungle," and they envisaged as its demonic master a
great dragon spirit—modeled on the boa constrictor—whom they called
Anti Viracocha, the Lord of the Andes. In this land it was possible to get
lost so easily, and an individual could wander interminably until he was
engulfed by the great *amarus*, "the boas." Had not Pachacuti himself
sent a whole army into the *hacha hacha* only to have it destroyed by the
giant serpents, after which disaster only an enchantment had saved a
second army? Or there was that other demon whom one placated by
addressing him as "Father." This was the *otoronco* or "jaguar." It was
even said that Pachacuti and his heir for a time themselves became
jaguars in that montaña and that they were responsible for engendering
there a race of half-caste Incas. Another son, they said, whose name was
Otoronco Achachi, never regained human shape but continued to rule
the land in his animal form.

That such stories were absurd the Incas well knew, but they took in
all seriousness the detailed descriptions of the tribes and nations thought
to inhabit the *hacha hacha*. Near at hand they well knew the Chuncho
Indians who painted their bodies red with the juice of the *mantur*-berry,
who danced to the sound of Panpipes, and who reluctantly worked in

177

the gold-washing camps supervised by Inca officials. Some of these Indians from Opatari occasionally even appeared in Cuzco bringing in nuggets and gold dust as tribute. The taste for human flesh in these parts was well known and was attributed to the *mama mirccuc coyllur* or "mother-eating star" which cast its rays so hotly down into their thick coverts, influencing the savages to devour their parents. About the folk beyond the fringe of the Chunchos one could believe anything. Here men had sired on female monkeys a half-breed race hairy and disgusting to contemplate. Somewhere out there also, near the *pachap cuchun cuchun*, "the corners of the earth," lived the *huarmi aucas*, the "women warriors" or Amazons, subservient to their empress and fully a match for men on the battlefield. Men called this land Peñeca. Somewhere out there also was the land of Paititi, a rich land and full of curiosities. In their younger days some of the Incas of Huascar's reign had officered parties out in the *hacha hacha*, and the tales they told were of terrible ambushes, of the thud of arrows into the tree trunk next to one, of the spilling over of canoes laden with fighting men into the clicking jaws of the piranha, or of outposts of Inca braves decimated, starving, and without hope of relief, yet still holding at bay the people of the forest, whirling their slings and brandishing their *champis* to the last, unsubdued masters of the world.

With the same gusto they spun out tales of the gods and of former times. Crouched around the warm fires in Cuzco on stormy afternoons, the *pallas* told their children the story of the water-maiden, a lovely *ñusta* in the sky who possessed a magic jar in which she kept rain and hail and snow. Her brother *Illapa* in sport hurls his slingstone at the jar, sometimes hitting it, sometimes missing. The whiplike lash of his golden sling was the quick lightning; the missle was the thunderbolt, and when he had aimed true, the breaking up of the enchanted jar was the splitting roar of thunder, *kakakakay*—and then out over the world would gush the torrents of rain or hail, or, like a falling of llama wool, the thick snows—according to what the *ñusta* had in her jar at the time.

For the more historically minded there was the wonderful tale of the magic mirror, of how the prince Pachacuti had seen this object fall from the heavens into the spring of Susurpuquio, of his beholding in

178

it the dazzling god who ordained victory for him and a long reign, and of how Pachacuti took this mirror with him wherever he went and read the future in it—wherefore he was unconquerable. Every Inca child knew by heart of the wanderings of Manco Capac in search of the city of Cuzco which had been promised to him by Inti, and of how he gave benign laws to all the neighboring peoples. Or perhaps it was a tale of how the emperor Inca Roca touched the ground on Mount Chaca with his left ear, bloody from being pierced in the knighting ceremonies, and thus miraculously opened up a spring which when properly channeled was led down the Sapi Valley to give increased life to the city of Cuzco.

The successive creations undertaken by the god Viracocha filled the minds of the young Incas with the idea of a divine plan. These more serious tales were told by the wise men, the *amautas*, to the young. They told that the first men, gigantic of stature, had displeased the Creator wherefore he had enchanted them into stone images still to be seen in Collasuyo. Or the story as told in another version related that the primal race became monkeys and was forever exiled down in the montaña. These stories only proved that ages could and did come to an end to be replaced by the novel and the unexpected. The Incas were aware that the coastal people told of one of these aeons which ended in universal fire; the aeon which preceded the present age they knew had ended not in fire but in flood, out of which had been saved selected prototypes of men of all Indian *ayllus*, but principally and by special sanction Manco Capac and his seven kin. A corollary to the wonderful Flood stories was the concept that the present aeon too would come to an end. Priestly speculation on this topic was naturally discouraged, however fearfully fascinating it might be. It had been the Creator, through his agent the sun-god, who had ordained Tahuantin-suyo, the schema of the present world, and to contemplate the end of this great empire could only be a shocking exercise for an Inca. In the backs of their minds, however, Incas and *pallas* alike knew that this was the way history worked, in creative bursts and annihilations; they were therefore not wholly unprepared to speculate on the end of the current aeon.

But there were other beings besides gods, *huacas*, and heroes, to speak of. There was the sea, Mamacocha, which most Incas had never seen but which all knew of, a vessel holding all the waters of the world and located down beyond the western *sallca*. Edged with deserts of sand and astounding cities, it secreted in its fastnesses "*huacas* of the abyss," vast monsters that occasionally rolled up to the surface, exploded great clouds into the air, and then dived down again no one knew where.

There were corresponding monsters of the *sallca*, dragons, bearded and of incredible length, which would appear out of the earth as portents. One such had arisen in Pachacuti's day out of the hill on the east of Cuzco, Pachatusan; it had passed over the city and subsequently disappeared into a body of water near Anta. It was connected with the disasters of that reign, terrible famines, earthquakes, and eruptions. In addition to such public prodigies there were the common demons and the evil beings that none could escape. Sometimes these beings came to one in nightmares; they could be stealthy vampires or *masaruna*, "batmen"; they could be heads that flew through the night whistling and chattering, *uma purik*, or phantoms and goblins. Witches were known to assume dreadful forms and appear in the shadows of the night. All of these apparitions came down from earliest antiquity, indeed from the *tutayapacha* when darkness alone was on earth. These specters were lumped together as the *achacallas*. Of them, surely the most bloodcurdling of all was the demonic *hapiñuñu*, a vile female who roamed the land with flaccid breasts that trailed the ground. Night time was the playground of these monsters, and mothers warned their children, then as now, against straying lest they be spirited away by these "clutchers."

Of the many terrors afflicting the Indians of Peru one variety had most particular pertinence to the Inca people—the *tapia*, those ominous signs or prophecies that threatened their lordship over the world. A corroding psychosis of suspicion and fear was the price the Incas paid for their dominion. The violence with which they threatened their subject peoples and the impulsive cruelties with which they occasionally treated them were only the outer signs that inwardly they felt themselves to be a people *chhiqquip muyoycuscan*, "besieged with perils."

This unending spiritual crisis of the nation was evident in the *tapia* which in increasing numbers were now being seen in Huascar's reign. Again and again the Inca magnates discussed the meaning of the terrible plague which had so recently visited the empire; they discussed interminably the *suncasapa*, "the bearded ones," about whom so little was known and so much suspected. All knew the story of Viracocha and how he had brought order to the world, moving north through Peru until he came to that far northern land where Huayna Capac had so recently died, and how going down to the coast he thence departed over the sea with his ministrant archangels. Before his death, Huayna Capac was said to have received an oracle that the twelfth Inca ruler would be the last, for Viracochas would then return and renew the world. Huascar was the twelfth ruler. Were the *suncasapa* the Viracochas of prophecy? Were they rather *supay* or demons? Or perhaps mere men and warriors from beyond the confines of Tahuantinsuyo?

It had not been long since Huascar had sent a delegation of distinguished Incas to his sister, the highpriestess of the Apurimac, for an oracle on the subject. The bloodstained and gold-sheathed post representing the vast mother in that part of the land had spoken *huatunasimi*, "obscure words." And what had they meant? Some said that the *huaca* had announced the overthrow of Tahuantinsuyo by the *suncasapa*. Others denied this theory. None of the auguries were unequivocally clear, but certainly it was not groundless to feel that power of the evil one was growing.

Such were the thoughts and speculations of the Inca people in the days of Huascar's visit to the city on Machu Picchu. Undoubtedly he asked of the oracle there, as we have opined, the true meaning of the future. For Huascar that meaning floated up out of the river, but whatever it was, it probably did not totally erase the purport of the Apurimac oracle to eat, drink, and be merry for the empire would soon be no more.

LASES TA COIA
CVCICHĨBOMAMA
MICAI

Reyno hasta ande suyo -

que

Pallas, Feasts, Dances, and Games

WITH THE ACTIVITY that attended the return of Huascar's court to Cuzco, some of the premonitions which may have affected the Incas in the fastnesses of the Vilcabamba Andes and in the capital disappeared. Cuzco was not a festive city in the true sense of the word, light-hearted and gay, but it was a city of recurrent pageants fiercely enjoyed. To this life the Incas returned. A people about to be destroyed is a people that finds it convenient to forget.

The position of the women of the nobility at the court must have been one of relative freedom. Every *palla* had around her a small retinue of *yanaconas* or domestics as well as certain Inca girls from the families of Outer Incas who acted as maids-in-waiting. Her own daughters or *ñustas* might form a part of this female coterie, or they might be found in the *acllahuasi* where their virginity was guarded and womanly skills learned until such time as they were assigned in marriage to eligible young knights. The *acllahuasi* could thus be used as a sort of finishing school. But if the father had formally devoted his daughter to the service of a god, she of course had left forever the protection of the family.

An Inca who possessed an extremely lovely daughter could always win the highest favor by presenting her to his emperor. His daughters by concubines were not technically *ñustas*, but if handsome they too could be used to purchase favor either with the emperor or with the gods or even, in unusual circumstances, offered as a sacrifice for the common weal.

When we consider how very few Incas of the Capac Ayllu there were —probably no more than four or five hundred—we can easily sense the elevated aristocratic standing of the *pallas* who were the pure-blooded and legitimate wives. They did not as a rule walk abroad but were carried in curtained hammocks—a very few even in the supreme dignity of a litter. They possessed property rights and establishments of their own, either within the *canchas* of their husband's family or as endowed manors outside of Cuzco. They were honored everywhere because of the purity of their blood; it is to be supposed, however, that as a group they built narrower cliques for themselves within the Capac Ayllu as a whole—no doubt in cruel competition with each other for influence. Rigor and arrogance probably marked their rule of the households under them, but this is a mere guess.

The great occasions for them were the ceremonies and banquets of the state festivals. For these events they went garbed in the richly somber or rainbow-striped *lliclla*, the woman's outer mantle which closed over the breast like a draped jacket pinned with a great silver *tupu*. Under this garment was worn the dress, a rectangular wrap-around falling from shoulder to ankles and decorated with striking geometric patterns. It was tied in at the waist with the narrow *chumpi* or girdle and opened at the side occasionally to expose the leg from the thigh down. The hair was worn long and neatly combed out and was arranged to fall down the back and over the shoulders outside the *lliclla*. Pinned onto the top of the head was the *ñañaca*, a soft folded mantilla or kerchief that fell back over shoulders and hair halfway down to the waist. The whole was a warm ensemble in keeping with the chill of the highlands, but it was also not unbeautiful; the full effect was certainly not that of charm but of a kind of womanly elegance. It attested to status; it did not incite or provoke. When to this national garment was added a *palla's* brilliant red face-painting and a stylish coca-bag, she was adjudged to be "a beautifully adorned woman," *pallahina huallparicuk*. "The manner in which they dress," says Cieza, "reveals the *pallas* of Cuzco to be the most distinguished and handsomely accoutered of all the women in the New World."

The festival banquets were solemn public affairs. They were served always in the morning, for breakfast was the principal meal of the day. If it were raining or hailing outside, these collations were held in

183

the roomy *carpa huasi* or covered sheds, but if the weather allowed, the Incas squatted on the ground in the square which for the occasion was strewn with rushes. They sat slightly separated each from his fellows but still grouped according to their *ayllus* and *panacas*. Fires blazed in front of them in cold weather. There entered then the *pallas* behind the *coya*, each of them carrying on her back a token jar of *akha* and in her hand a small bowl of hot cooked food. Each *palla* went to her husband in the same manner as the *coya* went to the emperor, and each proceeded to sit down immediately behind him with her back to his. The *pallas* then served the food out in dishes and passed these around back of them to their husbands. Thus they sat quietly busied with the food while their husbands ate the first dish in silence; next, the *pallas* ate, they and their husbands now being served by retainers. Frequently an Inca arose or sent a servant to offer a part of his dish to some other favored person at the banquet. Other than this small commotion, the meal was taken in absolute silence and with profound intensity. Meals were never affairs of gluttony. The cuisine was limited, porridges or *sancu* of various kinds being a staple preparation, generally made of maize, potatoes, quinoa or *oca*, with roast meats and fish added. Meat was rare and a real sign of privilege. The Inca lords had llamas from their herds brought in and butchered in an abattoir in the city in preparation for such an event. Favored relatives or retainers would receive cuts of the animal. All dishes were generously salted or sprinkled with the red pepper *uchu*, the two ever-present condiments, as much to create a thirst as to add savor to the food.

Following the meal proper the *pallas* poured out the initial goblets of *akha* for their husbands; after this ritual it was served in almost endless quantities by lesser females of the household who brought it out in large jars slung on their backs. This was the main part of the fiesta and generally lasted till sundown. Drunkenness was common but those with strong heads were admired. The custom of toasting others with drink was a common practice, the giver of the toast making his way over to the favored one with two full cups, one of which he offered and one of which he drank himself. *Akha* was a maize or *molle-*berry preparation of *muccu*, that thinly diluted paste made from the grain or berry which the women chewed and then spit out into jars for fermenting.

A *taqui* generally accompanied a prolonged drinking. This event was a dance participated in by individuals of both sexes who had been thoroughly stimulated by *akha* and who chanted phrases and verses after a lead caller. The dancing was often choral in style, generally hand in hand and circling. The rhythm was beaten out by the *pallas* and *ñustas* on tambourines or by one woman beating a *pomatinya* or "lion drum" large enough so that it had to be carried by a man; the jangling of the shell anklets worn by the dancing men added to the effect. Perhaps the most stylish of these dances and the one that has come down to the present day was the *huayño*; two partners, male and female, danced with crossed hands, in a circle, while the strongly repetitive verses were chanted by a chorus around them and time was kept by the tambourines. For certain occasions these *taquis* were allowed to become semipublic orgies, and at such times the puritanical rules of the Incas regarding sex were put aside, although the details concerning the *pallas'* part in these affairs are totally unknown. The *cachua* was an orgiastic dance in which men and women holding hands moved rhythmically in a big wheel. This dance took place only around the fires at nighttime. It is probable that there were areas under the great sheds used for the purpose of copulation on these occasions. Among the *acllas* we know that certain ones were trained to partake in these festivities. Perhaps they were "the painted ones" mentioned by Huaman Poma.

The emperor sat on the *usno* in the center of the square surrounded by the various *panacas* arranged in order of precedence. The moieties sat on his either hand, Upper Cuzco on the northwest side of the square, Lower Cuzco on the opposite side. It was the emperor who ate and drank first, and he alone who could offer toasts in golden cups to Viracocha. The *coya* and her women served him aided by the many pages in his court. His food and drink were tabooed, having been specially prepared, and what was left over was carefully preserved and hidden away to be ceremonially destroyed once a year. In formal processions the Incas, both men and women, circled the *usno*, one *panaca* following another.

The almost brutal splendor of these holidays was emphasized in the entertainment offered on such occasions. The emperor had his *ccamchu*, or "jester," whose skill consisted in jumbling his words and concepts to bring laughter. But hilarity was especially provoked by the hunchbacks, dwarfs, and harelips who were introduced; these unfortunates lived in a special hamlet nearby and were protected by the emperor who saw to it that they could breed only among themselves, thus producing more of their kind.

During the prolonged drinking these funmakers pranced about, human monsters hideous of aspect; there were "jokers" or *sauca rimac* from among the Huancavilca people, *farceurs* from the lowlands called *hayachucos*; there were *saynatas*, masked clowns who delighted the onlookers by pretending intimacies with the highest-ranking Incas and *pallas*. *Llamallamas* simulated animals engaged in ridiculous and provocative acts. Others engaged in ludicrous battle with the grass-stuffed mummies of old enemies, the so-called *runatinya* or "man-drums," beating the dried bellies of the trophies with sticks, poking them in their private parts, and shouting vulgarities into their dead ears. The humor was broad and cruel and consisted largely of bawdiness and of incongruities between man and the animals. The Quechua language lent itself easily to punning with all the genuine humor that issues from that basic exercise in contrived confusion.

It is doubtful that the Incas were a people much given to wit. Their genuine accomplishments, the rigor of their orientation toward dominion, and the fear consequent upon it must have always made humor, which ends in self-criticism, a dangerous relaxation. In the heavy drinking of the great fiestas, sometimes extended for days, the powerful social tensions between the two moieties as such and among the several *panacas*, as well as that unformalized tension between all the Incas and their emperor, must have provided many conflagrations of the human spirit. The tautness of the whole Inca situation and the ever-present competitions built up by the opposition between the Capac Ayllu and the Hahua Incas added to the need for laughter, but laughter among warriors easily becomes immoderate.

 QVINTA CALLE
CIPASCOVIA

Of Love and Sex

INCA CULTURE lacked sophistication in many areas; only recently they had been a raw young people of the *sallca* who had lacked a strong tradition and had to wait until Pachacuti created one for them. Certainly their history had too short a span to achieve the refinements and perversions of sexual culture so notable among certain other Peruvian groups. Where their sexual life differed at all, therefore, from what we would expect of such a recently gauche people, it is probably traceable to borrowings from the outside.

The transvestite homosexual was a prominent feature of the life of the Yauyos, for instance, and the Incas, having included the Yauyos in their empire, were well aware of their public houses filled with men who dressed as women and painted their faces. The Lupacas who lived on the shores of Lake Chucuito had an established practice of homosexualism and sodomy, while the ancient kingdoms of the coast had behind them countless centuries of varied sexual experimentation.

In this hot world around them the Incas appeared to be somewhat naïve and even puritanical. In general, the more epicene practices repelled them and became matters of adverse legislation and derision. It is, however, probable that by Huascar's time the Incas were being propelled to an elaboration of their own sexual practices as the coastal influences increased in Cuzco. The isolation which was so important a part of the *panaca* system must have served as a fertile seedbed for these foreign vices, and it is certainly true that under the mummified emperors the *panacas* did become protected centers of fornication. But it is, in any case, in the last degree difficult to be certain of the extent of

187

such practices. A great deal of what we have to say is therefore suppositious.

Women took a prominent part in the affairs of the Inca world, sharing as they did in the vast assurance of their male kinfolk. They considered themselves women of luxury. They painted their faces to increase their dark beauty, had attendants who kept their black tresses glistening and attractive and in some instances they indulged in sexual intrigue. *Ayuy,* "adultery," was far from unknown and was considered to be a more reprehensible kind of theft. A child badly crippled could be suspected of having been deformed by a mother's milk soured by sexual incontinence or unfaithfulness.

Chastity among the Incas was a state entered into by the girl only after her marriage. Before marriage, amorous adventures appear to have been easy and numerous for the daughters of Incas, and it was not uncommon for the most highborn *ñustas* from early girlhood to accompany the Inca armies in which their fathers were officers. On those extended campaigns the moonlit nights outside the circle of fires witnessed interminable singing, dancing, and copulation. It is in line with this sexual freedom of the young that the language had no word specifically for "a maiden or virgin." The word *ñusta* meant simply an unmarried daughter of the nobility, and it carried no necessary connotations of chastity. The corresponding unmarried girl or young woman aged fourteen to twenty of the classes below was a *sipas*, which word could be used indiscriminately either for "girl" or "concubine." Sexual freedom for the young was taken for granted. For a married woman it could call for death.

For the Inca men there were always, in addition the services of the state geishas, certain girls from the *acllahuasi* assigned as entertainers and available by the emperor's generosity or that of the local governor to travelers along the Great Road. These girls are not to be confused with the *mamaconas* who were the wives and concubines or women-in-waiting of the various gods, *huacas,* and past rulers and were therefore necessarily chaste. A woman sexually unfaithful to a divine husband was subjected to the most degrading and horrible of deaths.

But the Incas were still aware of various qualities of love. *Coyay* was love which prominently included pity and compassion. *Mahuay* was specifically exterior love and called to mind the attitudes of courtship, gifts, and words which openly discovered lovers to the world at large. *Munay* was love in general as well as being hidden or capricious desire. *Huaylluy* was romantic love which indeed was a real part of Inca culture and feeling. There existed love lyrics of many kinds, some mere snatches, others courtly lyrics, others lovers' laments likening their beloved to the orange flower of the *chinchircoma*, or to a dream reflected from the waters, or recalling the playful glances of her dark eyes. These were songs of the nobles and perhaps were sung as serenades or *aubades*.

The festival of the first menstruation for noble girls, the *quicuchicoy*, was held at the same time as the rites for the young men. Girls of eleven to fourteen years of age now became *ñustas*, cast off the headband of girlhood, put on sandals and assumed the striking red and white *acsu*, the garment that marked her as a marriageable woman. Because she was now a different person, like her counterpart of the knighting ceremonies, she was given the name by which she would from that time forever be known.

We have seen that in those parts of the festivities wherein the girls ceremonially cleansed themselves it was customary for them to bathe in the impounded waters of the Sapi just above the city. As they splashed about naked in the clear cold water, the young acolyte knights, perched on the boulders and terracetops above them, played on their flutes, or sang while watching the proceedings below them. They would make the great glen speak back to the sound of their shouts, calling out to the *yachapayak kaka*, "the mimicking rock," amusing the girls below and frightening the quail on the hillsides. This was the *huarmihapiy pacha*, "the woman-taking time," when the young men sought out their future wives.

If a *ñusta* did not at first respond to one's overtures, one might have recourse to a sorcerer skilled in love charms. The *huaca* of desire and mating was known as *huacanqui*; it was a powerful and explosive force and its manipulation was in the hands of a special class of sorcerers. The charms in which the *huacanqui* was most commonly found were

189

certain grubs, herbs and flowers like the carnation or the *villca*, or small stones; a small viridian fly was especially efficacious in this respect. For elder men who were losing their potency an effective *huacanqui* was the dried body of the tiny *causarca*, a lovely hummingbird not much bigger than a bee. This bird's name, derived from *causariy*, "to renew or resuscitate," came from its sudden reappearance every April. Its connection with a revived virility in men was obvious.

Love stories out of the past were numerous and stressed the demonically possessive power of love which often ended with the lover or lovers changed into a rock or peak such as Pitusiray above the Yucay Valley. The old men who knew the tales were the *huacanqui machu*, and their store of songs and legends was called upon at all fiestas. The subject of their lays they carried back to the very beginning of Inca history where the discovery of *huacanqui* and its fascinating power was attributed to Manco Capac's son, the second emperor.

But the subject of love could be new as well as old. When Rahua Ocllo had returned from the far north after the death of her royal husband, she had assembled a retinue of girls, all wellborn, from the provinces round about. This entourage was assembled so that she might arrive in a state befitting her dignity. One of these ladies-in-waiting was the lovely Chestan Xecfuin from one of the occupied valleys of the coast. The third son of the *curaca* of that province, who had earlier fallen in love with her, was called by Huascar to represent his father at one of the imperial gatherings in Cuzco, and this task he performed with alacrity—notwithstanding the deaths of some of his compeers in the high altitudes—so that he might be closer to his inamorata. In the court at Cuzco the prince found opportunities to meet secretly with his beloved and she soon became his wife. When she became pregnant, the young man petitioned Huascar that he might return to his home along with her so that his child could be born in a more temperate altitude. The request was granted and the child, named Cuzco Chumpi after the place of his conception, lived to become Don Pedro Cuzco Chumpi, a Christian. This love affair was no doubt well known to all the Incas of the time.

HUASCAR HAD RETURNED to Cuzco to celebrate the Situa. The dry season had been long advanced and the clouds could soon be expected to pour out their violent contents, bringing not only life to the *chacras* but also many illnesses to Viracocha's beloved children, coughs and aching bones and wasting diseases. It was a time both longed for and dreaded. This was the month of the Coya Raymi, the Queen's Festival, equivalent to our months of August and September.

Preparations for the festival were advancing. The serving-women of the lesser *panacas* could be seen every morning trotting down the narrow sunless streets of Cuzco in their bare feet with empty jars on their shoulders to fill them in the square shallow basins or fountains of the city. A vast amount of *ukha* had to be prepared for the great drinking to come. Files of llamas with packs of wool or bundled feathers or bags of coca-leaves released from private warehouses filed daintily and superciliously into the city. Young boys set off for the nearby *punas* to gather bundles of *ichu*-grass which would be scattered about in Haucaypata and Cusipata as pallets for the nobles to sit on. Messengers moved constantly between the royal *canchas* on the square and Huascar's palace above them on Collcampata, while groups of Inca braves gathered repeatedly in parts of the city to discuss and practice their parts for the approaching celebration.

This particular Situa was to be of special poignancy to the Inca folk, for they were aware of an unaccustomed misease. By now their emperor had become for them a completely alien and unpredictable master, and he had dramatized this fact by moving his palatial presence from among them in the city. One had only to lift one's eyes to see his newly erected residence just under the walls of Sacsahuaman. In the early history of the city this shelf on the hill had been terraced up to support the first large granaries, whence it had received its name, Collcampata. It was well provided with water and the paved road down from the fortress ran just under its southern corner. On this terrace there were no great works which would interfere with new building so Huascar had seized upon it as a satisfactory site for his palace; in addition, it was deep enough for a *carpa huasi*. It looked directly down into the city.

Whenever Huascar was in Cuzco, he seldom stirred out of this cyric of his. He had become openly contemptuous of the blessed dead, the *illapa* of his mighty ancestors. His *caumihua* or planted spies were everywhere. Detachments of armed Cañars loitered near the fountains and placed themselves strategically about the squares to see everything that was done. They were the *chapa*, "the police," loyal only to Huascar's *huatay camayoc*, or "sheriff," who bore the royal sandals at the end of a long staff as the badge of his special authority. It was no longer an uncommon sight to see a squad of these police striding rapidly out from the steep street leading from Collcampata to intercept an Inca going about his business or a woman at the fountain and to hear barked out the dreaded announcement *"Huatascca canqui!"* or "You are under arrest!" whereupon, at a quick shuffle, the offender was taken away, sometimes never to be heard from again, unless the wheeling of birds of carrion announced it a few days later over the Sankacaucha.

This period was the time of favorites, of the *quemiquiru*, who eased themselves into the painful privacy surrounding Huascar and who for a moment or two ruled through him by insinuation and whisper. We have previously mentioned two of the Hahua Inca *ayllus* which were especially notorious for thus betraying the emperor's confidence. They were the Equeco and the Quilliscachi from Anta, possibly the two moieties of that pueblo, and had been Incas since the days of Pachacuti. Their young men were powerful men of war, and their elders had long held the prerogative of inspection and intelligence in Tahuantinsuyo, posts which gave them such a potential power over the erratic mind of Huascar. His initial dependence upon these men of Anta, Incas by adoption only, was of course a cutting insult to the Capac Incas who were the true children of the sun. But this situation soon passed, for the emperor turned upon these Hahua Incas, as we have seen, and in an insane outburst ordered them decimated and their pregnant women butchered.

It was at any rate apparent by now to the Capac Incas that they had lost the power to regulate and police themselves. Only within the sanctity of the *panaca* could they feel themselves relatively secure, but the *panacas* were purely institutions of protocol—and in addition were almost all sundered from each other. The *panaca* was a retreat, but it was not a fortress. Only the common cult of the Chima *panaca* now held the Cuzco Incas together.

Increasingly also the Incas were leaning on that special class of servitors they called the *yanacona*. These domestics were drawn from recently conquered peoples and appear in certain cases to have passed their dependent status on down to their descendants. They were not like those groups of Indians assessed against certain provinces for periodic labor but were more in the nature of domestics permanently owned by certain Incas, *pallas*, gods, or *panacas*. Belonging to no nation or tribe, they were probably considered for purposes of classification chattel members of whatever *panaca* or *ayllu* their master claimed. Many appear to have been originally selected on the basis of rank, intelligence, and bearing, for some were even entrusted with such high responsibilities as *curaca*-ships. In the *panacas* their energy and skills led some to acquire positions of real control. In this last reign, two in particular, bearing the names Titu and Amaru, had virtually usurped the role—although not the title or prestige—of the major-domo of the Iñaca *panaca*. The emperor even went to the extent of bestowing *acllas* on some of his more beloved *yanaconas*. The danger of a final usurpation of power by this strategically placed class was never to menace Incas and *pallas* directly, but that these groups were weakened by their reliance upon their *yanaconas* is undoubted.

Over and beyond this weakness was the ominous feature that a part of the Capac Incas had for some years now been resident in Quito, two thousand miles away, under the leadership of the enigmatic Atauhuallpa. These were the ones who had not returned to Cuzco after the death of Huayna Capac. While claiming the privileges of true children of the sun they were in effect strangers, and their connections with the Cuzco moieties and *panacas* were so tenuous now as to be almost meaningless. Their women were mainly northerners and their sons careless of the sacredness of Cuzco.

Probably little of this division was consciously realized. The Capac

Incas, rich and arrogant as ever, had ceased to look into the face of reality. They carried on the cultus of the ancestral mummies as ever. Among them the *bon-vivant* companion came and went, living his life of pleasure and avoiding the harsh life which his warrior ancestors had marked out for him. He and his fellows were the *pococ*, "the ripe ones," or the *kallu*, "the smart ones." They played daily at the gameboard and envied the very great. They knew of the occasional bursts of largess for which Huascar was noted, and they hoped that something they could do would push them into his good graces. For if he could endow his favorite *yanaconas* with *acllas*, why might they also not receive a lovely girl as a plaything? Or the right to be carried about in a hammock? Or to eat off silver plate? Or a sinecure in the provinces—after all, had not a certain Huayna Pari been appointed to a *curaca*-ship on the shores of Lake Chucuito over the legitimately elected headman? And who could unseat him while Huascar lived?

Day after day the lives of the lords and the lesser Incas went on seemingly as usual.

SECTION 12. *Night and Day*

To ALL OUTWARD APPEARANCES each day did seem the same. Before the stars had paled, the fires were teased up within the open courtyards of the *canchas* or under the sheds. Only the Incas and the great ambassadorial magnates living around Cuzco had the luxury of fires in the dark before dawn along with abundant hot food. In the performance of these chores the dim figures of serving-women, their *llicllas* pulled close around them, moved in and out under the eaves of the apartments and slipped like shadows through the narrow doorways. The chill of the ground and of the andesite walls in the cold season was almost a torture to the shivering figures, and because of it one did not walk but trotted with small steps.

Then came the first glimmering of dawn when the eye could not distinguish between a ghost and a solid person; this moment was the *ramca ramca pacha*, "vision time," when the young lovers fled away like wraiths, indistinguishable from the shadows. There was a conceit

194

among the Incas that the morning star blazing so spiritedly in the pale east was a favorite engaged in motley dancing before his lord the sun, soon to appear; for this reason he was sometimes known as Aranyac, "He who dances in a mask." But his dance in any case was a silent one.

Sounds also announced the new day. When the *puco puco*, a small bird like a partridge, whistled his first notes on the terraces of Patallacta, one knew that the mists and phantasms of the night were dissolving and that the joy and the life of movement would begin again and that real men would walk in the streets of Cuzco. This was the "break of dawn," "the growing-white," quickly followed by the springing sun.

The smokes of the fires and the odors of the cooking filled the city as the resident *curacas*, their servitors, and the many purveyors of necessaries swarmed across the bridges and through the plazas into the city. Porters appeared to squat down at the *cancha* entrances, and the life of Cuzco began. It was an eminently silent life, however. The burden-bearers ran in silence, the Incas moved with decorum, the clots of *ñustas* or young men, even the processions of a *panaca* on its way out to serve one of its more distant *huacas*, all were affairs of dignity and few words. Perhaps the loudest sound would be the sudden barking of a dog in one of the back streets, but even this sound only accentuated the containment and the dignity of life in Cuzco.

After the sun had passed the zenith, the *ticnu* or "upright point," the melancholy of a cold people who loved the sun's warmth began to possess them. Upon the terraces east of the city one could still sit in a mellow sunshine, but down in the heart of Cuzco itself it was the *pircallantuk pacha*, "the time when the walls cast shadows."

Pallas and their women gathered under the *pisonay*-trees planted on the esplanade of Pumapchupan to feel the last of the afternoon sun and look down the valley at the busy scene presented to them, the beautifully channeled river bordered with lacy *molle*-trees, the Collasuyo road lined with branched cactus and filled with traffic, slow hammock-bearers, working gangs, knots of old women with downcast eyes carrying braided-grass slings or *chipa*, full of gleaming duck eggs, llama-herders bringing chosen beasts in from the upper pastures, dignified Incas moving off on imperial errands of inspection, and on either side the fields filled with serfs bent double over the harsh toil of wresting food from the ground. On the backs of these *yupacs* or "plow people" and in the knotted muscles of their calves resided all of Cuzco's prosperity. To the noblewomen watching them, beautifully wrapped as they were in mantles of fine *cumpi*, these barefooted thousands were the *yanca yahuar*, "worthless folk," whose crude customs and meaty faces caused them peals of laughter. The whole valley, both sides and level bottom, was terraced and green in the lambent sunshine, a monument to the labors of the worthless ones.

But very quickly the shadows lengthened and the *pallas* moved away in little groups, going back to the *canchas* or villas where they resided. Guards strode out of the city to take up their night watches at assigned stations, while others came into the city with their reports. Sunset was always appreciated as the last act of an imperial sun. It was *anta rupay*, "coppery burning" or sunset, and the *pallas* crossing Haucaypata on their way home blew kisses back to it in reverence.

When they stepped across the thresholds of the *canchas*, they had entered the closed and remote world which the Capac Incas had circumscribed for themselves within heavy battered walls. The *pallas* now moved through the gloaming of the inner patios preceded by their pages or girlish ladies-in-waiting bearing the *huaricolla*, the flower of the cattail soaked in tallow and flickering smokily, the only candles they had. Some of the *carpa huasi*, or apartments open on one side, held knots of squatting Incas talking in low voices around a fire, debating the few issues they had left to them, promoting the business of the *panaca*, or merely recounting the past and drinking the inevitable *akha*.

Night skies in the high sierra have the quality of deepening the location of each star, while the moon takes up the center of an almost palpable blue-black space. This sight was known to the Incas as *llipiyac tuta*, "the spangled night," for they were very conscious of the stars. The all-pervading static splendor of the heavenly lights was as beautiful to them as it is to us, but in addition they saw the night sky as the home of powerful and mysterious *huacas*, such as that which resided in the constellation of the Southern Cross in which they saw a female llama and her lamb peacefully grazing the celestial *puna* together. The moon and all her phases were also well known to the Incas. As *pacsa* she was "mooniness," her disc lightly covered with a veil of clouds, dispensing a milky radiance over all things, but as the mother of months she was *quilla*.

The old men told their grandchildren stories about her dirty face, received when her brother threw ashes at her, the warriors knew her intimately, for they had slept and kept vigil under her unblinking eye on many eves before battle, the wise men read in her the times of the festivals, *pallas* and *ñustas* felt close to her, for she regulated the periods of their menstruation and she was a woman herself. She was Mama Quilla, "Moon Mother," and her high priestess was the Coya Pacsa, "Queen Mooniness," a sister of the ruling Inca. She was the wife of the Sun, walked in his chambers after his departure, and mothered the Inca folk. The terrors of nighttime were not attributed to her. She was a comfort to all.

SECTION 13. *The Situa*

OF ALL the great periodic Inca festivals the Situa was the most moving, for it was the feast of salvation. An unreflecting and compulsive people, such as were the Incas, storming every citadel of power known to them, of necessity needed reassurance. The greatness of their need in this respect eventuated in the amazing theatrical apparatus of the Situa.

The Situa came in the month that alternated between August and September, that month which the Incas called Coya Raymi, "the Festival of the Queen," meaning the moon goddess. The sowing of the new seed had just taken place and it was still the dry season. The new year was thus about to start, with the whole valley anxiously awaiting the first rains.

The Creator, who had made all things, had placed the Inca people highest in his graces. They were the touchstones of the whole world's prosperity, and to them, therefore, it fell to intercede with Him in order that renewal and weal might be the order for the coming year. That goodness might accrue to them, first of all to them as the selected people and then to the swarming millions of Tahuantinsuyo—this

197

heartfelt need was symbolized by the Situa. It is of interest to see in what sense, therefore, they made their supplication and what they felt to be demanded of them.

Old evils and new ones were known to be in the city, diseases, misfortunes, ill luck, intrigues, doubts, conspiracies and secret thoughts, witchcraft and deformities of man and animal, death, drought, and dearth—all of these or the possibilities of them had to be expunged and wiped clear away if the new agricultural year were to begin auspiciously.

But the Incas conceived of the simultaneous necessity of renewing the heavens as well. In this sense the Situa was a great puppet show miming the actions of the gods and *huacas* as well as a ceremonial cleansing of the capital city. It would be unfair and untrue to call the Incas puppeteers, for this term implies that they had an awareness of themselves as the source of the action depicted. Nevertheless, their staging of this world drama in which gods, *huacas*, Incas, and men all intermingled was a masterpiece of consistency and high color and was eloquent of their presumptions. A race of conquerors almost without their peer in history, in the Situa they relieved their most basic fears and stated again their imperial prerogatives.

SECTION 14. *The First Act—In Heaven*

THE ACTION OF THE SITUA originated, as it were, in heaven. Informed by his subservient high priest, Challco Yupanqui, of the new moon which would appear the next day, Huascar gave the traditional orders to expel from Cuzco all foreign, afflicted, or impaired people. All people not Incas or their immediate retainers, all visiting provincials, even resident ambassadors from the client kingdoms of the coast, were ordered to remain temporarily out beyond a six-mile limit. Similarly all foreign *huacas* which had been resident during the year in Cuzco were for the time being dismissed along with their attendant sorcerers and priests, for they too were foreigners. The powers of the Inca universe were now about to sit in council, and for the short time of this conclave Cuzco had to close in on itself, to become once again the pristine home of the Incas and their gods, unsullied by any lesser presences. Purity was the keynote.

It was an august assemblage that met therefore in Coricancha. The Creator, normally represented in Coricancha by a bundle of the finest woolen *cumpi*, came this time in the *huaca* of his small golden image which was kept in Quishuarcancha. There attended also the thunder-god, in his triune person, Chuqui Illa or "Golden Treasure," Catu Illa, and Inti Illapa, the last named being the solid gold idol under the control of the Iñaca *panaca*, for it was the great Pachacuti's *huaoqui*. Down from the heights of Mount Huanacauri had come the indispensable *huaca* of the Incas' manhood, their genius, the ugly stone of the same name borne in a litter, ornately smothered in robes of great beauty and crowned with a diadem of feathers. The Rainbow came, the Morning Star who was Inti's page, and also the Pleiades, dispensers of plenty. Inti the Sun was the host god, the one with the most splendid retinue and the most desirable women.

Two other deities sat nearby in that synod, but they attended more as presences than as actors—Mother Earth and Mother Moon. The former probably had no concrete image to be adored and no special priesthood, for she was the ground upon which men and gods together walked and sat. She had the peculiar quality of belonging concretely everywhere and therefore being without a true focus. Mother Moon, on the contrary, was present as a small solid silver statue, squat and naked, the mother of all Incas. She was served by women only, under the rule of the Coya Pacsa, her high priestess and oracular mouthpiece.

Then came the eleven ancestors, each accompanied by the titular head of his *panaca*. The leading Inca magnates attended, some from the Yachahuasi, some famous as generals of armies or as successful builders and engineers, some especially venerable because of age. All together, gods, mummies, and men, they now entered into conference seated in hierarchial arrangement with Huascar, the living emperor, presiding.

Nothing is known of this particular conclave, but if we may interpolate from the situation of Tahuantinsuyo at the time, it was probably found necessary to organize the complete Situa, in other words, to omit nothing from the traditional rites, and even perhaps to add cer-

199

tain embellishments to them. The looming shadow of an Inca state in the far north whose relationships with Cuzco were dangerously unclear, the sporadic presence of the great plague still among the cities of the empire, the constant trickle of rumors concerning the *suncasapa runa*, "the heavily bearded men" along the coast, the whispered but well-known prophecies of the return of Viracocha, and finally the growing silence and reluctance of the great *huacas* of the empire to reveal the shape of the future—all these conditions must have impelled Huascar to lead the conclave in decreeing the utmost in ceremonial splendor for that year's Situa.

After the gods had ratified the decision, Huascar and Challco Yupanqui were solemnly escorted out of Coricancha to announce it to the Inca warriors waiting in Intipampa. This *cusi simi*, "the good news," was awaited by a heavily armed regiment of Incas. Trooping and shouting, they turned and poured up the narrow Street to the Sun to burst into Haucaypata and set off the celebration.

SECTION 15.

The Second Act—In Cuzcoquiti

AWAITING THEM in the vast square was a grand display. Four hundred Incas accoutered in beautiful feathered bonnets, vividly painted and armed for war, stood silently and at attention, one hundred on each of the four sides of the central *usno*, each group facing outward toward one of the four cardinal directions. Cuzco was now officially at war with those invisible and deadly perils which always menace a dominant people, and here at attention were her armies, each now to be launched against one of the four quarters of the universe. Every one of the soldiers

200

in these miniature, heraldic armies was a high-ranking Inca knight. The constituent parts of these armies are, therefore, of great interest to the historian of these people.

The army on the southwest side of the *usno* was comprised of men from the *panacas* of the first two Inca emperors and from the two *ayllus* of Masca and Uru, while those on the southeast side were from the *panacas* of the next three emperors, plus the *ayllus* of Sutic, Maras, and Cuicusa. This array was the official roster of Lower Cuzco. The little army of the northeast contained warriors of the seventh and eighth *panacas* plus the Tarpuntay and Sañu *ayllus*. The northwestern group, that with the most prestige, contained men of the sixth, ninth, and tenth *panacas* plus the *ayllus* of Chavin, Quisco, and Huacaytaqui. These two groups formed the city's upper moiety or, as they were specially called, the Cuzcos. Thus the ten nations and ten of the eleven imperial households or *panacas* making up the full caste of Incas were represented.

The enemy within the gates by now had been identified. Two judicial or confessional boards had been set up in the appropriate sides of the plaza, one for Upper and one for Lower Cuzco. Each was composed of a panel of six, no doubt representing among them all the *panacas*, and they in turn were split so that, in all, four courts sat corresponding to each of the four directions. These individuals had heard statements of the civil, criminal, and ceremonial wrongs which the Inca people were alleged to have committed over the year. Each *panaca* and each *ayllu* was responsible for bringing before the appropriate panel evidences of such derelictions on the part of its members. Sitting along with the judges of each panel was a *huchacamayoc*, a "crime expert," trained in the laws from his boyhood and able to read the tariff of delicts and their penalties on the *quipus*. If the offense were grave, the *huchacamayoc* handed the case immediately over to the emperor who sat enthroned on the *usno* serving as the court of last appeal. Thus all contaminations which had accumulated in and among the Incas themselves over the course of the year were heard and either absolved or punished—but in every case identified as enemies of Cuzco.

Only after this ritual was completed did Huascar give the signal for the onset of the war. As if at a magic touch the four armies suddenly awoke and with piercing yells and ululations broke away from the *usno*, each toward its appropriate exit from the square. As they rushed out they hurled javelins about, whipped the air with their slings, and slashed at empty enemies with their bronze star-maces—driving before them the identified evils, herding them and pressing them outward as strenuously as if engaged with invaders of flesh and blood. "Evils, depart!" was the shout they raised as they rushed through Cuzco.

Alerted by the approaching din, the men, women, and children of the city came to the doors of the *canchas* and villas, shaking out their mantles, rubbing their arms and legs, slapping their skirts, and repeating the cry "Evils, depart!" Thus they brushed out into the streets all their uncleannesses, diseases, and other misfortunes to be repelled by the charging troops. They called jubilantly to each other, "*Achallay! Achallay!*" or "How wonderful! How good!" with reference to the new situation created by the energetic attack on evil being carried out in front of them.

With dusk coming on and the new moon in the sky as the symbol of renovation, the din and shrieking increased within the city to become the *pancunco*, "the torches." Warriors dashed into the shadows on the edges of the square and up and down the dark streets hurling stones wrapped in flaming straw. Men, women, and children busily attacked each other with flaming faggots of *ichu*-grass, beating out the evils that still lingered in them and destroying them by fire. This universal fumigation continued until midnight, turning the city into a fantasy of sparkling lights and flambeaux chasing each other like fireflies through the darkness. A great relief began to possess the Inca people at this evidence of their purification, and they repeated over and over to each other the words of approval, "How wonderful this ceremony is! How splendid! Oh, may the Lord let us live to see such a fiesta another year!"

Meanwhile, the chosen warriors of the symbolic armies, sweeping the air before them, bounded outward along the four great roads of the empire. These men were the heroes of the Inca world, the very sinews of the state, the strong ones on whom all else depended. Those of the army of the west fought and danced their way along the Conti-suyo road to the watershed some six miles out where confederate Incas who lived in Yaurisque met them with torches and lances to carry on the act of expulsion as far as the pueblo of Tantar where the last relay picked up the mission to carry it just before dawn to the deep gorge of the river at Cusibamba. Here the exhausted runners in a final victory hurled the invisible enemy across the frontiers of Cuzcoquiti. Then they ceremonially cleansed their maces and javelins in the swift Apuri-mac River. Cuzcoquiti on this border was safe for another year.

The southern army rushed down the Collasuyo road as far as the Narrows where the next team relieved it, carrying the war on to Anta-huaylillas, which pueblo in turn passed it on once more until the last group dipped its weapons in the Vilcañota at Quiquijana. The eastern army took the Antisuyo road over the mountain to Chita and handed over to a group there that carried down to the Vilcañota at Pisac, there washing their weapons. The northern army pushed its way up the royal road over Carmenca and handed over at the *tambo* of Satpina. Here the burden was taken by Incas on to Anta whose relay then car-ried it to the lip of the basin at Vilcacunca where with a rush the last army carried it triumphantly down into the warm trench of the Apuri-mac, the northern frontier of Cuzcoquiti.

Thus all through the night of the new moon, while the Incas of the city were cleansing their city by fire, the panting and exhausted, but triumphant, armies hurled back the enemy who had infiltrated the beloved land that was their home. With the washing of the weapons under the morning star in the waters of the Apurimac and Vilcañota, the stains of the late year's evils were carried away into the distant voids of the great sea, Mamacocha, and there lost forever, nevermore to be chargeable against the Inca folk. A memorable night indeed!

The last purification began after the fires and torches had been ex-tinguished at midnight and each Inca *panaca* and *ayllu* had assembled all of its members, human and *huaca*, young and old, men and women, living and dead. Carrying their mummified ancestors if it was a *panaca*, or their principal *huaca* if it was an *ayllu*, each group moved out of the midnight city and along its particular *ceque* to an assigned spring or tank or *tincu*. Here all of them stripped and in the cold mists of dawn washed away the last scurf of sin and contamination. This yearly baptismal rite meant much to the Inca people, for it renewed them as families with no reference to the state or to the emperor. When their mummies, their *huacas*, and their family *conopas* had all been properly bathed as well, they had successfully completed this part of the Situa.

SECTION 16. *The Third Act—On the Altar*

THE SITUA proper could begin.

The central act, beginning with the dawn of that day, was the taking of the communion meal, the *yahuar sanco*, or thick "blood dough." Everyone adorned himself as splendidly as possible. The men wore large red and white flowers called *achancara* in their *llautos*, silver *canipus* on their brows, and golden medals or *purapura* won in the wars hanging from their necks. Tunics of soft and brilliantly checkered *cumpi* completed their costumes, and some carried bunches of gay feathers in their hands. Their wives and daughters had their faces painted vermilion in striking contrast with the whiteness of their teeth and the jet of their overflowing hair. The more prominent of the *pallas* wore beautiful striped garments, so-called *cuychi lliclla* or "rainbow sheaths," and all of the women had the customary warm mantillas or *ñañaca* pinned in their hair and falling over their shoulders. Enormous flat silver *tupus*, "shawl pins," flashed at their breasts.

Misery was not allowed to show any of its manifold faces during this great saturnalia. Even the lowliest retainers appeared in festive garb; no evil or bitter words could be spoken by anyone, no quarreling between the members of the two moieties allowed. This day and the three succeeding ones were to be the statement of a happy, purified, and harmonious people.

The *yahuar sanco* had been specially prepared in Coricancha by the sun-women, and by them it was now distributed to all of the *panacas* and to every other qualified inhabitant of Cuzco. It was a roughly ground maize-meal dumpling which had been slightly moistened by the admixture of the blood of the hundred sacred white llamas sacrificed for the occasion. Each person smeared his face with this doughy mass, and each *panaca* saw to it that the entrances to its *cancha* were also anointed; they painted the mouths of their imperial mummies with it and took bits of it out to the springs and other *huacas* on their *ceques* to be similarly offered. This substance was the blood and the biscuit, then, of a solemn communion meal; the taking of it was at once a grace, a symbol of plenty, and a renewed dedication to Inti. It was believed that this sacred food inside the body of a person would cry out and inform against him if he should contemplate treason to the Inca ruler or to the Inca gods.

The day closed when the images of the great Inca gods, from Viracocha down to the Pleiades, were brought into the communion by having doughy fragments of the same sacred food drawn across their mouths. This act completed the unification of the Incas and their gods —all made one in a common and prosperous overlordship of the world.

The Creator in company with his living viceroy Huascar, the twelfth emperor, had entered Haucaypata with great pomp that day, each of them, god and man, crowned with a diadem of iridescent *pillco* feathers. The courtiers and noblewomen of Huascar's immediate household came on behind, with the *coya* Chuqui Huipa, crowned like her husband, in the center. The richness of her apparel and the bright rouge of her face paint obliterated from her visage its habitual expression of fear and sadness. As yet she had produced for her brother-husband no heir-apparent; this achievement alone was lacking to fulfill the splendor of the occasion.

All took their places around the *usno*. Nearby was the mummy bundle of Huayna Capac placed in dignity on a low golden stool. Its gold-plated and empty face stared out upon the people over whom it had once cast far more imperious glances. Beside it stood the mummy's living wife and *coya*, Rahua Ocllo, with a fly whisk dangling from her hand.

Into this assemblage there now paraded the sun-god's image, the Apu Punchao, "Lord Day," sedately maneuvered about by his priesthood. To increase the splendor of the occasion, his entire harem of *mamaconas* came, led by the Coya Pacsa representing his legitimate wife. The dogma that he had fathered the Incas was symbolized by the inclusion in his train of the two wooden statues known as the Inca Ayllu and the Palla Ayllu, standing for the two sexes of the caste, for although Inti was the father of both Incas and *pallas*, they were supposed to be two separate creations.

The appearance of each of the other gods was heralded by the entry of his respective *yauri* or "scepter" borne at the procession's head by a priest. When all were arranged the repast began, followed by the *taqui*. The dance was unique to the occasion. The dancers were dressed in soft red mantles and wore flowers in their headbands. The song was called "The Field of Flowers" and expressed the beauty and delight that was to mark the coming year. The shrilling of pipes, the hooting of trumpets, the stamping of the dancers' feet, and the jangling of their shell anklets, all announced that such a desired condition of things had indeed already come to pass.

Interspersed with the various sacrifices made during these two days were prayers offered by Huascar in behalf of his people. Most of these prayers were addressed to the Viracocha "Just-Beyond" or "Imminent." They were simple and moving. "Where art thou? Without? Within? In the clouds? In the shadows? Hear me, respond and consent." These petitions pleaded especially for good harvest; empty bellies were all too quickly moved to treasonable designs. "Guard the emperor you have set up, the Inca whom you have created, in peace and safety. Let him defeat each of his enemies." From Inti those assurances were sought that mattered most deeply to his people. "May they not be conquered, nor despoiled, but let *them* be conquerors and despoilers."

In such attestations of pride the Incas most clearly revealed themselves as a marked nation, for by invoking the Creator they were appealing to an unconditioned god beyond the world for the maintenance of a narrow and finite *politique*. This festival thus reveals a spiritual focusing of great intensity, a remarkable sensitivity to the divine; yet the deeper foundations of this great people, as we have seen, rested on stones of arrogance and cunning. The quarries from which those blocks had been extracted were indeed Pan-Peruvian, and other kingdoms had struggled energetically to raise similar temples of pride. But the Incas had not cared to hew the crude blocks into softer forms. In brief, the Situa was basically designed to turn aside any convulsions that might unsettle their foundations or topple their lovely terraces into the shadowy ravines unseen but always suspected below.

The dramatic culmination of these intercessory rites came in the performance of the *huayaya*, the national dance of the Incas. From the small house in Coricancha where it was kept when not in use came the *moroy urco*, the "spotted male." This was a woolen cable braided of many colors, sparkling with gold attachments, and shaped with a head to resemble an *amaru* or giant anaconda. It was borne along, Incas on one side and *pallas* on the other, into Haucaypata where its spectacular length carried it around at least two sides of the square. It adorned and made more stately the decorous and hesitant steps of the *huayaya* which was danced about the *usno* whereon sat Huascar the emperor. Forked poles were set at intervals around the square, and when the coiling dance was ended, the *muru urco* was placed in those supports, its loops hanging limply and its golden bangles tinkling in the cool wind. It represented the strong soul of the Inca people and their lordliness.

So far the Situa had taken four days. On the first day had taken place the communion meal, on the second prayers and sacrifices to Viracocha, on the third day similar petitions to Inti and Illapa, and on the fourth to the female deities. The Inca folk had thus fulfilled their obligations.

SECTION 17.

The Fourth Act—In the World

CUZCO HAD BEEN tightly quarantined during these highly exclusive celebrations. Like a jewel in its casket the Inca people had been secreted away from the world's flirting glances. On the fifth day, the jewel box was opened to the admiration of all the people.

Trumpets and the thudding voice of the great festival drum announced the entrance of the *huacas* of the empire. These were the ones which had been invited or commanded to appear at this year's Situa, and they had been waiting at the outer stations of the city for just this moment. They were carried in on litters by their priesthood and accompanied in most cases by the *curaca*, or his ambassador, of that particular people. Bearing gifts to the Inca gods and *huacas*, they now entered Haucaypata by the entry appropriate to the quarter of the empire in which they resided. They proceeded slowly about the square greeting all of the Inca deities in turn.

From each of the four corners thirty llamas, pure-white and specially selected, were brought in and sacrificed, their blood being sprinkled over the *sanco*. This substance was then administered to the foreign chiefs and their *huacas* by the Hahuayñin *panaca*. For those not invited to that Situa, or too distant, portions of the *sancu* were set aside, later to be dispatched to them by special delegations. Treason could exist nowhere.

One more necessary act remained, the taking of the omens. The lungs of four specially sacrificed llamas, representing the four parts of the empire, were first removed and then inflated by mouth. In the cabalistic veinings and marks of these horrid balloons the sorcerers read the

208

signs of the coming year, whether it should be prosperous, whether flood or drought should mar it, whether the llama herds should multiply, and whether the emperor should enjoy good health.

The morose emperor sitting enthroned on the *usno* asked fierce and embarrassing questions of the heavens. Even the *curacas* from the most distant parts of the empire were aware that disturbing portents had of late become more common and that Huascar's terror had proportionately increased. The Capac Incas who were ranged about the *usno* trembled at his pointed questions and feared the answers. The readings of the future were, of course, at once both glozing and ambiguous, seeming to promise all but saying nothing. On such a note of artificial happiness the court might momentarily relax. But this forecast did not clear the northern heavens of those distant lightnings which had been over the long years flickering on and off like urgent signals in another tongue.

For the rest of the day and the next the subject nations present regaled themselves and their Inca lords by staging their *ayllu* dances, drinking, and feasting. The poor and the crippled, the dogs and the gangs of the lowly returned to swarm about the edges of the feast. The foreign *huacas* again presented themselves to the Inca gods, and those which had been domiciled during the year in Cuzco received permission to depart, while the newcomers along with their priests took up quarters in the divine dormitories provided for them in the city for the coming year.

One year was ended and another had begun.

IV
War Enters the Great City

Twice Huascar had ordered his brother Atauhuallpa to appear in Cuzco to do him homage. The fact that on one excuse or another Atauhuallpa had not done so was suspicious in itself, if indeed it was not positively a studied affront.

For several years Atauhuallpa had held the *de facto* office of viceroy in Quito. After Huayna Capac's death, Huascar had reluctantly been persuaded to recognize his brother's standing in that northern quarter simply because at that time there seemed little he could do about it. He had, therefore, tacitly confirmed him in Quito, allowing him even to use the formidable title of *Incap ranti*, "the one who exchanges for the Inca." Thus commissioned, Atauhuallpa had proceeded to tighten Inca control over the north country by a campaign against the Huancavilca Indians. He had been successful in this venture and was now further expending his energies with a noble building program in the already sumptuous provincial city of Tumibamba. But a secret message had come to Huascar from that city. It was an insinuation by the *curaca* of the Cañar Indians, whose capital city Tumibamba had once been, that this building program was for Atauhuallpa's glory and not for Huascar's.

It took approximately six days for a message to go by *chasqui* from Quito to Cuzco. This report was to be one of the last communications carried by the imperial post. The *chasqui*'s conch-shell trumpet sounded from the top of Carmenca as he paused in his breakneck pace to announce his coming. This individual was one of the *hatun chasqui* or "great runners," and he could be seen from afar by his cap of pure-white feathers which flashed in the sun as he sped along behind terraces, houses, and abutments on his way down. The purport of his message was soon known to all the Incas in Cuzco, and few there were who did not see in it a presage of harsh events to come. At this juncture Huascar was known to have upbraided not only his *coya* but his mother as well, viciously accusing them of taking the part of Atauhuallpa against him. Before the death of his father they had both resided at the court in

213

Quito—Chuqui Huipa in fact seems to have grown up there—and to his inflamed mind this former proximity spelled collusion.

Even more pressing news followed, that Atauhuallpa had just dispatched an embassy south to Cuzco on a matter of great urgency and that the party was in fact well on its way. It was known that the spokesman of this embassy was a young Inca named Quilaco Yupanqui who had been reared as a page in the household of Rahua Ocllo when she had earlier resided in Quito. This point seemed to Huascar to be another link between his women and the Atauhuallpa faction. To balance this suspicion, he could take a malicious delight in contemplating the young man's ancestry, for his father had been Topa Yupanqui, one of the magnates whom he, Huascar, had ordered killed at Limatambo a few years previously. It would, in any case, be a dramatic confrontation.

The day before the embassy appeared at the guard station on the Chinchaysuyo road just outside Cuzco, Huascar moved with part of his court to Calca in the Yucay Valley. This affront was intended to be a deliberate insult to Atauhuallpa. More insults would follow.

SECTION 2. *The Quilaco Embassy*

THE WAY TO CALCA passed over Pachatusan, that divide called "the Pillar of the World," which separated the Huatanay and the Vilcañota valleys. The easiest way over was to go via the Antisuyo road to Pisac first and then to turn downriver for the few miles left. The young ambassador, having been reared in the distant north under the equator, had probably never traveled this famous road before, although the many legendary and historic sites along the route were well enough known to him as a part of his Inca heritage.

Lodged briefly in Cuzco by his former benefactor, Rahua Ocllo, who had not accompanied the emperor to Calca, he shortly set out on the last leg of his journey, taking now only a few of his party with him. The cheerlessness of his welcome in Cuzco reflected the care with which his own people, the Incas, kept their distance from him, for while they hated their own emperor, Quilaco Yupanqui's master was too far away to rescue them from Huascar's wrath should they show undue friendliness to the young ambassador. Quilaco Yupanqui and his companions, accompanied by the porters who were carrying the magnificent gifts to be presented to Huascar, stepped out on the Antisuyo road on their dangerous mission.

They set forth under the stars with a skin of mist just beginning to shine on the valley floor. They crossed the Huaro Punco bridge, its woven floor suspended over the gully of the Tullu River, and emerged into the Rimac Pampa. To the north their road led up the steep pitch of Senca, "the Ridge"; from this point looking off to the left they could see a massive terrace shoring up the steep slope. Numerous villas on it, stuccoed and richly painted, looked down on the city; this terrace had once supported a well-cared-for potato patch belonging to Urcon, that former coemperor who had been hunted down and destroyed by Pachacuti in the tumultuous days of the Chanca war. Its fine soil had been carried in from a distance, and from this origin it had acquired its name *Allpa Suntu*, "Soil Heap." This airy suburban slope of the city, raised up on multiple terraces like giant steps, was, because of its view overlooking the city, one of the more desirable sections. Because of the many lovely bushes which had been planted there, it was sometimes referred to as Cantut Pata, "Terraces of the *Cantut* Flower."

The Antisuyo road climbed up through this suburb; parts of the road were laid out along terrace tops and other parts in neatly worked stone stairs winding up through the terrace walls. This whole area along the face of Senca had belonged in the days of the founding of the city to the Hualla Indians, and in fact the cave from which they as a nation had originally emerged was located in the steep and narrow Tullu gorge that cut down between Sacsahuaman and Senca. Their long-ago *chacras* had by now totally disappeared under the Inca masonry and terracing; that humble and bucolic yesterday could hardly be conceived by the imperial Incas of this later day. Echoes of the early skirmishes which had affrighted these slopes and brought the Inca nation into existence were only weakly heard now by the contemplative son of the Capac Inca. The deeds of that day, however, were told with a mighty difference by the Hualla *ayllu* still in existence.

At the summit of the steep climb just off the right-hand side of the road was Queancalla, "Pus Cliff," on which stood the four eastern sun pillars of the city, black in silhouette against the pale lemon dawn. Silence was all around except for the shuffling of quail in the grass, the panting of the heavily laden porters in the group, and the quiet crunch of gravel under the thoughtful feet of the ambassadors.

Once up on the rolling *puna* movement was faster. The little party came first to Illacamarca, the famous guard station on this road. The visitor today knows it as a ruined site called Puca Pucara, a strong place on a low rock with a splendid view eastward to the Ausangate massif. It is surrounded with alpine meadows which were called in those days Yuncaypampa, dry in the wintertime and showing only as the most modest part of its potential floral loveliness the unassuming yellow lady's-slippers which the traveler today indeed scarcely notices. In the spring the rains bring the *punas* alive with masses of flowers which make gay the valley of the pleasant Cachimayo flowing past the small fortress.

The road passes under the guardhouse and crosses the shallow Yuncaypampa Valley to drop over the next low saddle into the basin of Chita. But just before crossing the stream, one could look up the draw to the left to the site of Tambomachay, "Den of the Tambos," a spot famous in Inca history. Here a source of wonderfully clear water welling out of the slope had been enclosed in a tasteful masonry façade by the great Pachacuti. The waters of the spring fell over a green diorite lip into one basin and thence into another. Together they were called Quinua Pucyo. Two terraces, a parapet, and numerous niches for sacred objects completed the arrangement. It was an artful and splendid way of reverencing the *huaca* of these waters and, although today it stands in partial ruins, it is still imposing. Nearby in the same secluded glen was a hunting lodge where the same great emperor passed in revels the first day of his journey whenever he went to the Yucay country.

But the true import of this spot could only be appreciated by an Inca thoroughly steeped in the traditions of his caste. The highlands on the left of which flowed the pure waters were called Sapi, the "Root" or "Origin." It was here that the great Pachacuti had received the vision and that promise which not only had rescued the Incas from ignoble defeat but cast them in the role of world conquerors. The spring in which he had gazed to behold the vision could therefore rightly be called Viracocha Pucyo, "the Lord's Fountain." On that memorable day the true greatness of Cuzco had been born. The magic mirror which Pachacuti drew out of that spring was reputed to have been placed therein by Viracocha. In it all wisdom was reflected and the future clearly seen. These ambassadors from the north would gladly have read in it or on the surface of the pool the outcome of their present mission, for fear must have oppressed their hearts. But if they had seen that the journey which they were making would mark the beginning of the end of the great empire which was theirs, they would not in any case have believed it. Man does not believe what is contrary to his own interest. So the fateful heralds, having presented their credentials to the officer at Illacamarca, continued their way on up through the *huaylla* or "mountain pasture," as we might translate it, land that could not be farmed but which could be usefully grazed.

The plateau countryside through which Quilaco Yupanqui's party was then passing was filled with wide and wonderful vistas opening up everywhere. Chitapampa itself was rolling basinland intensively farmed and adorned with neat terraces on most of the surrounding hillsides. The word *chiu* means "a nursling llama which has lost its mother," a maverick; appropriately the *punas* round about were covered with vast herds of llamas belonging to the Incas and which were the source of much of their wealth. In fact the area was one of the most famous pasturegrounds in Cuzcoquiti. The placid lake of Quihuipay lay just over the swales to the north, its shores much frequented by the imperial herds whose gentle comings and goings in their drifting over the face of the land were like the shadows of clouds. In the damp hollows of the higher hills grew the *cuchuchu*, a wild and abundant plant whose roots were eaten by lonely llama herders and the busy partridge.

The road now led through several settlements and at one point passed the favorite villa and estate of Pachacuti's *coya*; here her mummy was still entertained on certain occasions to indulge her in her former delights and to receive her yearly income. Passing the villa, the party of

217

ambassadors and their porters stopped to perform the *mocha*, plucking a hair of the eyebrow and blowing it with kisses towards the *huaca*.

From here the way was downhill into the deep trench of the Vilcañota.

In the palace at Calca, Huascar was contemptuously awaiting the arrival of Atauhuallpa's messengers. For the constant feasts and drinking bouts which were always a part of the imperial way of life he had selected certain companions whose loyalties to *ayllu* and *panaca* were not so ardent as to cause him concern and whose easy ways earned them the name of *puccochicuk*, "the fat ones, the feasters." Some were half brothers who had survived his tirades and proscriptions; others were from Lower Cuzco families. Huascar's face was now set implacably against the Cuzcos of the Upper moiety; therefore their menfolk, formerly the greatest lords of Cuzco, now walked obsequiously behind his litter never forgetting those of their number who had already been dispatched because of some informer's whispered word. Their *pallas* remained in the background as much as possible, and their *ñustas* were no longer so arrogant in their beauty and high connections. The revolution which Huascar had wrought among the Inca people, overturning their whole social structure, almost reversing it in fact, was consuming that people's strength. The energies formerly devoted to maintaining the empire were now needed simply to survive the Byzantine snares hidden in their paths.

The rigor with which the Incas were treated in Cuzco was matched by Huascar's cruelty in the provinces. Inca rule abroad had never been mild, for only terror served them in keeping the defeated down; nevertheless it had been predictable. Now it became something of whim. A lovely *aclla* from the valley of Chincha down on the shores of the Pacific who had been selected for Huascar's harem was found to have been seduced by one of the local *curacas*. The Inca *huchacamayoc* or "inquisitor" summoned every *curaca* in the area and all of their sons over ten years old, marched them twenty-five miles through the desert to a high rock of punishment in the coastal sierra, and had the lot hurled to their deaths below.

When Quilaco Yupanqui was finally ushered into Huascar's pres-

218

ence at the end of his journey, he must have been aware of these and similar stories. In Cuzco he had surely been able to sense the bitter humiliation of the Capac Incas of the Upper moiety. And in such a world of frightfulness an ambassador's life was far less certain than the life of a warrior in the most atrocious press of battle. Quilaco Yupanqui indeed had cause to fear.

According to court etiquette, Quilaco and his fellows had put burdens on their backs on passing the last guard station of the Chinchaysuyo road. These burdens they had carried with them until now as tokens of their subjugation. And as they were finally ushered backward into the imperial presence, they removed their sandals in a final token of obeisance.

"*Sapay Inca Ya!*" or "Hail, unique Inca!" greeted Quilaco Yupanqui, bowing to the ground after blowing kisses at the emperor seated in front of him and waving his open right hand at him in the approved fashion. "*Intip churi, huacchac coyac*" or "Child of the Sun, most generous," he enunciated sententiously the parts of the titulary, ending again with "*Sapay Capac Apu Ya!*" or "Hail, only emperor!"

Huascar was seated in state on a low golden stool surrounded by the favorite women who held over his head the feather canopy or *achihua*, waved fly whisks at him, and held jars of *akha* which they continually offered him in gold cups. Two of the most beautiful of the younger ones held in front of him a long diaphanous towel so that his subjects saw him only as a shadowy figure through it. His latest intimate, Roca Inca, stood beside him.

Directly out of this interview in Calca was to come the stupendous fall of the Inca people, compounded of total division, supreme hatred, immense slaughter, and a foreigner's opportunity. The traveler looking about him today in the wide and pleasant square in Calca sees Inca walls much in evidence but finds it impossible to feel the fatefulness of that moment for later history. *Calca* means "a stony place." Peruvian history was to bruise its feet forever on these stones.

Quilaco Yupanqui offered once again to the emperor Atauhuallpa's assurances of fidelity and then turned to display before him the exceedingly rich gifts he had brought, not only of gold and silver but of priceless *cumpi* garments, the weaving of which had taken many lifetimes in the far north. It was a regal gesture and offered accommodation. Incited by Roca Inca and without even deigning to answer the ambassador, Huascar ordered the rich gifts hurled into the log fire burning nearby. This shock was great, but the cup of horror welled over when he ordered the mutilation and slow death of some of the members of the embassy standing stricken before him. Quilaco was spared to carry to Atauhuallpa with one or two other survivors the full impact of this unbelievable humiliation. These who were allowed to live had their garments cut off at the waist, had women's combs and pots of cosmetics thrust into their hands, and then, exposed to the ridicule of all, were hurled out of the royal presence. This obloquy was accompanied by the furious demand that Atauhuallpa appear in person.

Those of the embassy who had been killed were Incas. Those mutilated were Incas also, but in the public degradation of Quilaco himself, Atauhuallpa, who was the most renowned of all living Inca warriors, had personally been humiliated. Over this stony way there was no way back either for Huascar or for Atauhuallpa. The contemning and violent spirit of the Incas had at last evoked its nemesis.

The small and broken party, isolated, pointed at, and mocked all the way back over the gigantic downs of Pachatusan, returned to Cuzco. That city hushed and caught its breath at their ludicrous and pathetic arrival. Rahua Ocllo and the *coya* again gave them as much shelter as was compatible with their own safety until finally permission was received from Huascar that they might leave. Return word from Atauhuallpa to Huascar would next arrive on the point of a lance.

The Incas of Cuzco began to whisper to each other that Huayna Capac would return to rule them. Chuqui Huipa, the *coya*, retired even more into herself, indulged more than ever in the narcotic peace of coca-chewing, played interminably with her green parrots, and wondered not a little about the wide world over which she reigned. At least one of the ambassadors killed—like her husband who ordered the killing—had been a brother of hers.

ELQVARTOEDADDEINS
AVCARVNA

aucapachaurna

pucara

THE BARE HILL against which the city of Cuzco nestled was known as Sacsahuaman, "Speckled Hawk." It dominates the city, a great bleak headland looking eastward to those parts of the world called *intip lloc-sina*, "the place where the sun springs up." Even while the city lay cold and darkling below it, Sacsahuaman swam in light and was therefore a hill beloved of the *huaca* of dawn. No more logical place, therefore, could have been conceived as a site for the House of the Sun, an edifice begun in the days of Pachacuti and still in the process of completion in the days of Huascar. In our literature the House of the Sun, or *Intihuasi*, is commonly though erroneously referred to by the name of the hill on which it stood, Sacsahuaman.

The wreckage of this edifice of the Incas is one of Peru's major historic tragedies. "That work was conceived on such a majestic scale," said Cieza de León writing soon after 1550, "that even if their monarchy should have lasted to the present, it would still not have been finished." The figure he gives for the labor force engaged on it, twenty thousand men, is probably close to the truth. Four thousand of these prized the great blocks out of the Huayrancallay quarries nearby, while six thousand dragged them on log rollers and sledges to the site. The remainder were engaged in assembling logs, cutting poles, twining and repairing rope and cable, building earth mounds against the wall faces, and, finally, cutting and grinding the stones *in situ*. Seventy-five years of intermittent work, organized with deadly precision by the Inca lords, had brought the site almost to completion. It took the Spaniards far less time to dismantle it. Only eight years after Spanish depredations began, the *cabildo* of Cuzco became so alarmed at the little that was left of the structure—which was being used as a quarry for the building of Spanish Cuzco—that it prohibited further raids on the site. But that original vandalism was followed by centuries of treasure hunters who, in the years since, have grubbed out the site and scattered the remainder of its foundations. Only the great outer parapets remain intact enough to publish to the world the sinister power of the lords of Cuzco. They, at least, seem imperishable. "To set the base, they excavated down to the very rock," added Cieza; "this they did so well that the foundations will remain as long as the world shall last."

The *Intihuasi* was the *pucara* or "fortress of refuge" for Cuzco and stood on the peak and edge of Sacsahuaman, its back esplanades looking directly down into the city. Massive walls girdled it all around, but the side which looked away from Cuzco was of incredible strength—huge sharp cusps like saw teeth jutted out onto the plateau so that for an attacking force there was no escape from flanking fire. The triple circumvallation is typical of all Peruvian *pucaras*, but the masonry of the three superincumbent walls, one terraced back onto another, is probably unique in the world, the fitted irregular blocks being the largest in all military architecture. No engine however cyclopean itself could ever have breached those defenses. Each of the three walls bore the name of one of the great *cancha* areas down in the city below, Cassana, Hatuncancha, and Pucamarca, the most important spring nearby was named Calispucyo after the fountain in the city below, and the paradeground which the great walls overlooked was Chuquipampa, named after the open space outside the walls of Coricancha. *Intihuasi* thus was meant to be a spiritual distillation of the city of Cuzco below.

Inside the vast area were three towers painted with strong and satisfying colors, the center one being in reality a palace. This one was Moyomarca, "the Round Tower," given over to the emperor whenever he chose to hold court here, a massive and beautifully thatched castle, filled with private apartments and even provided with its own pressure-piped water supply led in from underground. It stood in the center of a great square *cancha* walled and terraced up with apartments for the royal women; it had areas for the brewing and storage of *akha*, esplanades with wonderful vistas, royal baths, and vast storerooms for Cuzco's treasures, objects of gold and silver plate, rare textiles in great abundance, the state litters, and the imperial regalia. The two other towers were higher; they were square and housed the troops who acted as a permanent garrison. Their purpose was purely military. Labyrinthine stone galleries underground connected all three tower areas. The whole was under a praetorian *sayapayac*, a Capac Inca closely related to and trusted by the emperor. His office was obviously crucial, for he controlled both the state treasury and the state arsenal. Under him was a small elite group of Inca knights, while the bulk of the forces were Cañar and Chachapoya warriors supplied from the *mitmac* population in the valley. The barracks they inhabited probably adjoined the armory, a series of hidden and interconnected rooms piled to the ceilings with slings, slingstones, quilted armor, reed and metal helmets, bows, arrows, javelins, shields, war clubs, and war hatchets of all descriptions. The Spanish conquerors estimated that *Intihuasi* could house ten thousand inhabitants in time of siege.

This, then, was Cuzco's *pucara*. Enough has been said here to reveal a very important feature about this fortress-city. Although it was built to stand as a place of refuge for Cuzco's people in the case of a sudden collapse of the imperial defenses—for such was the function of a traditional Peruvian *pucara*—in actuality it served the purpose of a standing threat to the Inca lords themselves. This conclusion is inescapable to one who studies both the site and the history of the last reign. Adding weight to this argument is the proximity of Collcampata, the site to which Huascar had moved his residence in the second part of his reign. Collcampata was just under the eastern ramparts. In case of need Huascar could have escaped an enraged Inca people into the safety of the *pucara* via the short steep climb at his back door. All the men and women of the Capac Ayllu carried in their veins the blood of the sun-god and were thus in theory freely privileged, but whenever they cast their eyes up from the city streets and plazas, they beheld displayed upon Sacsahuaman the seal of their subservience. Those perilous walls and those burly towers cautioned them daily to learn to love their poorly concealed slavery.

Across the leveled paradeground fronting on the *Intihuasi* could be seen one of Cuzco's greatest *huacas*, an immense rock outcrop of a curiously striated roundness. This spot was called in the popular parlance Suchona, "the Sliding Place," for those who were playfully inclined could sit and slide down in the smooth grooves of the rock. The whole complex was clearly holy, for it had been surrounded by a masonry parapet while various portions of the rock were carved out in the geometric and abstract fashion common to the Incas. On the rounded top was the Sahuacurinca, a *huaca* marked by inset steplike ledges marvelously broad and shallow. Today it is called the Throne of the Inca, and indeed, according to Cobo, it was used for just that purpose. In other words, it was a gigantic *usno*, although we are ignorant of what special ceremonies were carried on there. The probability is that the emperor watched military reviews from this elevated spot.

On the far side of the hill of the Suchona was another leveled space, amphitheatrically enclosed, with the sacred spring Calispucyo on the far side, and terraced up behind that a villa of Huascar's grandfather, Topa Inca. This whole area is indeed a fairyland of *huacas* and should be visited by every traveler who wishes to understand the Inca idea of the sacred. Whichever way one turns here, one sees a fantastic assemblage of broken and wierdly shaped blue rocks of all sizes, some honeycombed with natural passageways and fissures, but all of them with artificial cutouts pockmarking the surfaces. The sacred source of Calispucyo was used in the knighting ceremonies; it is probably marked by that house whose complex walls still stand on the edge of a grassy flat heavily mired with seepage from many springs. Here in these clear waters and in these restricted tanks the young boys being inducted into Inca manhood bathed, and from these basins were dipped waters reserved for the emperor's household, for the water was very holy.

Back of this area the land rose to the gibbous shoulders of Sapi, "the Root," already mentioned. Out of this mountain-mass came the river of the same name. On the summit was the stone of great sanctity named

Quisco which was the petrified body of the ancestor of all members of the Antasaya *ayllu*. The Antasayas indeed claimed to have founded Inca Cuzco and so felt that they could rightfully look upon their *huaca* as "the root" or origin of the city. In another avatar Quisco was conceived to have been the root of a quinoa plant which had been transformed into stone and which also received splendid sacrifices. It was popularly held that the life of the city of Cuzco was maintained only so long as this root was nurtured and grew.

It was this whole mysterious backland, so filled with evidences of primordial activities congealed now into hard stone, which had in the first instance given Cuzco its peculiar sanctity and made it into the central point of an empire. Besides, Sacsahuaman and its area strategically commanded the greatest road of the Peruvian sierra. Thus the logistics of travel, the heightened apprehension of *huaca*, and the fierce ambition of a tough mountain people had combined at this spot to evoke a truly imperial fortress city.

The man who conceived and planned the site in the days of Pachacuti was named Huallpa Rimachi Inca. His name deserves to be remembered as one of the world's master builders. Three other great engineers followed him, and their names too are recorded, but his was the Promethean touch.

ELOTABO CAPITAN
APOCAMACINGA

IN THE VERY CENTER of the Inca vocabulary was the word for war, *auccay*. It tells much about this people that the simple verb "to fight" had the meaning also "to enjoy oneself with the enemy, to play games." A Spaniard who knew them most intimately said of them, "In the days of the Incas there were more Indians solely engaged in war or stationed in fortresses on the frontiers than there are today who pay us tribute."

A true Inca was a man who longed for war, trained for it, was enduring on the long road and swift as a hawk in pursuit, boasted interminably about it, underwent hardships with dignity, reveled in the fray, and utterly disdained death in battle. He was not, however, a mere brute but a person of invention and stratagems, resourceful in recovering from setbacks, and never without a plan. He was always a dangerous antagonist.

To grasp the significance of war in Inca culture we have only to recall the investiture of the youth with his full Inca manhood in the *huarachicoy*. In this ceremony, which began the calendrical year, fleetness of foot, endurance of pain and exposure, obedience to elders, ability to drink interminably of *akha*, reverence for the great warriors of the past, and loyalty to the state were all significantly featured. The young knight took a new name because he was now, in fact, a new and a thoroughly proved person. The earplugs served as the sign of his status, bespeaking his Incahood; the sign of his vocation for war was the sling given to him by his *ayllu* elders. His feathered war bonnet crowned him with manly elegance.

He hoped for an assignment in the field and generally got one. He might be stationed in one of the provinces as an officer who organized

226

and trained the local militia. When and if this contingent were called up, it was he who brought it into the field behind its local *curaca*. Or he might be assigned as the equerry to some greater warrior, or even taken into that select bodyguard which surrounded the emperor; he might be assigned to one of the frontier garrisons, a lonely, difficult, and dangerous duty, or, more immediately, sent as a replacement to one of the Inca regiments on active campaign. Above all things he desired to prove himself either in close combat or in the storming of an enemy *pucara*. He preferred to fight, like the puma, among the rocks and grasslands of the *sallca*, but if his duty took him into the close thickets of upper Amazonia and the arrowy ambushes of the Chunchos, for this task, too, his courage was equal.

Interestingly enough, he had no word as such for "army." Instead he used the word for the moiety or tribal "division," the *suyu*, or more simply and inclusively he could speak of "the soldiers." The nucleus of the army was always two "divisions" of Incas, these two being the fighting men of Upper and of Lower Cuzco. These groups probably were composed mainly of the Hahua Incas or ordinary knights, the backbone of the Inca fighting machine, officered by Capac Incas. Probably these regiments were a thousand strong each. Around them were clustered the contingents from the subject peoples. Quechua was the language at every level of officers in the Inca camps.

The generalissimo of the army was the *aucacunap apu*, or "chief of soldiers." He was himself always of the Upper Cuzco moiety and was naturally a Capac Inca. Lower Cuzco was represented in this high command by the *aucacta yachachik apu* or "chief in charge of organizing the army," perhaps better translated as chief of staff, a position of importance equal almost to that of generalissimo. Commanding the two Inca *suyus* were the colonels or *huaminca pusariquen apu*, "officers commanding the veterans," each belonging to the Inca moiety which he commanded, and each expected to extract from the Incas under him their utmost in military skill and effort.

The Inca army was thus simply the caste structure transferred to the battlefield. This system naturally projected into the politics of the army command all of the traditional hostility between the two moieties.

The Inca army in a sense was therefore really two armies in alliance, traveling side by side but so competitive in spirit that there seem to have arisen occasions when they were unconcerned about each other's fate. They traveled and camped separately, sometimes widely apart, no doubt to prevent altercations. The imposition of the two general officers over this dual structure only partially solved the problem of integration, for the two generals themselves represented the two moieties. Lack of co-operation thus seems to have been endemic in the Inca army and to have led occasionally to such disasters as that which befell Huascar's early Chachapoya campaign under Chuqui Huaman. Full integration could only be achieved when the *aucacunap apu* was the emperor himself.

The lack of a specific word for "army" in the Inca tongue thus allows us to discover the one weakness of the Inca as a fighting man; his allegiance was ambivalently poised between two poles. On the one hand, he fought for the state, represented by the emperor and by the myth of the solar sonship of all Incas; on the other, he still had to defend the prestige of his own quasi-tribal *suyu*. It is probable that the disintegration of Huascar's troops in the War of the Two Brothers owed something to this unresolved tension.

Inasmuch as the great army had to stand muster in the field at every dawn, it was at such times under the immediate supervision of a sergeant major, a *hinantin aucacta suyuchak apu*, a "chief who assigns all the contingents to their proper stations," and he in turn had a subordinate sergeant to aid him. There was also his compeer and alter ego, the officer in charge of night billets and stations, the *sericac*.

The captains or *aucakpussak*, "leaders of soldiers," were the all-duty junior officers, training levies of subject Indians, officering intelligence patrols, *chapatiyak*, or garrisoning frontier posts. They carried larger shields than the rest as a sign of their office. It is presumed that the Hahua Inca knight had to earn this rank, whereas a young knight of the Capac Incas would in all probability be eligible for the rank immediately upon receiving the earplugs. This, however, is speculation.

The most colorful military spectacle of all came at the inception of a campaign, after the call to arms, the *caparisca*, had gone out. A review

of the troops, *yuptiracuy*, was held. Here the warriors called up were
assembled in their *ayllus*, each one equipped with his favored weapon;
they were led by their own *curaca* but operated under the superior
guidance of an Inca veteran or *huaminca*. The nucleus of the army
was, of course, the two Inca divisions in which each man was equipped
with the national sling at the use of which he was extremely dexterous.
Besides this weapon, for close fighting he carried either the *champi*,
the studded war club used for the crushing of skulls, or the javelin,
chuqui. Some also carried the halberd, the *yauri*, which could be used
for striking, stabbing, or hooking. On his head the Inca warrior wore
a bowl-shaped helmet made of plaited reeds, the *passana*, almost as
hard as tempered steel, and he carried a small square parrying shield
which was heraldically painted and from which hung an apron of colored cloth, feathers, or tassels. With face paint added and glittering
medals slung from his neck he was now *huallparicuscca*, "splendidly
adorned for war." He conceived of himself as a great bird of prey, a
raptor swift and savage. His friend he called a "hawk companion," his
war club was a "hawk club," when he raced after the enemy he "flew."
In rushing at the waiting enemy, he "swooped," *pahuapuy*. The word
for hawk, *huaman*, was the word he most commonly associated with
war, and it was a personal name he himself was always proud to wear.

The Inca warrior took special delight in his ability to storm the
enemy's *pucara* successfully, and his annals were replete with stories
of great sieges and the many inventions and sleights by which they were
brought to successful conclusions. The siege was the *auccay intuy*, "the
war encirclement," and offered plentiful opportunities for acts of individual daring and display. The *chapa* or "spy" came first on the scene;
his was a singularly dangerous assignment, sliding in and out of rocks,
viewing from close at hand the enemy and his works, noting his water
supply, the number of his women, the weaknesses of his dispositions.
When the war cry suddenly shattered the hot air of the great gorges
("*Chaya! Chaya!*" or "At them! At them!"), when the great *cumpas*
or stones launched from the walls by the besieged came bounding
down the steep slopes, and when the slingstones splattered all about
in the dust or thudded into the cactus, then the Inca was living at his

highest. For this existence he was made. When finally his victory cry came—"*Haylli! Haylli!*"—then might the enemy well lose heart. The Quechua word used for crushing the enemy was the same word for breaking and flattening clods with blows of a stone hammer, *maruy*. Victory was *atircuy* and was total; it was the winning of the field, it was the loot, the heads taken, the women rounded up, and it included the triumph celebrated back in Cuzco. More than anything else, perhaps, it was the humiliation and insulting of the defeated. And it was understood that what the Inca left behind him after such a passage at arms was a *chinnik purum*, a "desert of desolation," marked only by the heaps of dead and the horrid din of the vultures.

Nothing points up the profound martial orientation of the Inca quite so well as his use of the verb *hayllircoy*, "to triumph over," for he used this word not only to describe the end of the battle but also the successful completion of the harvest in the field. Even as a farmer he did not so much "harvest" as "conquer" his fields.

Section 5. *The Road to War*

What the Incas of Cuzco were unwilling to face was the fact that there were Inca squadrons in the north which owed little or no allegiance to Cuzco. Under their leader or *sinchi*, Atauhuallpa, these hardened veterans who had campaigned on the northern frontiers with traditional Inca *élan*, still showed no desire ever to return to Cuzco. They were the remnants of that officer class that years before had gone north with Huayna Capac. The sons whom they were rearing and who were already fighting at their sides had been sired on non-Inca women of the conquered northern people. It was admittedly a dangerous situation that their warlikeness was being maintained, indeed even sharpened, while their allegiance to the Capac Ayllu and the household of the emperor was so rapidly melting away. Under the equator inchoate and hidden forces were forming a new tough, bastardized Inca nation, as yet only dimly aware of itself and its possible role in history.

The first signs had indeed appeared during the previous reign when the Lower Cuzco regiment, led by Misi, broke with the emperor, thereby threatening a dissolution of the state. This split had been quickly patched up in Quito, but it had created disturbances back in Cuzco. When Huascar ascended the throne, his first act had been, as we have seen, to destroy his father's executors, men of the Upper moiety. Then he had publicly renounced his inherited connections with the Upper group, thus in one blow depriving the hitherto untouchable Capac Incas of their prestige in Cuzco. Yet at the same time, as far as we know, he did not commit himself wholly to the Lower group, although he may have favored them somewhat. At any rate an undeclared war, long in preparing and ominous for the future, now existed between the two parts of the Inca nation. Huascar had completed his divorce from the Capac Incas when he threatened the removal and burial of the royal mummies, and while he did not carry out this intention, his open hostility to most of the *panacas* further frayed the ties that had bound Inca society together. This situation had an effect on the Cuzco Incas opposite to that which was taking place among the Quito Incas, namely, of further eroding their war spirit; some of his captains indeed defected to the north. Incas in Cuzco now gained their standing as much by success in flattery and acquiescence in evils as by exploits in the army. The fate of Chuqui Huaman was instructive to those who wished information on the mettle of the lords of Cuzco.

When Huascar returned to Cuzco, he had determined to bring matters between Cuzco and Quito to a head. He issued a peremptory call to all *curacas* and governors to come to Cuzco to swear fealty in person. Those who did not attend were to be declared *aucas* or "traitors" and hunted down. In this way he presumed to discover his hidden enemies. But his ill judgment went further, for he ordered an increase of the tyranny at home. Those magnates of the city even remotely suspected of being affected to Atauhuallpa's party were narrowly interrogated and harrassed, while the *coya* herself, along with the queen mother who made little effort to hide her dislike for her son, were bedeviled with accusations of treason and conspiracy.

From all parts of the empire the surprised and apprehensive magnates hurried down the roads to Cuzco. Urco Colla, the *curaca* of the Cañar Indians of Tumibamba, answered the call, no doubt bringing with him fresh alarms concerning Atauhuallpa's designs. *Curacas* from the coastal regions appeared. Their homage obtained, they returned as uneasily as they had come.

Atauhuallpa did not come, for, with the humiliation which had come to him as a result of the rejection of his embassy, he now realized that the die was indeed cast. What added to his decision thus openly to harden his position was the sudden and astounding presence on the coast of two of the bearded strangers who had been marooned there by Pizarro returning to Panama from his second voyage. These events were made more ominous by his dying father's prophecy that these beings were Viracochas and that much trouble was in store for the Incas because of them. In addition, the recent oracle delivered by the Apurimac *huaca* announcing the end of an aeon was known to Atauhuallpa and called for action on his part if it were not to be used adversely against him. Accordingly, he had declared himself *capac apu* or "emperor" of Quito and assumed there the royal *mascapaycha*. In this action was implied the degradation of the city of Cuzco from its eminent station of holiness, for up to that moment emperors held their high position only because they had been crowned in Cuzco. Now there were two Inca emperors. Atauhuallpa, however, made no overt move, hoping that Huascar would accept the irregular situation and allow him without contest thus to seize a place in the equatorial sun.

The jaws of the Cuzco dungeons now gaped wide for new raven. The infamous Sankahuaci daily gulped down new rations of victims, Incas both highly and lowly placed, for Huascar's reaction to the news from the north had been typically ferocious; in that outbreak of the terror the *coya* and her mother escaped execution only by a handbreadth.

232

Whoever of the party of his father's executors had survived was now slaughtered out of hand.

While these events lowered over Cuzco, Huascar was meeting with his inner council to formulate some action that would bring the traitor down. His sycophants were keen to support him on an anti-Atauhuallpa policy but cautioned that deceit and cunning would achieve that objective sooner than an outright attack. They advised that a glozing message advising Atauhuallpa of the possibility of accommodation be sent forthwith. The following men were the councilors: Tito Atauchi, Topa Atauchi, the notorious Inca Roca, Huaminca Atoc, Urco Huaranka, Huanca Auqui, Paucar Usno, Hahuapanti, and Topa Atau. All of them would die violently.

A compromise plan was evolved. Two of Huascar's trusted captains, with names appropriate to their mission, Huaminca Atoc, "Veteran Fox," and Hancu, "Muscle," were to depart for Tumibamba to make certain of the Cañar nation's loyalty to the government. They were to raise troops as they moved north in whatever provinces seemed most likely to them, but in any case they were to raise up the entire Cañar nation. The reputed explanation of their presence was to be that they were there to sacrifice to the shade of Huayna Capac in the great provincial city which he had so largely built. They took with them a statue of Inti, with the purpose in mind of drawing away from Atauhuallpa those Inca retainers who still held to their tribal loyalties, for Inti was the father of all Incas. It was considered unwise to stampede the Cañars, so crucial to Huascar's plans, into any action before they could be recemented in their obedience and organized into strong anti-Atauhuallpa forces. Therefore these two spies were to suborn them with promises and threats before the actual army appeared.

The plan was, in general, good; it allowed for many contingencies and was typically Inca in its use of subterfuge. Neither of the chosen Cuzco commanders, however, showed the requisite valor and skill against Atauhuallpa's Incas of Quito. And, what turned out to be the fatal miscalculation, they apparently took no Inca troops north with them, relying on contiguous provinces for their levies. Either sloth or overconfidence was dictating to the Incas of Cuzco their own destruction.

233

SECTION 6. *Topa Atauhuallpa, Founder Prince*

THAT TOPA ATAUHUALLPA stands out in Inca history as one of their most notable figures is indisputable. His name meant Honorable Fortunate Turkey Cock, and his early and strenuous career had already proved this title a good augury. In contrast to his brother Huascar, whose genius for dividing and weakening his people was well known, Atauhuallpa felt that he represented traditional Inca valor and dignity. His blood was as royal as was Huascar's in the male line; his mother had been his father's cousin and belonged to the Upper Cuzco *panaca* of Pachacuti. He was a very great nobleman, and, what was more, a proved *sinchi*, or "war leader." At his coronation he took as his *huaoqui* a spirit whom he prophetically called Ticci Capac, "Prince of the Foundations," implying in this action that he, Atauhuallpa, was a second Pachacuti who, as all knew, had begun a new aeon. Atauhuallpa would again renew the Inca world, reaching down into its basements for the ancient virtues and refreshing the Incas in the fires of conflict, purging their dross and rededicating them.

The Incas who had stayed with him or defected to him since the death of his father were few in numbers, but in the short time that history was now to provide for them they would cast a spell of fear and darkness over the whole Peruvian world. And that ability, of course, was the mark of the Inca. The same can in no way be said of Huascar's captains whose names were to mean only misfortune and defeat.

Atauhuallpa seems to have set up the customary moiety system of command, with the two generals Challcochima and Quizquiz commanding Upper and Lower regiments, respectively. In filling up these commands Atauhuallpa must have created a new group of Hahua Incas to officer these two cadres and to command what few provincial recruits he could count on. The names of these northern Incas and bits of the histories are known and will be traced more fully later: there was Rumiñaui, of the most evil reputation and in the end a brutal coward; there were Huallpa Yucra, Una Chullo, and Ucumari, "the Bear," who were among the best known. Quilaco Yupanqui, the former ambassador, was also among the leading officers. He was to be seriously wounded in the vicious fighting around Jauja but would survive to become a Christian for the few remaining years of his life.

It is probable that only a few of those men were of legitimate Inca blood, and perhaps even fewer belonged to the Capac Ayllu. But in terms of the Inca ethic they were pure, for they shared a common hunger for war. The capacity of these men for the most revolting atrocities seems to us to be sheer sadism, but it is more probable that it was for them a learned virtue. Indeed nothing pleasant is known of any of them.

It was the Capac Incas under Huascar who failed in violence, the true test of Incahood.

SECTION 7. *First News from the Front*

THE WAR OF THE TWO BROTHERS began dramatically. Before Atoc and Hancu had arrived in Tumibamba, the Cañars of that city had invited Atauhuallpa to discuss with them their possible adherence to his cause. They had then treacherously seized him and held him incommunicado pending the arrival of the two Cuzco commissars. But these two arrived just in time to learn of Atauhuallpa's thrilling escape from prison, his sole confederate being the woman who brought him his food. The year was 1530.

Atoc had thereupon set about raising a small army from the Cañars and *mitmacs* in the area. The recent action of the Cañars, by earning for them the eternal hatred of Atauhuallpa, had irrevocably committed them to Huascar's cause. With this scratch group and with a few Inca reinforcements which had just arrived Atoc then won an initial skirmish, but this news in Cuzco was almost immediately followed by a succeeding advice of the army's defeat in battle at Ambato; the disaster was total, for both of Huascar's commanders were reported captured. It was known some time later that terrible tortures had been inflicted upon Atoc and Hancu and that their skulls had been made into drinking vessels for the now exultant Atauhuallpa.

Huascar responded to this setback by appointing Huanca Auqui, one of his favorite brothers, to the rank of general. This unfortunate appointment brought to the fore a man ill equipped to face the storm that was about to roll out of the north. He had been campaigning out in the Bracamoro montaña without any spectacular success when he was summarily recalled and put in charge of some new contingents sent north, with instructions to use in addition whatever Cañar regiments he could still recruit. Under him were placed Hahuapanti and Paca Mayta, two who would remain on his staff till the end. To mark the new appointment, Huanca Auqui was granted the signal honor of being carried about in a litter. It was assumed that this action was all that was needed to insure his success.

When the great battle was fought, the posts concerning it could scarcely be believed in Cuzco. Tumibamba, anchor of Inca power in the north and one of the most beautiful of Inca cities, had not only fallen, it had been destroyed stone by stone. The Cañars not killed in the battle at the gates had been later assembled and massacred, men, women, and children, in one of history's great orgies of blood. Huanca Auqui and his shattered few were in full retreat south.

Huascar proclaimed an *itu*, the solemn and silent two-day supplication of a city in distress, performed only on such extraordinary occasions. At last the Incas squarely had to face the fact that they had become a radically divided people and therefore a weakened one. And the feeling of weakness was new to the Incas.

Section 8.

Gods Before Generals

As THE FLOOD WATERS of defeat rose inexorably around Cuzco, the lords of that city turned away from the traditional Inca policy of resting the arbitrament of their destiny primarily on their regiments to one of reliance on the heavens. This development is not to be understood as saying that their history of imperial conquest had been unrelated to their sense of the divine. The organization of the powers of *huaca* and the centralization of the heavens under Viracocha had gone hand in hand with their conquests; deity was necessary to them, but deity had never before dictated their policy.

Now their policy, based on the legitimacy of an emperor crowned in the holy city, was demonstrably failing. Instead of sharpening their martial skills or reviewing the inadequacy of their commanders and fighting men or deposing their emperor, they turned wholly to their gods. For the first time in their history, on the eve of their great national disaster, they became a truly religious people, devout because they were indecisive, humbled because of loss of their self-respect, fearful for having lost confidence in their arms.

To the great oracles of the empire Huascar sent urgent messages entreating from them the signs of the future. The two greatest oracles, that at Pachacamac on the coast and that at Porcon in the central sierra, returned hopeful answers which, even as they were received in Cuzco, were overturned by equally swift news of fresh disasters in the field. To raise the regiments which were being so urgently requested by the commanders on the collapsing northern front the great magnates from those parts of the empire still free of war were now called to Cuzco

237

and ordered to provide fresh levies. These were forthcoming because of the habit formed after years of obedience to the principle of Cuzco legitimacy. But they were also brought to Cuzco for perhaps the equally cogent reason that they might not fall into the power of Atauhuallpa's advancing armies and thereby accrue as spoils to the enemy.

The case of Chucuito, a regional capital on the shores of Lake Titicaca, is instructive in this regard. A man called Vilca Cutipa had been appointed *curaca* of the people of this area by Huascar's father and then had been taken north with him to Ecuador. For the long drawn-out blood bath there Vilca Cutipa had provided six thousand warriors from his province. Of that number only one thousand lived to see their homes again. In spite of this fantastic depletion of their manpower, Vilca Cutipa's people still had to provide labor gangs for the continuous building going on in Cuzco. And now Huascar was demanding another muster of their men to fling into the war with Atauhuallpa. With the most strenuous efforts Vilca Cutipa was able to raise two thousand more men of whom one-half were to be quickly destroyed. Night settles rapidly on the altiplano.

The city of Cuzco overnight became an entrepôt for piecemeal groups of warriors from many nations moving through the area; they were assembled and equipped up on the flats of Sacsahuaman and then, once formed into larger groups, were moved swiftly up the Chinchay-suyo road under Inca officers. These officers were in some cases Incas with little training in battle or bivouac, young men brought up to be peacocks in the court rather than eagles in the field.

The cause of the frightened city was further hurt when Huascar, incensed at the news of a particularly serious reverse, ordered women's clothing, combs, and pots of rouge sent to his wretched generalissimo. This insult to Huanca Auqui's manhood was an incomprehensible action, for he was not at the same time cashiered. Even while publicly condemned as a coward, he retained something of his command. He continued for a short while to feed replacements from Cuzco into the maw of war.

In the understanding of the lords of Cuzco one paramount fact had at last to be admitted—a situation even more impressive than the failure

238

of their command. This fact was the withdrawal of Viracocha's support from the empire.

It was known that the *suncasapa*, "the bearded ones," had landed on the coast behind Atauhuallpa's forces. It seemed incomprehensible that they could be other than the *huaminca hayhuaypanti* of distant myth, the angelic warriors of Viracocha, but whether they came to bring the Inca empire to an end or to give it support in its agony was unclear. That terrible prophecy that was supposed to have pointed to Huascar as the twelfth and last emperor was, of course, never mentioned in Cuzco, but it was known to all and it continued surreptitiously to guide the people's thoughts. Huascar's councilors urged their now thoroughly distraught and vacillating emperor to make some attempt to discover the truth about these intruders into Tahuantinsuyo, and they finally prevailed upon him to dispatch an embassy down to the coast to ask their aid. It is perhaps significant of the suspicion which Huascar held toward his own people that he sent along with a Capac Inca of his court the *curaca* of the *Huánucos*, a once independent line of kings in the central *sallca*. This great provincial noble, Huaman Mallqui, had only recently been summoned to court in the convocation of *curacas*; he was now sent off with an Inca companion via the coast road to seek out the *suncasapa* and request their support. They were to be treated as gods and offered gold. It was at the end of summer of the year 1531 when this embassy set out. It was indeed able to locate Pizarro and his men, but the rapid pace of subsequent events rendered it fruitless and it never returned an answer to Cuzco.

In the fainter hope that some change in the army command might also be of benefit, the favorite Huanca Auqui was at last relieved of command and Mayca Yupanqui was sent north to replace him. But the number of capable men left among the Incas had now been reduced by attrition in the northern theater of war, by previous imprisonments and executions in Cuzco, and by sheer failure of nerve. Mayca Yupanqui was to prove no more able in command than his predecessor.

It was after the stunning defeat of the army at Yanamarca, contrary to the promises of the former oracles, that Huascar took a decisive step, not in his military posture nor as a civil administrator, but in his role

239

as arbiter of the imperial theology. He summoned to Cuzco posthaste all of the *huacas* of the empire still under his control and all of the chief wizards attached to their cults. Only Pachacamac was excused. Huascar had come to believe that an army in the field could be considered only a secondary resource. To reopen communication with Viracocha was now his sole preoccupation. The Creator had—for reasons unknown to Huascar but no doubt suspected by his people—turned his face away from his great imperial creation, Tahuantinsuyo. Direct appeal to him was known to be now unavailing. Lesser gods and *huacas* must be induced to intercede with him, adding their pleas to those of the gods of the Incas.

More than forty of the *huacas* from the provinces assembled for this curious confrontation. The Inca people, who had defeated those very *huacas* in the distant past and who had so often humiliated them since, now appeared before them as suppliants. On the day designated, when the *huacas* had all been assembled in a circle, each with its chief wizard nearby, the Inca forces in the north had fallen back to the Mantaro crossing and had there taken their stand. What perhaps no one knew or appreciated at the time was the fact that the cashiered Huanca Auqui had withdrawn from even that line along with some of his dispirited contingents. Thus Mayca Yupanqui guarded the bridge without a full complement of troops. Such a fatal division of the Inca forces on the line of battle appears to correspond to a division of the Capac Incas back in Cuzco.

It was an assemblage of the most exotic aspect which met in Rimac Pampa on the eastern edge of the city, and one in which an outsider unacquainted with Inca history would have found only an occasion for laughter. The *huacas* aligned in a circle were either shapeless lumps of stone, or stones which had been roughly carved out into unfinished geometric forms, or rough figures vaguely suggestive of human or animal forms. All were small and not so heavy that they could not be carried about in the hand or at least in litters. Those with recognizable forms were the *villcas*. Only the Inca people, their heads covered with their mantles, barefooted and penitent, could understand the true dignity of that dingy and mean-appearing circle of stones and stocks of wood.

To each one the appropriate sacrifices were made, and each was individually petitioned to carry the plight of the Inca folk to the Creator's ears, asking for his mercy and for victory over the rebels. Each *huaca* delivered its answer through its own priest and in its own way, some through fire, some through spiders, some through the falling of dried beans, and some through the veinings on the inflated lungs of sacrificed llamas. One and all assured Huascar, who personally stood among the stones, that they had learned of Viracocha's reviving interest in the cause of Cuzco and that a glorious victory would soon be announced from the Mantaro line.

Even as these signs of reassurance came from the ecstatic lips of the sorcerers, word came of the collapse of the Mantaro effort and the precipitate retreat of the shattered Inca army back to Cuzco.

Huascar's fury at this treason of the *huacas* knew no bounds. He addressed them, in a terrible tirade, as "lying tempters, rapacious thieves, insane devils," accused them of desiring the present outcome, and upbraided them with not doing their duty in bringing his pleas to the ears of the Creator. And he promised them his eternal enmity should the future deliver him from the immediate danger. The wizards who had interpreted the unfortunate prophecies were cruelly treated— some were probably killed on the spot—and the idols contemptuously abandoned. Once again there were left only the persistently deaf ears of Inti and Huanacauri to speak to.

All of the great Inca emperors from Mayta Capac on down had, whenever possible, mocked, persecuted, and diminished the *huacas* of their subject peoples. These *huacas* were now having their revenge. The Inca lords were at last aware that the unctuous oracles of the immediate past had been cunning traps into which they had fallen. They had believed them and acted on them. They had believed that the *huacas* were loyally supporting their cause in Viracocha's court, while in fact they were undermining Tahuantinsuyo. It was even possible that the presence of the *suncasapa* was a part of this widespread treachery of the Peruvian *huacas*.

It was a bleak prospect that faced the lords of Cuzco. With their army shattered at the Mantaro, the last line that could now be held was the Apurimac. To summon up the requisite levies would necessitate a last and a desperate demand upon the parts of the empire least capable of adequate aid, the distant south and the semiwild peoples of the montaña frontiers, none of them too reliable. A large portion of the Hahua Inca knights who resided in the Anta, Huatanay, and Vilcañota valleys had already perished in the mighty battles in the north, and the lands of the Collas and the Lupacas had sent almost their last men. The decision to squeeze the most distant parts of the empire was taken by the lords reluctantly, for they were not so besotted that they did not know that raw recruits were no match for Atauhuallpa's veterans. As a holding measure, Huanca Auqui, who was hovering indecisively around Vilcas with the last troops on station, was ordered to deliver a night attack on Atauhuallpa's forces in that provincial capital, but, typically, Huanca Auqui allowed his plans to become known and he was the one surprised and forced back to the Apurimac bridge. With him came Mayca Yupanqui and the other officers of his staff.

One single glimmer of light flickered in that night of fear. Huascar turned again to Huanacauri, the Inca's own war *huaca* and the only true custodian of victory. Fasts and mourning were decreed, and rich gifts of handsome young children were sent to the mountaintop, strangled, and buried at the feet of the ugly and powerful stone. At last Huanacauri deigned to issue an oracle to the effect that victory was assured if Huascar would in person command the Capac Incas. Huascar acceded to his councilors and gave orders for the crucial move out of Cuzco to be made under his personal direction.

SECTION 9. *The Last Review*

HUANCA AUQUI had been recalled from his command and had returned into the royal presence penitent and beseeching. Through some magic he had been able to restore himself in his brother's favor and was returned to his command at the Apurimac bridge along with some scratch contingents under his colonels Hahuapanti and Paca Mayta. The three of them joined up with Mayca Yuyanqui whose troops had now also fallen back to the bridge. With such inferior and demoralized troops they were ordered to deflect the enemy at that crossing, thus forcing him to fight farther upstream for the more difficult crossing of Cotapampa.

With the main force under Huascar went Inca Roca, Urco Huaranka, Titu Atauchi, Topa Atau, Paucar Usno, and a younger captain, Rampa Yupanqui. Apu Challco Yupanqui and Rupaca, the two leading priests, of necessity accompanied the army, for their auguries and sacrifices were essential to any success. This group formed the roster of the last Inca magnates, and of them only one was to acquit himself with honor.

We are already acquainted with Carmenca, "the Shoulder," that rounded mountain mass on the northwest of Cuzco over which came the Chinchaysuyo road. The road, paved and lined with planted trees, led over Carmenca's top and past Yahuira where the young knights received their breechclouts in the initiation rites. Here, as we know, Apu Yahuira, one of the Inca founders and the particular progenitor of the Maras *ayllu*, had been turned to stone, this event marking the spot as a *huaca*. Just beyond this point the road moved down to pass through a level place, stony and dry. A small group of dwellings called Quihuipay marked the spot where the memorable battle against the invading Chancas had been fought only some ninety years before. Quihuipay, which means "the Bend," is probably represented today by the hamlet of Poroy, not three miles from the city. This place was Yahuar Pampa, "the Field of Blood," as we stated, the high-water mark of Inca heroism. Because of its associations with victory against great odds as well as because of the near presence of the war-*huaca* of Yahuira, Yahuar Pampa was a place of good omen for the army that passed over its sacred dust. Farther on, at a place called Utcupampa or "Pitfield," the order was given to the host to assemble for review.

Tahuantinsuyo's last army was, if not the most formidable of her many armies, at any rate the most exotic in appearance. Seated in his palanquin, Huascar scanned the separate files of the fighting men of the many nations who had been drawn up beside their tents and arranged in their separate *ayllus* to acclaim him and to be counted. Many of these men, as has been said, represented the far southern and eastern parts of the empire—for little else was left to him.

243

The array was divided on this day into two army corps, the third being already on the Apurimac station under Huanca Auqui being held in readiness to threaten the enemy's rear if he should thrust onto the Cotapampa bridge. Rampa Yupanqui commanded the second army corps made of *ayllus* mainly from south of the Titicaca Basin, most of them Charcas from farther down the Bolivian plateau and some from distant Chile. The most remarkable were the half-naked forest groups of the Andes montaña who fought with exceptionally long *chonta*-wood bows and had a custom of eating their enemies. They were more splendid to contemplate than functional, however, for they shivered and weakened rapidly in the high altitudes where the battle was to be fought. The first army group was centered around the traditional cadres of Upper and Lower Cuzco, their numbers and their spirit much diminished but their pomp if anything increased. These two divisions were led by Titu Atauchi and Topa Atau, respectively, but both acting under Huascar as generalissimo. The knights of the Hahua Incas—tribes like the Papris, the Quechuas, the Mayos, and Chillquis, upon whom all Inca emperors since Pachacuti had depended for the dependable nucleus of their fighting men—were by now so depleted that they were conspicuous by their small numbers. The Cañar and Chachapoya *mitmacs* who lived close to Cuzco and whose younger men formed Huascar's personal guard were to be used for the van and rear of the first corps on the march.

Simply by lifting his eyes from that astounding assemblage of men before him, Huascar could look down the gentle meadows of the Cachimayo and far beyond to the quiet grandeur of Salcantay bearing snow fields on its brows as a queen wears her jewels. Salcantay was at that very moment looking down not only on the enemy's encampment just beyond the deep gorge of the Apurimac but upon Huanca Auqui's tattered squadrons drawn up to block them on the hither side of the river. Appropriate sacrifices were sent by swift ambassadors to the *huaca* of that mighty mountain that it might lend its support to the Capac Incas.

Nearer at hand was the rounded top of Churuncana where generals campaigning into the north always made their appeals to the Creator for victory. Accompanied by his council members who walked barefooted behind his *rampa*, Huascar was now carried up the bare slope. Priests from Coricancha came also and finally a group of small boys of about five years of age, elegantly dressed and jangling with golden and silver bangles. The boys had been selected out of the children's pound in the city below for their unblemished health and beauty, as the Creator would accept nothing but purity. Staggering drunkenly up the path, they had to be led by the hand for they had been plied with many cups of sacred *akha* to complete the festivity of their passing.

Near the top the emperor descended from his litter and in sign of abasement removed his sandals, all of his royal insignia, and placed a token burden on his back. Thus he humbly approached the stone on the bare summit in which resided the *huaca* of the place. All was quiet, except for the sudden shuffling sounds made by the lurching children, and the heavy breathing of the councilors and priests grouped nearby. Far below lay the encampment and out beyond that spot the fertile and agreeable plain of Anta; beyond towered the Andes, and beyond the Andes was the world.

The Incas who had assembled there waved kisses to the Creator and, plucking hairs from their eyebrows, blew them in the direction of the *huaca*. The emperor repeated his fervent appeal for victory and then offered the gifts he had brought. The boys were one by one led around the stone and then strangled by a priestly assistant. Shallow holes had meanwhile been opened up in the ground around the *huaca*. The workmen, who used only sharpened sticks for this sacred duty, trembled and grimaced with fear as they went about the work. Each child, wearing all his finery, was tumbled into a hole as soon as dead and instantly covered up; figurines of gold and silver were thrown into the graves with them to increase the richness of the offering. When the whole solemn *capac hucha* had been completed, the party respectfully withdrew, leaving the site to the cool airs of noontime, the yellowing *ichu*-grass all about, the small mounds of fresh earth, and the breath-taking view of the Peruvian *sallca*.

245

SECTION 10. *A Vigil of Women*

AT DAWN ON THE DAY before the emperor had set out from his city Chuqui Huipa, the *Coya*, had left her apartments clad in all her regalia. She was surrounded by her women and escorted by a small group of pages. Down the Street of the Sun the group proceeded decorously until it halted finally under the high walls of Coricancha. The *Coya* and those of her entourage who were *pallas* then entered the narrow doorway. The *pallas* remained in the antechamber as the *Coya*, guided by the high priestess, went on into the inner yard where the houses of the Inca gods were ranged about. She now offered the sacrifice of a white llama to the great face of beaten gold that adorned the façade of Inti's house; this was the image of him as Punchao, the Day.

She proceeded to a small repository shrine in which were stored the royal weapons: the golden halberd or *topa yauri*, which was the scepter, the solid gold war club, the *champi*, and finally the royal shield adorned with feathers and painted with the vivid blazon of the emperor. These articles were then carried reverently back to the golden face which was beseeched to bless the weapons with victory. She then brought the weapons, as was customary at the beginning of a campaign, to her husband; he had taken them, stepped into his open war litter, and had been born away up the Chinchaysuyo road for the review we have just seen.

Both the *Coya* and her mother remained in the city. The Incas described a deserted town as *racay racay*, a term which carries a meaning like "corrals" or "roofless and empty walls." Such almost was Cuzco the imperial city, at least as regards the absence of the normal sounds of everyday life. It had become a city almost emptied of men. An aged magnate had been appointed viceroy of the city in the imperial absence, and he was supported by the merest handful of Cañar troops. The great fortress had been almost totally denuded of its garrison, and the three portals were closely shut and watched from above. Whenever messages came into the city, the *chasquis* raced up to Sacsahuaman rather than down into the city to deliver them, for in Huascar's absence his viceroy resided there. The city of women below knew nothing but what the feverish palpitations of rumor brought to it. Fasting was mandatory; salt, coca, and *uchu*, the hot red pepper, "all adjuncts of the good life," were abjured. No loud noises were countenanced. The *ñustas* ceased to sing love songs and to beat the tambourine, for there were no young men to interest. The *amautas*, the wise old men who taught the youth, moved about the city, leaning on their sticks and trying in their withered way to believe that the miracle which had saved the state in the days of Pachacuti would be repeated. The *pallas* did visit each other, but they came with covered heads and frightened hearts; only occasionally were they seen on the terraces and clustered under the gnarled *chinchircoma* trees.

"*Ña, ña,*" the women greeted each other and asked was the news good, "*simi cusi cancchu?*" And then the stale rumors of yesterday would be repeated. "*Achallay!*" or "How wonderful!" one would exclaim and would then go home to sit patiently spinning with her ladies and children around her. No words of lament or anguish were allowed lest they poison the future and destroy Cuzco's hopes.

Then on a day a *chasqui* was seen racing up toward the fortress. The eyes of many women, old men, and wondering children followed the pinprick figure edging up under the colossal walls. Hearts quickened and mantles were bitten in the dark coolness of the city as the residents waited for the message to be passed on down to them.

A victory had been won! The second army under the valiant Rampa Yupanqui had caught the enemy napping out beyond the Apurimac, had decimated and scattered him, and killed Atauhuallpa's commander, the famous Tomay Rimac. The severed head of the latter had been shown to Huascar and was now on its way to Cuzco to be made into a royal drinking cup.

A few days followed during which the wings of the dread bird of death no longer shadowed the city. It was thus an unbelieving and a wholly unready city which received the next and the last message of all. A vast battle had swirled about the high slopes and *huaycos* beyond the Cotapampa bridge. An amazing victory had at first scattered the forces of Atauhuallpa. In the sudden relief and bravado of his victory Huascar had lost all sense of caution, had carelessly put off the ex-

247

termination of the enemy till the next day when he had fallen into their trap. Topa Atau had been ambushed, tortured, and forced to reveal Huascar's movements. And Huascar, like a fat pigeon had been taken and held fast, and most of the Inca knights had fallen defending him. The imperial army had instantly broken up and fled, great numbers being butchered along the road. The swinging bridge over the Apurimac fell intact into enemy hands. Titu Atauchi had been captured in flight. There was no word of Rampa Yupanqui.

The awful truth was certified when the first of the survivors began to appear, stumbling down the neat stairs of the Chinchaysuyo road and reeling with hoarse shouts of despair along the edges of the terraces.

Stunned and silent the women of the Incas awaited the beaten survivors, a sight none of them had ever seen before, a sight indeed which they could not properly believe. One by one the dirty, often bleeding, men, without sandals or weapons or pride, were received by their women and each huddled group retired into the *cancha* where it resided. Then from within the walls began to resound the high-pitched and chilling shrieks of the women as awareness of their plight gradually broke upon them. Most horrible were the sounds that arose from within the *acllahuasi*. *"Huay! Huay! Huay!"* sounded the shrieks of the chosen women locked in their narrow alleys and inner patios, aware not of definite news but only of some vague and impending disaster made the worse for being undefined; *"Anay ananay!"* "Woe! Woe!"

The sun finally set on the evil day. The fiery red clouds of the sunset, *anta rupay*, fell into mere embers and then fled away to leave overhead the vault of night glittering as with a million jewels, *llipiyak tuta*, "the spangled night." But Cuzco looked not to the heavens. Cuzco shuddered. The holy city was about to meet its fate, and never again would the *pacha yuracyan*, "the paling before sunrise," gladden the hearts of any of the Inca people. Yet even still they had no conception of the extent of the disaster that lay ahead.

ELVIOVENOINGA
PACHACVTIWC
IVPANQVI

Reynabjus · ta ihili y de to · Oasuior fulliera
padjaqen

NOT LONG AFTER the refugees from the Cotapampa front had appeared, the remnants of the second army began to come in. The Apurimac bridge had been lost, and Huanca Auqui had fallen back on Lima-tambo. This place, too, he had lost. A weak stand had then been made at Ichupampa, scene of the final de-feat of the Chancas many years ago, and there that army corps finally fell apart. Of the four generals at-tached to the group, the ill-starred Huanca Auqui is known to have made his way back to Cuzco along with Paucar Usno and Hahuapanti.

The pursuit was pushed, and in a short time, with stragglers from Huascar's shattered armies still stumbling into the city, the small Cañar garrison holding the walls on Sacsahuaman sent word down that the enemy vanguard was camped on the field of Quihuipay just across the Sapi gorge. Shortly thereafter, moving pinpricks of figures ap-peared along the top of Carmenca, announcing to the Incas below the arrival of the first enemy outposts.

Since Huascar and most of the magnates making up his imperial council were held captive by the enemy, no vestige of the former gov-ernment as such existed. The Capac Incas left in the city, being now freed from the tyranny of Huascar, could make decisions in accordance with their own temper as a people. They still held the fortress, and, in the ancient tradition, they could well retire into it for a heroic last stand.

The first herald from the enemy, one of Huascar's captured cap-tains, came to the apartments of the *Coya* and her mother to deliver his message. He brought word to the two women that Huascar was being well treated and that a general pardon would be extended to each and

249

every supporter of Huascar, as it was recognized that their allegiance to their emperor, however mistaken, had been natural. It was, after all, hostility between two brothers that had led to these events, and that particular contention did not really concern the Incas as a people. All that was required of them, so ran the terms, was to come to Quihuipay and there transfer their allegiance to their new emperor Atauhuallpa.

The Capac Incas came together for the last time in a meeting at which their remaining magnates as well as the distraught *Coya* and her mother were present. The membership of the *hunuc* "or council" was probably dominated by the discredited Huanca Auqui and his associates, Paucar Usno and Hahuapanti. No immediate decision seemed possible, so the *hunuc* requested of Atauhuallpa's two generals a period of three days in which to develop an answer. This period was granted, as it also gave Atauhuallpa's generals time to communicate with their master back in Cajamarca.

What the Incas as a people were debating in those three days was not their fate, for it must have been apparent to them that that had already been decided, but their integrity. Nothing is known of the city of Cuzco during those three days; nothing is known of its debates, of the reasoning of the parties, or of the making of the final and harrowing decision. Certainly that council was caught on the horns of one of history's sharpest dilemmas—a defiant stand could only be made as a gesture of support for a hated tyrant, a supine surrender would at least acknowledge the merits of a new emperor who by reason of his indomitable might was shown to be in the Inca tradition. The Capac Incas themselves had helped to forge the ineluctable horror of this decision. They ended by agreeing to a supine surrender. These were no longer the days of Pachacuti.

The fortress on Sacsahuaman was thus ordered to open its gates to the enemy, and on the fourth morning the population of Cuzco, saving only the *acllas* and some of the *mamaconas*, ascended Carmenca to drink from the sour cup of defeat.

SECTION 12. *Vae Victis!*

AGAINST THEIR ENEMIES in the past the Incas had customarily initiated proceedings with a combination of guile, threat, and terror to effect their ends. For this reason the Incas in Cuzco cannot have been unaware that the glozing words of Atauhuallpa's captains covered traps set to snare them or that they were probably being gathered together to learn a new lesson in brutality. The fact that they chose this alternative, rather than dying according to their ancient virtues, was an earnest of the extent to which they had degenerated as a people of war during the eight years of Huascar's reign.

They came onto the field of Quihuipay by their *panacas* and *ayllus*, men, women, and children, each group huddling together as if it could make a fortress out of the bodies of its members.

The events of that day and the succeeding day need not be lingered over. They still come off the pages of the old chronicles with a sense of utter scandal, of an experience in horror unique, unrepeatable, and unforgivable.

First the Capac Incas were told to worship formally Atauhuallpa who was placed before them in the person of his *huaoqui*, the Ticci Capac. They were then forced to witness their captive emperor, who had been brought in tied rigidly to a frame of poles, derided with obscene gestures and shouts of *"Coca hachu! ysullaya!"* or "Coca cud! son of a whore!" Rahua Ocllo was reminded that she had been only a concubine when she bore her son, and that, as a bastard, Huascar therefore had no more right to the throne than any of the sons of Huayna Capac. Her words were directed not to her tormentors but, properly, to her captive son, and they still carry in them all of the frustration and tragedy of the last reign:

"Wretched person! Your own cruelties and crimes have brought you here. Did I not warn you! And yet you murdered and dishonored Atauhuallpa's messengers; all of this you deserve and more. It is Viracocha himself who has put this fate upon you to pay you for the cruelty you have done your people! And we, your own people, must suffer too for what you alone did!"

251

So saying, she rushed up to the pinioned emperor, her son, and struck him in the face.

Haughtily, still unable to realize the scope of his fall, Huascar rejected his mother's passionate hatred by reminding her and Atauhuallpa's captains and everyone there that all of them were speaking out of turn, that this dispute was in fact a quarrel between Atauhuallpa and himself alone, that as subjects they could have no interest in it whatsoever; they were servants only. He then called on Apu Challco Yupanqui, Inti's priest, to testify to the validity of his coronation, contemptuously refusing to speak directly to Quizquiz as being a mere subject. The high priest's testimony that he had legitimately taken the *mascapaycha* from Inti's hand and fastened it on Huascar's brow was followed, of course, by a deluge of derision and insults from the men of Quito.

Accepting these slurs of illegitimacy and usurpation against Huascar, the Inca *ayllus*, squatting in the dust of that dreadful field and surrounded by Atauhuallpa's victorious army, were forced then to watch the war hammers at work on some of the pinioned officers who had fought under Huanca Auqui. After a selected group of these had been beaten to death, Huanca Auqui himself and his two captains, Hahuapanti and Paucar Usno, were hauled out of the press of squatting Incas to receive the punishment of the *hiuaya*, "the boulder," crippling blows on the back, not savage enough to kill—for these three would be wanted at the last exquisite torture session reserved for Atauhuallpa's eyes—but enough to satisfy for the nonce the pride of Challcochima and Quizquiz whose armies they had so often obstructed.

The Capac Incas were then dismissed with the sardonic adjuration to return to Cuzco since they had been mercifully pardoned. Biting and jerking their mantles in agony of spirit, the lords of Cuzco and their women returned to the holy city. "At this hour, O Viracocha, you who gave us our being, where are you now? How could this terrible thing happen? How could you have raised us up, if this was to be our end?"

The imposition of terror in Cuzco awaited only the liquidation of the Cañar garrison still in the fortress, for they represented to Atauhuallpa's generals the only coherent fighting force left to fear. It was well known that the Cañars, as well as some of the Chachapoya *mitmacs* living in the valley, had served as Huascar's personal henchmen. It was their nation in the north which had treacherously seized and imprisoned Atauhuallpa; for this act they were marked men. With no longer the favor of the emperor to count on, they surrendered, were marched out with their *curaca* Urco Colla at their head, and systematically exterminated, their bodies left in piles just outside of Cuzco. This deed done, Challcochima immediately left with a portion of Atauhuallpa's army on forced marches south to Lake Chucuito to forestall the defection of those difficult provinces and to block the escape of any Capac Incas into this region. This development left the sinister Quizquiz to administer the occupation of Cuzco; there had also just arrived an inquisitor and executioner dispatched with specific orders from Atauhuallpa's court in the north to aid Quizquiz in the extirpation of the Capac Incas.

All of Huascar's leading generals were now in custody; the *Coya* and Rahua Ocllo had likewise been seized to be held for the final reckoning. They were fully aware of what that reckoning would be, an entertainment prepared as part of a victory fiesta at which Atauhuallpa would preside. But meanwhile it had been decided to root out all of Huascar's seed. To this spectacle in extermination Huascar was ironically invited, being installed in Haucaypata where, trussed up on a rack of poles, he was forced to watch the women of his harem led out before him for the event. This group included all those with children and all those pregnant or suspected of being so. They were systematically butchered, disemboweled, and the unborn torn from them. Then all the bodies, a hundred or more, were spitted on heavy posts spaced out along the Chinchaysuyo road, the dead children and fetuses pinned in their arms. The line of posts was then extended farther out, and every one of Huascar's half brothers who had adhered to his party, every intimate of Huascar, male or female, and every one of his personal domestics or *yanaconas* was sought out from his or her miserable hiding place in the city and the surrounding countryside and dealt with similarly. This triumphal decoration of the main approaches to the city would then greet Atauhuallpa on that day when he was to be borne exulting into Cuzco.

In the days of his power Huascar had leaned for some of his support on the Capac Ayllu *panaca*, that one which possessed the mummy of Topa Inca, his grandfather. Probably many of his toadies and minions in fact came from that powerful organization. This situation was, of course, well known to Atauhuallpa, and he had given orders therefore that the Capac Ayllu *panaca* in particular be destroyed root and stock. Not only was the *pachaca* or major-domo of that royal household in Pucamarca done away with but all of the *mamaconas* assigned to the cult of the mummy and almost the entire body of officials and servants as well—in all some one thousand persons. To crown the work the central *huaca*, the mummy bundle of the great emperor himself, grandfather of Atauhuallpa as well as of Huascar, was dragged through the streets to the place of common execution outside the city, burned, and its ashes pounded into dust. Some members of the *panaca* did escape, taking with them Cusi Churi, Topa's *huaoqui*, and, with this object and the ashes of the mummy which they later rescued, they were able afterward weakly to reform the cult.

An observer of that day would have predicted that the whole future of Tahuantinsuyo would have to rest thenceforth on foundations different from those laid down by the former generations. The Capac Incas had advanced the fiction that a line of charismatic emperors went uninterruptedly back to the founder Manco Capac and that the presence of each one was necessary in the scheme of things. One can see then that the brutal disposal of one of the greatest of them all was intended to be a part of Atauhuallpa's new era—which he himself obviously intended to design. It was certain that the *panaca* system was to be either radically altered or destroyed.

To set the seal on the extinction of that old world and the beginning of the new, Quizquiz set about ferreting out and destroying as many as possible of the *quipucamayocs*, "the recorders," who had committed to memory the deeds of Topa Inca. Few indeed of the *amautas*, those learned custodians of the Inca past, were allowed to survive, and their *quipus*, wherever found, were burned. The ways by which these and similar victims were done away with varied from simple destruction to forcing victims to eat hot peppers till they died. The objective was, however, in all cases the same—the denigration of the Capac Incas.

The tale could be extended, but there is no need. History tells of no more condign yet still tragic punishment for a city setting itself high. But even this penalty was not to be the end. It may not be amiss to record that Huascar, watching his beloved sister-wives with their children being destroyed, cried out in his last recorded statement. "Ah, Viracocha! you who raised me up for so short a time, now bring it to pass that he who forces me to witness such things, should be himself so treated!"

Most curses, uttered by it matters not whom, have something of a habit of delineating the shape of subsequent events.

SECTION 13.

The Inner City of Women

OF THE LOOT gathered in after Cotapampa, the most eagerly lusted after was the contents of that remarkable warehouse, the *acllahuasi*. The possession of the wealth enclosed in that one *cancha* would suffice to make Atauhuallpa the most courted of all men. The treasure inside consisted of beautiful young women.

The location has been in general described. It was situated between Topa Inca's palace and that of Huayna Capac. It was a long rectangular *cancha*-area divided down the long axis by a narrow street or passageway flanked with apertures leading to small and complicated groups or cells or apartments. Each entryway was closed only by a hanging curtain before which sat a woman who served as a porter; it was her care to receive things which were handed in from the outside and to carry them in to the inmates, to pass things out, and, especially, to prevent unauthorized persons from entering. A narrow door opened out on the east end of this interior street and was guarded by twenty porters, all of them old men. A part of this long inner axial street is probably represented today by Avenida Arequipa. The largest of the inner apartment areas was at the southeast end of the vast rectangle, and this space housed the *Intip huarmi,* "the wives of the god Inti," others of the *mamaconas* who served in the cults of the gods of Coricancha, and perhaps some of the women of the emperor. This section, probably called Cusicancha and meaning "the Harem," was conveniently located near Coricancha, for the eastern doorway opened directly into Chuquipampa, the open plaza on which Coricancha also fronted. The other sets of *pitita* or inner apartment areas of the *acllahuasi* were assigned separately to two sets of women, the *acllas* proper, who were all virgins, and the majority of the ruling emperor's harem, the overflow in fact for which he had no immediate need. There were thus three classes of women within the *cancha*: cult women, imperial concubines, and unassigned virgins being held in reserve. Only the last two groups should be referred to as *acllas,* and only the area they lived in can therefore properly be called the *acllahuasi.* There may have been in all as many as three thousand residents within or attached to this inner city of women.

If the outworks on Sacsahuaman represent the capacity of the Inca people for the giantesque, the high battered walls of this particular *cancha* reveal, as nothing else can, their overriding acquisitiveness. Gold and coca were state monopolies and control over them was enforced with strictness, but the monopoly in women which the Capac Incas exercised was inordinate. Because of the great confusion in the early Spanish reports of the system, an account of the women who lived within those walls is of importance. The taking of women as loot is a commonplace in history, but then to transfigure what was loot into a yearly tax and to organize its storage, maintenance, and progressive screening thus skillfully—the whole culminating on every Inti Raymi in the delivery of the empire's most select girls—reveals an exceptional society.

The system by which this monopoly was organized is more compli-

cated than at first appears. The distinction between the two basic groups
of women, the *mamaconas* and the *acllaconas*, was that the former had
been formally and permanently assigned to the Inca gods or the imperial mummies; the majority of them belonged to the cults of Inti,
Illapa, and Mama Quilla. The *acllas* were, on the contrary, secular
in the sense that they were either unassigned to any specific use and
awaiting the emperor's will, or they were professional entertainers at
the *taquis*, or they were used by him as concubines in his own harem.
All of them appear to have been at least to some extent under the rule
of the mother superior of the whole establishment, the Coya Pacsa, who
was always, as already pointed out, a sibling of the emperor himself.
Her power of enforcing the required discipline, of seeing to the requirements of chastity and virginity, and of arranging affairs among the dis-
parate groups of women must have been considerable.

The *mamaconas* belonging to the sun-god were certainly of high
standing; if from a province beyond Cuzcoquiti, they were at least of
noble blood and always legitimate. The dignity of the god whom they
served demanded no less. But within their group they were generally
divided into the *Intip huarmi*, legitimate "wives of Inti," probably all
pallas, and "his concubines," *Intip chinan*, the latter being in caste inferior to the former. The wives were the only ones who had been
formally married to Inti with appropriate marriage rites.

The *mamaconas* were not too strictly secluded, for they were involved in a rotational system in carrying out the household duties of
their divine husband. They tended the sacred fire in Coricancha, brewed
the special *akha* which alone Inti and the other gods drank, and cooked
and served their meals. Thus they often had to leave the confines of
Cusicancha when they were needed in Coricancha or when their services
were required outside in the great religious festivals. Their persons
were sacred; even to touch their clothing was to court swift disaster.
Certain *mamaconas* also served the mummies in the *panaca* cults, and,
therefore, they were required to reside outside Cusicancha most of the
time; the relation of these women to the *Intip huarmi* is unclear.

When an Inca father dedicated a daughter to one of the gods or
huacas, because of her noble status as a *ñusta* she probably became a

mamacona directly, but non-Inca girls who were *mamaconas* had in all cases been assigned as such from the ranks of the *acllas*. The privileges of aristocratic birth were as carefully maintained within the walls of the *acllahuasi* as in the world outside.

In February the tribute of Cuzcoquiti was brought into the city for storage; among the more important items were the *acllas* of thirteen or fourteen years of age who had been winnowed out from their less beautiful sisters in the provincial establishments. Soon after their arrival they were brought before the emperor who then assigned them to their fates.

Once in Cuzco an *aclla* never went outside her prison walls unless assigned by the emperor as a gift to some meritorious captain or great provincial *curaca*, or as he might choose to take her along with the rest of his harem on some progress or campaign. He of course could use for his own pleasure any of these girls, but those not so favored by him formed a large pool from which he could draw at any time to give away, to use for sacrifice in time of great need or festival, or to offer to one of the gods as a living servant.

While thus waiting to know on what altar they were to be sacrificed or to what Inca warrior or distant chieftain offered, these young women served under a discipline both inhuman and exacting. Their days, interminably alike except when the emperor might appear, were spent in groups weaving the beautiful *cumpi*, or chewing *mocca* and spitting it into jars for fermentation into *akha*, or else in obsequiously serving their superiors. Punishments for even slight delinquencies must have been severe, and the bitter tyranny of prisoner over prisoner must have soured every aspect of life within the massive dark stones of their environment. The emperor's favorites and those of his harem who lived in the *acllahuasi* gossiped and intrigued endlessly for advantages for their children born and unborn. Some were trained specifically to be *taqui acllas* or "geishas," the only group perhaps ever allowed out into the world of Cuzco; they were entertainers with trained voices and a repertoire of songs sung to the rapping of a tambourine. Most of the *acllas* entered the harem while twelve to fifteen years old as *sayapayac*, "those who are always around and ready to assist," servants of the more beautiful or more favored. Under them were the *uiñaychicuc*, "those being raised," little girls being trained up as a servant class, some only five years old. Their lot was probably the most unenviable of all, for they were without even the protection of fully matured beauty. They were classed as domestics or servants, and probably some never became anything more.

The nubile girls were popularly classed according to a color chart in order of beauty. The most desirable were the *huayru* or the girls with cheeks as rosy as the red seeds of the *huayru*, a tree in the montaña. Those with very light olive or cream-colored complexions were the *yurac*, or "white" girls, many of them Chachapoya or Cañar Indians. The more yellow of skin were the *pacco*, or "fair." Lowly birth was a grave disadvantage even to a very lovely girl, and in general legitimacy and noble birth were required along with loveliness.

The lost lives of these women, the dumb inanition to which they were subjected, their sense of being items like stored sacks of corn or *chuño* or gold vessels, their deprivation from the life about them, their subjugation to the cruelties of the women over them is almost inconceivable. Finally the silent terror of the wholly unknown future—this situation was the fruit of a monstrous ingenuity which in the end defeated itself. It created a false center of life in Cuzco for the virile Incas; it nourished intrigue, provoked savagery, and deprived the women of their common humanity. The customary punishment for an *aclla* who was found sexually delinquent was to be stripped naked, along with her seducer, their arms pinioned, and then both hanged by the hair from the rock of execution at Arahua. Here they remained till death from pain and frost and rapacious birds intervened, a warning to all lustful young Incas who envied their emperor's male license. The families of both of the culprits were hunted down and destroyed and their houses, although they might be as far as two thousand miles away, razed to the ground.

One of the younger brothers of the emperor had been so tempted. Paullo Topa Inca was one who up to the end had managed to escape his brother's many proscriptions. During the near chaotic conditions in Cuzco as Atauhuallpa's army was pressing closer to Cuzco, he had apparently compromised himself with one of the imperial women. She herself had been buried alive as a punishment, but because Paullo was a Capac Inca, instead of the hanging reserved for commoners, he was sentenced instead to the pits in Sankahuaci, to die there a lingering death. When Quizquiz entered the city, Paullo was released by the invaders and again escaped death by proving to Atauhuallpa's executioner his allegiance to the Atauhuallpa party in Cuzco.

The cults of the Inca gods depended largely on the ministrations of the *mamaconas*. The possession of their quarters therefore gave Atauhuallpa control over Inca religion. Possession of the *acllahuasi* itself gave him the women necessary for recompensing his captains, and possession of Huascar's harem afforded him the opportunity of extirpating the royal line so that no claim could ever be made good against him on the basis of legitimacy.

Waiting for the new dispensation which was to wreck even the small security they had known up to then, *acllas* and *mamaconas* continued to spin the amazingly fine threads of dyed vicuña wool and to weave on their backstrap looms creations of somber beauty; they continued to chew *molle*-berries and maize and spit the *muccu* into vats. They combed each other's hair and adjusted their *ñañacas* with care, and when their work was done, they retired, each to her windowless cell, to listen throughout the night to the sudden shrieks of terror in the city outside, to the hurry of charging feet, and to the thud of stone war hammers on flesh. They must have known, from the Coya Pacsa on down to the most menial serving-girl, that both their lives and their beauty were at the hazard.

V
The Lords Perish

AN IMPERIAL FOLK who conceive of themselves greatly and who claim for their mission in history a pivotal importance must of course have an adequate language. But empires differ—some grow up suddenly and cruelly out of the dirt of the farmyard, some appear as the blossoming of old and sophisticated cultures, some are contrived by a single man, others are built slowly and unconsciously by many men, some are without any direction and rationale, while others have well-contrived doctrines to support them. The *runa simi*, "speech of men" —or Quechua, as we call it today—was determinative in the building and maintenance of the Inca empire. It was the only thing belonging to the Incas which they insisted on sharing with their subject people.

While the history of *runa simi* has not been established, there seems little doubt that the Incas spoke a variation of Quechua which we can identify as the tongue of the Tambos. As the Incas were rising in prestige, this dialect was one of the features which marked them off from other speakers of Quechua. When finally they became a sacred caste, their variant manner of speaking also became sacred. It was the *topa simi* or "royal speech." The Quechua that was taught to the sons of the important *curacas* resident in the court was undoubtedly the common variety spoken in Cuzcoquiti. Undoubtedly this dialect and the *topa simi* were mutually intelligible and differed only in the tabooed quality of certain words of the latter and in their pronunciation. No doubt also the latter could assume an especially baroque quality.

Much of the vocabulary of this early Quechua has disappeared, for the friars who compiled the first lexicons had a propensity to include pre-eminently those words which would be useful to them in catechizing their Indian charges and convincing them of their sins. In the process many—perhaps most—of the words and concepts relating to status, administration, technology, astronomy, cult, learning, and such have disappeared, for these were areas of which the Indians of New Castile in their later abjectness had no need.

In general then, only subsistence words survived. It is, however, of note that the words for war and things pertaining to war had a relatively strong survival value in the early dictionaries, probably speaking to the fact that the status of the warrior had always been, for each and every one of the subject peoples of the Inca empire, the very *summa* of merit. But even here we possess only a skeleton vocabulary left of what must have existed originally.

The idiom of the Viracocha cult, for instance, has survived to us only in the titles of the Creator and in a few extant prayers and hymns. The little that does exist perhaps warrants the cautious observation that at the time of the coming of the Spaniards the language had not yet become apt in expressing the spare and elevated concepts which were obviously emergent in the imperial cult. This situation we may attribute both to the short time that that cult existed and to the lack of any form of writing in Peruvian culture. But the lack probably also springs from the concreteness of the language. Two of Viracocha's commonest epithets are *camac* and *churac*, and these we translate as "Creator" and "Establisher," but the primary meanings of the words appear to be "producing fruit" and "putting down or placing inside," so that undertones of the growing season and of the storing of grain are still to be felt in the high hailing of the god.

The language abounds in allusion to the concrete. "To go swiftly" was to go *huayra huayralla*, "windlike," or *huaman huamanalla*, "hawklike." A speedy traveler was therefore *huayrahina puric*, "a windlike traveler." There existed totally different words for the washing of the face, the hands, the head, the clothing, the feet, or the whole body.

Yet the concrete words themselves often had a number of secondary or derived meanings, attesting to the fact that the flexibility which the language possessed lay, not in a rich vocabulary, but in the semantic elasticity of the words for the concrete. *Ñuñu* is the word both for "milk" and "a woman's breast"; there are no other words for either. The word *pacha* is one of the more curious of all of these cluster-words, for it means "earth," "time," "epoch," "place," or "world." The noun *cocha* means "sea," "pond," "lake," "basin," or "fountain." *Simi* means "mouth," "beak," "word," "speech," "command," "promise," "news." *Ñaui* means not only "face," "visage," "sight," but is the only word in the language for "eye." In this line is a heavy reliance on negatives to produce concepts such as "hugeness," "terror," "evil." There is no word in the language for "bad"—a truly remarkable omission. Speakers of Quechua had to say "not good." For "vast" they had to say "without measure," and for "cruel" they used "not ever-loving." It would appear to be in brief a tongue ill-formed for the logician or thinker.

So strong was the tendency to the concrete that categories were often derived from one of the specifics. "Red" is *llimpi*, but used with *ñauray* ("diversity, all kinds of") it means "colors." *Anta* is "copper" but, again with *ñauray*, becomes "metals." *Poma* is the "mountain lion," but *ñauray poma* again means "beasts of all kinds." This characteristic also indicates a language in which integrating concepts, such as collectives, are of minimum importance. There are words for "fruit tree" and "forest tree," but there is no word for "tree." Needless to say, there is no word for "nature" as over and against "history," and to achieve something of the concept the language used forms from the common word *pacariy*, "to dawn, to appear, to be born." There are no words to express "animal," "plant," "number," "weapons," and such. Regarding anything approaching the concept of "law," there is an absolute blank for the obvious reason that in the Inca world law was still only *apup simi*, "the word of the leader."

The meaning of verbs could be refined by agglutination. *Apani* is the simple verb "I carry." By inserting *mu* the idea of motion hither is obtained so that *apamuni* means "I bring." The particle *chi* gives the idea of causing someone to do something; thus *apachimuni* is "I cause to be brought." *Pu* adds to the verb the idea that the action is to the advantage of some person understood or mentioned, thus *apachimupuni*, "I cause someone to bring something for his advantage." *Naya* gives the sense of a strong desire involved in the performance of the verb's action, or points to one who is on the point of doing something; so *apachimupunayani*, "I am very desirous of causing someone to bring something to me for his own advantage." These additive particles, of which there are a great number, give a flexibility to the verb as it describes situations in which persons participate. They thus form a most useful device for a caste of nobles who could by means of it easily express their own superiority and the shades of prerogative of those who stood under them. This wonderful plasticity tended to balance out the poverty of specific verbal ideas.

But agglutination was even more a part of the skeleton of the language than this. Subordinate clauses as we know them are minimal in Quechua. The conjunction "that" does not exist in the language. Instead the subordinate verb form assumes a participial phase and can act as a noun or an adjective. Thus a sentence such as "I know a city whose inhabitants are always hostile to strangers" becomes "(I) (always of strangers enemy) (city) (know)." Indeed an entire sentence such as this one may become a noun, i.e., a substitute for a subordinate clause, if necessary, and then its translated formula would go approximately as follows "[(always of strangers enemy) (known city my)]."

Because of this fundamental orientation of the language, connective words are rare, and the thought moves along in a series of juxtaposed meaning-clusters, whose complexity and richness are theoretically unlimited.

If intellectual display was denied to a speaker of Quechua, not so elegance. The language lent itself spectacularly to the baroque, the precious, and the exuberant. It achieved this effect by the use of reduplicated syllables, by a large amount of onomatopoeia, by words of emphasis, and by the positioning of certain particles. When skillfully employed, these devices resulted in the "high speech" or *hatun simi*, which no doubt was influenced by the *topa simi* of the Inca lords. Indeed, one of the commonest names given to Inca boys was *Rimachic*, "One who speaks sententiously." Proficiency in excess and elegance of speech thus marked the true Inca, as did his terseness when dealing with inferiors. If men, inferiors were addressed as "my son," and if women, as "my child." But an inept speaker, one who foolishly mingled idioms of several languages in his speech was a *mirccasimicta rimac*, a "mixed-words speaker."

These qualities of elegance and showiness were made palatable because of the fundamental simplicity of the language. There was only one conjugation and no declensions at all, prepositional suffixes alone being used. A copious store of expletives and exclamations made easy the statement of complex situations and sudden sentiments in a single word. Words had no gender attributed to them and essentially no number, although a pluralizing suffix existed.

In matters of greeting also the Inca lords exploited the simplicity of their language, their urbanity being expressed more in the gravity of their demeanor than in a long parade of words. "Eat and drink," they would say to the august stranger and to their equals, "for you are in your own house. Have joy."

Quechua was penultimate in stress and thus flowed smoothly, there being few explosive masculine endings to create emphasis or abrupt pauses. For this reason and because of constantly occurring liquid consonants and diphthongs ending in the semivowels *w* and *y*, it is a beautiful language, Italianate in sound and often poetic in mood. The wind whistling in the branches or leaves of trees, for instance, was evoked in the verb *chiwiwiwiñichiy*.

An empire is just as importantly a concept as it is a way of organizing alien peoples and subgovernments. A successful imperial people must be able to articulate this concept in numerous ways, for the concept is a center of value which they must always be in a position to control. In other words, they must have the linguistic means to point to themselves as the agents for this center and to express clearly the mission upon which they are sent. One wonders after close inspection of *runa simi* whether it was indeed the tongue of such a people; the history of the Incas—for they were to be proved ultimately unsuccessful as an imperial people—appears to bear out this doubt. Their concept of governing at its best was *runacta michiy*, "to herd people," and the verb formed from the noun for "people," *runachay*, meant "to dominate," "subjugate, or "order them." The Quechua word expressing the relationships which the Incas felt they had with mankind in general was crass and concrete—to "man" the world was not "to staff" it but "to crush" it. It is not inconsistent with this feeling to find that Quechua had exceedingly powerful expressions for disgust, loathing, dirt, and contempt.

Perhaps the lords of Cuzco were still so close to their pastoral and agricultural origins that they had not developed an imperial concept other than that which could be expressed by numbers on the *quipu*. That part of the empire which included meaning and responsibility eluded them. Their language, consequently, did not speak of such things.

An important part of their culture was their system of personal names. Choice here was fairly limited. Men's names tended to be either honorific like *Yupanqui*, Esteemed; *Topa*, Royal; *Auqui*, Prince; or they tended to things of war, *Lloque*, Dagger; *Chuqui*, Javelin; *Huaman*, Hawk; *Tomay*, Siege; or to be expressive of prosperity, luck, or elegance, such as *Cusi*, Fortunate; *Inquil*, Flower; *Paucar*, Iridescent; or they were names of distinguished ancestors with no known meanings like Manco, Roca, and Mayta; or they were the names of tribes, animals, or birds. Sometimes three or four of these names were piled one on another to produce what seems to us a senseless juxtaposition, a mere desire to claim whatever there was of prestige in several unrelated names. It must be remembered that the name a boy was born with was not his knight's name. Thus the boy born and known as Huascar after the place of his birth received from his uncles on coming of age the name Titu Cusi Huallpa which had been the name of his father and of his great-great-great-grandfather. An Inca bore three names during his lifetime. The birth name merely recounted or recalled some circumstance at the time of his birth or was a good luck name serving to identify him. At the ceremony of the first haircutting, when the boy was about eight, he either took the name which at a corresponding age had been carried by his father or grandfather, or he himself chose to be called by the name of the Inca whom he served as a page. His third or knight's name was the sign of his prerogative as an Inca and was generally also a name in the family. If he were the emperor as well, he might take a fourth name, of his own choosing this time, and one which as a rule announced his connections with the unseen world and the gods. In this connection Huascar as we have seen took the throne name Inti Illapa.

Of all names the one that specially distinguished the Incas was Yupanqui. It was in fact so common that it could almost be considered the family name of the caste. The root meaning of the verb *yupay* was "to count," with the extended sense "to count as something or somebody." Thus *yupanqui*, the second person singular of the present indicative, gives as its meaning "you count as somebody." *Yupa*, the adjective, meant "decent, nice, proper." It was a singularly aristocratic concept that was involved in this word and its variations.

Girls similarly were given names at birth which they carried with them until the *quicuchicoy*. On becoming *ñustas* they too assumed noble names like Darling (literally "Golden"), Lithe, Halo, Star, Pretty, Happy. Often the names were connected with goddesses such as Ocllo or Coca, or with distinguished *pallas* of the past. A *palla* always had the word for "lady," *Mama*, prefixed to her name, a true honorific and one jealously restricted. The full name of Huascar's sister and wife was thus Mama Chuqui Huipa or "Lady Darling Joy." Paullo Inca's wife's name was Mama Tocto Usica, "Lady Maize-flower Sandal."

Section 2. *What Is Man?*

THAT WHICH ANIMATED all beings was *causay*, "life." Birds and fish and men all received it, and it was in each one of these instances the same thing. Nevertheless it was given in different quantities, conditions, and forms so that different species eventuated. Certain forest trees, for instance, all belonged to a certain *ayllu*; this was their "species." Mankind, when envisaged as all the people of Tahuantinsuyo, belonged to the *hatun ayllu*, the "great species."

One could distinguish the characteristics of each of such *ayllus*. The "beastness" of wild animals, their *llamacayñin*, consisted in their four-footedness, their inability to speak, and their lack of *sonco* or "reason." They were *upa*, "dumb," unable to communicate properly with others. Beyond the confines of Tahuantinsuyo some races of mankind partook of this nature; these were the barbarous tribes, the *uparuna*, who did not use a rational language but simply babbled stupidly.

The central fact about all *ayllus* is that they were known to have had a point of divine origin. The Inca insistence on the concept of a creation meant, therefore, that "nature" was simply an extension of what had been indelibly ordered at that dawn of time. Thus a person's nature or the character of his tribal culture, of his *ayllu* in fact, was his *pacariy*, his "beginning."

The verb *pacariy* we have seen to be one of the fundamental words in the Quechua language; in it and its many transmutations we begin to appreciate the Inca's grasp of nature. *Pacariy* means equally "to be born" and "to dawn." What was originally set, formed, molded in the act of creation is the "natural thing," *pacarisca*, and is thus always correct. Once born, nature cannot change without the intervention of injustice. The pattern of what is right is to be found, therefore, always with the ancestors. And the ancestors derived this pattern from receiving *causay* in that glorious and far-off dawn of being when the Creator first revealed himself in his works.

The nature of man is, of course, found in the fact that he speaks, but behind this is the fact that he alone of beings possesses *yuyana*, "imagination." The verb *yuyay* means "to take thought of or for; to have charge of." It implies responsibility perhaps even before it implies intelligence. Rational and judicious by nature, mankind is therefore *yuyayruna*.

But this rational being was still only *allpa camasca*, "animated clay," molded by the Creator into whatever shape he desired, and without this clay around him man was nothing. Against the time of death it therefore behooved a man to collect his discarded parts, such as nails, hair clippings, and castoff clothes, into one easily accessible spot so that he might later be wholly remade. For this end his body was mummified and his bones retained. Those unprovided with their carnal parts, their "stature," or those lacking a grave service after death were forced to wander as phantoms in the night, restless and perennially seeking. Death was an absolute of its kind and, of course, an evil, but death was unable to prevent the remaking of a person if all the correct precautions had been taken beforehand and if the person had aristocratic status while alive. This was because the *samay*, or spirit (literally "breath"), would be revivified and the *sonccoyoc*, or "rational soul," would thereupon reappear in the body.

Thus the Incas believed, in accordance with a widespread Peruvian conception, that a man could be reborn on earth at which time he would repossess all things which had formerly been his. This was the only

270

manner in which they could conceive of immortality, which they called "deathlessness," *mana huañukcay*, even as we do. All of this was quite consonant with the theory that mankind was under an almost mechanical kind of judgment as regards the afterlife; the Capac Incas went to a blessed state of composure and delight in the high heavens, and the common person passed down to the *supaypa huasi*, "the House of the Demon" below the surface of the earth where for a while he suffered disgusting and terrible things.

In some cases a soul might even become an *illapa*, a sainted essence possessed of much *huaca*, but this was considered rare and was the prerogative of only the most highly placed Incas, it being simply a continuation of the special charisma which they possessed when alive.

In holding these concepts the Incas did not materially differ from other aristocratic peoples over the world. Because of this fact, we can state that their experiences in history were common or universal experiences and thus important for us to understand. In an Inca's conception, man was a natural being but also in a curious way exempt from nature and outside of it. Nature itself was an effect of creation and therefore under the supreme direction of that god great enough to have evoked that special Creation. The Capac Incas fully acknowledged their dependence on that Creator. Death had no explanation to them and was an unacceptable thought. Their views of the other world were therefore conflicting and multifold, and they put their trust in no one of them alone.

As for the wide world itself, calamities of many kinds marred its normal serenity. Murders and mutinies, floods and famines kept bursting in upon man. Terraces could be shaken down in violent earthquakes, llama herds could be wiped out with the mange, and kings could be assaulted by slingstones and killed. Most often this *hucha* or "evil" was a direct offense against the Creation consciously intended by some person or *huaca*. In other cases, misadventures and suffering were sent by a deity or *huaca* offended at some person's *hucha*.

The noun *hucha* has been generally translated "sin" but is perhaps better understood more baldly as "evil." The verb formed from it, *huchallikuy*, meant "to put on evil," as one would put on an article of clothing. Included in the meaning of *hucha* are overtones of "meddling" and "busyness."

Such things as ritual dereliction or offenses against one's *ayllu* were generally understood throughout Peru as being *hucha*, but for the Incas *hucha* was either an offense against the Creator or an offense against their own persons and privileges by others. This latter offense of necessity had to be *hucha*, in view of the divine institution of their empire. *Hucha* in their understanding was thus either blasphemy or rebellion, and because, like magic, it was a force that worked secretively, it could at times even contaminate them, the elected people.

Hucha moved stealthily about in the shadows of the personality, whether human or *huaca*. It was a predator on the political body of men and in particular on the ruling caste of the Incas. To cope with it, of course, one had first to discover it, and this goal was accomplished by means of confession, a very old Peruvian practice. While public or forced confessions were the rule everywhere in Tahuantinsuyo, the Incas alone enjoyed the decency of private confession. This privilege came about because it would have been unseemly for a people who served as Viracocha's agents on earth to have been openly exposed to discovery and penalties. Therefore Incas and *pallas* when necessary confessed to a specially skilled class of priests from Viracocha's shrine city of Huaro. Not being a people much given to speculation about themselves, they did not search their own hearts deeply for the true home of *hucha*, but, clear at least in their understanding of the Creator's sovereignty, they did see him as alone able to destroy it.

Certainly in the Yachahuasi such things, neatly packaged and tied up, were never a part of the young warrior's curriculum, but some clear-thinking *amauta* must have more than once from that house of learning looked out beyond "the ends of the earth," the *pachap caylla caylla*, to incline his thoughts to the Psalmist's question, "What is man, that thou art mindful of him?"

The Return of the Pururaucas

ALMOST EVERY important family in Cuzcoquiti had suffered great injuries in the collapse of Huascar's rule. In some cases whole families had been obliterated. The punishment of proscribed persons extended into the countryside where small settlements of farmers who owed their service to them or groups of domestics attached to their houses were wiped out—pillars of smoke down the valley and up in the *huaycos* marked those broken communities of plowmen and servants. The birds of carrion wheeled ceaselessly over the rocky outcrop of Arahua, for their food was being abundantly supplied from Cuzco and the foxes were busy at night.

Although far from exterminated, the Capac Incas were no longer a cohesive group. Their legitimate *apu* was a captive whose approaching extinction was as certain as the setting of the sun. The *panacas* had been severely shaken by the almost total extirpation of one of the greatest of their royal households. For the moment they still carried out their cults and some preserved their wealth as before, but this situation would certainly change when Atauhuallpa was borne victoriously into the city at the head of a new nobility. Certain of the closer Hahua Inca *ayllus* had been thoroughly shattered by the war, having contributed many of their sons, while many of the more distant confederate Inca groups were radically reduced in numbers and strength. But what had suffered most was the prestige, the taboo attached to the city of Cuzco—its *huaca*. It was the insult to this concept which more effectively undermined the resistance of the Incas than even their drastic loss of members. In the past they had assumed that a spiritual rampart surrounded

273

the city, impenetrable and secure, guarded by the ghostly armies of Viracocha, the *pururaucas*.

At about this time orders arrived from Atauhuallpa to remove Huascar, his ranking magnates, and immediate family from their places of detention in Cuzco. They had been held there awaiting the arrival of Atauhuallpa himself, but disturbing news of the *suncasapa* had now caused that great conqueror to consider a longer stay in Cajamarca, and, not wishing to be deprived of the pleasure of exulting soon over his wretched brother, he had issued orders requiring his presence in Cajamarca. Challcochima had just returned from his parade of strength in Collao, and so he and his hard-marching army took the imperial prisoners north over Carmenca on what was to be their last journey. Quizquiz, the man of terror, continued to command the occupation, being carried here and there about the city in a litter, for both he and Challcochima had been granted this most signal of honors by Atauhuallpa as a reward for Cotapampa. He ruled from the Intihuasi as an ogre dominating an abject land from an iron castle. And his cruelties showed no signs of abating. The former lords of Cuzco knew now what the last draught of the cup of bitterness tasted like.

To this condition of things was now added the unbelievable.

Their conqueror, Atauhuallpa, had been captured! He had been seized in Cajamarca and was being held a prisoner by the *suncasapa*, even as Huascar was presently being held on the Royal Road north of Cuzco by Challcochima. Twice now the Incas' world had been overturned. Almost surely this was the *pachatikray*, the great "end of time" when all things were to be swallowed up.

That the *suncasapa* were indeed the legendary army of Ticci Viracocha, the Creator, seemed now to be a certainty. Whatever terrible and untoward events were in the making, it was they, Viracocha's veterans, the *huaminca* of the heavens who had long ago saved Cuzco in the historic battle with the Chancas, who were to be indisputably in the forefront of new battles. The lords of Cuzco raised their eyes from the ground to look about them, savoring this strange taste of hope. Would the city of Cuzco be saved again, and by the same archangelic army?

All Incas knew the ancient story; they had grown up filled with its mysteries and its heroism; looking about them they could behold the *huacas* of those warrior-wraiths placed here and there throughout Cuzco and its environs. These *huacas* were the *pururaucas*.

Years ago after the battle of Yahuar Pampa, Pachacuti had told his people how and why they had won such a memorable victory. The Creator had appeared to him in secret and promised him victory at a time when the cause of Cuzco appeared hopeless. In the heat of the battle, the Creator himself had hurled down against the enemy his *pururaucas*. These sky-born knights had turned the tide against the Chancas according to the divine promise, and then, even as the dust of the mighty conflict still hung in the air, they had suddenly congealed into stones, some small, some great, scattered widely about in Cuzco-quiti. In the work of reconstructing the Inca state afterward Pachacuti had ceremonially toured these environs and had pointed out to his awed people each one of those angelic allies as they lay about in the fields, on the hillsides, in the quarries, or on the mountaintops, locked in an ineffable muteness of stone. Those which were small enough to be removed were brought back to Cuzco with rejoicing and ensconced in niches in various parts of the city, many being placed in the outer walls of Coricancha. Those that were too ponderous or that formed a part of the living rock of Mother Earth were worshiped where they stood. Altogether they formed an army of unsleeping sentinels in and around the city. Each of the *pururaucas* had its own name and its own cult service on one of the *ceques*. So numerous and splendid was this array of guardian *huacas* both within and surrounding Cuzco that special priests were appointed to guide visiting dignitaries from one to another, so that they might properly worship the ghostly army and realize its full power. This mystical presence was the real reason that Cuzco could never be defeated. Mortal soldiers might fail but never those captained by Viracocha.

To the niches containing these *huacas* the Incas now raised their eyes, beginning to believe that it was they who had struck back at the desecrator of Cuzco's holiness, Atauhuallpa. The *suncasapa* were surely the *pururaucas*. If one needed additional proof, one had only to consider again the tale from the *ñaupapacha*, "the ancient times," which related how Viracocha had gone through the whole land from south to north, putting all things in their order, after which task, with his coequal helpers who were Viracochas themselves, he had vanished into the great waters off Ecuador with the vague and possibly menacing promise of return. And where had the *suncasapa* come from? They had come out of the sea off the Ecuadoran coast.

As the runners began to come in with reports for Quizquiz quartered in the Intihuasi, wild rumors in the city below gathered strength. The occupation forces now became uncertain and hesitant in their treatment of the Capac Incas, and a long pause in the half-life of the city followed. The entire atmosphere in Cuzco had in fact changed. Quizquiz was obviously puzzled and awaiting instructions. No longer did he have himself borne in his litter down the curving highway from Sacsahuaman to enforce his terrible inquisition; his patrols continued to move about in the environs as usual, but they no longer derided the Incas as they passed them by. They trod the streets and passed through the open spaces with more circumspection, awaiting further word on this most curious passage of history in which an emperor was held captive by an emperor himself a captive. The Capac Incas maintained that the *suncasapa* were Viracochas and that they would restore legitimacy by forcing the release of Huascar. Not sure of the truth of such asseverations, Quizquiz, as noted above, temporarily suspended action.

This period witnessed further overt cracks in the tottering structure of Inca solidarity. Ancient enmities fostered in the early history of the city began now to come to the surface. The Ayar Ucho *ayllu* for one resurrected its ancient claims to be the nuclear people of Cuzco. Their *ayllu* histories were exact on that point. The Creator himself in passing through Cuzco had blessed the rule of their great founder Alcaviza who with his people had occupied Pucamarca, a part of the city later to be pre-empted by Topa Inca and therefore in the center of the sacred triangle. They had at first successfully opposed the peoples moving in under Manco Capac and had boasted other great leaders, but pressures had become too great; they had been conquered and incorporated into the new Inca city under Mayta Capac, the fourth Inca ruler, and their own *apu* had disappeared into those pits dug in the ground where later was to be erected the infamous Sankahuaci. Finally, in the days of Pachacuti, the ninth ruler, they had been ejected from the city proper and forced out into the hamlet of Cayaocachi. They were and remained a strong *ayllu*, and the testimony of this fact was that their *ayllu huaca*, Ayar Ucho, was recognized as one of the original four Inca founders. They had long memories and never ceased to believe that the site of Cuzco had been stolen from them.

Such tensions, of which there were probably as many in Cuzco as there were *ayllus* represented among the Incas, had been controlled by the imperial office while it was strong. The release of this massive coercion from above allowed such anarchic tendencies inherent in the Inca social situation to reappear; this erosion, as we know, had been initiated by Huascar's denigration of the prestige of the Upper Cuzco *ayllus* and *panacas*.

The first clarification came with the arrival of a *chasqui* bearing Atauhuallpa's terse orders to strip Cuzcoquiti of all immediately portable gold and silver objects and to have these articles rushed by special carriers to Cajamarca. The precious metal was to be the ransom for his freedom from the *suncasapa*.

The morose Quizquiz complied. In part this action represented the snatching away of that share of the loot for which he, like Challcochima, had so tenaciously fought. It must have been difficult in the extreme for him, holding Cuzco as he did in his sole possession, to remain loyal to Atauhuallpa, an emperor who had thus weakly allowed the royal city to slip from his grasp at the very moment of seizing it. His relationship to the Capac Incas whom he had conquered had shifted considerably by this order, although in a direction he could not clearly see. All he knew was that both he and they now co-operated in looting the sacred city for the benefit of still a third party.

And then one day in May, two of the *suncasapa* entered the city accompanied by one of Atauhuallpa's captains as a surety for the correct accomplishment of their mission. They had been carried in hammocks at a fast pace all the way from Cajamarca. History vaguely remembers their names as Martín Bueno and Pedro Martín de Moguer, two of the uncouth soldiers under Pizarro whose exploits may have been, and indeed must have been, notable, but who are remembered only for this act. There may have been a third, Zárate by name.

The entry of this small group charged with the rapid collection of Atauhuallpa's ransom was sensational in its varied implications. Shattered as was the life of the Capac Incas, all who could emerged from their grief to witness the arrival of these beings from heaven.

That entry—so astounding in history—has gone almost totally unrecorded. The Viracochas left no adequate record of Cuzco, for they had no eyes for the world and its wonders except as they glistened. We know from later snippets of information, however, that the *suncasapa* were engaged at least once by the solemnity of the culture into which they had fallen, for when in the course of their search for gold they entered the cult chambers of the Tumibamba *panaca*, they did remove their footgear according to custom, out of respect for Huayna Capac's silent yet commanding presence. But they strode unfeelingly into the tabooed precincts of Coricancha—never before violated—and with bronze crowbars themselves prized off the extensive outer sheets of gold veneer, at which desecration their Inca attendants shrank away and covered their heads with their mantles. How great must be the *huaca* of these Viracochas that they could so insult and degrade the dignity of the Inca gods!

The *ayllus* at first felt suddenly freed of the yoke of the hated Quizquiz by the mere presence of these powerful Viracochas and hastened to deliver to them out of their own secret treasure-troves gold plate and other objects. Overruled for the moment by the presence of Atauhuallpa's envoy, Quizquiz offered no help to the Viracochas but did not molest them either.

The first enthusiasm with which the conquered Capac Incas had greeted these angelic deliverers rapidly faded. In purely mortal ways the interlopers misused the women of the city, and their every action spoke not of the iridescent squadrons of the heavens but of the coarse troops of earth. As these difficult facts secured acceptance, the Incas realized that although they had been delivered from one conquerer, they had simply acquired another. And insofar as Huascar also had earned their hatred and fear, they were now a destitute people, twice conquered, without legitimacy, and forsaken by Inti.

SECTION 4.

Andamarca and the News from the North

EVEN WHILE the *suncasapa* were in Cuzco supervising the collection of Atauhuallpa's ransom, the curtain was being rung down forever on the role of the Incas as a people descended from the sun.

It might have been hoped that the Viracochas in Cajamarca would have rescued Huascar from his captivity. Such did not occur. Huascar and the last of his blood were dispatched on secret orders from Atauhuallpa who feared lest Pizarro, his captor, should reseat Huascar on the throne of Tahuantinsuyo.

The cavalcade of wretches had been moved under heavy guard westward with Challcochima's army up to the *tambo* of Andamarca midway on the Royal Road. The prisoners were: Huascar; his *Coya*; Rahua Ocllo, the queen mother; Huanca Auqui, that unfortunate opponent of Atauhuallpa's great generals, his body already crushed by heavy blows; Inca Roca, the toady; Topa Atau, barely alive from the wounds received under torture at Cotapampa; Titu Atauchi, seized in the flight back; the three diligent campaigners, Urco Huaranka, Paucar Usno, and Hahuapanti; and, finally, Challco Yupanqui and Rupaca, priests of the sun. Huascar had had his shoulder threaded with a heavy rope for leading, but it is probable that the prisoners had not been further injured lest they expire before the appointed time.

At Andamarca they were led out by Challcochima's executioners, sadistically tortured, and then slaughtered one by one; their bodies were desecrated, cut to bits, and finally shoveled into the swift green river that leaped and roared and foamed nearby.

Huascar had been the architect of his own end, and it was he, as charged by his mother, who had included in it, as in the crowded last act of a bloody drama, the kinfolk left to him after the ravages of the plague and his many proscriptions had blotted out the others. The historian can only wonder at the awfulness of the fall.

Profound mourning ensued in Cuzco when residents learned the news, followed some time later by the report that Atauhuallpa himself had been garroted by the *suncasapa*. Little was changed; these acts were simply the expected sequels of disaster caused by Huascar's last, malevolent curses. Cotapampa and Andamarca had already altered *in toto* the world of the Incas. On that loom nothing that would be recognizable again was to be woven by them.

The Viracochas had left Cuzco. Quizquiz, still in command of the city, had nothing more to lose, no matter what transpired. He gave himself up to a debauchery of cruelty and lust, and the city sank moaning again into despair.

EL ONZE CAPÍTAN
RVMIÑAVI
TRAIDOR

SECTION 5.

The Last of Atauhuallpa's Generals

THESE TWO related tragedies had taken place in the first half of 1533. From that year until 1572 much is known of the trampings back and forth of the *suncasapa*, of their own series of brutal wars which thoroughly impoverished the land, of the tyrants whom they brought up out of the dust, and of the deadly chaos which they organized and always found so congenial—but little is known of the rapidly dissolving caste of Incas. What little there is, therefore, should be rescued so that the full tale of these remarkable people may be told.

The fates which befell Atauhuallpa's captains are an integral part of the story, for these men themselves wore the earplugs and were thus by definition Incas.

Rumiñaui, the man called "Stone-Eye" and Atauhuallpa's third ranking general, had been recalled to Cajamarca after the battle of Cotapampa and had been there with his master when the *suncasapa* had appeared. He had been in command of a strong regiment strategically placed in the environs of that city, but he had incontinently fled when the *suncasapa* seized his master. The man he was, and the type of man with whom Atauhuallpa would have had to deal had he lived, can be seen in the sequel to that flight. During the months of his royal master's detention by the *suncasapa* Rumiñaui set up a tyranny in Quito where he held Atauhuallpa's sons and a part of his women in custody. Atauhuallpa, although himself a captive, had sent a brother north to reclaim these children, if possible, and to rectify the situation. Illescas, the brother in question, failed and was treacherously slain by Rumiñaui

281

during a fiesta. He was skinned and made into a drum by this would-be emperor in Quito, and later, when Atauhuallpa's body was secretly brought back into Ecuador by his adherents, Rumiñaui saw to it that the mummy was destroyed and its pieces scattered. His last actions are veritable sagas of savagery. Forced farther back in Ecuador by the Spaniards, he systematically scorched the earth behind him. Of the many astounding Inca buildings in Ecuador, he left only smoking and overturned ruins. His masterpiece was Quito. Here he sadistically burned alive all the *acllas* and *mamaconas* whom he could not carry with him as he disappeared forever into the Ecuadoran Andes. His end took place in the montaña where a snow-clad peak today still bears his gruesome nickname.

The execution of Atauhuallpa had left a dangerous void in the authority which up to then, either legitimately or illegitimately, had been exercised over the great empire. This void Pizarro tried to fill by elevating to the vacant office of *capac apu* a young and inexperienced Inca named Topa Huallpa Inca, one of Huayna Capac's few sons who had been with Atauhuallpa in Cajamarca; he had escaped down the Royal Road the night of Atauhuallpa's capture but had subsequently returned to put himself under Spanish protection on hearing the news of his brother's execution.

After the extinction of Huascar and his party, Challcochima had turned his attention to exacting revenge upon the Huancas of the central sierra for the support they had given to Atauhuallpa's enemies. His army was still operative, and his cruelty was, if anything, stimulated by the fact that his emperor Atauhuallpa was at that time a prisoner in Cajamarca. When Hernando Pizarro and a group of Spaniards appeared in Jauja to see what could be done to immunize this potentially hostile army, Challcochima met them with Huanca heads, hands, and tongues spitted on the points of his lances. He was prevailed on to step down from command of that bloodstained army and to return to his captive master in Cajamarca, bringing with him the Indian porters and slow strings of llamas laden with the gold and silver objects destined for Atauhuallpa's ransom.

In Cajamarca Challcochima, no longer with an army at his back, was on the surface apparently loyal to his captive lord, but there is some evidence to suggest he had now written Atauhuallpa off and was casting about for a plan of action. After Atauhuallpa was executed, Challcochima was kept in partial detention by the Spaniards as they began to realize that, because of his fearsome reputation, he commanded the utmost respect among all levels of the Peruvian population. Thus when the Spaniards finally left Cajamarca for Cuzco, they took with them not only the puppet emperor Topa Huallpa Inca but Challcochima as well.

When this main body of Spaniards came to Jauja, they found that the large army which Challcochima had previously left there had broken away to the south where it was in a position to impede their passage to Cuzco. It was in Jauja that the puppet emperor died suddenly and very suspiciously. Some of the accompanying Incas insinuated that Challcochima was responsible for the event, that he had ordered poison to be introduced into the young prince's *akha*. Having no other candidate available at the moment to replace the youthful emperor, the Spaniards pressed southward without a *capac apu* in their entourage, but they kept Challcochima, now closely constrained, with them. Having crossed the Apurimac, they halted at Limatambo to take stock of the steep ascent which loomed ahead of them, not quite certain that Challcochima might not surreptitiously be involved in the ambush obviously being prepared for them at that place. Near the top of the pass of Vilcacunca, Quizquiz and his lieutenant, Yucra Huallpa, had thrown across the Royal Road an army formed by the Jauja detachments that had retreated to this point and his own garrison troops brought forward out of Cuzco.

The situation at this point was extremely complicated for the Incas who were left. The two brothers whose fratricidal hatred had so racked Tahuantinsuyo were now dead, and all was confusion. The captive Challcochima was being used by the Spaniards to the best of their ability against his former comrade-in-arms, Quizquiz, who now in an inverted role assumed the protection of the city of Cuzco which he had so recently terrorized. Behind him Cuzco had no love of seeing him victorious, for the only unchanging element in the whole situation was the residual hatred between the remnants of the party of legitimacy (who had by now forgotten Huascar's tyranny) and the Atauhuallpa faction which Quizquiz above all others represented. The relative freedom with which the invading Spaniards moved about in Tahuantinsuyo was a direct function of the disorganization and built-in hostilities of the Inca people.

There ensued a short and fierce clash between the Spaniards (aided by certain Indian groups who had thrown in their lot with them) and the forces under Quizquiz, but the pass was eventually forced and the Spaniards emerged into the lovely intermontane basin of Anta. Earlier there had joined them at the Apurimac bridge that son of Huayna Capac who was called Manco Inca. He had been a partisan of Huascar and was one of the few sons of Huayna Capac now left to claim the *mascapaycha*. At this time he therefore threw in his lot with Pizarro and petitioned him for the imperial office as his inheritance.

Behind this petition lay the statesmanlike work of an Inca called Titu Atauchi who had been one of Atauhuallpa's trusted officials at the time of his captivity. This person after the death of his master assumed command of one of the splinter armies of Tahuantinsuyo operating in the *sallca*. He had captured some Spaniards whom he wished to convince of his honorable intentions and to that end proposed a treaty between Spaniard and Inca. The terms were the restoration of Tahuantinsuyo under the only legitimate claimant to the *mascapaycha*, Manco Inca. All ordinances of that empire not in contradiction to Christian custom and Spanish imperial law were to remain in effect, and a symbiosis was to be established wherein on the one hand lands and *yanaconas* were to be offered to the Spaniards and on the other they were to provide for the Christianization of the Indians through the enterprise of the friars. Mutual nonaggression was agreed to, and Charles V of Spain was to ratify the agreement personally.

This was a notable formulation by a formerly pro-Atauhuallpa Inca, for it implicitly reunited all Incas again under an unquestioned legitimacy. It furthermore recognized that the Incas were no longer a dominant caste but would have to learn to share both their goods and their policies. As matters turned out, the Incas assumed this treaty was in effect; Francisco Pizarro allowed them to think so but himself had no intention of fulfilling its terms.

Because the Spaniards were so few they had great need of sheltering behind some façade of Inca government, and, for this reason, they gave the impression of acceding to this request. But they could not crown Manco Inca without disposing of Challcochima, for these two were the claimants, respectively, to the prerogatives of Huascar and Atau-huallpa, and the enmity between them was of the utmost virulence. Against Challcochima, accordingly, the charges of poisoning the former emperor were now brought out into the open, probably with the crime of treachery added. Challcochima, the most frightful of all Incas, was therefore publicly burned in Sacsahuana as a necessary sacrifice to the undying hatred of the Capac Incas for their Quito congeners. It was reported that with the flames licking about him he called out for his comrade-in-arms Quizquiz in a stentorian appeal that seemed to shake the heavens; Quizquiz with his shattered troops was camped nearby. But no succor came.

Still falling back, Quizquiz made a weak pretense of holding Cuzco near the famous Field of Blood, but with a hostile city behind him there was little to hope for and, finally allowing the Spaniards to move through after a night skirmish, he slipped past their flank with some regiments and fled up the Chinchaysuyo road behind them. The collapse of his terrible rule in Cuzco was sudden, and the remaining Incas in the city had little heart themselves for a fight with the *suncasapa* nor any ability left to concert meaningfully. As the invaders inexorably closed in on Cuzco, great smoke signals went up in advance of them, spelling in the dripping skies the message of their progress. Some of the splintered factions of the Incas, not wishing to accept Manco Inca as their *capac apu*, moved up to the top of Carmenca and, in confused fury, held up the advance for a while. With nightfall this part of the Inca people melted away, leaving the city unguarded against the next morning's seizure. It was with submission, therefore, and indeed with some gratitude, that the remaining Incas blew kisses to Manco Inca, their new *capac apu*, as he was escorted in his litter down into the city by the ironclad Viracochas.

Quizquiz, who was now north of the Apurimac, moved recklessly here and there in the dark Andes, no doubt with the eventual strategy in mind of joining Rumiñaui in Quito. But his movements show uncertainty. He was joined on the way by one of Atauhuallpa's brothers, a die-hard captain called Huaypallca, with a few warriors behind him, and with this outlaw army they fought several vicious battles with the handful of Spaniards scattered about in central and northern Peru. The Spaniard Benalcazar was in pursuit of Rumiñaui who had fled into northern Ecuador; Quizquiz was following Benalcazar, while behind him came another group of Spaniards under De Soto dispatched from Cuzco to track down Quizquiz—three pursued and three pursuers. Rumiñaui's end has been related. As for the feral Quizquiz, his authority over ragtag army was challenged in a deadlocked council of war, and he was speared to death by his brother-captain Huaypallca, who himself was dead soon after. So ended the generals of the forces of Atauhuallpa, like mad dogs eating each other up at the end. No loyalty was there.

Section 6.

Manco Inca's Reign in Cuzco

On the 15th of November, 1533, the full party, including approximately one hundred and seventy-five Spaniards, having moved down the face of Carmenca along the tree-lined terraces and thence into Cusipata, crossed the river and entered Haucaypata. For four months longer, while Cuzco was being systematically looted and the tombs in the environs sacked, it continued to be an Inca city. Indeed Manco Inca's formal investiture, following the terms of the Titu Atauchi treaty, took place as usual with the royal mummies in attendance in the open square—the only differences from former times being the poverty of the proceedings and the presence of alert and disdainful Spaniards. Then on March 23, 1534, in a ceremony at the foot of the public gibbet which the Spanish had substituted for the *usno* in the plaza, the *capac llacta* became formally a Spanish *cabildo* soon to be known as the Very Noble and Very Great City of Cuzco. The following day the first meeting of the Spanish *ayuntamiento* or city council took place. The city which less than a century before Pachacuti had re-established, naming it and envisaging it as a *pumap-uku*, a "lion-body," was now being carved up for a new set of lords. Manco Inca, who had formally requested that Francisco Pizarro implement the treaty two days after this arrival in Cuzco, must have begun to realize with this new founding the unreal quality of his hopes.

The first order of business after the election of the *cabildo* officers was the parceling out of lots to the victors. The frontage of a lot was put at two hundred feet, and these were at first measured out along the existent Inca streets and terrace faces. The favored locations were of course around Haucaypata and fronting on it. Francisco Pizarro received four contiguous lots in Casana, Pachacuti's *cancha*; Gonzalo Pizarro was assigned two lots in Coracora next to these; Hernando de Soto, two lots in Amarucancha, Huayna Capac's establishment. To Almagro went three lots in Collcampata, Huascar's palace, and to Juan Pizarro, the huge terraces of Coricancha.

Hatuncancha was sliced up into numerous lot fronts for the other deserving warriors of Spain, and the same was also done to that part of the city on the terraces across the Sapi. The church was alloted all of the frontage of Quishuarcancha, Viracocha's shrine. From this site the life-sized stone statue of Viracocha had already been removed and taken covertly to a spot far up the Vilcañota valley; thus the dwelling place of the high god of the empire was empty when the crucifix entered.

Only gradually did the Capac Incas awake to the import of the meetings of this first *cabildo*. To them Cuzco was of necessity the concrete expression of Inca life. They could not be expected to follow the meaning of the cabalistic signs put down on parchment by each one of the founding fathers with a scratching condor feather and a black dye.

At the time of his taking the *mascapaycha*, Manco Inca was about twenty years of age. He and his younger brother Paullo had grown up during the intrigues of Huascar's reign, for their imperial father had left them both as babies in Cuzco when he had journeyed north to Quito. The fact that these two remained alive at the end of Huascar's reign was a tribute either to their apparent innocuousness or to their skill in circumventing the quicksands of intrigue. Both had managed to flee the worst of the rigors of Quizquiz' occupation, Manco Inca escaping down into the montaña and Paullo to the island of Titicaca with a group of retainers which included his mother. Challcochima's swift foray into those parts had failed to track down and destroy these two male survivors of the Huascar party.

The younger of the two, Paullo, was the more interesting person. He was astute and less impulsive than his brother Manco Inca, and his high standing among the Inca people must have had the effect of considerably dimming his brother's luster. But Manco Inca had been closer to Cuzco when the Spaniards leaped the Apurimac frontier, and it had been he who had made first contact with Pizarro, supplicating his assistance on the grounds of being the oldest surviving son of Huayna Capac and therefore the legitimate claimant to the *mascapaycha*. Around that time Paullo had married his half sister, the priestess of the moon on an island just off Titicaca; she also had escaped the hasty probing of Challcochima's patrols. Her name was Tocto Usica and she was classed with the Vicaquirau *panaca*; her high place in Inca cult, ranking with the Coya Pacsa in Cuzco and the *asarpay* of the Apurimac oracle, gave additional prestige to the union, and both Paullo and she had proceeded to carry on Inca rule in a somewhat *de facto* manner over all of Collasuyo after Challcochima's departure. Paullo's influence extended even down into the Chilean parts of Tahuantinsuyo, and it was this fact alone which allowed Almagro to penetrate that area later. It is probable that Paullo remained in Collasuyo for exactly the same reason that Atauhuallpa had originally remained in Quito—suspicion that he would be destroyed by his brother, in this case Manco Inca, should he return to Cuzco. And that this fear reflected the realities of Manco Inca's court in the Spanish city of Cuzco is seen in the fact that Manco had two of his other remaining brothers so murdered. One of them was Pascac who was apprehended while doing homage to Manco Inca with a weapon concealed under his *yacolla*. Foreknowledge of the assassination attempt allowed the young emperor to turn the tables and have him killed instead. The other was Atoc Sopa in return for whose death Manco Inca promised Almagro that he would reveal to him the whereabouts of a buried treasure.

We can see from these incidents that the unwholesome flavor inherited from the court of Huascar, the poisonous breath of delation, and the dagger that smothered all its whispers, had not been purged away by the series of cataclysms that had fallen upon the Inca people. It is evident to the historian that in the culture which the Incas had built for themselves there was no remedy for this disease.

Yet the Incas continued to celebrate their festival calendar—they knighted their young men, celebrated harvest-home, honored their father the sun, and purified the city. But their activities were, as already indicated, radically reduced. For one thing Manco Inca, a slave to an incurable anti-Atauhuallpa passion, had followed Quizquiz north in the train of De Soto, hoping to satisfy his vengeance. He was thus away from his people when they needed him most to smooth the always harsh way of social adjustment. The Incas, unaided by their *capac apu*, could certainly not then have been expected to have established a policy. Nominally under their own ruler, they drifted this way and that on the turbid tides of New Castile.

What neither Manco Inca nor his people could have remedied in any case was the damage caused by increasing division in the ranks of their Spanish masters, for two factions had formed there, their basic quarrel having been occasioned by the loot. In history these parties are referred to as the Pizarrists and the Almagrists, and their bloody deeds and horrendous altercations make a fitting addendum to the War of the Two Brothers. Weakened by their own opportunist leadership—or lack of it—the Incas could only suffer further from this strife among their masters.

Unsatisfied with his share in the booty extracted up to then from Tahuantinsuyo, Almagro mounted an expedition for distant Chile, and he took with him the young Paullo, still not twenty years of age, chiefly because of Paullo's great prestige in those areas. Also he wanted an Inca counteremperor along with him should Manco Inca during his absence become too closely identified with the Pizarrist faction in Cuzco. A number of Paullo's noble relatives accompanied him. The expedition turned out to be a disaster.

As soon as Almagro had left the city, Manco Inca incautiously, although with some justice, demanded of the Pizarrists that the *modus vivendi* supposedly agreed to be reaffirmed by them and that Tahuantinsuyo as an empire be reconstituted with himself as its acknowledged master. This naïve misreading of the actualities of the situation elicited from the Spaniards nothing but contempt. But they also were uninformed, for they did not realize that as long as Paullo was alive and under the protection of the opposing Spanish chieftain, by just so long would mighty perturbations convulse the corpse of Tahuantinsuyo.

Spanish greed for gold produced the catastrophe. Manco Inca was badgered incessantly by the Spaniards to produce more of the precious metal. It was known or suspected that only a portion of that available had gone to Cajamarca to ransom Atauhuallpa. The finer pieces, statues of the Inca gods in solid gold, the famous serpent-cable of the Incas braided with gold and almost long enough to encircle Haucaypata, along with other objects well known from the recent Inca past had not turned up in any of the searches; they had been removed and buried in unknown or inaccessible places. In contemplating this treasure-trove so tantalizingly near, the Spanish mind became easily lost in the fumes of speculation and heated beyond the point of endurance. Pressure on Manco Inca increased to an unbearable point. Besides this situation, the Spaniards were aware by now that, from the point of view of pliability, they had probably invested the wrong man with the *mascapaycha*; they became openly contemptuous of Manco Inca, and his disclaimers of knowledge of the wealth buried under the earth they thrust aside. One method of extortion practiced by the Spaniards to elicit such knowledge was to gather Incas presumed to have information into the houses and then to set the great thatches over their heads on fire. Less extreme but more effective was the Spaniards' use of the *pallas* as informers. Marca Chimpu was one of the four sisters of Huascar who had managed to survive up to that point, probably because she had been a baby when her mother had taken her north with Huayna Capac. She was raped many times by the Spaniards in Cuzco and forced to reveal what she knew to the insatiable Almagro and others concerning the hiding places of Inca treasure. Relations between the two peoples sank to a level of mutual fear and hatred.

Manco Inca, now under suspicion, became a house prisoner in the city. He was incarcerated in the Intihuasi but later and reluctantly freed. His half sister and *coya*, a lovely young woman called Cori Ocllo, was coveted by Gonzalo Pizarro who may indeed have desired her primarily to help him found a dynasty of independent kings; the bitter feelings aroused over this unsavory episode contributed to the further collapse of Manco Inca's prestige. It is difficult to sort out the true from the untrue in the tales of mayhem and sexual lust that attach themselves to the Spaniards of this period and place; they are said to have urinated in Manco Inca's face, forced lighted candles up his nose, and raped his concubines under his very eyes. Certainly the historian can easily envisage it as possible, for the conquest of one people by another is always a tragic spectacle. The *suncasapa* in Peru in callousness, atrocity, and general infamy have certainly never been surpassed, and what is recorded above is found in a letter written to Emperor Charles V by two Spaniards who held property in Cuzco. The Spaniards were not given to recording their own misdeeds unnecessarily.

In any case Cuzco's early enthusiasm for the Viracochas had totally disappeared. Dazed by the daily insults offered them, by the thefts, looting, and seizure of their women, the Incas fumbled about in a night of ignorance and frustration. Looking for the last time into their heroic past, they finally dredged up their last measure of self-assertion as a people and challenged the *suncasapa* to a contest for the beloved city.

Section 7. *Auccay Yntuy—the Siege*

We have seen that Almagro, departing south into Collasuyo and the parts beyond, took Paullo with him. Paullo soon showed that he, alone of the Capac Incas left, appreciated the role his people must play in the future, and from this time on he committed himself to a policy of moderate co-operation with the *suncasapa*, although perforce he was for the moment identified as an Almagrist. Against him of course stood the faction crystalizing around Manco Inca and vigorously headed by a relative named Vilauma who felt that with resolution Tahuantinsuyo could be snatched back from iron-hearted *suncasapa*. Vilauma had accompanied Paullo and Almagro as far as Collao, but once there he had managed to leave the ill-fated expedition.

The famous siege of Cuzco, which was to last from the spring of 1536 well into the summer of the following year, was a part of a larger attempt to hurl the Spaniards out of the whole of Peru. Vilauma, an Inca with an Aymara name and probably not one of the royal family, was the person who engineered and masterminded the enterprise, and he came within a hair's breadth of success.

While down in Collasuyo he had apparently been laying the groundwork for the uprising. He had then been dispatched by his emperor on a seemingly innocuous errand up into Chinchaysuyo; in reality he was there to enlist the northern *curacas* in the scheme and see to its preparation. The typical Inca genius for organization is indicated in the execution of this vast conspiracy against the *suncasapa* who had come into their midst; it had to be on an imperial scale if it was to be successful. What made the task easier was the fact that Manco Inca as *de jure* ruler of Tahuantinsuyo had continued under the Spaniards to send out Inca governors into the provinces and thus maintained the semblance of an imperial administration. Nevertheless, when the rebellion did break out into the open, the hatred against the arrogant Incas was so implacable amongst such groups as the coastal peoples, the Chachapoyas, and the Cañar *mitmacs* in Cuzcoquiti that they actively assisted the Spaniards against the possibility of a revived Tahuantinsuyo. Furthermore, a few highly placed Incas threw in their lot with the Spaniards during the siege, bringing with them in some instances contingents of fighting men from their respective *ayllus* and some food to relieve the starving Spaniards. Bitterly were the followers of Manco Inca to castigate these men, charging them with being *aucas*, "traitors," and therefore the most despicable of criminals. It is to be supposed that the *ñustas* and *pallas* were also similarly unreliable in their commitments, for some of them were already the concubines of the *suncasapa*.

In order to act as suzerain over the enterprise, Manco Inca had of course to escape Spanish custody. This goal he accomplished by the infallible subterfuge of appealing to the Spaniards' greed for gold, their permanent Achilles' heel. He wished, he said, to celebrate the April harvest on his terraces near Calca in the Yucay valley. If allowed to do so, he would also see to it that the solid gold *huaoqui* of his father —up to then still missing—would be located and turned over to the Spaniards. They agreed. Once in the Yucay valley Manco Inca remained inaccessible to the Spaniards who soon became thoroughly alarmed at the possible consequences of his freedom. Manco Inca did celebrate the traditional rites there, but he used the occasion to reveal to Incas and local *curacas* his determination to oust the *suncasapa* because of their failure to maintain the agreement made earlier by Titu Atauchi, acting in his name, and Francisco de Chávez, who had acted for Pizarro. The Yucay valley itself, lined with its great palaces and fortress cities, Pisac, Huchuy Cuzco, Calca, and Ollantaytambo, could easily be entered by the Spaniards riding over Pachatusan from Cuzco, but they could not successfully storm the forts. Manco Inca established himself in Ollantaytambo and from there announced himself as fully sovereign over Tahuantinsuyo in the manner of his fathers.

On May 3, before dawn, the attack on Cuzco began, the traditional *tutapacuspa aucaycuy*, "rising in the night to deliver an attack." Scattered all over Peru—Benalcazar being in Ecuador, Francisco Pizarro in Lima, and Almagro far down in Chile—the Spaniards were in any one area a mere handful and the chances were all in favor of destroying them piecemeal. In the city of Cuzco there were at the time only about one hundred and ninety Spaniards and eighty horses supported by a certain number of Cañars and a mere handful of Incas. Around them on the hills that sunny morning there were encamped some of the hordes from the four quarters of the empire under the command of the resourceful and fire-breathing Vilauma—that relative of Manco who was responsible for the disposition of all contingents. His head-quarters was in the Intihuasi on Sacsahuaman from which he looked down into the heart of the city he hoped soon to reclaim for his people.

Even as the hills around Cuzco had seeded themselves with innu-merable Peruvians in arms, so had portions of the rest of Peru arisen. A formidable and fully confident army lay athwart the Capac Ñan between Cuzco and Lima, cutting the sierra off from any Spanish help from the coast. Lima was closely besieged by an Inca army, and severe battles were fought around that city and in the sand hills just to the north. On the death of the Inca army's leader in battle, Huallpa Roca who had been stationed in the fortress of Cuzco was sent as a replace-ment, but he defected to the Spaniards and another captain, Tisoc, ably but without success, filled his place on the Rimac.

The siege of Cuzco was most pertinaciously sustained by the Inca army, *ayllus* relieving each other in orderly fashion, but missed oppor-tunities were many. Vilauma had to refer major decisions to the em-peror Manco Inca who remained, as was a *capac apu*'s custom, taking his pleasure under the peaks of the Andes some distance away. The worst blow came when the invincible fortress was lost to the Span-iards. From here the Incas had been able to send great rocks bounding down the slopes and into the heart of the city. But the morale of their contingents had been seriously undermined by the calculated Spanish policy of destroying all of the women captured. Inasmuch as it was the women accompanying the great host who cooked, carried, and cared for their menfolk and provided them with sexual solace, this calculated cruelty had its intended effect. These Indian women seized while for-aging and filling their water jars were subjected to the most brutal uses. Their cries of terror from down in the city as they were being tor-tured chilled even the toughest warriors of the *sallca*, and the sight of the torn and hacked bodies spread out on the terraces in the morning sun for the inspection of vultures and kinfolk taught the Peruvian *huaminca* to read out of a new chapter in the book of war. In the Spanish *conquistadores* they had at last met their peers in terror.

Vilauma, the fierce captain, was not in the great fortress when it was taken. The intrepid Spaniards, a mere handful of them, fought their way up to Chuquipampa with their Indian allies and miraculously succeeded in forcing the three circumvallation walls. The final battle took place around the base of one of the towers within the Intihuasi and lasted for three days, at the end of which period thirst and panic had destroyed the morale of the fifteen thousand defenders. The tale was played out when the heroic Cahuite, last of the stern Inca captains, fighting in a Spanish helmet and with a Spanish blade, wrapped himself in his *yacolla* and leaped off the battlement to his death. While his men had stood about him on the towertop dazed and frightened, he had killed thirty of them himself as cowards and contemptuously toppled their bodies into the ranks of the Spaniards and Cañars below. He had fought like a lion and alone, rushing at the Spaniards as their ladders topped the battlements until finally he could do no more. Cahuite, otherwise unknown, is the last flicker in our sources of the independent fury and valor of the Inca knight.

Just previous to this episode, at the lowest ebb of their fortunes, the Spaniards had taken refuge in Hatuncancha for a last-ditch stand. The massive thatches of the city were naturally the targets of hundreds of flaming torches flung at them from the terraces, and the black pall of smoke, pinked out with occasional flickers and tougues of fire, became daily more and more suffocating. Those marvelous roofs burned for months, so thick and compactly contrived were they. Finally the rain of sparks and the choking air mixed with occasional cold rain so hampered the Spaniards that they were forced to camp out in tents in Haucaypata. Almost every Spaniard was wounded, many seriously; none slept except in arms and, were he a *caballero*, beside his saddled horse; they were cut off completely from Lima which was the only possible source of succor on a large scale, and they believed all Spaniards there to be dead—yet never once did they think of not sustaining the fight. Their heroism is as appalling as their brutality, and in the end, excelling the Incas in both, they won.

During the year of this memorable siege the appearance of the Upper Huatanay valley was wholly altered. The bulky terraces with their great perpendicular faces, sharp angles, and steep winding stairs, had radically reduced the effectiveness of the Spanish cavalry, and as a consequence they had been destroyed wherever possible, leaving rubble-strewn slopes that in the winter rains gullied rapidly. The green gardens that everywhere overhung Cuzco washed away with the terraces, their refuse dirtying the stream beds and roads. Inca suburban villas and apartments, having lost the strong support of the *callanca* terraces, became unsafe and fell into rapid decay or were demolished. Vilauma had cut all the *pacchas*, "the waterways" into the city, and the uncontrolled waters now washed down here and there, filling the flats with puddles and bogs. The reservoirs farther up the Sapi had been breached, and so the waters in floodtime came down in violent spates causing further damage and a spreading health hazard. The raging fires had destroyed almost every roof in the city and left the stuccoed walls open to the weather. Cuzco in that one year became a *racay racay*, a gutted city.

But one of the edifices escaped the general conflagration, the Suntur Huasi. Here the Spaniards daily worshiped and heard mass. At the very nadir of their fortunes, so runs the medieval legend of that dark day, the Spaniards, having no hope of help but from heaven, looked up and saw a woman "beautiful as the moon, select as the sun, terrible as armies in array." Sometimes she is said to have been clad in armor, more generally in her maternal blue mantle, but she is always described darting lightly here and there over the packed *ichu* of the roof, blowing out the torches hurled up to it with her own divine lips and fanning out the embers with her skirts. Other accounts said that the beautiful virgin scattered snowflakes over the burning roof and hurled hailstones into the eyes of the raging Indians below. Thus transpired the Miracle of the Matriz and the supposed spot is today commemorated on plaques in the façade of the church of the Triunfo fronting the Plaza de Armas. The ever-grateful Spaniards even remembered the date as the twenty-first of May. Cuzco had always been holy. Viracocha had blessed it and put it under the protection of the *pururaucas* in the Chanca war. But the *pachatikray*, the "overthrow of time," had indeed taken place and new gods walked the walls of heaven. When the story of the Miracle of the Matriz appeared in the years that followed the siege, there could be no reason to doubt it, and it spoke to the Indians of the Huatanay valley, as well as to the Spaniards, with complete authenticity. It was not the Incas' story, but they did not on that account doubt it.

The competing legend had it—perhaps more realistically—that St. James, the war saint of the Spaniards, seated on his white charger and brandishing his sword, fought miraculously against the Inca hordes. But if so, he gave himself away most interestingly when he began hurling thunderbolts, for by that act he revealed to later Incas his true identity—he was none other than Illapa, the god of thunder, here in his anger turned against them.

What finally could be borne no longer by the varied regiments under Manco Inca were the unplanted *chacras* back home, at that moment raising for them and their children only crops of weeds and famine. Inevitably the host began to dwindle as one *ayllu* after another slipped away, and with each such defection the pressure on the Spaniards lessened. Down on the coast the siege of Lima had also been thoroughly broken, and Spaniards were known to be on their way to Cuzco's relief. After the loss of the Intihuasi, Manco Inca had thought it expedient to strengthen the fortifications of Ollantaytambo. However intelligent his action, it nevertheless spoke eloquently to all concerned of the failure of his campaign.

Eventually the last *chaya! chaya!* was heard ringing off the heights and the last slingstones rattled down into the city. Abandoning Cuzco, and Incas fell back to Ollantaytambo, the sole fortress left to them.

Vilauma had escaped and separately from Manco Inca continued to carry on guerrilla warfare for four or five more years in the difficult country of Contisuyo to the south. With his capture and death all determined resistance based on the Inca idea of the recovery of Cuzco ended. The damage had been incalculable. More than twenty thousand Indians died in the siege of Cuzco itself. The burning of *tambos* and the failure of *chacras* all over Peru brought on at least four years of terrible famine in which died great numbers of children and youths particularly. The extinction of Inca power in the provinces allowed the local *curacas*, hitherto responsible to the central power, to set themselves up in unrestrained local tyrannies, thus deepening the chaos.

When the siege of Cuzco was raised in the year 1537 and the famine was beginning in the land of Peru, it was said by one of the more perspicacious of the Spaniards resident in Cuzco: "I believe it can be affirmed that the Spaniards did more damage in four years alone than the Inca ruler achieved in four hundred."

When all the embers remaining from the rebellion had been stamped out, the Very Noble City of Cuzco received in 1540 from the court in Spain a coat of arms commemorating the days of her agony and triumph. This design displayed a golden castle on a red field, the whole surrounded by a gold band containing eight condors. The castle was the captured Intihuasi, and the condors told of the eight months of feasts which they had had on the bodies of the Inca slain.

Section 8. *Manco Inca, First of the Vilcabamba Emperors*

Manco Inca had with him in Ollantaytambo besides some remnants of the army his *coya*, Cori Ocllo, many women, and a small retinue of Incas under the newly appointed captain general, Cusi Rimachi. Just as importantly, he had with him the relics of his religion which included some of the mummies of the emperors and their *coyas*, the stone of Huanacauri, and the image of the sun. For a while he felt safe in Ollantaytambo, for the site had under his direction been almost completely rebuilt, the steepness of the ascent and the violence of the river at its feet being of advantage to those who might wish to stand siege there. In all he was here about a year and a half carrying on the leisurely and luxurious duties of an Inca emperor, raiding the Spaniards at every opportunity, still able to command some labor gangs from the environs but forever deprived of that indispensable adjunct of Inca royalty, the city of Cuzco.

Once during the year of Cuzco's agony, Spaniards from Cuzco had ridden with their Indian auxiliaries over the flats of Anta to drop down into the Yucay valley and attack Ollantaytambo. This foray had been easily repulsed, and the Spaniards had been forced back across the river.

But in the last analysis Ollantaytambo was indefensible unless the strategic location of Pachar just upstream could be permanently manned and held. Fierce drawn battles in this area finally convinced Manco Inca and his brother Cusi Rimachi that they could afford little more of such fighting and they prepared to make the move which was inevitable for all Peruvians who had already become bandits—flight into the montaña.

The city of the Vilcamayo oracle, Machu Picchu, in all probability had already been evacuated and its remaining women added to Manco's entourage. The poisonous fer-de-lance could now slither across the splendid stairs without fear or sun himself upon the worked lip of the basin; the condor could light unmolested on the rotting thatches and the waxy begonia grow on the esplanades; no more oracles would ever again be read there from the river's hollow throat.

The news had come to Manco Inca that the Spaniard Almagro had unexpectedly returned from Chile bringing Paullo with him. It was this piece of news which precipitated action in Manco Inca's camp, for it was also known that Almagro had encouraged Paullo to assume the royal fringe and declare himself the legitimate emperor. Manco Inca saw the possibility that the allegiance up to now given to him by the remaining Incas might melt away in favor of his more popular brother. He consequently made an effort to treat with Almagro on the subject. Not unexpectedly Almagro repulsed this approach, for Paullo was exceptionally popular.

The move into the back country where he was less exposed had in the event now become pressing for Manco Inca. Ollantaytambo he had defended up to this point because it commanded the only two gateways into the Vilcabamba montaña. Back of Ollantaytambo is the Panticalla Pass, excessively dangerous because of sudden rockfalls, precipitous trails, and death from freezing. Over that terrible path now, carried sedately by the last of his Lucana bearers, passed Manco Inca, king of the bandits certainly but hardly an emperor as well. The year was 1538.

From the trans-Andean provinces of Huitcos and Vilcabamba he proceeded to rule as any robber-baron would rule, periodically issuing forth over the glaciers of Salcantay to raid the *tambos* and Spanish posts on the old Capac Ñan. The Incas had remained as vengeful as ever, and Manco Inca, who did not forget the Huancas' easy defection to the Spaniards, more than once harried that exposed population. He fought now on horseback and brandished the steel arms of the enemy. True to the anti-*huaca* tradition of his house, he mistreated Huarivillca, the potent idol of those people, dragging it behind his horse after having cruelly slaughtered all of its priesthood. The people and the lands he continued to lay waste so far as it was in his power. The central sierra, already racked by famine, was further crippled by these devastations. Once back in his pocket of the Andes, Manco was relatively immune from hot pursuit, but, having no policy other than that of irritating his enemies, his achievements could accumulate to no purpose.

A serious foray into the montaña by a force of Spaniards under Gonzalo Pizarro finally reached him. Paullo and two cousins—the three of them pro-Spanish—accompanied the column either as guides or as ambassadors, according to the vicissitudes they might meet. A fierce engagement was fought along the lower Urubamba, and the two cousins fell into Manco Inca's hands. In the subsequent victory feast they were treated as *aucas*, ingeniously tortured, and decapitated so that Manco Inca might drink from their skulls. Paullo, the third brother, escaped. But in that mighty world of hot canyons and icy peaks the tides of fortune shifted easily, and during a drinking bout the Inca camp was ambushed. Manco Inca himself escaped by leaping into the river, but his *coya*, two of his sons, and his brother Cusi Rimachi, as well as several captains, were taken. In the loot were a few ancestral mummies.

Riding back into the Yucay valley, the Spaniards left their accustomed record of savagery. In retaliation for the killing of their two Inca ambassadors the Spaniards attempted to rape Cori Ocllo in the square of one of the Inca communities where they stopped, but to prevent this indignity she befouled herself. All the way back to Ollantaytambo they molested her but were unable to break her spirit. Finally in frustration Francisco Pizarro ordered her placed alone in the center of the plaza of Ollantaytambo—her brother and the captains being forced to watch—and from a distance as in sport they shot arrows at her.

Folding her *lliclla* over her head, she died pierced through and through. Next Cusi Rimachi was burned and the other captains served up as torches at each stop up to Yucay. The life of one of Manco Inca's sons, Titu Cusi, they preserved. This child was put under the care of one of the Spaniards so that he might grow up in this household in Cuzco; but he was shortly thereafter kidnaped and brought back to Vilcabamba, his father's refuge capital.

Manco Inca's end was appropriate to the rough drama in which he had been chosen to play a part. He was set upon and killed by brutalized renegade Spaniards who had fled to his mountain barony to escape Spanish justice. They were, of course, apprehended by the Inca captains and tortured to death. The Inca army, or band as it should be more correctly called, at this point could have numbered no more than three thousand conditioned fighting men.

By now the famine was severe and thousands of Indians were dying in southern and central Peru. Many of the warehouses which had been filled to bursting with the grain and *chuño* of the empire had been wantonly burned by both Spaniards and Incas as they carried their weapons against each other up and down the land.

"What is certainly most melancholy to contemplate is that the Incas, though idolaters, knew how to govern and to reclaim lands for cultivation whereas we Christians have simply destroyed kingdoms. Wherever we have gone, discovering and conquering, there it appears that great fires have raged."

Thus wrote one of the conquerors. And another one, who wrote only thirty years after the Spanish entry into Cuzco, credited that entry with reducing the population of Peru to one-fourth of its former number.

COREGIMIENTO
ELCOREG.ºIPTINIE
Kandavda 9an.do ymirando laguerguenza delas mugeres

pro 'inçias   Pas

SECTION 9.

The Very Noble City

FATHER VALVERDE, Cuzco's first bishop, in the year 1538 came to revisit the city which earlier he had entered with the conquering army of Pizarro. He failed to recognize the city after the depredations of the siege. "Now most of the city is tumbled down and burned," he wrote. "Few stones of the fortress are standing. It is a wonder when one finds any house in the environs with more than walls."

Between this date and 1572 the Spanish reconstruction of the city of Cuzco was completed. It took thus a trifle more than a generation to make anew the visage of the city as well as the faces of its population. Almost nothing of this process is observable by the historian because it took place amidst ferocious civil wars among the Spaniards and alarms and suspected treacheries among the Incas. But what can be seen should be related, for, as the city progressively lost its *huaca* and became Christian, by exactly that much did the last flicker of the spirit of the Incas gutter and die down. City and people, as we have already pointed out, were one.

When Paullo had returned from Chile wearing the *mascapaycha* given him by Almagro, he was looked upon by all the Indians of Cuzcoquiti as their natural leader. An overt contest among those loyal to him and those loyal to Manco Inca did not arise, inasmuch as the latter seemed permanently immured in his distant valley over the Andes. Paullo in fact seems not to have pressed his claim too sharply, being content from 1539 on to exercise a certain *de facto* power while apparently waiting for Manco Inca to die before fully legitimatizing himself and establishing a house. He was intelligently pro-Spanish and

302

through this allegiance perhaps lightened somewhat the bitter plight of his people.

Nevertheless, it was Paullo who in a concealed shrine next to his residence on Collcampata cherished some of the older Inca *huacas*. It was here, therefore, that the Incas of the interim years continued surreptitiously to celebrate the *huarachicoy* until finally the Spaniards located the obnoxious and potentially dangerous *huacas* and removed them along with their attendant *villcas* and rich offerings of *cumpi*. Huanacauri had already vanished with Manco Inca into the montaña. With the passing of these *huacas* of Collcampata into the hands of the Spaniards there was effectively removed the traditional mechanic by which the Inca caste was recruited and maintained, for the earplugs could be legitimately bestowed upon young Incas only by Huanacauri or proper substitutes in the festival of the Capac Raymi. Nevertheless the genius of the Inca people for ceremony continued to appear in new and substitute rites which they created for the underground perpetuation of their identity as a people, although this activity became more dangerous and difficult with each passing year.

It was perhaps because of this situation that Paullo finally took the step of renouncing his familiar gods in favor of the god of the Christians. In 1543 he was baptized as Don Cristóbal; his sister-wife became Doña Catalina, another sister became Beatriz Huayllas Ñusta, and his mother, Doña Juana Añas Collque. These conversions openly marked—but did not further divide—the Incas into two opposed groups, those carrying on the struggle against the Spaniards under the dynasty of Manco Inca in Vilcabamba and those who now accepted the Spanish presence in the city of Cuzco. Christianity indeed was becoming something of an element even among the Vilcabamba Incas. Many others of the ranking Capac Incas, spurred on by Paullo's example, came now to Mary's Church in Haucaypata to be baptized. It is probable that the change was neither abrupt nor difficult, and it offered the Incas a kind of protection, meager to be sure but better than their status as worshipers of the devil. In any case, Paullo's conversion was a watershed.

In recognition of the importance of the event the Spanish crown in 1545 granted to Don Cristóbal Paullo Topa Inca a coat of arms which incorporated the elements of the blazon of the Inca *capac apu*: the palm tree; the jaguar and the two serpents each wearing the *mascapaycha*. Forty-two crowns were said to represent the forty-two kingdoms which had formerly been included in the wide reaches of Tahuantinsuyo—as a memory of faded glories. Paullo now resided officially in Collcampata which estate had been allotted to him upon the death of Almagro to whom it had been assigned in the original Spanish allotment. Here, in the apartments built by Huascar, he lived, surrounded by a pathetic imitation court and wonderfully revered still by the population around. His piety was great and it was he who founded in 1545 the first chapel in Cuzco, that of San Cristóbal. This chapel he situated on the terrace of Collcampata which had been one of the few to survive the general wreckage on the slopes round about; it may be presumed that this Christian shrine became for the Incas and other Indians a new *huaca* in the environs and one which in a sense belonged to them alone. It would later become a parish church wherein his own descendants were to be baptized. In spite of his acknowledged Christian piety, his *huaoqui* was adored with traditional Inca rites on his death in 1549, and his palace was the scene of the traditional clustering of Inca warriors to prevent usurpation. And when the year of mourning had elapsed for him, his people roamed the *sallca*, carrying his garments and his weapons and wailing for him as was usual, with a three-day *taqui* at the end and much drinking of *akha*. His mummy, of course, was not available, for he had been buried as a Christian.

If the terraces and buildings of Collcampata had remained fairly intact, owing to their location well up the side of Sacsahuaman and therefore a site not greatly desired by the Spaniards, the same cannot be said of the city below.

Mary's first church, which had been in the Suntur Huasi, gave way to a cathedral church in 1538 which, however, was designated for erection on the terrace where stood Quishuarcancha. The Suntur Huasi seems to have been torn down at this same time to make the square in front of the cathedral more commodious. In 1560, when some important building was contemplated, the fortress on Sacsahuaman was officially designated as the quarry out of which would come the stones for the new cathedral.

Soon the other Inca structures fronting Haucaypata were reworked, torn down, or reassembled. Casana, belonging to Francisco Pizarro, had its magnificent Inca façade pierced with doors many times wider than true Inca doors and with exceptionally capacious window-doors, again non-Inca. The visitor who stands in the Portal de Panes today can contemplate this weird architecture "which mingled two cultures" still extant. Here and there throughout the city *cancha* walls were breached for new doorways or slit open so that narrow streets could be run through where none had been before. In 1545, eight years after the siege, the Spaniards were living in these formerly Inca edifices, most of them then only slightly altered. By 1558 most of the great Inca palaces had been demolished and essentially replaced by other structures.

As for the great square itself, somewhere around the year 1560 the Spanish *corregidor* of the city ordered that the sand which for a hundred years had surfaced it be removed and replaced with rubble and packed earth. This action he took partly to destroy the still powerful *huaca* connected with the place and partly to recover the multitude of gold and silver offerings which were known to be buried there. The sand was thought by the Incas to have come from the shores of Mamacocha, the mother of all waters. Earnestly they petitioned the magistrate and even offered what pittance of wealth they still possessed if he would desist from this destruction, but he refused.

The south side of the Sapi received extensive remodeling, for much of Cusipata was eventually to be broken up into lots and streets and filled in, the house of Garcilaso de la Vega being one example of this post-Conquest building. Of the wide spaces of Cusipata only the plazas of San Francisco and Regocijos remain today. Parts of the terrace frontings in this area were retained, but, where necessary, steep streets were driven through them and grim house fronts implanted on the sides. The gigantically blocked and stepped appearance of Carmenca, once broken by a few solid *cancha* and house walls, lined with trees and esplanades and winding stairways and showing rich agricultural terraces on the lower skirts, was done away with overnight. The failure of the Spaniards in this early reconstruction of Cuzco to control the seepage and runoff soon undermined what little terracing was left after the siege, and bare dirt slopes became commonplace as more and more of the area reverted to the condition of a tasteless and almost empty suburb. In 1550 imported oxen were plowing these lower slopes as open land where today are the busy streets around the market. The Sapi became a dumping ground and was notorious for the heaps of dung and rubbish which adorned its bed and banks.

Because of the docile bearing of the Incas under Paullo, the reconstruction of the city was easy. Many of the Spanish *vecinos* were also holders of large *repartimientos* of Indians, generally in Cuzcoquiti itself. This labor supply represented a remnant of that which had before been available for great works under the Incas, such as the building of the Intihuasi or the channeling of the Huatanay; now it was parceled out among the Spaniards in smaller *encomiendas*, and each *encomendero* used his own as he saw fit. Stoneworking skills were naturally plentiful among the Indians, and soon every Spanish *vecino* had a home for himself in Cuzco of remarkable Inca appearance but tiled and not thatched. If the Inca walls were preserved, they were given a coat of lime; if the walls were low, additional floors were added and there appeared as well a few incongruous wooden balconies. Some of the Spaniards, however, were not so hasty and at a more sedate pace built themselves town houses much in the Spanish style. The main quarry for all this building and rebuilding was the Intihuasi. The dismantling of the great fortress and its inner city had begun as soon as the siege was broken, mainly by Spaniards feverishly searching in its subterranean passages and rooms for buried treasure. When the building of the new cathedral began in 1559, the stones were taken from the tumbled heaps that had once been walls and re-used in Christian foundations. So far had the destruction of the fortress proceeded that two years later the *cabildo* had to prohibit further raiding of the ruins.

So melted away the Inca city of Cuzco.

But the outward appearance of the city changed no more rapidly than did that integral part of it that was the flesh and blood of its erstwhile possessors. The Incas, no longer the lords of Cuzco, lived in the city on sufferance. Most of them had been relegated to the *barrios* round about, their affluence had disappeared, and their deadly enemies of former days, Cañars and Chachapoyas, now insulted them openly in the streets as arrogant police for the Spaniards. The stone statue of Viracocha the Creator which had formerly been in Quishuarcancha and which had subsequently been hidden far up the Vilcañota valley had been located by the Spaniards and smashed into bits. This act had gone far to erode the Incas' faith in themselves as an elect people. The *panacas* retained some of their integrity, but their respective cults had to be carried on in covert. The mummies and the *huaoquis* of the dead emperors were kept secreted in hamlets round about in Cuzcoquiti and received only such stolen worship as was possible. Their wealth in gold, silver, retainers, and income had totally disappeared. The pitiable and cautious adoration accorded to them was a token only of their reduced powers and posed only a potential threat to the Spaniards.

Nevertheless, the cult of the *ccallaric machu*, "the old grandfather" and the very root of their family being, was clung to more desperately by the Incas as their social conditions rapidly deteriorated. They accepted the fact that Cuzco would never again be their city and that therefore, in one important sense, they had ceased to be fully Incas. They attempted to remain at the least a people with a tradition and a viable life in the present. Thus the Christian family of Paullo, upon his decease, still had a *huaoqui* made of him incorporating within it some of his hair and nail parings. They did not conceive of this act as anti-Christian. They simply saw it as a symbol of the only way in which they could survive. It was, in other words, essential to them in their identity as Incas, doubly so now that their city Cuzco had been filched by the Spaniards.

Virtually enslaved in the years following the siege, described as "so unprovided for that it is a pity to behold them," their few supports rapidly crumbled under them. Legally they were a free people and exempt from the tribute and exactions which the Spaniards levied on other Peruvian Indians, but this favor had little meaning in view of their poverty. A few of the more highly placed were meagerly supported by the Crown and, as mentioned before, even allowed still to live in Cuzco, but their numbers had radically decreased and the ties with custom and traditions were being snapped, one by one.

Quizquiz had had the mummy of Topa Inca burned. Gonzalo Pizarro burnt the mummy of Viracocha Inca on one of his more unsavory treasure hunts. In both cases the men and women of the respective *panacas* later collected the ashes of these great ones in order to continue their cults. These burnings left intact, of the great rulers, only the mummies of Inca Roca, Pachacuti, and Huayna Capac. In the year 1559 the magistrate Polo de Ondegardo made a notable and generally successful attempt to destroy the remaining *panaca* system. To this end he had the hamlets round about Cuzco searched wherever suspicion pointed to the continued and clandestine worship of mummies, *huaoquis*, or ashes. After a hot chase, Huayna Capac's mummy was tracked down in the dead of night and was found secreted in a house in Cuzco on the road leading up to Sacsahuaman. It was still surrounded by the half-dozen *huacas* of the Ecuadoran peoples whom he had conquered while alive. These tatterdemalion little figures ranged about it were its only court except for two Incas of the Tumibamba *panaca* whose piety and loyalty thus also came to an end. The other two imperial mummies were similarly found, as well as that of one of the *coyas*. Pachacuti's mummy had with it still the *huaca* of the Chanca Indians, most formidable of all the Incas' many enemies a century and more past.

The mummies were dispatched to Lima where they were interred within the grounds of the Royal Hospital of Saint Andrew. As cults the *panacas* were no more, although memberships in them continued to be counted for another half-century as they were, after all, *ayllus*. In 1560 the Indian population of Cuzco was divided into four Christian parishes corresponding to what had formerly been the communities of Carmenca (Santa Ana), Cayoacachi (Santos Reyes or Belén), Totocachi (San Blas), and Collcampata (San Cristóbal). Churches were erected in each one, new points of control and indoctrination which would combat the immemorial concept of *huaca* and weaken the cohesiveness of the Indians.

The appearance of the mestizos as a class was the most bewildering phenomenon of all for the Incas to combat. Their *pallas*—those who survived—were prized by the Spaniards, first for their beauty and second for their social claims. The children of mixed blood born to the *ñustas* and *pallas* usually were considered illegitimate by the Spaniards but, curiously enough, in the mothers' understanding were considered to be fullblood Incas and as such were assigned to *ayllus* and *panacas*. It was in no sense a matrilinear tradition that produced this anomaly but rather the belief on the part of the conquered that the Spaniards were the favored ones of the gods and, therefore, were true sons of Inti. As such the sons of the Spaniards were Incas. Don Cristóbal Paullo Inca was able to have his marriage to his half sister recognized by the Christian church and thus to continue in his line pure Inca legitimacy for one more generation, but this arrangement was uncommon. The exclusiveness of the Inca caste had been rigorously maintained since the days of Pachacuti. As a pragmatic matter of blood and descent it vanished with the second generation after the conquest.

The removal of the *panaca* as a center of wealth, the adulterating of the Inca blood, the reworking of the physical city, and the Christianization of many prominent Incas and *pallas*—these factors together in noiseless battle overthrew the Incas more crushingly than had the battle of Cotapampa. "Twilight," *cipi pacha,* came very early for the Cuzco Incas, but this time it was not to be followed by a *llipiyak tuta,* a "night of sparkling stars."

SECTION 10. *The Vilcabamba Interlude*

MANCO INCA was assassinated in his remote capital in the year 1545. He left behind him three sons and one daughter, aged two, at the time of his death. Each one of the sons was to rule the rump empire in Vilcabamba; in the order of their rule they were: Sayri Topa Yupanqui, Titu Cusi Yupanqui, and Tupac Amaru. The daughter, Cusi Huarcay, would be married to the first brother and have the dubious distinction of being the last known *coya* with any claim to legitimacy in Peruvian history.

After many and urgent solicitations by the Spaniards and the Incas of Cuzco, the first of these rulers finally emerged from his mountain eyrie and declared himself a vassal of the Spanish crown. Inasmuch as Paullo Inca had just died, at the time no conflict seems to have arisen in the claims of the two families to the *mascapaycha*. The entry of Sayri Topa into Cuzco was attended by all the great *curacas* around and was the occasion of a traditional triumphal entry. Seated in the imperial litter with his sixteen-year-old *coya*, Sayri Topa was said at that time to resemble closely his famous grandfather, Huayna Capac. In Cuzco they were both baptized as Christians and their incestuous marriage legalized by the archbishop of Lima.

Sayri Topa was given an important *encomienda* of Indians in the Yucay valley and along with it the title of Marquis of Oropesa. He died within a year of his return, in 1560, leaving his honors and estate to a daughter. This fullblood *ñusta* would soon be married to a Spaniard who in this way secured the splendid estate but whose historical claim to fame would be that he found and captured the last Inca emperor in the *hacha hacha* of Vilcabamba.

The second brother, Titu Cusi Yupanqui, was illegitimate and thus not entitled to the *mascapaycha*. Nevertheless, when he heard of his brother's death, he proclaimed himself *capac apu* in Vilcabamba and then in a return to his father's disastrous policy mounted a series of damaging raids on a number of Spanish posts and settlements. At the same time he was treating with the ambassadors sent by the Spaniards to entice him out of his lair. He finally became a Christian and was formally christened Don Felipe, while his *coya* took the name Doña Angelina Polan Quilaco. This conversion naturally did not prevent him from consorting constantly with his familiar *huacas*. He was able to maintain himself as *capac apu* with some of the pomp traditional to that office. He ate off silver plate and was constantly attended by twenty or thirty young women. But his dark and pock-marked face showed in its severe lines the harshness with which life treated an emperor who dared no more than hide out in the fastnesses of the *hacha hacha*, a part of the world which once his ancestors had treated as only fit for the living of wildmen.

Certain friars had courageously entered his refugee capital, unsupported by Spanish swordsmen, and had undertaken a program of conversion. For a while all had gone well until the friars exorcised the devil in one of the great rocks near the capital community of Huitcos. Tension between the two religions, that of Christ and that of the sorcerers, swiftly rose to a crescendo. At a critical juncture an illness, which was unfortunately attended by one of the friars who acted in a medical capacity, seized Titu Cusi Yupanqui. His death and the consequent events provided Peru with its first Christian martyr. Fray Diego Ortiz' story is one of the heroic sagas of the Christian faith but need not be detailed here.

During the indecisive reign of Titu Cusi Yupanqui the hostility of the Peruvian Indian for his Spanish oppressor had crystallized out into a new and morbid manifestation. The appalling cruelty of the Europeans had created throughout Peru the notion that they killed Indians to get their fat, with which unction alone could a certain disease which afflicted them back in Spain be cured. This vulgar explanation for the Spanish incubus was no doubt held by the majority of the Indian population which needed a rationale, no matter what, for the unbelievable things which were happening to them. But the remnants of the Incas, who had had a divine mission in their own history, knew differently. This terrible half-war, the crushing mastery which Spaniards exerted over Incas, was in reality a reflection of an upheaval in the heavens.

When the Pizarros entered Peru, they brought with them not only Christ but his fierce and lordly captain, Saint James, as well as Mary and many other saints. This Christian host had plainly defeated Viracocha, his divine captains, Inti and Huanacauri, the *pururaucas*, and others. But this defeat was only the beginning of the *pachatikray*. It was disclosed by oracles that in this new aeon the sea would rise and in a great flood sweep the evil Spaniards away. It was to be therefore a *lloclla aunu pachacuti*, a "destruction of the world by flood." In this twilight of the gods, Jehovah, Christ, and the Saints would meet two heavenly hosts of *huacas*, one led by Pachacamac, the Creator from the coast, the other led by Titicaca, the powerful oracle of Lake Chucuito.

Admittedly the Spaniards had everywhere overthrown, crushed, burned, and broken up the *huacas*, but the spirits of these insulted *huacas* had passed into the filial fragments of their own destruction and had become determined and deadly spirits, their numbers now marvelously multiplied. Christ and his cohorts could not withstand such an aroused power of *huaca*; they would be crushed, the Incas would be reinstated, and the Peruvian peoples would become possessors of their own again. The outcome of the war was, in fact, certain. The *huacas* had already planted worms in the bodies of the Spaniards, of their horses, and of all Indians who collaborated with them, and these would eat their hearts away.

This religion appeared in southern Peru about 1565. It was propagated by means of the "Dance Sickness," *taqui oncoy*, and represented a radical departure from the Inca imperial religion which formerly had been hierarchical and exclusive. The Dance Sickness was a return to the basic levels of shamanism, which was what was left to the Peruvians after the collapse of the Inca gods. The *huacas*—a whole new host— no longer needed specially trained and licensed oracle priests; they now enunciated their desires and commands by taking possession of no matter whom, for they had left their normal abodes in rocks, springs, mountaintops, and trees and now went about looking for Indians in whom they could live and whom they could use for the spiritual conflict that was coming.

The Dance Sickness spread far and wide over Peru, carried by itinerant and uprooted shamans. Wherever they stopped they poured powerful and menacing sermons into the ears of the distraught Indians; they adjured them to have their houses ready if the *huacas* should come to live with them. When an Indian as a result of one of these seances fell writhing on the ground or stamped and danced about screaming nonsensical words, shaking all over or hacking himself with a knife, or when he leaped to his death off a high rock—these acts were signs of his possession. The possessed one would then, if he chose, produce a small object which would turn out to be the son of one of the mighty *huacas*; he would name it, cherish it, pour *akha* over it, and finally dedicate himself to restoring its ancient powers.

Because of its inherent lack of direction, this dangerous malady of the conquered lasted only till 1572 when incontrovertible events proved that Armageddon had already been fought and that Christ and the army of saints had long since conquered. The new religion significantly failed to predict that the *huacas*, if and when victorious, would restore to the Incas the fullness of the land thereafter. The name "Inca" had lost its magic.

BVENGOBiERNO
LAPRECIODETOPAA
maropnga   ynfan lt Rey lo lleua preso congu co
rona el capi   tan martin garcia oto yo ta~

en el cuzco   *capilon*

Don Pablo Tupac Amaru and the Last of the Incas

THE YEAR 1572 marks also the extermination of the Incas as a caste and a nation. After this date the historian cannot use the designation "Inca," simply because they as a people ceased to exist.

Just before he died, Titu Cusi Yupanqui had been offered a pardon and safe-conduct if he would emerge from his province on the far side of the Vilcabamba Andes. Envoys hopefully bearing these advices had been sent into the montaña by the new viceroy, Francisco de Toledo, who was determined to end once and for all the anomalous situation of such a robber state on the borders of New Castile. The viceroy's initially generous impulses were brought to a sudden conclusion when he learned that one of his ambassadors into the montana had been brutally killed by the Incas. This atrocity had occurred because Titu Cusi Yupanqui was already dead, his successor was not yet in command, and there were no adequate restraints on those captains whom Titu Cusi had sent to guard his borders. The fact of this interregnum was not known, however, to the viceroy and for the deed and the insult he blamed the new and youthful emperor, Tupac Amaru. His implacable anger was now to set in motion the events leading directly to the extinction of the race of Incas.

This last of the sons of Manco Inca was dangerously inexperienced. When Sayri Topa had died, the bastard brother, Titu Cusi Yupanqui, had usurped the rule from the boy Tupac Amaru who, being legitimate, should have succeeded. Titu Cusi expediently thrust the prince into the deep seclusion of one of the temple *canchas* in Vilcabamba, and there he remained for the years of Titu Cusi's reign. Thus, when he did assume the *mascapaycha*, he inherited from his dead brother a group of intransigent captains most difficult to control; on the other hand, he also inherited the hostility of New Castile's powerful viceroy, an enemy to be dreaded even by one seemingly safe in the fastness of the trans-Andean Vilcabamba.

A sizable group of Spaniards, strongly supported by the Cañars of Cuzcoquiti, now entered the area. These Cañars, whose hatred for everything Inca was undying, had with relish offered to spearhead the operation into the *hacha hacha* and track down this new *capac apu*. The stage was thus set for the denouement, with old and new rancors motivating both antagonists.

The revived war between the Vilcabamba Incas and injured Spanish pride lasted a short but terrible six months. In the sequel the defenses of Tupac Amaru's remote kingdom collapsed, and, having lost a bloody battle in one of the more spectacular spots of that spectacular province, he and the last of his captains, carrying with them only their gods, fled incontinently into the lower montaña. He left sons, daughters, and women as booty for the Spaniards.

A battle-hardened and jungle-adept Spaniard, Martín García de Loyola, volunteered with twenty others to plunge down in pursuit of the fleeing emperor. In the sequel the Spaniard proved more intrepid than the Inca was full of guile, and the vast uncharted tangle of the lower Urubamba witnessed finally the capture of the pathetic group of refugees some seventy-five miles out in the jungle. Martín García was to have connections with the Incas other than those of a captor, for he married a daughter of Sayri Topa; he was to be the husband of a first cousin of the man whom, as a common criminal, he now dragged back to Cuzco along with his remaining and inglorious captains. All the prisoners were incarcerated inside Huascar's fortified palace on Collcampata. His two leading captains, Atauhuallpa Inca and Cori Paucar, were tortured and executed. Others of the luckless lords of the montaña, less guilty in the eyes of the Spaniards, had only their right hands severed. The mummies of Manco Inca, Titu Cusi Yupanqui, and his *coya* Mama Kanka, captured as part of the loot, were publicly burned. The statue of Inti, cast in solid gold, came at last into the grasp of the Spaniards and was melted down to pay for the debts of Philip II in far-off Europe.

The viceroy gave no heed to the multitude of voices from both races pleading that the chief prisoner be sent to Spain for King Philip's personal adjudication, and he saw to it that Tupac Amaru was out of hand found guilty of rebellion. The day was set for the execution far enough in advance so that the *curacas* from the farthest limits of Cuzcoquiti might come to witness it and understand once and for all the sovereignty of the Spanish crown. But more than the *curacas* came. It seemed in that abeyant period that all of Peru was moving in toward Topa Cuzco. They came meanly or in protective groups munching their little *chuño*, suckling their thin babies, trotting and hurrying along the roads which had been paved by their former lords the Incas. They poured down in upon Cuzco, still blowing kisses to the holy city that had so altered its appearance in forty years. The dust of their coming rose high and lingered over the shrunken valley like a golden haze. So great was the crowd pouring in from the four quarters that the Spaniards became uneasy, and no doubt the viceroy, ensconced in a screened window over the square, was himself apprehensive.

He need not have been. The prior of San Domingo, that monastery placed on the site of Coricancha, had succeeded in teaching the condemned Tupac Amaru the catechism and had then baptized him into the Christian faith. He was named after the greatest of Christianity's advocates, and so he would come to the scaffold as Don Pablo Tupac Amaru. His captains, as has been stated, had already received their portions of Spanish justice. He was to be the last.

The condemned emperor was brought down into the square on a mule draped in black velvet. His arms were pinioned behind him, and he was escorted by an impressive regiment of Cañars eager to see his blood poured out on the ground. As the usual crier went before the prisoner proclaiming the death of a traitor and the corresponding majesty of the king of Spain, a sister, Doña Maria Cusi Huarcay, widow of Sayri Topa, appeared in a window overlooking the macabre scene, sobbing and hysterically saluting him as the *sapa capac apu,* "the only lord" of Tahuantinsuyo. With difficulty she was restrained from hurling herself into the street below, and the reformed procession was freed to move on.

The pillory stood in the square in front of the cathedral, and as Don Pablo Tupac Amaru mounted it, such a shriek arose from the Indians crowding the square as seemed to block the heavy clouds in their flight across the sky and to arrest them in a stupendous immobility of sorrow. It was a sound the Spaniards had never in their lives heard before, so fierce, so anquished, so menacing that the Quechua-speaking friars who accompanied the condemned man begged him to halt it.

His arms were quickly freed and, facing Carmenca, he raised his right hand slowly and then as slowly brought it down, a most lordly gesture. The instantaneous hush that followed was as shocking as had been the uproar, and for that one brief moment the Inca race again dominated all of Peru. His words were remembered as follows:

"Incas and *curacas,* you who have come from the four quarters, know that I am now a Christian. I must die and I die in the law of Christ. Formerly I and my ancestors told you that you should worship Inti and the *huacas.* All that was a lie, a trick. We also told you that whenever we entered Coricancha we used to speak to Inti and he would answer us, and therefore you, our subjects, had to obey those commands. That too was a lie; Inti could not speak, for he was only a lump of gold. My brother it was, Titu Cusi Yupanqui, who taught me to deceive you in this way, to pretend to speak to the sun and to thus ensure your obedience."

So had come full circle the notable saga of the Incas, a people who had fashioned an affluence, a unique way of life, and a religion to support it. While it may be doubted that Tupac Amaru spoke exactly those words—for the friars were the ones to report them and their own interests are evident in the translation—the full sense of his passing is certainly contained in them. The inadequacy of the creation of the Inca folk was here openly admitted. And they stood there then, those who were left, as they had been in the days of the *ccallaric machu*, a people trying to be born, naked and casting about for a seat under the sun. Their piety was as clearly expressed in this address as was their cynicism. But they had told their tale and were done.

Don Pablo placed his head on the block. Grasping his short hair, the Cañar executioner struck off his head with one blow and then held it aloft for all to see. The iron voices of Mary's Church, of San Cristóbal, of Belén and the others at the same moment burst out with a startled clangor, while the vast crowd fell down writhing and shrieking on the ground. Out in the valley the bells of San Sebastián, the old Inca *ayllu* of Sañu, took up the clamor and passed it down to the end of the stricken valley whence it pealed away into the distance. The body was removed for burial and the head placed on a pike. All through the night the crowd of Indians stayed where they were, howling and moaning under the head. Lest it become a *huaca*, the viceroy ordered it taken down at the coming of dawn and buried with the body.

In this same year the viceroy instituted legal proceedings against the remaining members of the families of Manco Inca and Paullo Inca. The parish of Collcampata (or San Cristóbal), as if in derision, was reassigned to the Cañars and Chachapoyas who had contributed so much to the defeat and death of the last Inca emperor. Property still owned by Incas was confiscated. Of the thirty-six Capac Incas left, their *pallas*, and their children, no matter how young, all were ruthlessly turned out of what poor homes they had in the ramshackle suburbs of Cuzco and herded off to Lima whence they were to be sent to Mexico.

The group included the small daughter of Tupac Amaru and two of his sons, one of them a three-month-old baby, also called Don Pablo. The rigors of the forced journey made on foot over the high passes and in the hot *huaycos* caused several deaths. Some arrived in Lima, but in any case all were either transported or dead of exposure and neglect within three or four years at the outside. All of the mestizos in whose veins ran dilute Inca blood were tortured, charged with treachery, and exiled from Peru to parts distant, and they too died soon. A very few detached and degraded individuals of the blood of Manco Capac were not considered dangerous and were left to sink into anonymity among the base commoners out of whom they had once come. Seventy years after the Spanish entry into Cuzco the *panacas* claimed to have 567 members, but these were thoroughly bastardized. In the year 1610 the last members of Paullo's direct line became extinct in Spain.

SECTION 12. *Retrospect*

THE WRITER may be permitted a final word about these people whom for some years now he has made so intimately his own.

In describing them, I believe I have given way to no excess of depreciation or of adulation. I have been appalled at the immensity of their grasp and their greed. I have been oppressed by their savagery while still trying to see it as a condition of their times. I have without question been able to feel their wonderful vitality, and I have faithfully tried to give the reader some appreciation of their lucid grasp of the essential oneness of the divine. Circumstances have unfortunately obscured for us those finer sensibilities that many of them, both men and women, must have evinced in acts of loyalty, love, and reason. I wish it had been possible to report these deeds, but an age of violence preserves mainly the remembrance of violent deeds.

Bearing this thought in mind—for we must so honor them—I have found in them what all of us have known since Adam delved and Eve span: that man in his pride will rise up and insult his Creator, that he will refuse to believe heartily in his own creaturehood, and that he will never escape the consequences thereof. I see these facts as inescapably present in the tragedy of Inca history. These are perhaps the only *facts* that historians can really report—and they appear with particular vividness in the lives of these people. It is a solemn sight and meaningful beyond the mere minutiae reported.

Notes on Illustrations

IN INCA STUDIES there is nothing comparable to the Mexican codices or Sahagún's *Historia generál de las cosas de Nueva España*. The reason is threefold: first, the Incas did not possess a graphic system comparable to those of the various Mexican groups; second, Atauhuallpa's generals in the occupation of Cuzco destroyed quantities of what archival material did exist; and, third, the Spaniards in Peru were immensely superior to those of Mexico in the arts of vandalism and rapine. For these reasons Tahuantinsuyo as a proper subject of history has suffered immeasureably.

Therefore, what does exist to illustrate Inca life and history is triply precious. Huaman Poma's *Nueva crónica buen gobierno* is a case in point. It is a long, rambling, and confused account in manuscript of the Inca past and of the plight of the Indian after the Conquest. It was written by a Peruvian Indian in execrable Spanish, with much Quechua interlarded, somewhere around 1613—eighty years after the entry of the Spaniards. It was first published in facsimile edition in Paris in 1936. This edition is referred to herein as GPF.

The most accurate and interesting parts of the manuscript are the illustrations. Out of a very large number there are some 145, many repetitious, which concern the period of the Incas, their history, and their way of life. A few have been from time to time reproduced in various works by authors both good and bad. One of the more egregious errors made in most of these works has been a confusion between illustrations depicting Incas and those depicting other Peruvian Indian groups. Of the 39 illustrations I have chosen from GPF to add to the value of this work, all concern Incas unless otherwise specified.

For the expert there is a large amount to be gained from these illustrations. For the reading public their fidelity to the details of dress and of social and ceremonial life, added to their gauche but decorative charm, should prove of interest. They have aided me in the conception and writing of this book.

Frontispiece

Depiction: Early colonial Cuzco.

Remarks: The caption reads, "The great city and capital and royal court of the twelve Inca kings—Santiago del Cuzco in the heart of the kingdom, and a bishopric." It is to be noted here that the city's patron saint in the early period was Saint James who had aided the Spaniards in breaking Manco Inca's siege. With the exception of the areas marked Cusicancha and Pumapchupan in the center foreground and Carmenca under the arch, this view of Cuzco maintains a consistent orientation. It is as if one were standing where the cemetery is today and looking to the northeast. The view is therefore directly opposite to that of the Monroy Panorama. To the left the Huatanay (more properly the Sapi at this point) flows out of the hills at Huacapunco, passes through the city, and moves down to San Sebastián (off the right edge of the page but mentioned here as Cachi because of its saltworks). The square Haucaypata is shown reserved for the Spanish, while the Indians with their llamas are relegated to Cusipata where they are also shown sitting under their booths or *carpa* at the market, *catu*. The present market is not far from this spot. The two squares are separated by a block of Spanish buildings erected over the underground Sapi. The upper left-hand corner of the illustration shows the heights of Sacsahuaman (here referred to as Senca Urco), the ruined blocks of the fortress (*pucara*), and the *Suchona* or "Sliding Place" (here depicted as a steep inclined plane). Just under the fortress is San Cristóbal; nearby is Pincollona Pata, probably a part of Collcampata. Carmenca is placed on the wrong side of the river—it should have been in the lower left-hand part of the picture. San Blas is correctly identified on the slopes of Senca. Coricancha shows the Intipampa square and the tower of the Dominican monastery. The Tullu River is not shown. On the south side of the Sapi, Illapa Cancha is shown as a curious non-Hispanic structure in the area of the present Prefectura. Behind and above it was the Cantut Moya, "the Garden of the *Cantut*-Flowers, a former planted terrace or pleasure ground on the slope of Carmenca. The tall bell tower on the south corner of Cusipata is meant to represent San Francisco (compare with Monroy Panorama) and is in approximately the correct position. The parish of Belén (old Cayaocachi) and the Hospital (here spelled *Ispital*) both still exist in the spots designated. The site of the Inca prisons, the Sankayhuaci and the Piñas Huasi, is across from Coricancha on the south side of the Sapi; it is indicated by the kneeling and pinioned prisoners. The running waters of Cuzco are indicated in the right-hand corners of the illustration. These are the Viroy Paccha and the Cantoc Uno (whether these are correctly located is problematical). The Quispicancha shown in the Huatanay as it flows south is intended to indicate the pueblo of that name which was actually some twenty-two kilometers downstream. This whole scene relates to Cuzco as it was at the beginning of the seventeenth century well after the reductions of Toledo. What we see here is a city thoroughly remade but one that still tenaciously maintained the names of former Inca sites and buildings. In conjunction with the Monroy Panorama, this illustration well describes the outward Hispanicization of the city.

I, 1.

Depiction: The coat of arms of the Incas.

Remarks: The Inca coat of arms was quartered (as many European blazons were), the quarters possibly being red and blue alternately, JADG 17f. The following elements are listed in the sources as appearing in the quarters: a bird (identified as either a condor or the *coriquenque*-bird, which was a variety of eagle, GHLQ 69; EQD 12; LBVA I, 29; II, 60, 141; RFC 255), a jaguar behind a tree, the *mascapaycha*, and two serpents each wearing the *mascapaycha*. If we may judge from SPYP 217f. and GHLQ 99, the tree is the *chauchu* or "stock" of the royal line and consequently represents Manco Capac (here and in SMN 381 the tree is specified to be the *chonta*-palm which grows in the montaña). In some sources the tree is called a tower but this assertion is erroneous. The jaguar, *otoronco*, probably represents Pachacuti (to whom we undoubtedly owe this final formulation of the Inca coat of arms) and is intended to show that ruler as a second founder. Here he is called Otorongo Achachi Inca, the Noble Jaguar Inca (note that a famous general of the succeeding generation bore the name Otorongo Achachi, SG 48). The *coriquenque*-bird may well be the original fetish of Manco Capac, otherwise called the Inti-bird; at any rate it was the imperial bird of the Incas. From its other name, *allkamari*, we know it to have been an eagle speckled black and white, GHLQ 19, 600; JLD 36; EQD 12. The *mascapaycha* was the fringe worn on the forehead of the *capac apu*, red for the ruling emperor, yellow for the emperor-designate. The two crowned serpents, I suspect, have to do with the division of Cuzco into the two moieties. Some of the sources (JA V, 4; JADG 17f.; MMCB I, 21; BC XII, 36; RGI II, appendix, 32; VEC 1517) add the rainbow to this collocation of designs in the blazon. Where the rainbow occurred, it symbolized Huanacauri. Thus the entire set of symbols presented could be read as: "The house of Pachacuti who took the crown and received the power of the royal fetish as was his by right of descent from Manco Capac; it was he also who established Cuzco of the Incas in its two parts." It should be noted that the essentials of this coat of arms were confirmed to Paullo Inca in 1545, BC XII, 20; SMN 381.

I, 2.

Depiction: Inca ceremony of mourning.
Remarks: While the Spanish caption reads "January," the Quechua gives the names of the months of December and January, the Capac Raymi and the Samay Quilla. These names mean, respectively, "the emperor's feast" and "the month of rest." Both months together began the Inca calendar. What is displayed here is a ceremony of mourning which customarily took place in Samay Quilla, GPF 237, 285. The Samay Quilla was a month dedicated to Viracocha, ARGCS I, 24, inasmuch as the Creator was he who received the sins of the Incas and the contaminated sacrificial ashes thrown into the Huatanay River at this time. Here all the Incas, men and women, sit silent and unsmiling, their eyes on the ground.

I, 3.

Depiction: Warehouses and a *curaca* giving an accounting.

Remarks: These particular warehouses, *collca*, belong to the tenth Inca emperor, Topa Inca Yupanqui, who is here shown demanding an accounting of their contents. These storage rooms are of the party-wall type with each cubicle roofed with a rounded thatch. The person reading off the measurements and numbers on the *quipu* (knotted string) is identified as the *suyoyoc apu*, "the chief administrator of the province." His name is Poma Chaua—one of the ancestors whom Huaman Poma claimed—and therefore this scene is supposed to take place in Huánuco in the central sierra. It should be noted that the *curaca's* hair is long and he does not wear the earplugs. Also, the *canipu* he wears on his forehead is horseshoe-shaped—not the type worn by the Incas.

I, 4.

Depiction: A hanging.

Remarks: This place of execution is within sight of Cuzco. It is just downriver and on the south side of the Huatanay. The general area is identified as Arahua, and the specific rockside shown is called Copper Rock (i.e., red rock), Anta Caca. The Spanish identifies the woman as one of the *acllas*; the Quechua identifies her as one of the *tasqui*-age group, (more fully *tasqui sipas*, fourteen to twenty years old, GHLQ 594). She is described as "seduced" and as "one of the sinners." Her paramour hanging beside her could not be an Inca magnate since his hair is not cropped short. The executioner, who from his earplugs is an Inca, belongs to the Equeco *ayllu* from the Pampa de Anta. The leading men of this *ayllu* by hereditary right were hangmen. The culprits were left till dead of exposure.

I, 6.

Depiction: Manco Capac.

Remarks: The object in Manco Capac's left hand is that version of the *suntur paucar* carried in processions as a symbol of the ruler. It is a staff topped by a mop of brightly colored down with three feathers emerging from it. He is wearing the smaller cockade version of it in his *llauto*. *Suntur paucar* seems to mean a "mounded many-colored thing," referring to the brilliance of the feathers of which it was composed, GHLQ 281 f., 332; BC XII, 36. Hanging from his wrist is his *runcu* or "coca bag," strikingly patterned. He holds the *topa yauri*, "the royal scepter." The caption reads, "This Inca reigned alone in Cuzco—Acamama." Akha Mama is a rare designation for Cuzco. It would equate the city with the *huaca* (female) who brews and makes abundant the fermented maize drink of the region. Cuzco would thus popularly be "the home or source of beer."

<h2 style="text-align:center">I, 10.</h2>

Depiction: Toasting the royal mummies.
Remarks: In the background is a *pucullo* or tomb, GHLQ 547f. In this illustration the tomb merely serves to identify the general subject referred to as burial; Inca emperors were not buried but remained in their palaces. The caption mentions the two words for corpse, the *aya* which is any dead body or mummy and the *yllapa*, GPF 287f., 377f.; BLCL 25; CL 30. The word *yllapa*, GHLQ 367, is the name given to thunder or lightning. The word was also later used to designate the Spanish artillery. Technically thus, the mummy of an emperor was a "thunderbolt," although we might better translate it as "the illuminated," "the sainted," or "the blessed." Here the mummies both of an emperor and his *coya* have been brought out into public for one of the many celebrations in the Inca calendar. The reigning emperor is piously toasting his dead predecessor. He holds two golden cups. Out of one he drinks himself while he offers the other to the *illapa* by pouring it into a *vilque*, BC XIII, 10; PPR 264, a vatlike jar placed before the mummy on such occasions. When full the *vilque* was poured out into the large receptacle in the square of Haucaypata designed to drain away underground, CM 37, 44; PPR 264.

<h2 style="text-align:center">I, 13.</h2>

Depiction: Rahua Ocllo, Huascar's mother.
Remarks: The *coya* Rahua Ocllo is being assisted by two ladies-in-

waiting of her entourage. The long flowing hair of the true *palla* is well depicted here. Braids were never worn. Her hair is being rinsed out and combed. The word *taksay*, JLD 996; GHLQ 335; LDST 157, is used for washing both clothes and a woman's hair but for nothing else. Over the *coya*'s head is held the *achihua*, a beautifully feathered canopy reserved for royalty alone. The Spanish caption correctly connects her with the northern provinces where, as the *coya* of Huayna Capac, she resided for more than ten years.

I, 14.

Depiction: Huayna Capac in his war litter.
Remarks: Huayna Capac is shown being carried "swiftly" into the press of battle by his Lucana bearers (note that their headdress differs from that of the Carabaya carriers in GPF 331). This litter is identi- fied as the *pillco rampa* or "scarlet litter" (in distinction from the "crys- tal litter" of GPF 331). The *pillco* was a bird of scarlet plumage, GHLQ 285. The *rampa* is not to be confused with the *huantu* which was any kind of carrier but generally a hammock, GHLQ 178, 311, 407, 566; LDST 286. I am unable to account for the crosses which decorate this litter and the one in GPF 331. One would have expected to see used as decorative symbols the sun, moon, rainbow, and serpents, BC XII, 36; CL 20.

I, 16.

Depiction: A ceremony of mourning.
Remarks: The Spanish reads "a procession, fasting, and penance"; the Quechua reads "penitential invocation, fasting, grief." For the word *huacaylli* see GHLQ 165, 167; BVP 161; JLD 1083. The ceremony is undoubtedly the *itu* which was a national abasement; it was often performed because of drought, which was most menacing in October, GPF 254f. For the occasion men and women painted their faces with lampblack and *ñuñunya*, a bitter red stain (used also by women weaning their children—they smeared it on their nipples, GPF 285; GHLQ 263; JLD 710). The custom of women's painting their faces with the juice of the red *ñuñunya*-fruit also existed among the Aymaras, LBVA

II, 237. The celebrants here cover their heads with their mantles as a sign of mourning. The only sound comes from the *huaylla quepa*, the conch-shell trumpet from the seashore, GHLQ 192, 685. As a further sign of humility, all sandals have been discarded.

II, 1.

Depiction: A palace.
Remarks: This illustration is of great interest, for it is about the only detail we possess on the subject of the royal palace. With the exception of the *suntur huasi*, the buildings here should be imagined as being within the walls of the royal *cancha*. The audience chamber or throne room was called the *cuyos manco*. It is shown here with a *punco camayoc*, a "porter," sitting at the entrance. This entrance is really meant to depict the entryway to the appropriate section of the *cancha*, not to the *cuyos manco* itself. The *cuyos manco*, so I believe, was a *carpa huasi* such as the building shown beside it—that is, it was of rectangular plan and open on one of its long sides. This arrangement, under a peaked and thatched roof and with fires burning in the center portion, gave adequate protection, light, and warmth for the royal consultations and receptions held therein. The *carpa huasi* shown is probably intended to represent the great sheds (called *galpones* by the Spaniards) attached to some of the palaces and used for celebrations during stormy weather. In the interior of the palace can be seen the joined cells of the treasury, a set of storage spaces called *churacona huasi*. The inner, harem quarters are called the *quenco huasi*, "the house of many passages"; its labyrinthine character is suggested here by showing it as an irregular U-shaped ground plan. Standing out in front of the complex (presumably in Haucaypata) is a tower building called the *suntur huasi*, so called for its rounded mound of thatch. There is no information about its use.

II, 3.

Depiction: Ñustas bathing.
Remarks: The caption reads *araui pincollo uanca*. The *araui* was a lay chanted or sung about the past deeds of the ancestors, GHLQ 152, 446;

GVCR VI, 9; MMCB III, 6. *Pincollo* is the word for flute, and *huanca* was a song sung at sowing and harvest to the sound of a flute, JLD 1095. The young Inca neophytes for knighthood have been gathering bundles of *ichu*-grass in preparation for the celebration of the *huarachicoy*. They are shown piping traditional songs on the high slopes where the Sapi flows out of the gorge into the city of Cuzco—the spot is identified correctly as Huacapunco. They are sitting on the slopes of Sacsahuaman, but other high places round about are identified by name as well. The *ñustas* are ceremonially cleansing themselves in the flowing river as a part of their puberty rites. Other fountains and basins besides the spot where they are find mention in the illustration. The girls are listening to the boys singing and fluting; they are making the Inca gesture of greeting with the raised and pointed forefinger.

II, 4.

Depiction: An Inca in prison.
Remarks: The caption reads, "Prisons of the Inca rulers and their councils," and the Quechua word for "prisoner," *piñas*. In this case the prisoner is a high-ranking Inca, a *huchayoc auqui* which means "a delinquent nobleman." His caste is marked by the earplugs. He is probably being starved to death as was the anticipated fate of Paullo Inca. In rough translation his Quechua lament reads as follows: "My thoughts bear me away; my lament finishes me. I shall forever curse this evil heart of mine. Alas, for the past! O dungeon, O prison, allow me to go free!"

II, 7.

Depiction: Chief constable.
Remarks: This official is an Inca of Upper Cuzco. His office is specifically identified as that of the *capac apu huatac*, "the emperor's constable." The word *huatac* (*huatay camayoc* also, GPF 111; GHLQ 186) is a participial form of *huatay*, "to bind, seize, arrest." He is thus "the one who arrests." On his *llauto* is pinned the *canipu* of an Upper Cuzco lord, and he wears the double feather (called the *kausu*, LBVA I, 371; II, 48) in the headband which was the sign of a pureblood Inca.

Note that the emperor himself wears this article when he does not wear the *suntur paucar*, GPF 364. In the *llauto* are also thrust sprigs of what may be begonia flowers, the *achancara*, GHLQ 12f.; JLD 26; LBVA II, 6 (the *achancara* is the only flower which I find mentioned as an adornment for men). The sign of this nobleman's commission is the emperor's *mascapaycha* which, because of its excessive *huaca*, is here carried on the end of a wand. It was his duty to arrest highly placed persons. He was generally, if not always, a member of the Anta *ayllu*, GPF 184.

II, 9.

Depiction: Return of Huayna Capac's mummy to Cuzco.
Remarks: The mummy of Huayna Capac, here classed as an *illapa*, is being carried down the Capac Ñan or "Royal Road" from Quito to Cuzco. In the funeral palanquin are two other mummies; one is that of a woman of his harem who either performed the suttee herself or was forcibly destroyed to keep the emperor company. Seated in front of him is the body of a page who was undoubtedly his favorite cup-bearer, *upiachic*, LDST 181. This child was not sacrificed in the *capac-hucha*, for in that case he would have been buried near the *huaca* to which he was offered. In his hands has been thrust a small jug of *akha* for his master. Mummies were preserved in a squatting posture with the knees up and the hands crossed over the chest. If Huayna Capac had been simply a *curaca*, he would additionally have been wrapped and bundled in many layers of rich cloth, but inasmuch as he was the emperor—who was considered to be alive in a very special sense—he was not swaddled. Thus he could still wear his special items of dress and regalia, as well as look out on the world.

II, 12.

Depiction: Emperor and *coya* worshiping the gods.
Remarks: The caption reads "idols of the Incas—Inti, Huanacauri, Tambotoco—in Cuzco." Three stellar deities are shown overhead: Inti, the sun; Mama Quilla, the moon; and a starlike figure which is to be identified with the god of the storm and the thunderbolt, Illapa. Under

them are the two powerful mountain *huacas* of the Incas: Huanacauri (here represented as a masonry enclosure and a crude idol on the mountaintop) and Pacaritambo with its three orifices out of which came the Maras, the Sutics, and the Capac Incas. The kneeling posture of the worshipers is a contamination from Christianity, but the raised hands are forming a typical gesture of greeting. In view of the solemnity of the occasion, the *capac apu* has removed his *llauto* with the *suntur paucar* and the *mascapaycha* attached; he has placed it on the rough steps of an *usno*. Behind the *coya* is the heir apparent, already a full Inca as can be seen from his earplugs. He also has probably removed his regalia. Whereas his father's *mascapaycha* was red, his was yellow.

II, 14.

Depiction: Potato harvesting.
Remarks: The man with the *taclla* or footplow is here identified by the term *pachaca*, literally "servant." The usual term for the laborer on the land was *yapuc*, LDST 155; GHLQ 415, 558. The scene takes place in the month of *Aucay Cuzqui*, the "germination-plowing," our month of June. The caption reads, "The time when one is assigned to digging potatoes." The heavy digging belongs to the men, while the kneeling women sort out the potatoes and bag them for deposit in the root cellars. In the background is the *pacra pampa*, GHLQ 271, the "barren land" not subject to cultivation, otherwise known as the *puna* where only a pastoral life could be lived. While this was going on in the fields outside of Cuzco, in the city itself the Incas were observing the Inti Raymi.

II, 15.

Depiction: Incas plowing.
Remarks: The caption reads *haylli chacra yapuycuy pacha*, "time for plowing the victory field," equated with our month of August. This event followed harvest and broke ground for the next year's crop. This scene of the lordly Incas contrasts vividly with the preceding one in which the subjects are lowly commoners. Here the emperor, three of his great noblemen, the *coya*, and three *ñustas* are ritually breaking

ground on the famous *haylli chacra* called Sausero just outside Cuzco. The emperor is casually throwing his mantle back over a shoulder preparatory to thrusting his golden *taclla* into the sacred earth. His headband is adorned with sprigs of flowers, the one over his left ear being from the *cantut*-bush. The *coya* is providing her husband with two golden cups of *akha* so that he may drink a toast to his father Inti, shown as a figured sun-disc above him. The occasion is conceived to be a splendid victory, for the women are responding to the men's chant with the *haylli*! or "hurrah!" used in communal enterprises all over Peru (for the *haylli* among the Aymaras, see LBVA I, 115; II, 126). The men's chant is simply a mixture of traditional shouts which men used in calling to other men, *Yau*! *Yau*! (GHLQ 365), mixed with the *haylli*! It ends however with the emperor's announcing, "There it is, *Coya*!" while his nobles add, "There it is, *palla*!" This ceremony is a part of the month of plowing of the new shots (see previous illustration and BC XIII, 27).

III, 2.

Depiction: Worship of an idol.
Remarks: The emperor in humility has divested himself of his headgear and is offering a black llama to an idol which is undoubtedly Illapa, the god of rain and storm. It is the month of March and the *pacha pocoy* (less often *pocoy pacha*, GHLQ 292) or "ripening of the earth." It was a time of torrential rains, and little consequently could be done in the fields or open plazas. The emperor is in front of an *usno*, a rock carved out in asymmetrical steps and niches. This *usno* is a *huaca* itself and therefore can be adored for its own sake. On it the small idol has been placed. Insofar as this object is here an image it can be referred to as a *villca*, although the image also continues to be a *huaca*, as does the *usno*.

III, 5.

Depiction: The emperor consulting a sorcerer.
Remarks: The emperor is shown adoring his father the sun-god. It is the month of July. The harvest is in, and now has come the season

of *chacra ricuy*, "looking over the fields," and of *chacra conacuy*, "assigning the fields." A sorcerer who is a Colla Indian (as can be seen from the curiously shaped pendant under his chin) is reading the auguries in the fire which burns in front of him. He is depicted as a wizened old man. He is a sorcerer of the type called *visa*, GPF 330; SPYP 234, which apparently means one who summons by whistling, GHLQ 351 (probably also GHLQ 670). The word also appears as *viha* in AEI 3. The Hualla *visa* is identified in GPF 280 as a priest of the sun. Huallas could never be the high priests, for this position always went to a Capac Inca.

III, 6.

Depiction: Sacrificing to Vilcañota.
Remarks: The cross-barred chin pendants on all three figures as well as the *canipus* shaped like crescent moons mark this scene as connected with Collasuyo. The two types of headdress shown differentiate two of the important nations of Collasuyo, the Collas and the Lupacas (or Canas?), PPR 281. The long hair also sets them apart from the caste of the Capac Incas. A black llama is being offered to the *huaca* as well as three curious bound packages. The mountain is the great mass formed by Ausangate and Quenamari, GVCR VII, 11; JA III, 17, but the specific spot is undoubtedly the shrine of Vilcañota mentioned in CL 28. The spot is the watershed between the Vilcañota country and the Titicaca Basin—as such it was as sacred to the Collas as it was to the Incas. The *villca* is perched in a cleft high up in the mountain above the pass where hot springs and melting snows mingled to form the Vilcañota River.

III, 7.

Depiction: Huacas of the montaña.
Remarks: The caption reads, "Idols and *huacas* of the Antisuyos." The illustration depicts a scene of worship by the uncivilized Chunchos of the trans-Yucay country. They are offering incense and a small child to the jaguar, the *otoronco*, one of the formidable *huacas* of the forested hill country of Amazonia. The bow and arrow were never used by the

333

Incas as a weapon. The peaks on the left stand over the Yucay country and guard the pass to Paucartambo and the montaña. Sahuasiray is the peak at the far left. The two-pronged crag, Pitusiray, was reputed to be a young woman and her lover who were changed to stone, MMCB 429. These peaks were notable *huacas* long before the Incas entered the Yucay valley. In this illustration Huaman Poma has compressed two geographies, that of the Yucay valley and that of the montaña beyond it and over the passes. Machu Picchu is on the edge of this country.

III, 9.

Depiction: Inca woman dancing.
Remarks: The *coya*'s full name as given here is Cusi Chimpu Mama Micay which means Joyous Halo, Lady Micay. Strictly speaking she was a *palla* only by marriage, for she belonged to an *ayllu* in the Yucay valley before her marriage to Inca Roca, the sixth emperor. She was, however, of high rank and brought to Cuzco as her dowry important water rights. Here she is shown at a *taqui*, dancing, singing, and drumming. She is elegantly garbed and could be described as *pallahina huallparicuk*, "beautifully adorned like a *palla*," GHLQ 471. Over her sarong she is wearing a *cuychi lliclla*, "rainbow (i.e., striped) mantle," GHLQ 566, and on her head the folded kerchief or *ñañaca*, the sign of a lady. She is preceded by an Inca page, a *catiycachaquen huarma*, "a boy who goes in the following of a master or mistress." He is shown in the attitude of greeting. Behind the *coya* comes one of her more lowly servants, barefooted and without the mantilla.

III, 10.

Depiction: A young woman.
Remarks: A *sipas* or *tasqui sipas* was a girl aged fourteen to twenty, GHLQ 594; JLD 917. This type of young woman, if pretty and of sufficiently good birth in her native land, would be found there in the provincial *acllahuasi*. Here she is carrying her distaff and *puchca* or spindle. That she is not a *ñusta* or Inca girl is evidenced by the fillet or *uincha* around her temples, by the lack of the kerchief or *ñañaca*,

CM 87f.; SPYP 221 f., and by the fact that she is barefooted. A *ñusta* would have discarded her *uincha* and would have adopted sandals after her puberty ceremony. She is wearing the long wrap-around gown, the *anacu,* and the mantle or *lliclla* pinned over the breast with a *tupu.* This *tupu* is small, a fact which again shows that she is without caste. Around her waist is the *chumpi* or girdle. Huaman Poma's statement at the bottom concerning the age of the *sipas—de la edad de treinta y tres años*—is ridiculous.

III, 15.

Depiction: The *pancunco* ceremony.

Remarks: As a part of the Situa in the month of August–September (Coya Raymi—the Queen's Festival) there occurred the nocturnal fire-cleansing rite. Here we see the Incas hurling pellets of flammable material about the city with their slings. They have discarded their cloaks as if for combat. In each case their tunics are differently patterned. Their *campus* show them to be of differing moieties; the round one represents Lower Cuzco, and the one shaped like an ax-blade is from Upper Cuzco. The burning torches of *ichu*-grass and the fiery projectiles were called *pancunco,* GHLQ 277; GVCR VII, 7; CM 41.

III, 17.

Depiction: Emperor and his court.

Remarks: The emperor is splendidly attired, his tunic being wholly of the rich patterning of *tocapu.* He wears the knee and ankle fringes and carries the mace. On his right is a leading magnate from Upper Cuzco (identified by the *canipu* shaped like an ax-blade) and on his left a magnate of Lower Cuzco wearing the disc-shaped *canipu.* Behind them stand great *curacas* from the four parts of the empire. The Indian with the feathered war bonnet represents Antisuyo. Next to him is one of the chiefs of Chinchaysuyo, identified by his headdress and horseshoe-shaped *canipu.* On the opposite side are two *curacas* from Collasuyo, representing Lupacas and Collas, each with a different headdress. Next to them is a *curaca* from Contisuyo wearing the colored string *llauto,* a pompon, and two side rolls attached to it. The caption roughly identifies all these as the *camichicoc,* "councilors," and *apucona,* "rulers." The *curacas,* however, were never members of the royal council; Huaman Poma is mistaken on this point.

IV, 3.

Depiction: Attack on a *pucara.*
Remarks: This illustration gives the feel of incessant war and the lack of security in the world out of which the Incas appeared. Neither band is composed of Incas, for neither wears the earplugs; they are all identified as *auca pacha runa,* "men of the wartime," which designated the age just preceding the Incas' rise to power. Here a group of warriors has pursued a people up to their *pucara* or walled mountaintop fortress. Those besieged are hurling stones down on the enemy. Lances with feathered and tasseled collars are used as well as slings. The warriors are wearing hard reed helmets, and some wear around their necks gold or silver medals earned in previous battles, the *purapura,* SPYP 235, 266; GHLQ 296f.; RFC 258. The shields, which are used for parrying in close combat, have fringes draped from them.

IV, 4.

Depiction: Inca army in action.
Remarks: Here the Incas are shown advancing upon an inferior people in Chile whose lack of caste is shown by their bare feet, long hair, lack of adornment, and reliance upon only one weapon. The Incas wear the hard feathered helmet and fight with shields, slings, lances, and halberds. Leading the Inca regiment is a great *huaminca* or veteran warrior whose heroism is attested by the medal hanging from his neck. He is identified as Apu Camac Inca (Huaman Poma's historical statements are almost always worthless). This conquest of the southern countries took place during the reign of Topa Inca, whose brother is said to have been this Apu Camac Inca, GPF 158.

IV, 5.

Depiction: Incas settling boundaries in the empire.

Remarks: The two Incas are identified by name as Conaraqui Inca and Unacaucho Inca, from Upper and Lower Cuzco respectively, GPF 353 (note that the verb *raquiy* means "to divide up, to parcel out"). Their work of defining provincial boundaries took place under Topa Inca, according to Huaman Poma (there was a leader of the Cuyos in the days of Pachacuti called Apu Conaraqui, SG 34, but the person represented here could not be he). In the background is one of the fine masonry *sayhuas* or "markers" which the Incas erected throughout the empire designating the *topos* or "stages" of five miles along the roads (CL 15, 21; GPF 355), the provincial boundaries, the royal parklands or *moyas*, etc. The two Incas shown here are understood to be supervising the placing and erection of such structures. Note that for such a vital piece of work, each of the Cuzco moieties had to be represented.

IV, 8.

Depiction: Emperor addressing the *huacas*.

Remarks: A very interesting scene showing an Inca emperor—one incidentally who was known for his hostility to the *huacas*, SPYP 247; RGI I, 167—addressing a circle of these idols in Cuzco. Collectively they are identified as *huaca villca*, "sacred idols." The emperor approaches them with the proper gesture, the index finger pointing upward. Behind them Mount Huanacauri is shown identified as "Huanacauri, the *huaca* of the Incas." Some of the *huaca villca* are fully carved images, some are crudely shaped, and others are simply small *usnos* (asymmetrically stepped and carved stones). They have all been summoned to Cuzco for the yearly questioning. They are thus in Rimac Pampa where this rite customarily took place. They are being asked to prophesy the luck of the coming year. Their oracle-priests are not shown here. The emperor addresses them as follows, hoping to discover one who may wish to injure the year's crops: "Sacred idols, which one of you is saying, 'Let it not rain, but let it freeze and hail'? Answer now without delay." And the idols each reply, "Not I, eldest Inca." The term *curaca Inca* here seems somewhat unusual—at least I have not met it before.

IV, 11.

Depiction: Pachacuti, the ninth emperor.
Remarks: His full name is given here, Pachacuti Inca Yupanqui. The first name describes his accomplishments; it means "The Renovator of the Times." The second name gives his caste, and the third name was one of the common ancestral names and may be therefore considered his family name. He is shown in a warrior's stance whirling his sling, the traditional Inca weapon. In his left hand he carries the *champi*, a star-headed war club of gold. His string turban supports the pompon or *suntur paucar* and an abbreviated *mascapaycha*. His *yacolla* is knotted over one shoulder to give him freedom of action.

IV, 13.

Depiction: Acllas.
Remarks: The three main activities of the girls in the *acllahuasi* were spinning, weaving, and making *akha*. Here, under the direction of a mother superior, they are performing the first task. One girl on the left appears to be carding wool. The "abbess" of the "nuns" is in the Quechua language one of the *mamacona*, a plural form meaning "mothers, matrons, ladies, or sacred women." Cobo translates the word in the latter sense of sacred women as "lady mothers," BC XIII, 37, because they were either the wives or concubines of some one of the gods. The *acllas* or "selected" girls are all virgins awaiting assignment and being trained while they wait. As yet they have no status comparable to that of the *mama*. For the process of spinning and weaving, see BC XIV, 11.

V, 3.

Depiction: Inca giving gold to a Spaniard.
Remarks: Few documents offer as clear a conception of the baffled wonder with which the peoples of Peru viewed the European as does this naïve picture. It purports to be Huayna Capac conversing with Pedro de Candia, one of the important members of Pizarro's gang. The men represent their races. The Inca says in Quecha, "Is it this gold which you eat?" while handing the Spaniard a bowl filled with gold

338

nuggets. Pedro de Candia, surrounded by vessels of precious metals, replies in Spanish, "Yes. We eat this gold." An important feature of this picture is the presence of an *usno* inside a *carpa huasi*. The Spaniard is portrayed kneeling humbly before the Inca emperor who is sitting on the low golden stool of royalty. Needless to say, neither Pedro de Candia nor any other Spaniard ever saw Huayna Capac.

V, 4.

Depiction: Huascar led prisoner.
Remarks: Atauhuallpa's two great captains are shown on either side of the captive Huascar, Quizquiz to the left and Challcochima to the right. Both are shown as *pakuyoc*, GHLQ 271, or men "who wear the earplugs," that is to say they are identified as Incas. The former by his *canipu* is classed with Upper Cuzco, Challcochima with Lower. This information, plus the fact that Quizquiz wears a medal while Challcochima does not, appears to rate the former more highly. The legend on Huascar's tunic reads, "He ended his reign dying in Antamarca."

V, 5.

Depiction: Rumiñaui butchering Illescas.
Remarks: The third of Atauhuallpa's famous captains, Rumiñaui, is here shown eviscerating Inca Illescas in Quito. It is notable that Huaman Poma here wishes to show Rumiñaui as a non-Inca, for he wears his hair long, has no sandals, earplugs, or other signs of elegance. Elsewhere, GPF 379, he is depicted as a true Inca. He has just murdered Illescas who was one of Atauhuallpa's party and is opening up his carcass preparatory to stuffing it with grass. The corpse would then become a *runatinya*, a "man-drum" to be beaten and insulted during drinking bouts. The knife shown is the *tumi*, GHLQ 346, a common Peruvian type. As here it was used for slitting and cutting, not for stabbing. Knives in general were *cuchuna* or "cutters," and one with a point was a *quiruyoc cuchuna*, "a cutter with a tooth," GHLQ 466.

V, 6.

Depiction: Manco Inca as emperor.

339

Remarks: In true imperial fashion Manco Inca is shown surrounded by his great captains who throng about the bottom steps of the *usno.* The two captains from Upper Cuzco in the foreground are saluting him with the raised forefinger, and he replies in kind. The *usno* is shown as being an isolated and stepped stone, although we must not imagine the steps to have been as regular as drawn here. Because Manco Inca is surrounded by Incas dressed for war and not for fiesta, it is evident that this gathering is supposed to have been in the Urubamba valley whence Manco Inca escaped in order to concert plans for the uprising.

V, 9.

Depiction: Spaniards uncovering a woman.
Remarks: The caption reads, "Government in the provinces—the governors, priests, and deputies continually go about exposing women." The scene depicts the brutal, nocturnal irruption of Spanish officials into the sleeping quarters of an Indian woman. It is stated that this event takes place in the provinces. Scenes such as this one were an undoubted part of the early Spanish occupation of Peru. One can thus see why the caste of Capac Incas—which was based on a line of pure blood —so quickly disintegrated.

V, 11.

Depiction: Tupac Amaru captured by Spaniards.
Remarks: Two of the Spaniards responsible for the capture of Tupac Amaru are delineated, one carrying the loot, the other leading the Inca on a chain. Curiously Tupac Amaru is shown wearing a European-style crown as well as the *mascapaycha* and *suntur paucar.* Almost certainly this depiction is an error, although Huaman Poma makes a point of mentioning it in the caption. The Spaniard on the left is Martín García Oñaz de Loyola, a lieutenant who made the actual capture. The other is probably Martín Hurtado de Arbieto who commanded the enterprise. He is shown carrying two idols identified in Huaman Poma's text as the gold image of Inti (here seen with rays emanating from it) and below it the stone of Huanacauri seated on a miniature *usno.*

340

The stone is incorrectly depicted, for in actuality it was of medium size, was faceless and spindle-shaped, BC XIII, 15.

V, 12.

Depiction: Emperor and *coya* in litter.
Remarks: The tenth emperor, Topa Inca, and Mama Ocllo, his famous *coya*, appear in the covered litter or *rampa*, GHLQ 566. This specific one is called the *quispi rampa*, or "crystal litter." Their bearers are identified as natives of Carabaya, a mountainous region northeast of Lake Titicaca. Lucanas were usually the carriers of the royal *rampa*. The long hair and distinctive headgear of these Indians differentiate them not only from the Incas but from other Indian groups. The palanquin is covered with an *achihua*, a canopy made of the feathers of rare and gaudy birds. This type of *rampa* was used for the great state festivals. For long journeys the *rampa* had curtains which effectively screened the emperor from sight.

Notes on the Writing of the Book

A BOOK such as this one, which is of unusual format, needs some words of explanation and acknowledgement.

First of all, the reader will have noticed that little or nothing has been done with the economic life of Tahuantinsuyo. The reason is that economics is a part of the polity of the state and, as such, is not pertinent to the story of the Inca *ayllus*. John V. Murra of Yale has done more in this field than any other comparable investigator, and the interested reader is referred to his careful articles and monographs.

This work differs from my earlier *Empire of the Incas* significantly in the massive support added by the lexicons. The main dictionaries from the earlier period used were Holguín (and its later corrected and augmented version by the Redemptorist Fathers), Torres Rubio, and Santo Tomás. Useful hints, insights, and corrections were provided by the modern lexicons of which I used a variety, Lira being the most important. Bertonio's dictionary of Aymara for the earlier period was also consulted and added its share of knowledge.

I repeat my remarks from *Empire of the Incas*. No system of the spelling of Quechua words has been adhered to here. In every instance the expert has the citation to the word itself as it is discovered in the dictionaries, while the merely interested layman wants only an approximation to the sound of the word anyway. There is an even more compelling reason for this happy-go-lucky attitude, namely that in many cases we have no way of knowing which of two, three, or four possible words may be hidden behind the façade of a single Spanish spelling. The scholar certainly belongs here but not the purist.

Toward the writing of this book I have received suggestions and bibliographical help from Donald F. Solá and Gary J. Parker of Cornell University as well as Murra of Yale.

342

Florida Presbyterian College has generously provided financial aid for travel in Peru and for the purchase of books. The necessary accuracy and patience in typing and retyping a difficult manuscript as well as in reading proof has been provided by Miss Margaret Messer. I gratefully acknowledge the aid of these people and this institution.

The map of Inca Cuzco is based on the written sources, pieced out with some observation and deduction from the lay of the land. It is no sense claims the accuracy that would come from a study of the archaeology of the site, for the simple reason that no good archaeological survey is available. Most of the remains of Inca and early Colonial Cuzco are sealed up under the streets and houses and within the walls of the contemporary city. Today's over-all ground plan resembles the ancient city in its broad outlines, but in details a great deal has been changed, for, among other alterations, the Spaniards drove streets through *cancha* walls, tore out terraces, and thoroughly altered the water supply. The loss of the records of the first *cabildo* (later replaced in summary fashion) has been in this sense tragic.

There are numerous guidebooks to Cuzco, none of them satisfactory. Most of them stress the Colonial period, and here they are useful. For the Inca period they simply repeat a common stock of obvious information and, all too often, a common stock of errors. A partial list follows:

Rafael Larco Hoyle. *Cuzco Histórico*. Lima, 1934.
E. Alberto Rozas L. *Cuzco, Ciudad monumental y Capital Arqueológica de Sud America*. 3d ed. Cuzco, 1962.
J. Uriel García: *Guía histórico—Artística del Cuzco*. Lima, 1925.
Luis Valcárcel. *Cuzco*. 4th ed. Lima, 1950 (?).
Humberto Vidál. *Visión del Cuzco*. Cuzco, 1958.
R. P. Zárate. *El Cusco y sus monumentos*. 2d ed. Lima, 1940.

Bibliographical Code References

AC Anon., *Anales del Cuzco, 1600 á 1750*, Lima, 1901.

ACCM Antonio de la Calancha, *Corónica moralizada del órden de San Agustín en el Perú*, Barcelona, 1638.

ADS Anon., *Discurso de la sucesión y gobierno de los Incas*, in *El Cuzco y el gobierno de los Incas*, Lima, 1962.

ADVP Anon., *Descripción del Virreinato del Perú*, Rosario, Argentina, 1958.

AEI Pablo José de Arriaga, *La Extirpación de la idolatría en el Perú*, Lima, 1920.

ALLC Anonymous letter contradicting the opinion of Las Casas in *Coll. Doc. Ined. Hist. Esp.*, Madrid, Vol. XIII (1848), 425–69.

ARGCS Alonso Ramós Gavilán, *Historia del célebre santuario de Nuestra Señora de Copacabana*, Lima, 1621.

AZH Agustín de Zárate, *Historia del descubrimiento y conquista de la provincia del Perú*, Madrid, 1853.

BC Bernabé Cobo, *Historia del nuevo mundo*, in Biblioteca de Autores Españoles, Vols. LXXXXI and XCII, Madrid, 1964.

BCP Raul Porras Barrenechea, ed., *Cartas del Perú, 1524–1543*, Lima, 1959.

BE B. C. Brundage, *Empire of the Inca*, Norman, Oklahoma, 1963.

BLCL Bartolomé de las Casas, *De las antiguas gentes del Perú* (containing the chapters on the Incas taken from his *Apologética historia*), Lima, 1948.

BOD Baltasar de Ocampo. *Descripción y sucesos históricos de la provincia de Vilcabamba*, in *Coll. Libros Doc. Hist. Perú*, series 2, Vol. VII, Lima, 1923.

BVP Blas Valera, *Relación de las costumbres antiguas de los naturales del Perú*, in *Tres relaciones de antigüedades peruanas*, Asunción, Paraguay, 1950.

344

CA Anon., *La Conquista del Perú*, in *Proc. Amer. Acad. Arts and Sciences*, Vol. LXIV, No. 8 (1930).

CL Pedro Cieza de León, *Segunda Parte de la crónica del Perú*, Madrid, 1880.

CLPP Pedro Cieza de León, *Primera Parte*, many eds.

CLTP Pedro Cieza de León, *Tercera Parte*, partially published in the *Mercurio Peruana, revista mensual de ciencias sociales y letras*, Lima, 1946–.

CM Cristóbal de Molina de Cuzco, *Relación de las fábulas y ritos de los Incas*, in *Coll. Libros Doc. ref. Hist. Perú*, Vol. I, Lima, 1916.

CMS Cristóbal de Molina de Santiago, *Relación de la conquista y población del Perú*, in *Coll. Libros Doc. ref Hist. Perú*, Vol. I, Lima, 1916.

CP Raul Porras Barrenechea, *Cronistas del Perú*, Lima, 1962.

CV Miguel Cabello de Valboa, *Miscelánea antártica*, Lima, 1951 (all references are chapters in Part III).

DF Diego Fernandez, *Historia del Perú (Libro tercero de la segunda parte)*, Lima, 1876.

DSB De Sartiges and Botmiliau, *Dos viageros franceses en el Perú republicano*, Lima, 1947.

DTR Diego de Trujillo, *Relación del descubrimiento del reino del Perú*, Seville, 1948.

EQD see Dict.

FCL see Dict.

FEC Horacio H. Urteaga, ed., *Fundación española del Cusco y ordenanzas para su gobierno: restauraciones mandadas ejecutar del primer libro de cabildos de la ciudad por el virrey del Perú, Don Francisco de Toledo*, Lima, 1926.

FJ Francisco de Jerez, *Verdadera relación de la conquista del Perú y provincia del Cuzco*, in *Biblioteca de autores españoles: Historiadores primitivos de Indias*, Vol. II, Madrid, 1853.

FMA Fernando Montesinos, *Anales del Perú*, in *Juicio de Límites entre el Perú y Bolivia*, Vol. XIII, Madrid, 1906.

FSP Fernando de Santillan, *Relación del orígen, descendencia, política y gobierno de los Incas*, in *Tres relaciones de antigüedades peruanas*, Asunción, Paraguay, 1950.

GCIQ see Dict.

GDST see Dict.

GGO Gregorio García, *Orígen de los Indios del Nuevo Mundo*, Madrid, 1729.

GHLQ see Dict.

GHV Francisco Lopez de Gómara, *Hispania Victrix (La historia general de las Indias)*, *Primera parte*, in *Historiadores primitivos de Indias*, Vol. I, Madrid, 1852.

GKA George Kubler, *Art and Architecture of Ancient America*, Harmondsworth, Middlesex, 1962.

GOR Fray Gabriel de Oviedo, *Relación de lo que subcedió en la ciudad del Cuzco*, in Carlos Romero, ed., *Inédito sobre el primer Tupac Amaru*, *Revista Histórica*, Vol. II, Lima, 1907.

GPF Huaman Poma de Ayalá, *Nueva crónica y buen gobierno*, Paris, 1936 (facsimile edition).

GSC Gutierrez de Santa Clara, *Historia de las guerras civiles del Perú*, Madrid, 1905.

GSP E. George Squier, *Peru, Incidents of Travel and Exploration in the Land of the Incas*, New York, 1877.

GVCR Garcilaso de la Vega, *Comentarios reales de los Incas*, several eds.

GVHG Garcilaso de la Vega, *Historia general del Perú, segunda parte de los comentarios reales*, several eds.

HB Hiram Bingham, *Machu Picchu, a Citadel of the Incas*, Yale, 1930.

HBLC Hiram Bingham, *Lost City of the Incas*, New York, Atheneum, 1963.

HSAI *Handbook of South American Indians*, Vol. II, Washington, D.C., 1946 (exclusive of Rowe's article; see RIC).

HV Humberto Vidal, *Visión del Cuzco*, Cuzco, 1958.

IDI *Información de las idolatrías de los Incas e indios y de como se enterraban, in Coll. Doc. Ined. rel. Descub. Amer. y Oceania*, Vols. XXI and XXII, Madrid, 1874.

IH Roberto Levillier, ed., *Información hecha en el Cuzco por orden del rey* in *Gobernantes del Perú*, Vol. IX, Madrid, 1925.

ILPO Polo de Ondegardo, *Informe del licenciado Juan Polo de Ondegardo al licenciado Briviesca de Muñatones sobre la perpetuidad de las encomiendas en el Perú*, in *Revista Histórica*, Vol. XIII, Lima, 1940.

ISP *Informaciones sobre el antiguo Perú*, in *Coll. Libros Doc. ref. Hist. Perú*, Series 2, Vol. III, Lima, 1922.

ISP–HP *Relación de Hernando Pizarro acerca de la conquista.*

ISP–IH *Información sobre idolatrías en Huacho.*

ISP–TY *Relación de señores Indios que sirvieron a Tupac Yupanqui y Huayna Capac.*

ISP–VC *Declaración de los quipocamayos a Vaca de Castro.*

ISP–VT *Informaciones al virrey Toledo.*

JA José de Acosta, *Historia natural y moral de las Indias,* Mexico, 1940.

JADG Juan Ambrosetti, *Un documento gráfico de etnologia peruana de la época colonial,* Buenos Aires, 1910.

JB Juan de Betanzos, *Suma y narración de los Incas,* Madrid, 1880.

JCR J. Jijón y Caamaño, *La religión del imperio de los Incas,* Vol. I. Quito, 1919.

JLD see Dict.

LAC Lope de Atienza, *Compendio historial del estado de los Indios del Perú,* Quito, 1931.

LBVA see Dict.

LCI Juan Larrea, *Corona Incaica,* Cordoba, Argentina, 1960.

LCVP Luis Valcarcel, *El Cuzco precolombino,* in *Revista Universitaria del Cuzco,* No. 45, 1924, Cuzco.

LDB Reginaldo de Lizárraga, *Descripción breve de toda la tierra del Perú, Tucumán, Rio de la Plata, y Chile,* Madrid, 1909.

LDST see Dict.

LTOP Roberto Levillier, *Don Francisco de Toledo, supremo organizador del Perú,* Vol. II, *Sus informaciones sobre los Incas,* Buenos Aires, 1940.

MAH Fernanda Montesinos, *Memorias antiguas historiales y políticas del Perú,* Madrid, 1882.

MDK see Dict.

MGP Juan Matienzo, *Gobierno del Perú,* 1910.

MMCB Martin de Morúa, *Historia del origen y genealogía real de los reyes Incas del Perú,* Madrid, 1946.

MMDN Morúa, *Declaración del nombre deste reino del Perú con las ciudades que hay en él,* in *Historia del origen y genealogía real de los reyes Incas del Perú,* Madrid, 1946.

MP Anon., *Misión de las provincias de los Huachos y Yauyos,* in *Revista Histórica,* Vol. VI, Lima, 1919.

NC Anon., *Nouvelles certaines des isles du Pérou,* in *Cuadernos de Historia del Perú,* No. 2, Paris, 1937.

NCC *Noticias Cronológicas del Cuzco*, in Manuel de Mendiburú, *Apuntes históricos del Perú*, Lima, 1902.

OV Gonzalo Hernandez de Oviedo y Valdéz, *Historia general y natural de las Indias*, Madrid, 1851–55.

PHA Luis A. Pardo, *Historia y arqueología del Cuzco*, 2 vols., Cuzco, 1957.

PO Polo de Ondegardo, *Informaciones*. His *Errores y supersticiones de los indios* (PO:Error) and his *Fundamentos acerca del notable daño* (PO: Fund) are both in *Libros y Doc. ref. Hist. Perú*, Series I, Vol. III, Lima, 1916. His *Linage de los Incas* (PO:Lin) is in Vol. IV, same series, 1917.

PPR Pedro Pizarro, *Relación del descubrimiento y conquista de los reinos del Perú*, in *Coll. Doc. Ined. Histor. Esp.*, Madrid, 1844.

PRN Fray Pedro Ruiz Naharro, *Relación de los hechos de los Españoles en el Perú*, in *Coll. Doc. Ined. Hist. Esp.*, Vol. 26, Madrid, 1855.

RFC *Relación de las fiestas que en la ciudad del Cuzco se hicieron por la beatificación del bien aventurado padre Ignacio de Loyola*, in *Revista Histórica*, Vol. XII (1939), Lima, Peru.

RGEP *Relaciones geográfico-estadísticas del Perú . . . las instrucciones y memoriales que mandó despachar su Majestad en 1577*, in *Coll. Libros Doc. ref. Hist. Perú*, Series 2, Vol. V, Lima,1925.

RGH see Dict.

RGI *Relaciones geográficas de Indias, Peru*, 4 vols., Madrid, 1881–97.

RIA John H. Rowe, *An Introduction to the Archaeology of Cuzco*, in *Papers of the Peabody Museum*, Vol. XXVII, no. 2 (1944).

RIC John H. Rowe, *Inca Culture at the Time of the Spanish Conquest*, in HSAI.

RIP John H. Rowe, *Eleven Inca Prayers from the Zithuwa Festival*, in Kroeber Anthropological Society Papers, Nos. 8 and 9, Berkeley, 1953.

RMNL *Navigazione e viaggi raccolto de M. Gio Battista Ramusio*, Venice, 1545 (extract in Spanish in *Revista del Muséo Nacional en Lima*, Vol. IV, No. 2).

ROCW John H. Rowe, *Origins of Creator Worship Among the Incas*, in *Culture and History*, New York, 1960.

RSC Anon., *Relación del sitio del Cuzco*, in *Coll. Libros Raros y Cur.*, Vol. XIII, Madrid, 1879.

RZ Jerónimo Román y Zamora, *Republicas de Indias; idolatrías y gobierno en México y Perú antes de la conquista*, Madrid, 1897.

SG Pedro Sarmiento de Gamboa, *Segunda parte de la historia generál llamada Indica,* Buenos Aires, 1942.

SMN Santiago Montoto, *Nobiliario Hispano-Americano del siglo XVI,* in *Coll. Doc. Ined. Hist. Hisp.-Am.,* Vol. II, Madrid, n.d.

SPYP Juan de Santa Cruz Pachacuti Yamqui Salcamaygua, *Relación de antigüedades deste Reino del Perú,* in *Tres Relaciones de antigüedades peruanas, Asunción,* Paraguay, 1950.

TCYI Diego de Castro Tito Cusi Yupanqui Inca, *Relación de la conquista del Perú y hechos del Inca Manco II,* in *Coll. Libros y Doc. Hist. Perú,* Vol. II, Lima, 1916.

TRA see Dict.

UGMP José Uriel García, *Machu Picchu,* in *Cuadernos Americanos,* Vol. CXVII, No. 4 (July–August, 1961).

UGS Jose Uriel García, *Sumas para la historia del Cuzco* in *Cuadernos Americanos,* May–June, 1959.

VEC Antonio Vazquez de Espinosa, *Compendio y descripción de las Indias occidentales,* Washington, D.C., 1948.

VGD *Visita hecha a la provincia de Chucuito por Garcí Diez de San Miguel en el año 1567,* Lima, 1964.

VMP Luis E. Valcarcel, *Machu Picchu,* Buenos Aires, 1964.

VRQ Juan de Velasco, *Historia del reino de Quito,* 3 vols., Quito, 1841–1849.

DICTIONARIES AND OTHER LINGUISTIC AIDS

EQD *English-Quechua Dictionary,* Cornell University, 1964 (mimeographed), with introduction by Donald F. Solá.

FCL J. M. B. Farfán, *La Clave del lengua Quechua,* in *Revista del Múseo Nacional,* Lima, 1941–42.

GCIQ Sergio Grigorieff, *Compendio del Idioma Quichua,* Buenos Aires, 1935.

GDST Fray Domingo de Santo Tomás, *Grammática o arte de la lengua generál de los indios de los reynos del Perú,* Lima, 1951.

GHLQ Diego Gonzalez Holguín, *Vocabulario de la lengua general de todo el Perú llamada lengua Qquichua o del Inca,* Lima, 1952.

JLD Jorge Lira, *Diccionario Kkechuwa-Español,* Tucuman, Argentina, 1944.

LBVA Ludovico Bertonio, *Vocabulario de la lengua Aymara*, Julí, 1612 (facsimile edition, La Paz, 1956).

LDST Fray Domingo de Santo Tomás, *Léxicon o Vocabulario de la lengua generál del Perú*, Lima, 1951.

MDK Cesar Guardia Mayorga, *Diccionario Kechwa-Castellano, Castellano-Kechwa*, segunda edición, Lima, 1961.

RGH *Arte y diccionario Qquechua-Español de Diego Gonzalez de Holguín corregido y aumentado por los RR. PP. Redentoristas*, Lima, 1901.

TRA Diego de Torres Rubio, *Arte de la lengua Quichua, con las adiciones que hizo el p. Juan de Figueredo*, Cuzco, 1963.

Notes on the Text of the Book
by Parts and Sections

PART I

SECTION 1.

THE WORD *sallca* is best translated "highland"; in the Ayacucho dialect (VEC 1338; EQD 100) it is the equivalent of *puna* in the Cuzco dialect. The word is *páramo* in the far north and in Ecuador. *Sallca,* "highland," is opposed to *yunca,* "lowland," GHLQ 669. *Puna* has also the specific meaning of high, treeless land fit only for llama-grazing. The name of the lake is undoubtedly the same as that word we meet in GPF 186, 224, 305, 330, 336, 353. Analyzing all of these occurrences, one would think there would have to have been a verb *lucriy* having the meaning "to work at the building of terraces." Possibly confirming this supposition is the presence in Ayamara of a verb *lukhritha,* "to dig the earth," LBVA 197. A *lucri* would therefore have been a terrace. For a *chacra* called Lucri Ochullo, SPYP 247. I am convinced that the word given in SG 30 as *sucre* and meaning "agricultural terrace" is in error for *lucri.* In a Spanish manuscript hand, "l" and initial "s" could be confused.

For the festival of the *rutuchicoy,* "the hair-cutting," SG 13; CV 9; BC XII, 4; XIV, 6; CM 82, 87. The date 1493 comes from SG 69. For Huascar's name, GHLQ 185, 681. For Rahua Ocllo as not the *coya* at the time of Huascar's birth, CV 21; GSC II, 50. For the birth of Huascar before his father began to rule, SPYP 259. For his birth in a settlement called Huascar Quihuar, SG 63. For the site as being beside Lake Muhina, CV 24, and called Huascar Pata, SPYP 266. In the early seventeenth century there was a *repartimiento* near Quispi-cancha and Quihuares called *Huascar Quihuar del Rey,* undoubtedly referring to the birthplace, VEC 1869.

351

Section 2.

For the word *aucanacuy*, GHLQ 37. A city, *capac llacta* (GHLQ 470) or a "rich community," is contrasted with the *uchulla llacta* (LDST 34), "small community" or hamlet.

Section 3.

We have chosen to call the area around Cuzco from which the city drew its immediate sustenance *Cuzcoquiti* (GHLQ 102, and see analogy with Rimakquiti, GHLQ 617), although *Cuzcoquimray* (GHLQ 309) would have been equally as good. Both *quiti* and *quimray* mean "environs, province," GHLQ 645. Quotation from Cobo, BC XII, 36. Quotation from Cieza, CLPP 92. For *Topa Cuzco*, MMCB III, 73; IV, 2. Quotation from Sancho, CP 103. For other descriptions of the city, BLCL 2; NVBR; OV XLVI, 13; LDB I, 80. The heavy foundation courses of stone were the *callanca rumi*; the smaller ones above, the *checosca rumi*, GHLQ 44, 107, 222, 670. The word for "thatch" was *curahua*, GHLQ 428 (see also JLD 334 for a cognate). The two streets that led up to the heights were Pomacurco, "Lion Trunk" (for *curcu* as "tree trunk" see EQD 140; GHLQ 56), leading up past the north side of Collcampata, and that which passed up on the other side, its name is not certainly known.

For the masonry gutter down the middle of the street, BCP #86 (p. 127). A house in general was a *huasi*, but a house with a superadded floor or garret was a *marcahuasi*, GHLQ 231. For the terraces, PPR 292, 297; CL 51; SG 30. The common word for terrace was *pata*, a "step"; agricultural terraces were *palta* from *palltay*, "to put one thing on top of another," LDST 40; GHLQ 274. Sarmiento gives another word for an agricultural terrace, *sucre* (SG 30) which must be an error for Huaman Poma's *lucre*, see Notes, Part I, sec. 1. For the plastering of the huts, JB 16. For planting of cactus fences, GHLQ 152. The plant used in the plastering process was the same branched cactus used to make the fences, JB 16; GHLQ 144, 448; JLD 234, 324; *Revista Universitaria del Cuzco, primer semestre de 1961*, p. 46. I have heard this plant also called *atakiska* in Chincheros. The population figure of 25,000 (which is a mere guess and probably on the low side) I derive from BCP 215 in which it is stated that Cuzco proper had between 3,000 and 4,000 habitations. For population types living in the valley, see GVCR VI, 3; CMS 141. For yearly street-cleaning *corvée*, CLPP 93. For the *yanca ayllu*, GHLQ 364, 450. For *curacas* who had to spend part of the year in Cuzcoquiti, CLPP 74. The warehouses were the *churaccuna huasi*, GHLQ 122; GPF 329f.

For the basic economic province centering on Cuzco with a radius of 150 miles, GVCR V, 8. The Spaniards exhaustively described the contents of these warehouses, see, among others, BLCL 5, 18; PPR 271f; DTR 63; JB 12; Sancho de la Hoz, quoted in BCP 104f. For the general system of provincial warehousing culminating in Cuzco, see BC XII, 30; CLPP 75; FS #41; PPR 271. For the word *capaccay* meaning "wealth" and "empire," GHLQ 135, 661. All traffic in and out of Cuzco was stopped after sunset, BLCL 24; RZ II, 14. For the four areas around Cuzco corresponding to four areas of empire, VEC 1500; AZH I, 9; GVCR VII, 9. For the high percentage of *mitmacs* in the population of greater Cuzco, CLPP 92. For the groups repre sented, CLPP 93. For regulations regarding headgear, CLPP 93; GVCR VII, 9; PO: Inf. 141; IH 276. For headgear of the Collas, PPR 281; IH 285; GPF 169. For headgear of the Cañars, CLPP 44. Headgear was known as *umamaytucuna* (i.e., "head-wrappings"), GHLQ 513. For prohibition against leaving one's village, ISP-TY 68; SF #13; PO: Inf. 141.

For the number of habitations as 20,000, BCP #215, p. 312. This figure for the near environs of Cuzco comes from Bishop Vicente de Valverde and checks well with the number of inhabitants in an area 30–35 miles around as amounting to 200,000, CMS 141. The figure of 100,000 houses to be seen from Sacsahuaman given by Sancho de la Hoz (quoted in BCP 104; MMCB IV, 2) is meant to include outhouses of noble estates and warehouses as well and is thus not out of line with the other two estimates. The limit of Cuzcoquiti (for the purposes of the Situa festival) to the southeast is given in BS XIII, 29 as Quiquijana and confirmed in CM 38. Urcos seems more likely, FSP 47. Vicos is also given, ISP-TY 59, and is very close to Urcos, VEC 1869. Not Pisac (as one would expect) as the northern limit but a place called Ahuisca is given in ISP-TY 59; FSP 47. I am unable to identify Ahuisca. The Contisuyo limit was the Cusipampa River, BC XIII, 29.

There is a Quechua verb *cuscuy*, "to variegate, to work with many colors; to enamel," GPF 191; GHLQ 58, 514; LBVA I, 225; II, 63. It is one of the few Quechua words in the old dictionaries from which "Cuzco" might be derived. Another possibility is *cuscu*, "ground barley; a kind of maize," RGH 60. The modern word (Ayacucho dialect) *qusku*, "mottled brown and white," is pronounced differently from the name of the city of Cuzco, EQD 36, 88, but this fact does not necessarily rule out a connection, especially in view of *sacsa* (see Sacsahuaman), EQD 88. For Sarmiento's etymology, SG 13; see also MMCB IV, 2. There is no evidence that "Cuzco" means "navel," as is commonly stated, although Huaman Poma's statement that the city was originally called "Acamama" (Mother of Beer) may be partially correct insofar as it was a popular designation of the place, descriptive of the vast quantities of *akha* produced and drunk there, MMCB I, 2; GP 31, 34. The verb *cuscoay*, LDST 54, is derived from the name of the city and therefore does not explain the meaning of the word. Quotation, ILPO 132.

SECTION 4.

FOR SAKRA, BC XIII, 15. The site would have been somewhere near the modern university. For the word *sakra*, LDST 57, 230, 345; GHLQ 75, 518, 524; JLD 868. For *tancar*, BC XIII, 15. For word *tancar*, GHLQ 337; JLD 959f., 997; EQD 16. For the plant itself, the *solanum pseudolycioides*, Revista Universitaria, Cuzco, 1961, p. 45. November was the *ayamarcay quilla*, "the month of carrying the dead," MMCB III, 72; GPF 256f. This period seems to be confused with festival of *Cantaray* in October in ACCM II, 12. Note that *Cantaray* is the name of the month of October in JLD 306; DF X. *Cantaray* means the making of that special *akha* used in the knighting ceremonies, CM 59. For the rites at the *ayamarcay*, ARGCS I, 22; MP 184, 188.

I have in this book used the Quechua word for the Peruvian drink commonly called *chicha*, and I have used the spelling *akha* (JLD 33) to keep it apart from *aka*, the Quechua word for "excrement," JLD 31. For *acoy* as "corpse," LDST 89. See also *accoya*, "livid, pale, dying" in Aymara, LBVA, I, 322; II, 5. It is probably connected with *acoy* (JLD 34), "to pulverize, to make into sand or dust." Tancar was just downstream from Cayaocachi, CV 20. Cabello Valboa is confused in suggesting there were two prisons, one at Tancar and one at Uimpillay (CV 20); there was only one—Uimpillay (LDST 166) was in the region called Tancar, and Arahuay was a rock just above and behind Uimpillay, BC XII, 26. The hanging-rock at Arahuay is called Antacaca, GPF 188. The names Arahuay and Uimpillay are indeed used interchangeably, GHLQ 33. If one checks the front map in RIA, one can see the archaeological site Limpillay at the juncture of the Huatanay and the Tancarpata. Hanging, which was the usual mode of execution at Arahuay, is even known as *uimpillupuyay*, "to hang by the heels or hair till dead," GHLQ 684.

For site of Huanaypata, CV 10; BC XIII, 15 (wrongly spelled Guanipata). I do not understand the translation of Huanaypata as "a precious thing," SG 13. For *Surihuaylla*, "Ostrich Meadow," BC XIII, 15; GVCR V, 10. There is a possibility that *suri* may here mean a kind of alpaca, JLD 940; SPYP 221. For the salt spring, LDB I, 63. For present-day paganism in San Sebastián, see Gorge C. Muelle: "La Chicha en el distrito de San Sebastián," *Revista Arqueologica Univ. Cuzco*, No. 1, 1945. For the channeling of the river to Muhina, JB 13; LDB I, 65. For the tale of the Sañu sorcerer, CV 9; SPYP 215; SG 12. For Huanacauri as a flood *pacarina*, BC XIII, 15. For *huaylla*, LDST 55, 62, 69; GHLQ 428.

For the name of the sanctuary as *Chimpu*, "Halo," or *Kahua*, "the Lookout," CV 9. The Chachapoya hamlet of Vilcarpay (BC XIII, 15) still exists under that name at the head of the Tancarpata gully. For the only clear picture of Huanacauri and the approach to it, see RIA 41–43, Plate IV, Figs. 3–6. Double bridges were not uncommon in Peru (OV XLVI, 11; BLCL 20); they differentiated classes and sexes. The third bridge here was probably reserved for the emperor and the *huaca* when it came down from the mountain. For the sons of Huanacauri, BC XIII, 15; MMCB I, 2.

Section 5.

I assume from GVCR I, 20 that Sañu was an Ayarmaca community. There is no certainty regarding the original name of this people, whether *Ayarmaca* or *Ayamarca*; I have chosen the former as being more probably correct inasmuch as it is the form used by SG plus the fact that *ayar* is a name or title used in the earliest levels of Inca history, as witness the original four brothers whose names all began with Ayar. The element *maca* may thus be the word "striker," GHLQ 221; JLD 611 f. For the Tocay Capac Ayllu and its continuing importance, LTOP 168. The number eighteen comes from GVCR I, 20. For the Chachapoyas resident on Carmenca, CLPP 78. For the quotation from Cieza, CLPP 78. There was a small pueblo called Larapa or Rarapa east of Cuzco; it is probably to be connected with the gully called today Larapa entering the Huatanay just west of San Gerónimo, BC XII, 9; XIII, 14. For Oma, CL 33; BC XII, 6; JB 18.

The *ayllus* from San Sebastián roughly up to the Lucre area were Ayarmaca, GVCR I, 20. For the Omas as confederate Incas, JB 18. The fall festival of the *Puzquiayquiz* (DF 10) or *Puchayquis* (ACCM II, 12) is undoubtedly to be explained from the verb *puchcay*, "to spin," GHLQ 292. For the Narrows, CM 38 gives *acoya puncu* while BC XII, 4 gives *ancoyac puncu*. The simplest thing is to relate it to *akkoya*, JLD 34, which is a word applied to crushed rock, sand, or rubble. For Huana Cancha, SG 12, 34.

For the battle cry, GHLQ 38. *Llullpac* is the same as *llumpac*, GHLQ 217. For the sacrifices on Llullpacturo, BC XIII, 15. This site was apparently on or near a mountain called the Lesser or Dwarf Huanacauri, BC XIII, 15; CM 28f. For the Quispicanchi and Muina area, CLPP 97. Quispicanchi which lies at the foot of Mount Pinahua today, is probably the successor to the old community of Pinahua often mentioned in our sources along with Muina. The communities in the Lucre basin are given in SG 25 as Muina, Pinahua, Casacancha, and Runtucancha. For the god Pachachulla Viracocha, CV 12, 14; BC XII, 6. The sources quite apparently attempt to disguise the fact that this armed attack on Cuzco by Muina was successful. That it was a defeat for Cuzco is proved by Lloque Yupanqui's reputation as weak and cowardly, GSC III, 49; DF V; ARGCS I, 3; ACCM I, 15; GPF 97, among others.

The name Lloque undoubtedly means "javelin, dagger" and not "left-handed," LDST 311; GHLQ 216; JLD 589 (in which it seems to mean "sharp"). A glaciated mountain-mass or *quenamari* is also called a *lloque*, SPYP 231. For Pachachulla Viracocha, see John H. Rowe, "The Origins of Creator Worship among the Incas," *Culture in History*, Columbia, 1960. Dates for Viracocha Inca, the eighth ruler, are from CV 13, 14. For the attack on the Yucay area before the reduction of Muina, SG 25. For Pachacuti's name, GHLQ 16, 17, 525; MMCB III, 57. For *purum llacta*, GHLQ 297. I assume the destruction of Muina on the basis of analogies in Inca history—there is however no specific record of it (see SG 24).

I have identified Pikillacta with a *churaccuna llacta* without sanction of any text, but it seems to me that this phrase describes what the site's function was. A synonym of *Churaccuna huasi* is *collcampata*. The word *collcampata* in the meaning of "checkered" was applied to certain weaves, MMCB III, 21. This term is merely a derivative from the ground-plan appearance of the typical planned and conjoined storage bins erected by the pre-Columbian groups of Peru. See in SPYP 226 the bottom figure in the illustration, the divinized *Collcampata* or community storage bins represented by a checkerboard. I agree with the recent suggestion of E. Harth-Terré *(Pikillacta, cuidad de Pósitos y Bastimientos del Imperio Incaico,* Cuzco, 1959) that Pikillacta was a store-city. The first two paragraphs in BC XII, 30 should be read in this connection. One should refer to the plan of the site given at the end of Harth-Terré's sensible monograph as well as to the excellent air photograph in GKA, Plate 162 (see also p. 312). It is quite possible that the contiguous ruins on the north mentioned in Harth-Terré, p. 16, are those of old Muina.

For the wall and guard station at Rumi Collca, CLPP 97. For Huaro, BC XII, 6. *Huaro* is translated "pebbles, gravel" (RGEP 101; GHLQ 621) and therefore means in a loose translation "Stone Pile." The modern verb *waruy* means "to pile stones," EQD 98.

SECTION 6.

FOR QUOTATION from Polo, PO: Inf. 146. For the Inca sense of their own aristocratic standing, BC XII, 4; OV XLVII, 8, 13. For the *Intip churin,* GVCR I, 26; OV XLVII, 8, 13. For Mama Ocllo, CV 22, 28; CM 86. For the meaning of the word *ocllo,* GVCR IV, 7. For the meaning of *huaco,* LDST 78; GHLQ 453. Today *huaco* means "cheek," EQD 23.

The cult of Mama Ocllo followed the Incas wherever they went, ARGCS I, 29. For *pallas,* VEC 1502; GVCR I, 26; GHLQ 273. For *iñaca* as a synonym of *palla,* GHLQ 368; LDST 96, 335; LBVA I, 325; II, 175. It is therefore also found as a synonym of *mama,* GHLQ 584, which explains why today it has degenerated to mean a "nurse," or "governess," JLD 285. Finding the word as a male name (as in NCC 38) must therefore be an error for "Inca." For *ñusta* and *auqui,* CM 62, 67; GVCR II, 27; GHLQ 38, 545. For the *Mancop churin,* SPYP 273; BC XII, 4. Manco's full name was probably Ayar Manco (royal descendants received this name, CV 19; SG 40), the Capac or "king" having been added as a title bestowed much later. For Huanacauri as a "father," CM 63.

SECTION 7.

FOR THE GENERAL MEANING of the word "Inca," BC XII, 4. A man became an *auqui* upon initiation; he only really became an *Inca* when he married, GVCR I, 26. For *auqui* as "nobleman," GHLQ 38. For *canipu,* GHLQ 50 and MMCB 421 (where it is wrongly spelled); RFC 258; GPF 354, 362, 364. The earplug was the *pacu,* GHLQ 271. The word for ear is *rinri* or *rincri*; an Inca was therefore a "golden ear" or an "earplug man," *cori rincri* or *pacuyok,* see for variations GVCR I, 26; GHLQ 38, 69, 271, 545, 610. Quechua is rich in allusions to "good blood" or nobility, GHLQ 20, 21, 32. A word rather loosely synonymous with *curac* is *pihui* (EQD 53; GHLQ 119, 545; JLD 812; JB 16) which means "first-born."

For *yanca ayllu,* GHLQ 450. For the basis of the Inca's claims to privilege, PO: Inf. 152. Head-binding of babies was practiced by the

Incas (MMCB III, 4; JB 18; SPYP 219, 224), as it was by other Peruvian groups, but this practice apparently was something of a rarity or it would have been more graphically commented on by the chroniclers. It was in no sense a special mark of an Inca. For *curac*, GHLQ 56, 545. For Yupanqui, see notes, Part 5, sec. 1.

For the Capac Incas, GVCR IX, 40. If we use BLCL 12, 24 as a means of counting the Capac Incas, we find "more than 300" Capac Incas which, with their immediate and legitimate families, might come to about 1,800 in all. Quite in line with this estimate is the army of 2,200 Inca warriors raised from all the *ayllus* on the death of Pachacuti (SG 48), which army must have contained all of the fighting men of the *panacas* (Capac Incas) as well as of the *ayllus* (Hahua Incas) of Upper and Lower Cuzco. For a threefold division of the Inca caste, the Capac Incas, the Hahua Incas and the Uaccha Incas, see GPF 243, 337. For marriage to foreign princesses of high caste, GVCR I, 26. Huaman Poma has simply not subdivided the Hahua Incas, as we have done.

The threefold division in SPYP 273 of "caballeros," "caballeros particulares," and then confederate Incas (Hahua) simply omits the bottom class, the *Uaccha* Incas. For the term *caylla ayllu*, GHLQ 616. For the creation by Pachacuti of the class of Hahua Incas, GVCR V, 23; CL 45; JB 13. For the status of the Hahua Incas in the environs of Cuzco, GVCR VI, 23. A large proportion of the Hahua Incas must have been made up of the descendants of these *curacas* to whom Pachacuti gave women of his lineage, i.e., legitimate by this definition, JB 12. For the long hair of the Hahua Incas, JB 18; PPR 267. For the *takya huarmi*, RGI II, 60. In Spanish the difference between Capac and Hahua Incas comes out as "señores" and "orejones," JB 16. The guess of 15,000 as the population of Hahua Incas has little more behind it than the chance remark in BLCL 24 that there were 6,000 *pallas* in the neighborhood of Cuzco.

For the status of the emperor's sons, CL 10; CV 16. Both SPYP 273 and GPF 34f, 337, 740 agree that the following belonged to the Hahua Incas: Quihuar, Masca, Tambo, Chilque, Mayo, Quechua, Quilliscachi, and Papri. Huaman Poma adds the following: Anta,

359

Huaro, Lari, Equeco, Huaroconti, Acos, and Poques. For the special prerogatives of some of these *ayllus*, GPF 306, 308, 310, 354, 356; GHLQ 139, 308; CM 23.

For pages, *catiycachaqquen huarma*, GHLQ 613 (from the verb "to go behind someone," GHLQ 51). Each of the principal *pallas* of Cuzco had fifteen or twenty ladies-in-waiting, a majority of whom were young girls, BLCL 24. For the training of these young people, the most important notices come to us from PPR 267. For the *huaccha cconcha*, or "poor relations," JB 16; GHLQ 67. The real meaning of *huaccha* is "orphan" (GHLQ 167), and the meaning of *cconcha* is "nephew (on the sororal side)," GHLQ 67. Thus a *huaccha Inca* was a by-blow of some Inca noble whose father did not claim him.

SECTION 8.

THE AYMARA *hatha* is the equivalent of *ayllu* or *yahuar* in Quechua, LBVA I, 121, 293; II, 28. At the same time *hatha* is more specific than *ayllu*, for it means "seed" (of plants, animals, men), LBVA I, 428; II, 124. The Aymara equivalent of the founder of the family is the "grandfather" or "root grandfather," *achachi* or *tunu achachi*, LBVA I, 7, 48, 157; II, 5, 364 (note that the Aymara word *achachi* appears with some frequency as an Inca personal name). For *ccallaric machu*, GHLQ 61. *Ticci* and *sapi* can also be used to designate the founder of a line, GHLQ 341.

For *villca*, LDST 143, 173; the other word for "grandchildren" may be used, *hahuayñin*, LDST 159. *Haway* is given in RIC 251 as "grandchild," while *wilka* is translated as "great-grandchild." The fact is they appear to have been synonymous, JLD 236; EGD 62, or of vague meaning, JLD 236; FCL 14. The equation of *aylluncuna* with *yahuar puru* (GHLQ 614) means that the *ayllu* was conceived to be a relationship of blood. Members of an *ayllu* were all "brothers," *ayllu huauque*, GHLQ 190. For *ayllu*, LDST 143, 159, 173; GHLQ 40, 523, 616. St. Tomás interestingly gives *villca*, "grandchildren," as a synonym of *ayllu*, and also *hahuayñin*. Family fetishes were called generally *conopas*, AEI 2, 8, 10; JCR 99, 102; ACCM II, 11; MP 184. For ancestral sparks in the fire, ACCM II, 12. For bezoars,

GHLQ 40; LBVA II, 127. A *tampu* was a stage on a journey and thus could be either a campsite in the open or an inn established on a traveled road. It is usually translated as "inn," but in "Pacaritambo" the other meaning is more appropriate (see JLD 960; SG 11).

The interpretation of the origins of Cuzco here differs markedly from the one which I advanced in BE I. Since writing that volume I have realized that the cause of so much of the confusion in this legendary period is the using of the names of *sinchis* as the equivalents of the *ayllus* they led and vice versa, as well as identification of *ayllus* by the name of the *huaca*. Once I realized this fact fully, then the numbers of peoples involved in the foundation were seen to fall off—thus simplifying the picture. From its name, Antasaya, that group should by rights be derived from the pueblo of that name in the present Pampa de Anta. SG 9–15 is the prime document here.

For the general quarrelsomeness of the invading elements, LTOP 188. For Pachacuti's reform of the list of *ayllus*, SG 19, and for the list, SG 9. The Sanus settled in Upper Cuzco under Lloque Yupanqui, CL 32. The Mascas could not have been defeated; they probably came in by treaty, bringing with them their *huaca* called Huari Huaca, CV 13. The statement that there were only two principal lineages *(ayllus)* comes from GDST 128 (the Tambos are the Sutic, SG 11); MMCB I, 15 ("Marca" is here erroneously given for "Maras"). There is no word in Quechua as specific as our "moiety"; the word *saya* will do duty for both *ayllu* and "moiety."

I found the hint for my reconstruction of the Inca social system in GDST 128, where it is stated that the two principal families were the Sutic and Maras. By definition then, they must be the Tambos whom Manco Capac is said to have led. No explicit statement gives me the right to equate Hanan Cuzco with the Cuzcos, and Hurin Cuzco with the Tambos. I derive the inference from Molina, Hymn #10, RIP 93, where Cuzco and Tambo are the only two named groups of Incas, obviously the two moieties. For Pachacuti as the organizer of the membership of the two moieties, BLCL 17.

For other references to the Cuzco moieties, CM 44, 78f.; GVCR I, 16; MMCB I, 15; PO: Error, III; MAH 6; BLCL 17. The Cuicussa undoubtedly was a people originating close by; the name appears as an isolated knob near Huanacauri, BC XIII, 15. For the Capac Ayllu, GVCR IX, 40. For the division in modern San Sebastián: Oscar Nuñez del Prado C., "Apuntes etnográficos sobre San Sebastián," in *Revista de la Sección Arqueológica de la Universidad Nacional del Cuzco,* No. 3, 1946.

SECTION 9.

FOR THE WORD *pana*, GHLQ 277; JLD 732. It is doubtful whether there is a connection between *panaca* and *apupanaca*, the title of the officer in charge of the selection and oversight of the provincial *acllas*, JA V, 15; BC XIII, 37; BVP 174. Sarmiento says *panaca* means "family," or "descent," (SG 14), as does RGH 261. In GDST 128 we find *ayllu* and *pachaca* as synonyms meaning "lineage"; *pachaca* here is almost certainly to be translated as a collective meaning "servants." Once it is spelled *panacay*, IDI XXI, 179. It is consistently spelled *panaca* in GDST and LDST, as if it were a formation from *pana*, "right hand." Whatever its meaning, *panaca* is adjectival with the noun it modifies (*ayllu*) generally omitted.

We know that a noun in Quechua can be further nominalized by the addition of the suffix -*ka* (JLD 291), so that *panaca* would then mean "sisterhood" or "sororal association" as it related to a special male person—this one seems at present the best explanation of the word, but one would much rather derive a meaning from it such as "brothers and sisters," *panantin*, JLD 732; GHLQ 544, as seems demanded by its translation as "descent," SG 14. The best descriptions of the structure of the *panaca* are in SG 14, 19; JA VI, 20; BLCL 17; RZ II, 12; GVCR VII, 9.

For the office of the *pachaca*, GHLQ 270. The basic meaning of word is "servant"; see GHLQ 363 where it is found as a synonym of *yana*. I base my statement that the issue of Inca members in a certain *panaca* were not bound to that *panaca* on the single instance that Tocto Usica was of the Vicaquirau *panaca*, but her sons were of the Tumipampa *panaca*, SG 62. For lists of the *panaca* names, CM 38–40; BLCL 17; GVCR IX, 40; MMCB I, 15; GSC III, 50; DF 7; ISP-VC 12; RZ

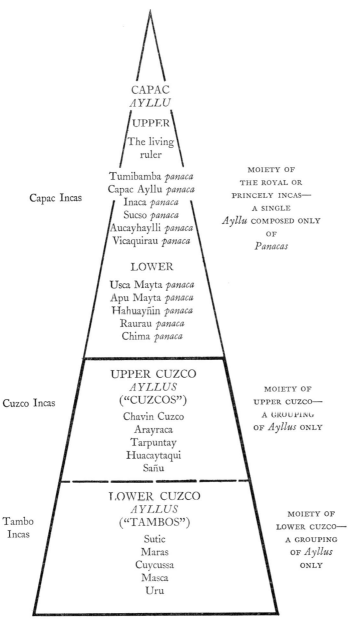

CAPAC
AYLLU

UPPER

The living
ruler

Capac Incas

Tumibamba *panaca*
Capac Ayllu *panaca*
Inaca *panaca*
Sucso *panaca*
Aucayhaylli *panaca*
Vicaquirau *panaca*

MOIETY OF
THE ROYAL OR
PRINCELY INCAS—
A SINGLE
Ayllu COMPOSED ONLY
OF
Panacas

LOWER

Usca Mayta *panaca*
Apu Mayta *panaca*
Hahuayñin *panaca*
Raurau *panaca*
Chima *panaca*

Cuzco Incas

UPPER CUZCO
AYLLUS
("CUZCOS")

Chavin Cuzco
Arayraca
Tarpuntay
Huacaytaqui
Sañu

MOIETY OF
UPPER CUZCO—
A GROUPING
OF *Ayllus* ONLY

Tambo
Incas

LOWER CUZCO
AYLLUS
("TAMBOS")

Sutic
Maras
Cuycussa
Masca
Uru

MOIETY OF
LOWER CUZCO—
A GROUPING
OF *Ayllus*
ONLY

PYRAMID TABLE OF INCA *Ayllus*

363

II, 12; BC XIII, 13–16. For all the *panacas* together forming the Capac Ayllu, GVCR VII, 9; IX, 40.

For Auccay Haylli (GHLQ 38) as a man's name, ISP-VC 12. *Iñaca,* "lady," appears to be sometimes confused with the *ñañaca,* which was a woman's headcloth or kerchief, often beautifully patterned or striped in colors; see GPF 122, 126, 130, 136. For Pachacuti's reorganization, BLCL 17; JB 17; ADS 28. Quotation on possession of a man's mummy, ALLC 448.

The Inca *panaca* was probably suggested by the sierra custom of keeping the corpse in the house for a month before burying it, meanwhile offering it feasts and gifts, RZ III, 9. By simply omitting the eventual burial from this institution, the skeleton of the Inca *panaca* is evident. For mention of *panaca* property-holding as being separate and distinct, ALLC 465f. For imperial competition with the ancestors for wealth, BC XII, 36; PPR 238f. For retention of an emperor's wealth by himself after death, CA 266; ALLC 467f. For Inca Roca as the originator of the system, JA VI, 20.

For membership in the *panaca* by choice and by assignment, PPR 239f., 267. For statement that most Incas were enrolled in the *panacas,* PPR 264. For Pachacuti's *panaca,* SG 47. For Topa's *panaca,* CV 31. Another name for Pachacuti's *panaca* was the Hatun Ayllu. The statement that Pachacuti's *panaca* was joined to that of his son Inca Yupanqui (GVCR IX, 40) probably refers to the substitution of Topa Inca for Amaru Topa Inca as coregent. When Amaru Topa Inca was coregent, he had already undoubtedly set up his *panaca,* but when he had to give up the crown, he must have been puzzled about what to do with his projected *panaca*—this situation probably suggested to his father, still alive at the time, the possibility of joining it to his own. Topa Inca's *panaca* then received the name Capac Ayllu *panaca* ("the King's Family *panaca*") to firmly attest the legitimacy of his rule, although most curiously it seems to have been put under the captaincy of the deposed heir, BLCL 25 and probably NAH 6. For *panacas* as centers of vice, BC XIII, 10; PPR 268, 276.

For Spaniards' burning members of *panaca* alive, BC XII, 11; JA VI, 20. For concept that dead emperor was to return in the flesh, ALLC

466. For assignment of *yanaconas* to the *panaca*, FS #36. For their attainment of positions of power, JA VI, 21. For tale of dead emperor's giving girl in marriage, PPR 239f. For royal mummies as *illapa*, GPF 287f., 377f. It is given as *ylla* in CL 30. For *illapa cari*, GHLQ 367. But the *illapa*, more specifically, was the divine spark in an emperor, and it could desert him if he were disobedient to Inti, BLCL 25. For the confusion as to whether the dead ancestor was in heaven or on earth, IDI XXI, 168f., 209; GVCR I, 22; II, 8. For fertilizing power of mummy, BC XIII, 10.

For Inca Roca's connection with water, BC XII, 9. There were still members of the Sucso *panaca* alive in 1654 (HV 151), but this fact does not prove an extended period for the life of the *panaca*, for the mummies and *huaoquis* had long since vanished. One of the modern *ayllus* of San Sebastián is called Sucso; see Oscar Nuñez del Prado, "Apuntes Etnográficos sobre San Sebastián" in *Revista de la Sección Arqueológica de la Universidad Nacional del Cuzco*, No. 3, 1946. For Yahuar Huacac's mummy, JA VI, 20. For Pachacuti's mummy at Patallacta, BC XII, 13; JA VI, 21. For location of Lower Cuzco *panaca* palaces, JB 16; VEC 1502f., 1507f.; BC XIII, 15.

SECTION 10.

SARMIENTO TRANSLATES *purucaya* as meaning the entire mourning service for a dead ruler (SG 31), but inasmuch as he is making the point that Pachacuti created these observances, it refers obviously to the processional ritual of the *panaca*. It is translated in GHLQ 297 as the dirge sung in the processions, the words being "*caymi saminchic, caymi marcanchic*." The songs themselves, recounting the deeds of the past emperors, were called *haravi*, GHLQ 152, 446; BC XIV, 17; MMCB III, 6; CL 11, 30. For good descriptions of the *purucaya* processions, BC XII, 2; RFC 258f. For the *unancha*, GVCR VII, 6; SPYP 256, 258, 260f. For the *pacarina capac unancha*, SPYP 217f. The ancestral trees were, for the father the *cori chauchu* (golden stock), and for the mother the *collque chauchu* (silver stock); the early friars used these words for Adam and Eve, GHLQ 99; SPYP 218.

The *rampa*, or covered litter, was distinguished from the *huantu*, the litter without a canopy, generally a hammock, GHLQ 566. For the various items of the regalia, BC XII, 36. The *suntur paucar* is depicted in GPF 86. For the *topa yauri*, GHLQ 347; Juan Larrea, *Corona Incaica*, Universidad de Córdoba, Argentina, 1960, pp. 59–94. The *capac unco* was apparently also called the *tarco huallca*, CV II, 18, 31. The descriptions of the dress of the emperors is taken from GPF 86–116. Historical accuracy is never to be expected from Huaman Poma, but it is possible that in a matter in which he was drawing on colored depictions—as here—he can be accurate; in any case, the types of *tocapu* and the variety in it are usefully set forth. For the special livery worn by all the members of a *panaca* in common, BC XII, 2. For the *puru puru* of the Chima *panaca*, BC XII, 4; RFC 259. The *puru puru* was a circlet or headdress of short feathers, GHLQ 298 (see variant form *pullu pullu*, GHLQ 294). For *yuyaycucuy*, GHLQ 373.

For descriptions of the feasting of the mummies, BC XIII, 10; PO: Fund. 123f.; PPR 204, 264. For the *haravis* of Pachacuti, RFC 257; JB 13; GGO 3. For *haravi* of Huayna Capac, CLPP 53. For the *harauicos*, GVCR VI, 9; JLD 227. For the four or five older men charged with this duty by each successive emperor, CL 12. For other remarks regarding this class of *amautas*, BC XIII, 1; ISP-VC 4–5; ACCM I, 14. The mimings were called *yachapayay pucllay*, GHLQ 659. One that lasted well into colonial times depicted Pachacuti's exploits in the montaña, RFC 259f. For the victory song of Pachacuti's *panaca* with reference to the Chanca war, RFC 257; JB 13. For *huayma pacha*, GHLQ 193, 679; JLD 1128.

SECTION 11.

FOR THE PERUVIAN CUSTOM of feasting the dead a month in the house before burial, RZ III, 9. For the mummy niches in Coricancha, SPYP 249; BC XIII, 10. For Manco Capac's idol, SG 14. There is a real confusion between this statue and that of Huanacauri. For the oracular man and woman in the *panaca*, BC XIII, 10; PPR 238–40. For the *mamacona* with the gold mask, CA 256–58. For the *yanaconas*, FS 36.

For the common Peruvian rite of annually taking the mummy to his former haunts, ARGCS I, 22; MP 184, 188; RGI III, 150; PPR 254f. The word for "echo" is *ancaylli*, GHLQ 25, but more specifically, see GHLQ 127. For the *huaoqui* in general, BC XIII, 9; JA V, 6; SG 14; BVP 149f.

For the monthly banquet, BLCL 26. For the *huaoqui* of the Creator (named *Turuca*; if *taruca*, "deer"?), BC XIII, 14. Of Manco Capac, SG 12, 14. Of Sinchi Roca, SG 15. Of Lloque Yupanqui, SG 16. Mayta Capac had a *huaoqui*, but it is not named (SG 17; BC XII, 7) unless it was the Inti-bird belonging to his great-grandfather, SG 17. Of Capac Yupanqui, BC XII, 8. For Inca Roca, BC XII, 9. *Huauque* is translated "friend" in Aymara, LBVA I, 45; II, 154. The fact that Capac Yupanqui and Inca Roca both had *huaoquis* named after the *ayllu* is evidence that these were assigned *huaoquis* of a later period, obviously Pachacuti's reformulation.

Yahuar Huacac had a *huaoqui*, but it is not named, BC XII, 10. Of Viracocha Inca, BC XII, 11; SG 25. Of Pachacuti, JA VI, 21, BC XII, 13; XIII, 7; SG 31, 47 (here Inti Illapa is synonymous with Chuqui Illa). Of Topa Inca, SG 54; BC XII, 15. Of Huayna Capac, BC XII, 17; SG 62. For the idols attendant upon Huayna Capac's mummy, BC XII, 17. For the Chanca god's accompanying Pachacuti's mummy, PO: Fund. 97. For the name of the *huaca*, SG 27.

SECTION 12.

CONCEPTIONS of newness, invention, or beginnings seem to have been congenial to the Incas; see, among many other references, GHLQ 266–68, 558. For *paccarik pacha*, GHLQ 267. And for synonyms, GHLQ 610, 642. For *huarachicoy*, GHLQ 182. No regularized calendar was imposed upon Tahuantinsuyo as a whole, ADS 27f., 31, because of the disruptive effects of such a rigid system in a land of so many contrasting altitudes and climates.

For listings of Inca festivals and month names CM; CV 19; ARGCS I, 24; JB 15, 18; VRQ II, 39f.; DF 10; ACCM II, 12; MMCB III, 71f.; AEI 5; PO: Error 8; BC XII, 37; BC XIII, 25–30 (these references should also be supplemented with what is found in GHLQ

367

under month and fiesta names, 33, 39, 41, 59, 141, 154, 381, 504, 551, 603, 611, 669). Complete accuracy in matching our month names with Inca month names and, finally, either of these with the fiesta names cannot be expected, for, depending on whether a particular chronicler met the Inca calendar at 12,000 feet or 3,000 feet, the month designation and its accompanying festival could shift almost around the year. For the *huarachicoy*, CM 59–76; JB 14; CL 7; DF 6; BC XIII, 25; LAC 27. I have given a compendious account of this festival in BE VII, 4.

There is confusion in our sources concerning the *purapucyo*, for BC XIII, 26, puts it in the second month, whereas JB 15, 18, makes it a part of the *situa* in the tenth month. In both, a *mayocati* (see CM 83) or "River Following" took place, that is to say an escorting of the ashes of sacrifice down river, but the ceremony of the second month, the true *purapucyo*, was addressed to the river itself as a placation and a thanksgiving, whereas the ceremony of the tenth month was a part of the *situa* purification. I therefore follow Cobo's lead (CV 19 and DF 10 back him up, although they have garbled the word *purapucyo*). The month of March was also called *paucar huaray*, the time when most of the flowers bloom, GHLQ 282. *Huara* is instead connected with the word for breechclout in GPF 238f., but this interpretation is unlikely. This month name is mentioned in DF 10; VRQ II, 39f. (where it is wrongly spelled *huatay*); CM 85.

Our sources spell the *arihua* differently, possibly reflecting a confusion in the Inca mind between *ararihua*, a person who guards the *chacras* from birds and theft (GHLQ 33; JLD 58), and some form from *ayri* (GHLQ 41, 539), a cutting ax. As far as we know, the name of the festival *arihua* is untranslatable. Note that GHLQ 33, 41, 381 spells the word two ways, *ayrihua* and *arihuaqui*. The *aymoray* and Inti Raymi are taken up in detail in Part II, secs. 14 and 15, of this book. For the irrigation ceremonies of the eighth month, BC XIII, 28. For the month of July as being traditional for the redividing of communal lands, GPF 248f. The month just preceding the Situa ceremony is sometimes called the Anta Situa; Anta probably refers to the community of that name, GHLQ 551; VRQ II, 39f. For the August sowing,

BC XIII, 28. The *huayara* (BC XIII, 28) is undoubtedly the same as the *guayyaya*, BC XIV 17, and the *yahuaira*, CM 33–35.

The *situa* is taken up at length in Part III, secs. 13–17. Almost every source spells the word *puchay* and not *puchcay*, which is the correct form; I have no idea why this uniformity in error exists. It is described in CM 58. The *cantaray* is described in BC XIII, 30; CM 59. For the *itu*, BC XIII, 30. This periodic *itu* is not to be mistaken for the *itu* celebrated in times of special calamity, BC XIII, 31. For the *huacaylli*, JLD 1083; LBVA II, 141 (among the Aymaras); GHLQ 167 (here the words of the dirge are given as also in GPF 190f.); BVP 161. That the rite customarily took place around October is evident from GPF 254f. For *carpana allpa*, GHLQ 656. For the *ayamarcay*, the "carrying of the dead" (corresponding to our All Souls), GPF 256f.; MP 184, 188; ARGCS I, 22; PPR 254f.

The *pucullo* of GPF 257 is *pucru* in GHLQ 548. In *pacha pocoy* I take the first word to mean "whole, entire," GHLQ 269, rather than "earth."

Cuzqui means "marginal, unirrigated land" (GHLQ 72), and the verb derived from it means "to work such land, to plow it"; see also GHLQ 59. *Yapuy* is the common word for "to plow." I have chosen to translate *hatun* as "common" rather than "great" here, although either is possible. The word *aucay* (or *auhay*) means "to put up shoots, to germinate," RGH 39. Rowe is therefore wrong in reading it as "warrior" in RIC 310. The word *Chahuahuar* is a mystery to me. It is not improbable that it has something to do with the annual redivision of *ayllu* lands (see GPF 248). For *yapa*, GHLQ 409.

For the two seasons, BC XII, 37; MMCB III, 70. Our sources on the *sucanca* are generally in disagreement, the numbers of the pillars ranging from sixteen (GVCR II, 22) to twelve (PO: Inf. 131; JA VI, 3; PO: Error 7) to eight (JB 15) to four (BC XII, 37). The eastern set stood on what is today Socorropata, formerly Queancalla, BC XIII, 13. TCYI 68; GPF 316, 1051. The opposite set stood on Carmenca in a spot called Chinchincalla, BC XIII, 16. For other references to the *sucanca*, ADS 29–31; VEC 1497; CLPP 92; SG 30. The word *sucanca* may be a formation from *sucay*, "to draw a line, plow a ridge," GHLQ 331; JLD 933. Again it may be related to modern *suka*, "afternoon," EQD 3; JLD 933, which has the merit of explaining why only the western or late afternoon set was called specifically *sucanca*. Using JB 15, Rowe adduces the designation of the towers to be *pacha unancha*, "time marker," HSAI 327. But note that *pachap onanchac* in LDST 50 means an "astrologer."

SECTION 13.

HUAYNA CAPAC took over Inti's "mayordomazgo" (SG 57) and called himself *Intip michi* (I have here translated "pastor del sol" into Quechua). For his divinization, GVCR IX, 1. Divinization of any outstanding leader, whether Inca governor or local *curaca*, was common in Peru, MP 184, 188. For Manco the Younger, RHA 30. Cusi Rimay, the first *coya*, produced a girl but no boys, FMA 93; SG 60; CV 21 (SPYP 259 disagrees and says she had Ninan Cuyochic whom Sarmiento specifically says was a bastard).

For the Mama Coca episode, SPYP 259f. For the use of *sapa* in imperial titles, GHLQ 78. For the title "shepherd of the sun," SG 57. For the Tarpuntay, CM 34; BC XIII, 33; SG 11. For Huayna Capac at Lake Chucuito, ARGCS I, 30. I am indebted for the translation of Yatiri from Aymara to ROCW 411.

SECTION 14.

FOR AUQUI TOPA INCA as "secretary" of the royal council and governor-viceroy of Cuzco in absence of Huayna Capac, FS 9; ISP-TY 60; SG 60; CV 21. The council of five was a *hunu* (GHLQ 203) or a *camachinacuy*, GHLQ 47f., 440; GPF 111. The names of the four men on the council (all of them uncles of Huayna Capac, CV 18) are known: Coyochi, Achachic, Hualpaya, Larico, FS 9; CV 18; ISP-TY 60. For the yellow *mascapaycha*, VEC 1573.

There is no doubt that Huascar was legally and formally made coemperor by his father previous to the northern campaign, CV 21; FS 18; SG 60. For officials sent at this time from Quito to take a *residencia* in Cuzco and an imperial census, CL 64. For appointment by Huayna Capac of his generals, SG 60; CV 21; SPYP 260. I believe that the

370

name in question here is *Mihi*, "cat," and not *Michic*, "pastor," as both CV (21, 22) and SPYP (260, 264f.) use it consistently. The full name is given in SPYP as Misi Ñaca(c) Mayta. This reference certainly seems an error, for one would not expect a name "Curser" (i.e. *Ñacac*) to be worn by an Inca. For *mihi=mici*, GHLQ 238, 532 (see also JLD 648), with the pronunciation of the middle consonant being in both cases an "s" sound; see *misi=gato*, EQD 22; Caesar Guardia Mayorga, *Diccionario Kechwa-Castellano*, segunda edición, Lima, 1961, p. 122.

For promotion of *curacas* for the campaign, SPYP 260. For decision to send back from Vilcas to bring Huanacauri, SPYP 260. For the division between emperor and Mihi's men, BE XII, 6. Whether the tumults in Cuzco mentioned from Topa Inca's reign (CL 56) belong in this category of internal divisiveness between the Incas and their ruler is uncertain. For the Sutic and Maras as two great *ayllus* of Lower Cuzco, GDST 128; SG 11. For the census ordered by Huayna Capac, CL 64.

SECTION 15.

THERE MAY BE some possible connection between *huallpa*, "turkey," GHLQ 531 ("cock" in LDST 140), and the verb *huallpariy*, "to arm oneself, to deck out, to dress up," GHLQ 416, 544; LDST 46; JLD 1091. In BE *cuyochic* is erroneously translated as "rainbow" (*cuychic*); rather it comes from the common verb "to move or wave," GHLQ 594; JLD 348. Mama Cusi Rimay had no male issue when she went north with her royal husband, CV 21. The problem of Ninan Cuyochic, as I pointed out in BE 372, is confused, but on reviewing the evidence I am still basically of the opinion I expressed there. Both SPYP 259 and BC XII, 17 say that Ninan Cuyochic was Cusi Rimay's issue, while CV 21 and SG 60 say that she had no son. Out of such a direct contradiction in the sources I have assumed an adoption as best resolving the difficulty. Nowhere is an adoption stated, however. Quizquiz' statement regarding Huascar's status in regard to legitimacy quoted in CV 31 speaks to the same purpose.

The name spelled *Atahuallpa* means "chicken," GHLQ 168, 511, 531, 636; LDST 140. The full name of the prince was Atau Huallpa

(SPYP 268; BC XII, 18). *Atau* means "success in war," GHLQ 36, and therefore the full name means "Turkey Fortunate in War." In BE I had overlooked Huascar's presence in Quito at the call of his father, NCC 67; FMA 26 (Montesinos here calls Huascar by the name Tupac Yupanqui, but it can be easily shown that it is in reality a reference to Huascar). The reason that our major sources do not contain this item is probably that the Huascar party suppressed it as being hurtful to its claims against Atauhuallpa. This is a datum hardly likely to have been invented by our two sources; furthermore, it is sustained in BC XII, 18 where it says that Huascar "agreed" to the naming of Atauhuallpa as governor of Quito.

Date of the Chiriguana invasion is a probable date based on 1525 as the death of the leader of that expedition; see C. E. Nowell, "Aleixo García and the White King" in *Hisp. Am. Hist. Review* (November, 1946). For Yasca, SG 61; CV 23. For red warpaint, BLCL 18. For *purapura*, RFC 258; SPYP 235; GHLQ 297. The house where the dried enemies and their skulls were kept was the *llasa huasi*, "the house of spoils," SG 37; DTR 63. For Pinto's mummy, SG 60; CV 23. For *pachap cayllan cayllan*, GHLQ 440. For *pacha puchucay*, GHLQ 269. For related concepts, GHLQ 270, 550.

For prophecies of Viracocha's return in a final cataclysm, IDI XXI, 152; MMCB III, 57; GHV 233; LTOP 7, 135; GSC III, 56; GVHG I, 32. For a fuller treatment of concepts of cataclysm, see Part II, sec. 11. The story of *Cumpi Illa* is known only from CV 21, 26. It is probable that the festivities (during which Huayna Capac took Rahua Ocllo as his *coya* in Quito and Huascar received Cumpi Illa in Cuzco) took place two or three years after Huayna Capac left for the north, perhaps 1513 or 1514.

SECTION 16.

FOR THE TERM *pahuac oncoy*, GHLQ 459, 629. For other words for pestilence, GHLQ 425. Any disease with pocks or spots was always *muru oncoy*, GHLQ 252, 666. For *yacollo*, GHLQ 447. The nature of this pestilence is uncertain, see BE XII, 8, and p. 376. For *canillipuy pachacta*, GHLQ 49. For the deaths in Cuzco, CV 24; SG 62. For the *itu*, BC XIII, 31 (FS 31 says the fasting was for a five-day period). There is an Aymara word *hitu* which is the exact equivalent of the Quechua *chimpu*, "the circle around the sun or the moon" (LBVA II, 139; GHLQ 110, 469); it is possible that this meaning has given its name to the circling procession of the Inca *itu*. The "sign" the *chasqui* may have carried was a baton painted in various colors. General ideas could be conveyed by this means, the specifics being carried by word of mouth.

In BE, I gave 1526 as the date of Huayna Capac's death. I now believe this date to be in error, and I am prepared to accept the 1524 (very end of the year, says OV XLVI, 9) which is given in SG 62, 69; FJ 334. The year 1525 is given by CV 24 (but note that his arithmetic in CV 32 gives 1524); VRQ II, 66; ALLC 445, 448. If Cotapampa was fought in the spring of 1532, then Huascar would have reigned just a little over eight full years.

PART II

SECTION 1.

FOR THE TRANSLATION of Haucaypata, VEC 1505; GVCR VII, 10. For the dimensions, GVCR VII, 10. It is certain that the two squares were contiguous and that no special edifices separated them until the Spaniards built houses over the buried river, GVCR VII, 10; IX, 1; GVHG VII, 2; ADVP 94; CMS 175. For its surface of sand, PO: Fund. 109–11; PO: Inf. 171. For the Capac Ñan, BC XIII, 13. For the Chiripacha, BC XIII, 14. The *huaca* of the Contisuyo road was *Usi*, BC XIII, 16. For *haucacuy*, GHLQ 155, 546. Undoubtedly the square was also paved with cobbles (BCP #86, p. 127) and not everywhere strewn with sand which, because of the slope, would have gullied in the rains; in any case it was strewn with reeds for the important fiestas, JB. 13.

For the *usno*, CM 37, 44; PPR 264f.; JB 11; SPYP 219, 259; BVP 144. The word in Aymara has the same uses; it is primarily a term or land-marker (LBVA I, 429), and secondarily a stone altar on which to place *huacas*, LBVA I, 41. The word is spelled *husnu* in

Aymara. For use of the *usno* as a place from which to muster and review troops, SPYP 261 (thus CL 23, 62 calls it a war stone). As a *huaca* in its own right the *usno* received adoration, BC XIII, 14. *Usnos* existed in other parts of the empire, CV 21. The word *usno* is defined as a stone altar for sacrifices or a tribunal in GHLQ 403, 684; LDST 36. The verb based on it is given in JLD 1056 as "to plant boundary stones, to delimit." Inca Roca was "gran hablón y hablaba con trueno," GPF 103.

Casana is translated in GVCR VII, 10 as "cosa para helar"; he interprets this word in the sense of freezing with admiration (VEC 1505 follows this translation). A similar use of the meaning of *casana* occurs in GHLQ 137, 444. For the name Condor Cancha, BC XIII, 13. Casana was occasionally confused in the chronicles with Huayna Capac's palace on the opposite site of the palace. In the *cabildo* of October 29, 1533, Francisco Pizarro received Pachacuti's palace, a property with a 200-foot frontage and extending 800–1,000 feet back along the Sapi River, PPR 318; FMA 83; FEC 35–37. For Inca Roca's palace at Coracora, GVHG V, 39; GVCR VII, 10; VEC 1504.

Hatun Cancha was the largest ward in the whole city (PPR 264, 292), and we must envisage it as something akin to the great enclosure rectangles of Chan Chan on the coast. Its exact location and its extent are major problems in trying to reconstruct Inca Cuzco. When we realize that the Capac Yupanqui (VEC 1503; MMCB III, 44) and the Inca Yupanqui (GVCR VII, 9) referred to as building on the site are to be equated with Yahuar Huacac, the seventh ruler (whose throne name was Inca Yupanqui, SG 23), we can then clear up the major difficulties and at last place every one of the Upper Cuzco palaces. For confirming reference to Yahuar Huacac's palace as near the cathedral and the *galpones*, VEC 1508.

For the site of Viracocha Inca's palace, GVHG II, 24, 25; GVCR VII, 9; AC 123; VEC 1503. For Quishuar Cancha, CM 16f., 36; MMCB III, 44; BC XII, 12; XIII, 4. For the location of the statue of Viracocha, BVP 144 (this statue was never located by the Spaniards, CL 30). For the high walls of Hatun Cancha, PPR 292. For the single entry and the dwellings, FEC 38; PPR 264, 292.

The Suntur Huasi would have stood in the northeast quadrant of the square if the tradition is correct that the Triunfo stood on the site, HV 46. It is also described as being in front of Amaru Cancha, GVCR VII, 10. These two site identifications are not necessarily incompatible. The Suntur Huasi is depicted in GPF 329 with windows high up under the eaves, while Garcilaso says the thatch was high and peaked and culminated in a pole, GVHG I, 32. Garcilaso translates the meaning of *suntur* as "superior, excelling," GVHG I, 32. This interpretation agrees with the "pleasing, elegant," of GHLQ 332. Because this *suntur huasi* was circular, it appears in GHLQ as "round house." The primary meaning of *suntur* is "a pile" or "a mound"; for confirmation see the cognates in Aymara, LBVA I, 120, 126; II, 328. Also JLD 938. The *suntur huasi* is thus "a mounded house," referring to the construction of the thatched roof without a ridgepole. I have no idea what the building was used for. Manco Inca's forces refrained from burning it which restraint may show a cultic use, GVHG II, 24—or could Suntur Huasi be simply a descriptive name of Quishuar Cancha? For the name Calispucyo Huasi, BC XIII, 13.

Most chroniclers refer to Topa's palace as Pucamarca, the general area northeast of Haucaypata and including the *acllahuasi*, FEC 38; GVCR VII, 9; VEC 1503; ISP-VT 135. Topa's palace was where San Agustín was erected, SPYP 249—thus the block from Arequipa to the Tullumayo and from Hatunrumiyoc to Maruri probably belonged to Topa Inca, although his palace proper need only have taken up a part of this space. For a narrower site within Pucamarca, LVCP 22. My suggestion that the *acllahuasi* was built by Topa Inca is based solely on the fact that it was a part of Pucamarca, FEC 38; SPYP 277. The only thing we know about Topa's palace is that it contained a shrine of Chuqui Illa, the first person of the Illapa Trinity and considered to be the father, BC XIII, 13; CM 36. His father's *huaoque* was Inti Illapa, and Topa, Pachacuti's son, may therefore have taken Chuqui Illa as a special *huaca*, although Chuqui Illa appears once to be simply another name for Inti Illapa, CV 15. Further notes on the location of the *acllahuasi* will be found in Part IV, sec. 13.

For the site of Amaru Cancha, GVCR VII, 10; SG 63; BVP 145.

For the site under the Spaniards, GVHG V, 9; RSC 111; J. Larrea, *Corona Incaica*, Córdoba, Argentina, 1960, p. 158. The best description of Amaru Cancha is in PPR 317f.; here is the only reference to the two flanking towers. The *galpón* attached may have had two entrances instead of one, RSC, 111. For some general description of a royal palace, BLCL 2; MMCB I, 21; III, 3, 7.

Carpa means primarily an "awning" or "arbor," GHLQ 50; LDST 224. Thus by extension it comes to mean a "tent" or "booth," LDST 250; JLD 307. The word *carpa huasi* (in Aymara *carpa uta*, LBVA I, 105) means any construction with a shedlike roof or awning and with one of its sides at least open, i.e., "portico, towngate, entry," GHLQ 638; "spinner's shed," LDST 51, 250; "auditorium" or meeting place of the city magnates, LDST 52 (the last reference is a special Inca construction which VMP 30 erroneously calls a *masma* and derives from the Yucay valley, the word is really *carpa masma*, GHLQ 50). We have the *carpa huasi* depicted in GPF 329f. where the open side is clearly indicated.

For descriptions of the *carpa huasi* (called by Spaniards "galpones," OV XLVI, 16; GVCR, *Advertencias* at the beginning of the book); BC XII, 32; PPR 317; VEC 1361, 1505; GVCR VI, 4; VII, 8 and 9. For the three *galpones* on the square, GVHG II, 24. For all four *galpones*, VEC 1509. Only the Collcampata *galpón* was standing when Garcilaso left Cuzco in 1560, GVCR VII, 8. It must be the one referred to in FEC 44 as the "Galpón de Atabalipa." For the Casana *galpón* as standing on a terrace, FEC 37. For *pitita*, GHLQ 631, 676; JLD 795. A house with a second story or garret was a *marca huasi*, GHLQ 449, 671.

Doors were generally curtains shrouding an entrance, BVP 169. A door which could be effectively bolted was a *cullu puncu* or a *vichcana puncu*, GHLQ 645. My identification of the *kenko huasi* with the *coya*'s apartments is not certain. However difficult of interpretation, the list of areas and apartments of the palace given in GPF 329f., 338f. is invaluable, for it is the only such list we have. Here are listed (with my translations where possible) his "cosas" in the palatial complex: *cuyos manco, kenko huasi* (labyrinth), *moyo huasi* (round house),

376

carpa huasi (shed house), *suntor huasi* (pleasure house), *uayacondo huasi*, *marca huasi* (treasury), *puñona huasi* (sleeping quarters), *chura-cuna huasi* (storerooms), *aca huasi* (place for making and storing *akha*), *masana huasi* (clothes-drying shed), *camachicona huasi* (council hall), *uaccha huasi* (house for the poorer sort), *carpa huasi* (sheltered festival hall), *quispi huasi* (crystal house), *cucho huasi* (corner house), *corpa huasi* (guest house). The *cuyos manco huasi* was a *carpa huasi*, open on one side, where the great magnates gathered in council, GHLQ 58; SPYP 256. It was, in other words, "the palace," MMCB III, 3. A descriptive term for it was *camachinacuna huasi*, "house of councilors," GHLQ 440, 449, 459. It is portrayed in GPF 329, 400. It is erroneous-ly made synonymous with Quishuar Cancha in GPF 401. The Spaniards understood it as a Casa de Cabildo. There was probably one in each royal *cancha*.

I am not certain about the name of the women's quarters in the pal-ace; they may have been the *cusicancha* "joy enclosure" (GPF 338) which descriptively would be known as the *kenko huasi*, "house of labyrinthine passages," but this attempt is only guesswork. At any rate the harem within the palace is not to be confused with the harem out-side, namely that part of the *acllahuasi* called Cusi Cancha. For the *paucar cussilla*, GHLQ 73. For the treasury, MMCB III, 5. For the *churacona huasi*, GPF 329f.; GHLQ 122. For the interior patios and gardens, GVCR VI, 1; GPF 334. For the *llasa huasi*, DTR 63; SG 37. For the storerooms, GHLQ 122; GPF 329.

SECTION 2.

MOST OF THE EARLIER MAPS divide Upper from Lower Cuzco along the street of the Triunfo. This position is erroneous and arises from the identification of Garcilaso's Antisuyo road with the present Triunfo, GVCR VII, 8. The site of Coricancha actually marked the division. Numbers taken from our sources can only be understood in an approxi-mate sense. For the 4,000 attached to cult, CMS 145. For the 200 *mamaconas*, PPR 267. For the marital couch, PPR 267. For *mama-conas* interceding with Inti for the emperor, VEC 1523. For the *coya pacsa*, CM 43, 62. For Mama Ocllo's temple, VEC 1514. For her

377

personality, GPF 139. I have described Coricancha at some length in BE so need add only a few notes. For the sacred fire, BC XIII, 13; BVP 144, 169. For Mama Ocllo's special position, VEC 1514. For the size of one of the larger temple-houses (twenty-five paces long by fifteen wide), BLCL 9.

For a good description of all the shrines, VEC 1514–18. For the weapons chapel, MMCB I, 22; BC XIII, 13. For the *moroy urco*, CM 80; BC XIII, 26; CL 49; GVCR IX, 1. For Tampu Cancha, BC XIII, 15. For Inticancha, BC XIII, 16. For the stone marker of Ayar Auca, SG 13; MMCB IV, 2; MMDN 2. For Ayar Auca, CV 9; JB 4. This source is no doubt the origin of the Señor de la Columna or the Señor de Huanca of Spanish times, HV 121, 140f. Adjoining Inticancha on the south was an old residence called Human Amean (Huaman Cancha?), SG 14. It was probably, in fact, the same property. The small plaza in front of Coricancha's main entry was called either Intipampa (GVCR VII, 9) or Choqque Pampa, BC XIII, 13.

The pound for sacrificial animals and children was not below Coricancha (LVCP 23) but on the Intipampa, IDI XXI, 196. The name of the pound is given as *Chiquina Pampa Yaurinauca y Patequel*, of which we can probably read "Choqque Pampa Ayar Auca [...?...],", IDI, XXI, 196 (we know that the stone marker of Ayar Auca was in this area, SG 13.) For Quenti Cancha, Chumpi Cancha, Sayri Cancha, and Yarampuy Cancha as the original names (variously spelled, of course), LTOP 185; ISP-VT 133; BLCL 7; SG 13; CV 10. For Cuzco Caca, SPYP 216. For the maize gardens of Coricancha, PPR 266f. For the fact that the second, third, and fourth emperors (fifth not mentioned) had their palaces here, VEC 1507.

For the names of the four *canchas*, SG 13; CV 10. A deep gully about one hundred feet to the west of modern Avenida del Sol must mark the old stream bed. The Street of the Seven Crosses has been modernly cut through the gravel point and gives the visitor a good view of the unstable nature of the ridge. For the planted park at Pomachupan, BC XII, 8. For the point of land as holy, CM 83. For the house where the sacred ashes were kept, BC XII, 36; XIII, 25.

SECTION 3.

FOR THE WORD *huatana* as a place for tying up animals, GHLQ 186. My suggestion concerning the reason for naming the river the Huatanay is a guess. Note that in Aymara there is a word *huatanaui* meaning "a drain for carrying off wastes, a sewer," LBVA II, 153. Did a cognate exist in Quechua?

For the Purapucyo festival, Gavilán quoted in Larrea, *Corona Incaica*, Córdoba, Argentina, 1960, p. 217; JB 15, 18; BC XIII, 26; CM 83f. *Purapucyo* probably means "the fountain of the full moon." This event took place in the month of Samay or January. The part of the *purapucyo* which saw the ashes escorted down river was the *mayocati*, "river-following." For the Inca park at Pumapchupan, BC XII, 8. I have considered sin and confession in BE. For the *opacona*, BVP 159f.; JA V, 25.

Quechua has many words connected with water, as might be expected. *Pucyo* is a natural spring, LDST 139; GHLQ 530. A bubbling hot spring was *pullpuk unu, et al.*, GHLQ 530. A spring gushing out of rocks is *ullco colla*, GHLQ 354. A fountain or piped water falling or gushing into a basin is *pakcha*, LDST 139, 188, 295, 334; GHLQ 268, 445, 530. *Pakchay* today means "to fall or spout" relating to water, EQD 50. A waterfall is correspondingly a *pakcha*, EQD 74; 146. *Huncolpi* is a jet or spout of water, LDST 139, 295; JLD 263. *Cocha* is a standing body of water, a pond, tank, lake, sea; see, among others, GHLQ 518. A water pipe is *pincha*, LDST 338; GHLQ 286, 445, 529f. An open conduit or irrigation ditch is *rarca*, LDST 25, 292, 346; GHLQ 313, 445. It is today pronounced *yarka*, EQD 41. *Patqui* is a channel, GHLQ 281. The Sapi arose in the spring of Tocori, BC XIII, 15, 28. This spring was on Mount Chaca, CL 35. The emperor bathed in the *Sapipakchan* to retain his vigor. This tank is referred to in BC XIII, 13, 14 (in the latter simply as Pacha).

For the paving of the Huatanay, GVCR III, 23; GVHG I, 32; JB 13; LDB I, 65, 82; CL 35. For the gully of Choqquechaka, RMNL IV, 1. *Sapantiana* seems to have been in Choqquechaka. It might well be the reservoir mentioned in the text. Sarmiento translates *chacan* as "waters," SG 19. This cannot be the specific meaning, however much it may be the sense. *Chacay* is given in GHLQ 90 as "to plug, to lay athwart or across," from which we could derive some such noun as "dam," "reservoir," in other words a constricted and controlled water area, perhaps best translated "water system." *Chakan* is given as an Inca reservoir, a man-made cave near the city, LVCP 25; I know nothing of this. For the drainage ditch from Lake Piuray, BC XIII, 13; GVHG II, 27. This Chincheros water was still used to run the fountain in Haucaypata in 1583; see NCC 229.

The two systems (Upper and Lower) are well attested, SPYP 216; SG 19; CV 13. We must emphasize that we know nothing at all about the courses of the two water systems, whether they had a single or multiple sources, or how their waters were apportioned. It is possible that the Upper system was Piuray water and the Lower came from the Upper Sapi. For *carpana allpa*, GHLQ 656. For ownership of waters by Inca Roca's family, BC XIII, 28. The Viroypaccha is mentioned by only two sources, BC XIII, 13; GPF 316, 334, 1051. It is obvious from BC XIII, 13 that the Viroypaccha and Pillcopucyo are intimately connected—the first probably pouring into the second.

For the Cantuc waters, JLD 432. The location of the water is corroborated in the plan of Cuzco, GPF 1051. I am making the assumption that Ticatica was the source of this drinking water on the lower slopes of Carmenca. It was the city's main supply of potable water even in the days of Toledo (FEC 92f.), and it came from a reservoir less than a mile from the city, GVCR VI, 4; FEC 97.

Very possibly the Ticatica reservoirs from Inca times are to be seen in the remains of Curacapampa today, RIA 51. These ruins are undoubtedly some of the dams which were opened up for the *purapucyo* ceremony. The source spring of the Ticatica waters was called Callanca Pucyo, BC XIII, 13. For Ticcicocha, BC XIII, 13. Ticcicocha is given in BC XIII, 13 as the name of the *pucyo* in Collcampata as well as the tank in Casana into which it finally led. It was, of course, the same water. In the name Ticci is probably a reference to the Creator Ticci Viracocha. The spring Haucaypata is erroneously spelled *Aacaipata* in BC XIII, 13 (Chuqui Illa, the god of storm, is also misspelled).

We know the spring was close to the Spanish *cabildo* (BC XIII, 13) which itself was in the *galpón* of Coracora, FEC 37; BC XIII, 13.

For the oral tradition of Añas Kucho, Skunk Corner, HV 25. I am assuming this name goes back to Inca times, but there is no specific evidence to that effect. It does, however, ring true insofar as it locates the spring that watered the area of Haucaypata. There were the Calispucyo near Topa's palace (BC XIII, 13) and the one behind Sacsahuaman, CM 75; BC XIII, 25. The word *calis* describes the special small jar used for *akha* in the *huarachicoy* ceremonies, JB 14. Note that when the young girls in this ceremony are identified, they are called "Callis-carriers," *callisapa*, CM 67. For the Coricancha fountain, BLCL 7; BC XIII, 16; GVCR III, 23. For Mutkapucyo, the Spring of the Mortar, BC XIII, 15; the extension of Tullumayo Street still carries the name of this fountain of Inca days at this spot—it may well have carried the runoff from the Pillcopucyo. Many of the fountains of Cuzco ran into and supplied each other, JB 16. For Collque Machacuay, BC XIII, 16; GVCR VII, 8. Specifically, *machacuay* is a poisonous snake; GHLQ 241. The fountain of Chilquichaca (Chaquilchaca?) may have been supplied by this system, BC XIII, 16.

For the time of the *quicuchicoy* as November–December, GPF 257; as February, ARG I, 24. The young women are undergoing certain ceremonies in connection with the *huarachicoy* in CM 61f., 66f., 87f. For the *quicuchicoy* as the *huarmihapiy pacha*, SPYP 221f. For the red and white *ancallu acsu*, CM 66; 87f.; GHLQ 25; JLD 46. For other remarks on the *quicuchicoy*, ARG I, 23; PO: Inf. 139; BVP 169 (confused). The picture of the girls bathing is drawn from GPF 316.

SECTION 4.

THE PLACE OF THE PRISONS is accurately shown in GPF 1051. See also MMCB II, 2; CL 26; BC XII, 26; CV 20. The two prisons at the river junction are called Sanka Cancha and Hurin Sanca, BC XIII, 13. *Sanca* means "pit," JLD 876; this meaning is preferable to "a vision or spook," GHLQ 311, 447; JLD 525. Hurin Sanka or the Lower Pit is probably a designation for the Piñas Huasi, GHLQ 451 (*pinas* is given in LDST 63, 339 as "slave" or "wild and savage"). The generic term for prison is *huatayhuasi*, "house of tying." For variants GHLQ 186, 414, 447, 501, 584, 641 f. For the prison as a *huaca*, BC XIII, 15. I know of no good translation of Cayaocachi; the one in LVCP 21 is unsatisfactory. For the antiquity of Cayaocachi, SG 14; FS 2. It was Pachacuti who forced the Allcaviza Ayllu to live in Cayaocachi (JB 14), but earlier Mayta Capac seems to have initiated this policy, see ISP-VT 131.

For the Ayar Ucho Ayllu, LTOP 186–88; ISP-VT 135, 137f. The House of the Sun appears not to have been on the peak of Puquin, which was called Viracocha Urco (BC XIII, 16), but on a smaller eminence at its foot (CM 77). For present evidences of Inca remains on Puquin, RIA 52. For the archival treasures, CM 4–6. For Intipata between the Sapi and the Chunchullmayo, FMA 111. For *mana huañunca huasi*, BC XIII, 15f. It is a good guess that the Manahuañunca Huasi was that villa of Mama Ocllo which her son decreed to be a *huaca*, BC XIII, 13. A place named Manahuañuncca appears south of Mount Puquin on the map of Cuzco environs in Rozas L., *Cuzco, Ciudad Monumental y Capital Arqueológica de Sud America*, 3d ed., Cuzco, 1962. For Llimpipata, FMA 111; HV 63. For the remarks on La Merced, FMA 111; HV 63f., 69.

For *Callanca rumi*, GHLQ 44, 670. Cusipata had no buildings surrounding it, GVCR VII, 11. For the market, GVCR VII, 11; ABC 81; MMCB IV, 2; MMDN 2. For the terrace where San Francisco is now as well as the large terrace above it, GVCR VII, 11. The terrace on which San Francisco stands was well watered and even as late as 1550 was still being plowed to crops, NCC 156, 158. It is quite uncertain whether the terrace torn down to build San Pedro was the one on which San Francisco stands or the next one above, HV 143f. For the Pachacutean terraces here planted to maize, PPR 292; SG 30. A great number of errors have crept into our knowledge of Incaic Cuzco (from Spanish and modern confusions and errors in manuscript and printings) as between *Tococachi*, the area of present-day San Blas, and *Totocachi*, the area on the south side of the Sapi across from Casana. Fasts were held by the rulers in *Tococachi*, says SPYP 228, 245, whereas NCC

192 spells the name for San Blas as *Toctoccachi*. For Pachacuti building at Patallacta, SG 41. Both Patallacta and Illapa Cancha were included in the hillside area called *Totocachi*, BC XIII, 7, 13; SPYP 228, 245.

For the terraces in the area, FEC 37, 44. Illapa Cancha is shown in GPF 1051 accurately situated. For *purina*, LDST 40. For hand-planted *chachacoma* trees, BC XIII, 13. For the detail that the Chinchaysuyo road came down "back of the garden" and then crossed the river to ascend to "the houses of Huaxicar," FEC 37. Cantut Moya is accurately placed on the plan in GPF 1051, just back of and above Illapa Cancha. The plan shows here a curious line of domed buildings at this point which give the impression of being strung out along a terrace top. Carmenca is placed on the wrong side of the river on this plan. It seems plausible to posit an Inca bridge over the Sapi where Amargura meets the Tambo de Montero today, but I have no textual evidence for such. It is generally supposed that Carmenca means "shoulder blade" (LVCP 21), but GHLQ 516 and JLD 438, 520 give "shoulder blade" as *ccarmin*. The name Carmenca applied only to that spur between the Sapi and the Aya Huayco. The next spur on the northwest was Picchu, the top of which was called Yahuira. The railroad climbs up this spur, whereas the auto road ascends via Carmenca. The entire mountain mass was designated as Pantanaya ("Place where one desires to wander about"?), BC XIII, 16.

For the feud between Cayaocachi and Carmenca, SG 24. For the 15,000 Cañars moved into Cuzcoquiti by either Topa Inca or Huayna Capac, ISP-VT 123; CL 56. For Cañars in Carmenca, MMCB III, 17. Elsewhere it is said to be Chachapoyas in Carmenca, CLPP 78. For *Incapmichhusccan runa*, GHLQ 237 (see also SG 39 for a more specialized meaning). For Urcos Calla, BC XIII, 13. For the location of the Sucanca, CLPP 92; VEC 1497; BC XIII, 15f. (the part of Carmenca upon which the Sucanca stood was called Chinchincalla—perhaps the same as Chinchacuay of BC XIII, 16). For the shrine of Viracocha's concubines, BC XIII, 13. Picchu is given in JLD 751 as a "cud of coca." Huaman Cancha must have been in the suburb called Quillipata, GVCR VII, 8; VEC 1496. For the ceremonies on Picchu, BC XIII, 13, 25; CM 71f. The special identification of Picchu with the Maras Ayllu is strengthened when we recall that that *ayllu* used Picchu as its burial ground (see BC XIII, 13 for the tomb of Vica Riui). Almost certainly Yahuira is an Aymara word and comes from the verb *yauriratha*, "to cut the hair," LBVA I, 458. Note that haircutting was a part of the *huarachicoy*, part of which was celebrated on Yahuira, CM 61. Apu Yahuira does not appear in the Founding Legend of Cuzco.

For the Contisuyo road as the road to Tampu, BC XIII, 16. The check point and *huaca* of first sight on the Contisuyo road was the Mascataurco, a name that appears to be garbled, BC XIII, 16. For Raurana, CM 67. It is also called Yaurana, CM 70; JLD 1185. For Choco, BC XII, 12; XIII, 16. For Choco as provenience of Mama Anahuarque, CV 15; RZ II, 11. For the Chanca attack on Cuzco through Choco, SG 27. The stages of the route out the Contisuyo road were Churicalla (6 miles), Yaurisqui (9 miles), Tantar (12 miles), the Cusibamba River (20 miles), CM 40. Pacaritambo is put at 18 miles, ILPO 152. I believe the present-day Mollemolle River and its tributary, the Llaurisque, are the old Cusibamba. Thus the Contisuyo relay team members in the Situa festival would have washed their weapons in the waters of the Huanoquite and Llaurisque rivers where they join to form the Mollemolle River. On our present maps Churicalla is Churucalla, Yaurisque is Llaurisque, and Tantar is Tandar Hacienda.

The name Cusibamba appears on our maps as a group of houses about one-half mile south of Llaurisque. I have subscribed to Pardo's identification of the site of Paccaritambo, PHA I, 7–53; it should be noted that on the modern maps the small community called Pacarictambo is only a trifle (a mile?) south of where Pardo locates the rock of Pomaurco. Pacaritambo is translated in SG 11 as "Casa de producción." While the rock may well have been the *pacarina* of one of the *ayllus* ancestral to the Incas, almost surely it was Pachacuti who designated it as the *pacarina* of all the Incas.

Section 5.

WE KNOW from Atauhuallpa's particular hostility later on to the Capac

Ayllu *panaca* that it must therefore have ardently espoused the cause of Huascar. It is purely inferential that this *panaca* aided him at the start of his reign. For Huascar's appointment of a private army of non-Incas, SPYP 267. Huayna Capac's high priest in the north was Cusi Topa Yupanqui, SG 62. This man is not the same as Cusi Yupanqui, who was Atauhuallpa's inquisitor general, SG 67. For Huascar's council, CV 24. For Huascar's largess and opening of the *acllahuasi*, SG 63; CV 24; SPYP 266. Huayna Capac had left 4,000 women in the Cuzco *acllahuasi*, CL 63. For Huascar's retreat to Muhina on death of his father, CV 24. For building in Amaru Cancha, CV 24. There is no record of which brother filled the post of major-domo of the Tumibamba *panaca*, but it stands to reason that no one hostile to Huascar could have had it. Almost certainly Huascar made the appointment. For death of Ninan Cuyochic, SG 62; CV 24.

SECTION 6.

IT MUST BE NOTED that the only reference we have to the conspiracy of the brothers and the resultant disclosure and punishment comes from CV 24 f. It is not mentioned at all in SG who in general is the source of a great deal of the information in CV. Its nonappearance in other sources can be explained by seeing the conspiracy as part of the succeeding massacre at Limatambo; as such it would be absorbed into it. In any case, both sets of executions (assuming there were two) must have taken place at almost the same time. If Titu Atauchi was the president of the council, as appears probable from the way the story is told, he will have held the office of president of the council or Second Person, *Incap rontin* GHLQ 454; MMCB III, 6; LDST 226; IH 280. For the girls in Rahua Ocllo's train, LTOP 112 f., 151 f.

SECTION 7.

FOR THE WORD *huatac*, "the sheriff," see GPF 342. *Huatac* means literally "the one who binds."

SECTION 8.

TARAWASI is the modern name of the farm on which the ruins stand.

The *tara*-pods are used in tanning, EQD 19. Limatambo was the colonial name and probably the Inca name. The area round about was settled by *mitmacs* from Nazca, VEC 1484. For Tarawasi today, *Los Trabajos Arqueológicos en el departamenta del Cusco, Informe de Luis A. Llanos sobre las ruinas incaicas de Tarawasi*, Lima, Imprenta del Museo Nacional, 1937. Llanos suggests that the original name of this post may have been Suntur Huasi (the river being the Sunturmayo and some terraces nearby being called Suntur). There is a clear photograph of the interesting porch in HSAI, Plate 76.

SECTION 9.

FOR THE STORY of the Limatambo massacre, CV 26f.; SG 63; SPYP 267. The visualization of the scene is mine. For the party of the executors, SG 63; CV 24. Among the executors who were killed at Limatambo were Colla Topa, Catunqui, Tauri Machi, and Auqui Topa Yupanqui. Colla Topa was of the Sucso *panaca*, SG 60; CV 21. The death of the high priest at the same time is most probable, Cusi Topa Yupanqui, SG 63. For *colla* as "sprout, shoot," GHLQ 632. For Colla Topa's career and appointment as chief executor, CV 21; SG 60; CL 68, 70. For the exclamation *anay*, GHLQ 25, 426. For the details of the keening and mourning rites, BLCL 15; SPYP 243; RZ III, 9. I make the assumption that Huascar appointed his own officers to head the northern regiments; there is no evidence for it. The great rock near Villcaconga cannot be missed. That it was a *huaca* was certain, but the assumption that it was a *huaca* connected with the road is mine.

The site of Ichupampa is given as approximately fifteen miles from Cuzco, SG 26. I have identified the site a trifle farther out, putting it at roughly the spot today occupied by the Ichupampa Hacienda. At any rate it is "back of Sacsahuana" (i.e., west of modern Anta), CV 14. For the site of Sacsahuana, JB 10; this assertion does not necessarily contradict a specific location of the Chanca *pucara* at Ichupampa. I have settled on the spelling of Sacsahuana for the community in the Pampa de Anta, and the spelling Caquia Saquisahuana for the Yucay community: see notes to Part III, sec. 6. The Spanish sources confuse them. *Sasahuana* means, according to RGEP 101, a stone *huaca* in the form of an animal. For the detail on Sillabamba and Carua Ticlla's house, CV 26f.

For the lupine, JLD 966; GHLQ 339; LDST 362. Sillabamba is present-day Surite, RGEP 101; RGI II, 200f. Surite ("plumage, crest of a helmet") was the native, non-Quechua name of the place which the Incas called Sillapampa, "gravel plain, field of rubble," RGEP 101; JLD 910; GHLQ 449, 621. For the *puna* and *huayco* area around Chinchaypuquio, RGEP 111–13. For Rahua Ocllo's properties there, LTOP 112f., 151 f. For the causeway, RGEP 105. For the abundance of Inca pleasure sites in the Pampa de Anta, CLPP 91. For Anta (Sacsahuana) as an important *tambo*, RGI II, 200f.; CM 39; GPF 1090; RGEP 100–102. The word *Anta* means "copper." Conchacalla (SG 27), still existent today west of Anta, appears to have been a Quillescachi community, for it was here that the Chancas picked up the Quillescachi guide who later defected. For Equeco and Quillescachi as living in the Anta area, MGP I, 1. For the Equeco as synonymous with "spy," GHLQ 139. See also Notes, Part III, sec. 11. For the Quillescachi as synonymous with "tale-bearer," GHLQ 308; GPF 363.

Yahuarpampa, "Bloody Field," was the name of the battle. The name of the meadow where the fighting centered was Quiachilli, BLCL 16; BC XIII, 13; CV 14. The small community nearby was called Quiuipay, GVCR IX, 37, SG 65; SPYP 276. See also BC XII, 10; PPR 262, 293, 340. The word means "a turn in the road," JLD 414. The actual site of the battle was probably in the stretch of road just west of El Arco and before one reaches Poroy. Undoubtedly the site of Poroy today was the old *tambo* of Satpina (Sacalpiña?), CM 39, 89. The name Poroy, however, does go back to the Inca period; see Poroypucyo, BC XIII, 13. For Urcoscalla, CV 25; BC XIII, 13.

SECTION 11.

FOR THE INCA'S LACK of interest in speculation, GVCR II, 21. For the Incas' claim to precedence in time, JA I, 25; PO: Inf. 152. For Huascar's excoriation of the *huacas* as evil demons, SPYP 272. For *apucay*, GHLQ 31, 552, 577. The statements on the Inca concept of truth are, of course, highly subjective. There are no specific citations proving these assertions, except perhaps such as may be derived from a study of the uses of *checca*, "truth, order, straightness," GHLQ 103f.; LDST 260.

For *pacarichisca pacha*, GHLQ 610. For the original *allicac*, GPF 65f. For the word, GHLQ 21. A *pachatikray* ("world reversal") and a *pachacuti* ("world overturn") and a *pacha puchucay* ("world finishing") are all synonymous, GHLQ 269, 525. For the (*lloclla*) *unu pachacuti*, "(flood) water cataclysm," GPF 51; GHLQ 270, 489. For the universal deluge among the Aymaras, LBVA I, 191. For an end of the world by fire, GHLQ 270. For a foundering or swallowing-up, GHLQ 550. For an end by earthquake or pestilence, GHLQ 16f., 525, 678f. The *pachacuti* was, in any case, always a divine judgment, MP 192; MMCB III, 57; IDI XXI, 152; LTOP 7, 135. For the word among the Aymaras, LBVA I, 448; II, 242. Any calamity or disaster such as a great famine (GPF 109) or the crumbling of mountains (GPF 94) could be taken as a throne name by a king. The word implied disaster (GHLQ 16f.; BLCL 16), yet as a name it equally implied the new age that would follow such a disaster, BVP 162; JB 17; ISP-VC 19. For an end to the world in drought, GHV 233; GSC III, 56. For Viracocha's part in the coming end of the world, MMCB III, 57; LTOP 7; IDI XXI, 152. Whether or not the so-called *capac huata*, "the august year," of 100,000 years' duration (MAH 7) is to be connected with the *pachatikray* is uncertain; this instance is our only reference to it.

For the theory that all things had a mother, BLCL 12. (A curious gloss on this subject is that Bertonio suggests the translation of "mama" from Aymara as "great," but only when the word modifies "sea," "potato," or "toad," LBVA I, 253.) It is perhaps not far-fetched to see a connection between on the one hand, the four years of schooling and the four *amautas* in the Yachahuasi (MMCB III, 4) and, on the other, the three or four *amautas* chosen at the beginning of each reign to record its history (CL 12)—in other words, a small group of highly selected sages. Under these top sages were many others charged with various aspects of learning, at least a thousand of them, says BC XIII, 1.

For *haraui*, GHLQ 152, 446; ACCM I, 14; CL 11 f.; FS 1; GVCR VI, 9; MMCB III, 6. For the Yachahuasi, GVCR VII, 10; MMCB III, 4; ISP-VC 4f.; BC XIII, 1; BLCL. I have here accepted the statement of a four-year course in the Yachahuasi, but we have only the rather poor evidence of MMCB III, 4 for it.

SECTION 12.

I AM ASSUMING Huascar's coronation took place the year after his father's death; see Notes, Part I, sec. 16. I read the name usually heard by the Spaniards as Chuqui (Lance) Huipay as really Choqque (Pure Gold) Huipay. *Huipay* describes a joyous and abandoned dance interspersed with leaps and delighted shouting, JLD 1159. The full story of Rahua Ocllo's opposition to the marriage is given only in CV 25. *Piui*, "first-born," can be applied to sons or daughters, GHLQ 545. For Huascar's throne name, SG 63; GVCR VIII, 8; IX, 1; SPYP 266f.

The name Huallpa means a cock-bird such as the turkey or rooster, LDST 140; GHLQ 531. The word may be connected with the verb *huallpariy*, "to arm oneself, to accouter oneself splendidly," LDST 46; GHLQ 416, 544. Note the modern adjective for "fierce, manly, strutting," *wallpari*, JLD 1091. For the fast previous to the coronation, OV XLVI, 17; FJ 345; CL 7. There is a fair amount known about the *capac hucha* ceremony, BC XII, 34; XIII, 21; SPYP 220, 229f.; SG 13; MMCB III, 44; JB 11; CL 28; ARGCS I, 5f.; FS 27; LTOP 128, 170; ACCM II, 12; CM 88–91, 93–95. The word is generally spelled *capacocha* but is really *capac hucha*, "the kingly matter," SPYP 229. It was descriptively called *cochaguas*(?) or *cachaguaco*(?), CM 93, 95, which might be emended to read *cacha huahua*, "messenger children," i.e., children sent to Viracocha as a petition for the emperor.

A special sacrifice, at the coronation, of a young virgin was made on a hilltop just east of Cuzco called Pillco Urco, BC XIII, 14. The details of the fealty ceremony are taken from BC XIII, 36. The feathers were called *tocto*, BC XIII, 36. The interpretation of the feather ceremony is purely mine. For the artificial animals in the park of Sapi, SPYP

ation of "tender." For additional information on this word, see notesing name is correctly given as

266. Sapi here could either be the park in Pomachupan or the one on the terraces of Totocachi; I have treated it as the latter. For Huascar's residence in Amaru Cancha, SG 63; CV 24.

SECTION 13.

THE TERMS "brother" and "sister" used in this section are intended to cover half brothers and half sisters as well. Our sources are inadequate for us to make a clear distinction between them. For Tocto Ocllo Coca, SPYP 259; SG 63 (erroneously given as Tuta and Tupac in CL 62, 69). The word *tocto* does not appear in the older dictionaries. In TRA 173 it appears as "bee" and "honey" (but in 142 "honey" is given as *misqui*, and in 123 "bee" is given as "huancuyru"—the standard translations), in MDK 89 as "down of birds," and in GPF 300 as a word meaning "savory, tasty." It is from the last that I have taken my translation of "tender." For additional information on this word, see notes Part V, sec. 1. The word *Atahuallpa* means "hen" and was applied to the chicken when it was introduced by the Spaniards (LDST 140; GHLQ 168, 511, 531, 636); as such it is therefore no candidate for the correct reading of an Inca's name. The name is correctly given as Topa Atau Huallpa in SPYP 268; BC XII, 18; this name is translated therefore as Royal and Victorious Turkey Cock.

For *atau* and *cusi*, GHLQ 36. For Topa Huallpa Inca as identified with Atauhuallpa's court in Quito, ISP-VC 32; BC XII, 20; PPR 252 (VRQ II, 22, 107 wrongly makes him Atauhuallpa's son). The only full reference to the Pomacocha war is in CV 25; for a different reference, SG 63. For Topa Atau, SG 65; BC XII, 19. References to Huanca Auqui are many; see, among others, SPYP 269; SG 63; CV 28–31. For Atoc, CV 27f.; SG 63; BC XII, 18; SPYP 268f. For the word *huaminca*, GHLQ 536.

For Mayca Yupanqui, CV 30. If Titu Atauchi was engaged in his knighting ceremonies when his father left for the north (c. A.D. 1511), then in 1532 (Cotapampa) he will have been about thirty-six, granting he attained the status of Inca at age fifteen. For Topa Atau, SG 64f.; CV 32. Huallpa Roca was sent by Manco Inca from Sacsahuaman to reinforce the siege of Lima, PPR 301; he seems to have defected to the Spaniards afterward, ISP-VC 36–42. For Cayo Topa's defection, ISP-VC 36–42. Contrary to this reference is RGI IV, p. xiiiff., in which a Cayo Topa dies fighting on the Inca side.

Material on Inquil Topa is in TCYI 70, 77, 127; DF 5; GSC III, 50; GPF 114. Contradictory accounts of his end are given in TCYI (Emzil here stands for Inquil). For Pascac, TCYI 59f., 177; ISP-VC 36–42. For Tisoc, TCYI 48, 90; ABC 82; BCP #215f.; GHV 239 (in GBH 189 and AZH III, 5, 7 he is said to have fought in the siege of Lima). A pro-Spanish brother, Huaypar, Huaspar, or Uaipai, is mentioned in TCYI 70, 77, 89.

For material on Vilauma, TCYI 48, 62f., 66, 90; OV XLVII, 9; AZH III, 1, 3; ISP-VC 35, 52; BCP #215, 233. All of our sources agree on the spelling *oma* in his name. Undoubtedly this name is Aymara, "Blood Drinker" (for *vila uma haque*, "a fierce or cruel person," LBVA II, 385), and has no connection with the Quechua ecclesiastical title *villac omo*, "advising sorcerer," JLD 1150; RIC 299n. It seems improbable that the title of the high priest would ever be given as a personal name, although we know that *coya* (the title meaning "queen," although perhaps originally simply the word "love") could be used as a personal name; see Coya Miro, one of Huascar's concubines, SG 67; CV 31. Another fact in support of our theory concerning his name is that he bore it when he was a mere child and at a time when his father possessed a high priest, CV 21. His connections with Aymara-speaking areas is obvious. On the other hand, some of the sources identify him as "the bishop," in spite of the fact that his career seems to have been martial rather than ecclesiastical. TCYI has it that after capture in the montaña, he was burned in Ollantaytambo; a far more credible statement is that he was captured in Contisuyo, BCP 233.

For Manco Inca's escape, ISP-VC 27. For Paullo's flight to Lake Chucuito, ISP-VC 27, 33. Huari Titu and Conono are little more than names, MMCB III, 17; DF 5; CL 68. For Huaman Titu and Mayta Yupanqui, BC XII, 20; PPR 232f.; CV 25. The fate of Illescas was well known, VRQ II, 111f.; AZH II, 8; MMCB II, 14; GPF 114, 141, 163. For Huayna Pallca, VRQ II, 62f., 127; GHV 236. For Atoc

Sopa, BC XII, 20; PPR 274. For Cusi Rimachi, FMA 90, 92; TCYI 90. For Coya Miro and Chimpu Cisa, SG 67; CV 31. A legitimate sister, Marca Chimpu, is mentioned in ABC 82.

For Mama Huarcay, VEC 1594; GVCR IX, 37; DF 5; GSC III, 51. For Cori Ocllo, TCYI 89. For the *azarpay*, PPR 345. For Huayllas Ñusta, VEC 1595; GVCR IX, 38; PPR 345; she is said to have been the daughter of Cusi Rimay, Huayna Capac's first *coya*, FMA 93, an assertion which is highly unlikely. For Tocto Usica, SG 67; CV 31; ISP-VC 45ff.; ARG I, 31; VEC 1591.

SECTION 14.

FOR THE VERB AYMORAY, LDST 23; GHLQ 40, 588. For the associated verb in Aymara meaning "to fill sacks up to the brim," LBVA II, 29 (the noun *aymura* here means "a full sack"). The *aymoray* could also be called *aymorana*, which is the grain being harvested, MMCB III, 71; JLD 80. The actual fallowing was the *cusquiy*, GHLQ 59, 154. The period of harvest was known as *hatun pacha*, "the great(est) time," GHLQ 154. See also GPF 1143. For the four synonyms of putting the grain in bins, GHLQ 654. For the five words for grain bin, GHLQ 54, 287, 686. For the *chahuay* specifically, GPF 1143; GHLQ 54 (also 686 ?). Note that RGH 269 gives a word *pihuac* as "granary"; one suspects this is a variant from *pirua*. For the *sunchu* used in the making of bins, GHLQ 332; LBVA I, 440. It is stated that the various kinds of bins were for different grades of grain, GPF 1143. For the reserved grain, GHLQ 232. Polo says that it was not uncommon for flood, hail, or drought to kill three out of every five harvests, ILPO 168.

For the magical strength of the *pirua*, PO: Error 8; ARG I, 24; BVP 136f. For *capac collca cuyllor*, GHLQ 440 (note that the constellation could also be called "Sickness," Oncoy, LDST 65, 295; RGI I, 205f.). For the fruitful powers of Collca and its pre-eminence, ACCM III, 2; BC XIII, 6; CV 15. For the celebration of the Aymoray in Rimac Pampa, BC XIII, 15. Rimac Pampa was sometimes called the Lower Haucaypata, BC XIII, 32. For location of Huanaypata, CV 10; BC XIII, 15; SG 13. For Sausero, BC XIII, 14, 27f.; CM 86

(Garcilaso has confused Sausero with Collcampata in GVCR II, 22; V, 2). For Mama Huaco, BE I (note that in this book my geography of the Wandering is unclear). Sausero was the arable land first seized from the Huallas). Sausero was a *marca chacra*, a "field set apart (i.e., for the deity of the place)"; all Peruvian communities had one, GHLQ 232; AEI 15 (where it is erroneously spelled *marcachara*). *Ocllo* appears to mean something like "pure, virgin" if GVCR IV, 7 can be trusted. Sausero was also known as Hayllipampa, BC XIII, 14. *Haylli* is best translated "hurrah!" and was used in many communal enterprises—see also LBVA I, 115; II, 126.

The harvest song is given in GPF 245 as "Ylla sara camauay mana tucocta surcos cayqui ylla mama acoya." I read the *surcos cayqui* as *hurccuscayqui* (from the word *hurccuy*, GHLQ 204); *acoya* seems to mean "pulverized earth" (JLD 34) in which case it means the land ready for sowing. For the Mama Sara doll, PO: Error. VIII. In Chuquimarca I have taken the meaning "precinct" from *marcachay*, "to reserve or set aside," GHLQ 232. For a general review of the archaeology of the Kenko area, PHA I, 173–82. My identification of Chuquimarca with present-day Kenko is based on BC XIII, 14 where a sacred spot commemorating the place where the sun used to sleep is referred to (it is alternatively called Chuquicancha in CM 91 f. and BC XIII, 32). From these accounts it is evident that it was an important and impressive "temple" in this vicinity—Kenko is the only spot that could possibly correspond to it. What adds perhaps to the identification is the presence there of a rock in human shape much venerated and called Una Huallpa, BC XIII, 14.

For the theatral area, RGI III, Appendix, p. 10. Because of the execrable spelling of the early sources and the many careless copyists who followed them, the readings Inca Ayllu and Palla Ayllu are not absolutely certain, CV 18; CM 31, 43. Inexplicably Molina calls both these figures "wives" of Inti, although we would prefer to see them, according to the founding legend, as children; I can only believe that he was misinformed, and I have so altered the evidence. There is, however, the strong temptation to read them as Palla and Iñaca and see them as both female (as Molina) and representing the Upper moiety, or fully noble woman, the Palla, and the Lower moiety, or almost as noble woman, the Iñaca.

The four llamas carried in the procession were called *cori napa* and *collque napa*, "gold" and "silver" respectively, CM 32. For the *chacra ricuy*, GPF 248f.; it was also called "field redistributing," using the verb *kkonakuy*, JLD 465.

SECTION 15.

FOR THE CULT JOURNEY of the Tarpuntay priests to Vilcañota and back, CM 28ff. The Inti Raymi was a matter of interest to the Spaniards and is variously reported, CM 24–32; BC XII, 30; XIII, 15, 27f.; CMS 160ff.; JB 13–15; RZ I, 21; BLCL 12; CL 30; ADS 40f.; GVCR VI, 20–23; BV 186–89. It was Pachacuti who named the ceremonies at the eastern entrance to Cuzco the Yahuarinchay Aymuray, JB 15 (for *yahuarinchay*—"to bedaub with blood," GHLQ 362). *Lucanas* were the preferred litter bearers; Huascar used them, as did other emperors. They were called "the Incas' feet," BC XII, 36; GPF 338; SPYP 276.

For the special wood burned in Cuzco rites, BC XII, 33. For the *napa*, BC XIII, 25. For the yearly tribute delivered as a part of this festival, BC XII, 30 (note that ILPO 147 wrongly places this rite in the month of February). For the formula *huaccha coyac*, "friend of the poor," FS #46; LDST 138; GHLQ 168, 590; JB 14. The *Incap rantin rimac* as the title of an office had variations such as *apup rantin*, *huchacta yachak*, *camacta yachak*, etc.; see GHLQ 199, 454; LDST 226; GPF 112. The Spaniards translated it as "second person" or "adviser"; it is very difficult to distinguish it from the office of the secretary of the imperial council. The yearly reassignment of *chacras* always followed harvest, coming in July, the month called *Chahuahuar*; it was called either *chacra ricuy* ("field checking") or *chacra conacuy* ("field exchanging"), GPF 248f. For the contemporaneity of alloting of wives and assignment of *chacras*, ADS 39f.

Villcacona means simply "the *huacas*." If the annual questioning of the *huacas* was omitted, the Incas became exceedingly anxious, CL 29.

For Raquiancalla, BC XIII, 15. The spot where the *villcas* were assembled was also called Villcacona, BC XIII, 14, 32. For *huatunacta rimay*, GHLQ 189, 514. For the events of the annual collocation of *huacas*, see CL 29; FSP 60; CCDM. For synonyms for a prosperous year, referring always to rich green fields, GHLQ 131, 567, 574, 598, 609, 618, 644. There is a record of the mock fight between Canas and Cañars from the colonial period in a fiesta in late May; I am sure that this is a fragment from the earlier Inti Raymi, so I have read it back into the description of that celebration, RFC 258. For gambling in the Inti Raymi, GPF 243. For the ceremony of chasing and slaughtering the four llamas in Sausero, BC XIII, 27.

SECTION 16.

HUASCAR'S WRATH is specifically said to have fallen on the Equecos and Quilliscachis, MGP I, 1, and this event is corroborated by BC XII, 35, even though here the ruler is unnamed. The description of Huascar's special dress comes from GPF 116. For a *huacmansayak*, GHLQ 164. There is amazing agreement on Huascar's evil propensities, only CL 69 offering an opposite opinion. For his refusal to banquet with his people, BC XII, 18. We can understand how Huascar would have become envious at the wealth of the royal mummies from PPR 238.

For Huascar's decision to cut himself off from Upper Cuzco, SG 63. Atauhuallpa's mother was of the Iñaca *panaca*, SG 63; CL 62. Colla Topa belonged to the Sucso *panaca*, SG 60; CV 21. The statement that Huascar favored Lower Cuzco is based on CM 72 where it is shown that he added to the *huaca* of the Maras on Yahuira (and the Maras belonged to Lower Cuzco, SG 11). I am making the assumption that the wall with niches still to be seen at Collcompata belonged to Huascar's new palace. For his residence on Collcampata, SG 63; CMS 175. For the interest of the Antasayas in the site of Collcampata, LTOP 185. For their ancestral *huaca* here, BC XIII, 13. For the house of Cori Ocllo, wife of Amaru Topa Inca, BC XIII, 13. In the same chapter Cobo confuses her with Mama Ocllo, the wife of Topa Inca.

For the Fortress of Huascar, NCC 85. Collcampata was by many of the early writers (e.g., GVCR II, 22; V, 2) confused with the *chacra* southeast of the city called Collcapampa, SG 13.

PART III

SECTION 1.

HUAYNA CAPAC'S VISIT to Titicaca is mentioned in SG 59; CV 21; CL 62; ARG I, 18, 30, but only the last gives details as to his cultic innovations there. The statement concerning Huascar's new syncretistic god in Titicaca is found only in SPYP 267, but SPYP 227f. corroborates it. It is certainly evident that Huascar instituted important changes in the cult in Coricancha.

SECTION 2.

FOR THE MEANING of *huac*, JLD 1072; GHLQ 164; EQD 134. Today in the Ayacucho dialect *waka* means "sacred," EQD 113. It is an error to derive *huaca* from either the verb *huaccay* "to weep," or *huaccay*, "to make animal sounds." The first error is made in GHV 227, 232. Nor is there a connection with *huaca*, "fissure, split, cave," as in *huacca senca*, GHLQ 165; GPF 276. In none of these cases do the medial consonants match the corresponding sound in *huac*, "apart"; compare JLD 1072, 1076, 1081. Thus *huaca* is in no way connected with shrieking or lamenting. The numerous meanings which hide behind the colonial Spanish spelling *huaca* are well pointed up in GVCR II, 4, 5; III, 9. For *huac suyu*, GHLQ 164. A person of another moiety, for instance, was a *huacmansayak*, GHLQ 164.

The "remoteness" that is an integral part of the concept of *huaca* can be judged by noting the fact that there seem to be no cases of possession in Inca religion, however common it may have been in other Peruvian religions. Note that *huaca* today can mean "crazy," EQD 33. A stone that suggested in its form some animal was called a *sasahuana*, RGEP 101. These stones could be crudely shaped to point up further the resemblance. The standing stone at Kenko is such a *huaca*. The word appears to be Quechua. For the wierdly shaped potato, *llallagua*, which received veneration, MMCB III, 49. For *huaca* as a phantom or bogeyman, GHLQ 516. For *huaca* as always connected with the unusual, MMCB III, 60. For the many words for "luck," GHLQ 36, 309, 527. For every need's being a *huaca*, see FSP 59. For the stealing of *huacas*, MP 184. For a *huaca*'s ability to be elsewhere, MP 185. For its power of proliferation, FSP 59. For substitute *huacas* used by the traveler, MP 189. For *samana*, JCR 85, 91 (quoting Arriaga and Oliva). For the ability of *huacas* to speak, FSP 59.

Basically the words *huaca* and *villca* are interchangeable (TCYI 80; GHLQ 693; MP 181), but the former was more common, BC XIII, 1. There does seem, however, to have been a tendency to use *villca* specifically for an idol, BVP 138; GPF 224, 261 (note that the large and poisonous species of spider was referred to as a *villca uro*, LDST 45, 369); this use is supported by the name Villca Rimac, "idol which speaks," GDST 156. The word *villca* in any case seems to have been Aymara and was the word used in that language for "sun" as well as for any shrine of a god, JCR 78; the meaning "idol" is thus a meaning imputed to the word by those speaking Quechua. Oracular power is almost implicit in the definition of a *huaca*; see FS 30.

For the concept of Supay as in opposition to Viracocha, BVP 138; TCYI 31. Any discussion of *supay* must take into account the predilections of the early friars in their lexicons always to read the word in terms of the European devil. Therefore, what is said here on the subject should be put to a searching critique. The best discussion of Supay is in BC XIII, 36. So pervasive was the Inca concept of *supay* among the Aymaras it displaced their own special bogey, which they called *hahuari haque*, "the dead man," LBVA I, 170, 239, 250; II, 108. For the destruction of a *supay* in a *cutipacha*, MP 192. For *supay* as good or bad, LDST 40, 99. A verb *supayay*, "to bedevil," must have existed, as we have a participial formation from it, *supayasca*, "possessed," LDST 99. For Inca's view of these *huacas* as "lying devils," SPYP 272. For possession by a *supay*, GHLQ 88; 477. For possession among the Aymaras, LBVA II, 328. I am making a distinction between possession by a *supay* (or the act of becoming a *supay*) and the cult frenzy of the oracular priest, the *utirayay* or "rapture," BVP 156; GHLQ 359.

Another word for "inspiration" (used of *supay*) is *samay*, GHLQ 76f. I assume the transformation of a person into a *supay* from the term *supay tucuk* "one converted into a *supay*," GHLQ 88. For *purun huaca*, MP 184. For *huaccap ñan*, GHLQ 165. For the *apachic*, JCR 281f. There are many references to the *apachita* in Peruvian literature; see, among others, PO: Fund. 190; GVCR II, 4; MP 183; MMCB III, 50; SPYP 219f. Today one may speak of an *apachita* or a *sayhua*, EQD 119. For the silence with which the Indians traveled, CMS 148. The verb *apachiy* means "to cause to carry," GHLQ 30. Note the modern understanding of the *apachita*, JLD 52. Garcilaso's remark that *apachicta* represents a dative is incorrect, as it is an accusative form; I am unable to comprehend the reason for his remark. Whether a *huaro*, "a heap of small stones gathered together when fields were being cleared" (RGEP 101), was considered to be a *huaca*, I do not know. Elsewhere than in Cuzco the *apachita* could be called *cotorayac* (if *cotoraycu*? "a stone for the mound"?), PO: Fund. 190; MMCB III, 50.

For the *usno* as an altar or place of sacrifice, BVP 144; LDST 36; GHLQ 403; GPF 262. For the *usno* in Haucaypata, CM 37, 44; CL 23, 62; BC XIII, 14; JB 11; SPYP 259. For the *usno* as a tribunal, SPYP 219, 261; GHLQ 684. Note that there was an *usno* in Tumibamba, CV 21. For *marcayoc*, AEI 15. The word *marcayoc* undoubtedly refers to the field "reserved, set apart" for the community *huaca*, the word for "field" being omitted. For the field in which it stood, the *marca chacra*, GHLQ 232. For the identity of name in the case of a pueblo and its *huaca*, AEI 19.

For remarks on the *huancas* or *marcayocs*, MP 183f., 194; RHA 32; AEI 2; ACCM II, 10; MMCB III, 49; RGH 127; for *callaric machu*, GHLQ 61. For Huanacauri as the *huaca* of the founder of the line, IDI XXI, 168f. The Incas were undecided about the identity of the founder who had been changed into the sacred stone of Huanacauri; it could be variously Manco Capac or any of the other three brothers.

398

For other statements on the ancestral stones, CM 6f.; AEI 5, 15. For examples of other *pacarinas*, GVCR IV, 5; RGI II, 40; CLPP 97. *Paccariy* means "to dawn; to appear; to be born"; *pacarina*, therefore, means "the place of first appearance." For other forms of the verb used with the meaning of *pacarina*, SPYP 218. For *samana*, JCR 85, 91.

For material on the stars as protector-beings, BC XIII, 6; CV 15; BVP 137; PO: Error. 1; JA V, 4; ACCM II, 11. The word *chinchay* is curious. Modernly *chincha* means only "north," JLD 122f. I find no meanings explicitly given for it in the older dictionaries. If one compares *acco chinchay* (GHLQ 16) and *chuqui chinchay* (GHLQ 454), the translation "star" seems to be called for, and I have so translated it here. However, in no text that I know does it substitute for the common word for star, *coyllur* (but see GHLQ 16). The identification of *choqque chinchay* with Sirius comes only from JLD 135. For *collca*, GHLQ 440; LDST 65, 295. For stars concerned with war, commerce, and disaster, BVP 137, 143. For the mother-eating star, GHLQ 242. What area the Chacana ("Steps") presided over (SPYP 226; GHLQ 90) is unknown to me.

SECTION 3.

QUOTATIONS, GVCR VII, 8; JA VI, 19. For Cuzco as Viracocha's city, SG 28. For the custom of appointing as successor to a *curaca* the son born to him in Cuzco, PO: Inf. 194. The *ceque*-system is known to us from Polo's detailed chart reduced to text in BC XIII, 13–16. This is the primary document and needs a definitive and exhaustive study. For remarks on the *ceque*-system, including its use in other communities of the empire, MMCB 9, 14; ILPO 183; PO: Fund. 56f., 114; PO: Inf. 184. The number of *huacas* ranges from 350 to 450 in the above sources.

Tincalla means the action of flipping several drops of *akha* to the gods or *huacas* before drinking oneself; the word is *tinka* in its less ornate form. The listings for the Chima Panaca are found in BC XIII, 16. There is no certainty that the *caya* in Cayallacta is to be translated "dried oca" (see JLD 494; GHLQ 52), as it might be an erroneous spelling of *calla*, of which there are numerous meanings; this instance is an example of common carelessness of the Spanish orthographers. Again it might be a word for "gold," LDST 179, 270. *Topa* means basically something like "illustrious," MMCB IV, 2. For the necessity of a Cuzco coronation in claiming legitimacy of rule, CL 7. For Huascar and his father referred to as "Cuzco," FJ 325f.

Section 4.

THE STATEMENT is commonly found in our sources that all gods and *huacas* were arranged as a hierarchy of intercession under Viracocha; see, among others IDI XXI, 184, 168f.; LTOP 129, 138; BC XIII, 4, 7, 23; PO: Error. 1. There was in the minds of the Incas a confusion as to the relationship of Inti and Viracocha (CV 9), but in theory Pachacuti had resolved it (CM 16).

Section 5.

AN EXPLANATION of the initial statement is in order. For "priest" the earliest friars used the descriptive terms "servant of God, giver of the God-man, surrogate of God, maker of the Mass" (LDST 206; GHLQ 664). The word *umu*, which we best translate "sorcerer," they did not use because of its connotations of oracle reading and black magic. The basic role of the *umu* was that of a foreteller, LDST 29. A synonym of *omu* is *laica*, AEI 3; JLD 553. Garcilaso explicitly denies the occurrence of a word for priest in Quechua, GVCR III, 20.

For the status of the Tarpuntay as of Upper Cuzco, SG 11. That certain priesthoods could be hereditary we know from CV 12. It is certain that Tarpuntay refers only to the priesthood of Inti and is quite distinct from the priesthoods of Viracocha and Chuqui Illapa, CM 34f., BC XIII, 33. For the role of the Tarpuntay in the *huarachicoy*, CM 59–76. In other ceremonies, BC XIII, 25f. For the Tarpuntay's special responsibility in one of the Antisuyo *ceques*, CM 39. For the title *villac omu*, RIC 299n. There was among the Spaniards in Peru a lamentable ignorance concerning the Inca priesthood and particularly the office of high priest (the reason is correctly reported in BLCL 10).

In spite of CL 30, the close dependence of the *villac omu* on the emperor seems clear, BVP 150; GVCR II, 9; ARGCS I, 12. For his vicarious fasting after battle, LBVA I, 263; II, 311. The statement that his office was called *Intip apu* (SG 29) is difficult to accept, for *apu* is a kingly or a military office; we are helped in CMS 146f. by hearing of the office as the *Intip yanan* (I correct this title from *Indivianan*) which means literally "the sun's servant." The personage in legend who preached the religion of Tonapa Viracocha is called a *pacchacan* (SPYP 211), and I suspect that this title, "major-domo," truly designates the office of high priest.

There was one "bishop," always an Inca, for each province, says GVCR III, 24. He is called *hatun villca* in BVP, but this term is very suspect, both because of the unreliability of Blas Valera as a source and because the title does not seem to consort with the office, for it means "the high or great idol." No other source, to my knowledge, gives us the Quechua title of the "bishop." His very existence therefore could be challenged, for Garcilaso himself as a source is only a little more reliable than Blas Valera. I suspect that Blas Valera has confused this hypothetical office of "bishop" with the office of *villca camayoc* (CM 95) who had charge of provincial *huacas* in each of the four quarters.

It is my belief that the governors of each province had "episcopal" duties in regard to the Inca cults carried on in their jurisdiction. For the *yacarcas*, CM 21; BC XIII, 36. For the high reputation of the sorcerers from Conticuyo, BC XIII, 34; PO: Error 11. They were the Contiviza and Huallaviza, RGI I, 167. For the many skills of the sorcerer, CV 12; AEI 3. PO: Error 10. The excommunicators were called *runañacac*, "man-cursers," MP 185, 189. For *huaca camayoc*, CM 72.

SECTION 6.

FOR TRANSLATION of Vilcañota, LBVA II, 175, 386. Garcilaso uncertainly translates it as "a sacred thing," GVCR VII, 11. I refer here to modern Lake Titicaca under its former name, Chucuito; Titicaca is explicitly the name of one island in it. Cieza claims Vilcañota as the empire's third greatest *huaca* (CL 28) and mentions there the sacrifice of children. The story of the scandal at Pomacanchi occurs only in SPYP 267; however shocking it seems, it is certainly an action which

Huascar might have taken. For *samay*, LDST 157. For *purina*, LDST 341; GHLQ 297. The checkered tunic was *ahuaqui uncu* or *casana uncu* (GHLQ 18, 362, 444, 447), while the colored tunic with trim was the *cuchu uncu*, GHLQ 53. The *yacolla* can be seen worn in different styles in GPF. *Yacolla* is also given as *yacollca*, GHLQ 362, 447.

Tocapu is primarily applied to royal habiliments with variegated and rich patterns, CL 6; GHLQ 344, 463; LBVA I, 468; II, 357. Thus is derived the epithet applied to the Creator and perhaps meaning "in whom all things are included" (CM 11) or "wise," LBVA I, 138, 146, 419. Rowe translates this epithet as "most excellent" (RIP 87) as it exists in connection with the allied word *acnopu*. In JLD 979 it means "trimmed textiles." I suggest the possibility that each stylized square in a band of *tocapu*-trim was a symbol having to do with rule or dominion and that Viracocha is conceived as girded in a cabalistic garment on which is esoterically displayed the meaning of all things—this interpretation at least would explain Molina's rendering. A shirt also appears to have been worn under the *uncu*, probably for warmth, GHLQ 349. For the *pillaca llauto*, CL 7; GHLQ 285. For the *canipu*, GHLQ 50; MMCB IV, 421 (story of Chuquillanto). For *runcu*, GHLQ 321.

The picture of the girls gathering flowers and roots is from GPF 227f. The Quechua word for maguey is *pakkpa*, JLD 727; see also GHLQ 271. For Pisac meaning "partridge," GHLQ 287; JLD 792. For a song regarding the *tuya*-bird, GSP 516. *Tuya* may also be translated "lark," EQD 77. The willow was the *huayao* or *huayaco*, GHLQ 191, 666; BC VI, 2. For the *moyas*, PO: Fund. 78, 87–89; BC XII, 29; GPF 330; UGS 146f. For the latest thinking on the institution of the *yanaconate*, see Murra in VGD 438–41. For Huascar's landed estates near Pisac, UGS 147. For *Calca* as "stony place," LDST 184, 348. Today it means "gravel," EQD 63. We know that Huascar was in the habit of visiting his palaces in Calca, CV 26. The element *sahua* in the name of the mountain probably relates to copulation (in reference to the Chuqui Llantu myth?), GCIQ 146, 311; EQD 30 (*sakway*, "to copulate," modern Ayacucho dialect).

The location of Caquia Xaquixaguana is difficult, principally because there was confusion in the minds of the Incas as to the meaning of the name and also because of the fact that in the Pampa de Anta there existed the place called Xaxahuana. Sarmiento consistently spells it Caquia Xaquixaguana (SG 25, 28, 32) which I believe is the best spelling. Here Xaqui is to be read as *sakkey*, "inheritance" (JLD 296, 428, 868; GHLQ 511, 619). The Xaguana is a problem. Could it be read as *kkhawana*, "lookout, cynosure" (JLD 526; GHLQ 131), the meaning of the whole thus something like "Demesne Lookout"? This attempt is at best a wild guess and does not take into account an initial "Caquia"—if such really belonged to the name. I consider the identification of Xaqui Xaguana with the ruins of Huchhuy (or Chico) Cuzco (VMP 24; PHA I, 333–47) as accurate. For other references to the site, BLCL 16; VEC 1871; CM 17; CL 38, 41; JB 6, 7, 9, 17. The site of Viracocha Inca's last days is called Pomamarca in SPYP 239. There is no doubt that the Yucay valley was indeed the site of Viracocha Inca's city (CL 43; CLPP 94; JB 10; PO: Lin. 49), Garcilaso notwithstanding (GVCR IV, 24; V, 20). What clinches the identification with Huchhuy Cusco is the fact that the female descendants of Sayri Topa possessed as *repartimientos* the contiguous pueblos of Xaquixaguana and Paulo de Quilleuay. Quilluay on the modern map is only two miles upstream from Cuzco Chico and on the same bank of the Urubamba, thus making the identification certain. Note that the site possessed its own warehouses, Oscar Nuñez del Prado: *Exploración arqueológica en Raqc'i (Urubamba)*, *Revista Tradición*, Cuzco, Vol. 1 No. 1 (January–February, 1950).

I have taken the facts concerning Topa's properties from UGS 146; unfortunately this document comes to us piecemeal and secondhand so there is no way really of authenticating the information. Whether the Aymara word for a tall bamboolike cane (*chinchiru*, BC V, 83; the Quechua *ipa*) is related to the place name, I do not know. The blue rock *huaca* in Chincheros is called Titicaca by the local people. For the Inca road from Chincheros down to Yucay, GSP 486. For the old (pre-Pachacuti?) terraces and potato bins of Rakchi, see Nuñez del Prado cited above. For the archaeology of Ollantaytambo, PHA I, 211–48. Pachar is the true gateway to Ollantaytambo; the Spaniards could not

move against Ollantaytambo until they had first forced Pachar, TCYI
75. For the burial of the imperial viscera at Ollantaytambo, GVCR
VI, 5; GVHG II, 23. Some doubt may be cast on this information inasmuch as there is much confusion in our sources between Ollantaytambo and Pacaritambo, both occasionally being referred to simply
as Tambo. There was an Inca community where the Pampacahuana
entered the Urubamba; it is locally called Patallacta, HBLC 107. For
the *via sacra* out to Machu Picchu, HB 23–30.

SECTION 7.

THE NAMES of Machu Picchu and Huayna Picchu go back at least to
the middle of the eighteenth century, UGMP 177f. Machu Picchu has
had an immense amount of fluff written about it—a very natural result,
for its very namelessness lends itself to conjecture. My own very feeble
guess as to its original name might be *Sacsasiray* (TCYI 71), but this
information is intended for burial in footnotes only. The fundamental
work is Hiram Bingham, *Machu Picchu, A citadel of the Incas*, Yale,
1930 (HB). A more popular work using the same material and offering interpretation is Hiram Bingham, *Lost City of the Incas*, paperback
edition by Atheneum, 1963 (HBLC). For Inca roads and communities in the area, Paul Fejos, *Archaeological Explorations in the
Cordillera Vilcabamba, Southeastern Peru*, New York, 1944. Jose Uriel
García possesses some documentary evidence which is perhaps of importance but which no one is able to validate since he sees fit not to
publish it except in almost useless references; see his "Machu Picchu,"
in *Cuadernos Americanos*, Vol. CXVII, No. 4 (July–August, 1961)
(UGMP).

For the pottery see Manuel Chavez Ballón, "La Alferería de Machu
Picchu," in *Revista del Museo e Instituto Arqueológico del Cuzco*,
No. 19 (July 1961), Cuzco. An architectural interpretation is offered
in George Kubler, "Machu Picchu," in *Perspecta*, Yale Architectural
Journal No. 6. The latest survey and attempt to identify the name of
the site is Luis E. Valcarcel, *Machu Picchu*, Buenos Aires, 1964. Hiram
Bingham's excellent piece of discovery and clearing of the site is in no
sense matched by his interpretation, which is fanciful, unsupported

by any knowledge of Inca history, and based on one of the weakest authorities in the whole range of colonial literature. My own interpretation that Pachacuti began work on the site and that each succeeding emperor added his own ward is not inconsistent with the archaeology of the site or with the facts of Inca history (see BC XII, 12) but must not be read as anything but sheer imagination. My statement of the probable motives behind the building of the city is based on what I believe to have been Inca religious psychology. Needless to say, these theories are only my suppositions and they are no more "proved" than the wildest statements in the guidebooks. Outside of the scientific description of the ruins themselves, nothing about Machu Picchu can be documented as "fact." It is because of this uncertainty that I did not even mention the city in BE.

I naturally have no record that Huascar ever journeyed to the site of Machu Picchu. It is a fair assumption that at some time in his seven-year rule he did so, and I have used this assumption to develop further the picture of the Inca people. For *ch'in*, JLD 117; EQD 47, 119, 143; the word "silence" does not give the full flavor of the meaning, although basically it gives the sense. For *chinnic llacta*, GHLQ 111, 670; LBVA II, 86 (my translation is a free one). A deserted town can also be described as *racay*, LDST 345, or *purum llacta*, GHLQ 645. For *mayup ccauñiynin*, GHLQ 663. Chuqui Llantu illustrates the difficulties of translation from Quechua through early Spanish orthography. Depending on which gutteral is intended in the first word, the meaning might be Swift Shadow or Golden Shade (with "golden" probably carrying the meaning of endearment, i.e., "darling," "sweet," LBVA II, 89). And even the second word might possibly mean "foliage" or "greenery," RGH 192. For the story of Chuqui Llantu, MMCB IV, section following chap. 16. It will be noticed that I refer to the so-called Intihuatana as an *usno*. This word in Quechua refers to a stone land-marker; it carries a secondary meaning of a sacred stone upon which fetishes or the statues of gods, or offerings to them, were placed or on which a ruler could sit and partake of the *huaca* in the stone. For *usno*, JLD 1056; GHLQ 358, 403, 684; LDST 36; SPYP 219, 261.

We know that Pachacuti built in and around Ollantaytambo, SG 40. Of Topa Inca in the area there is no record, but Huayna Capac also was active in adding to the fortress of Ollantaytambo and in the nearby areas, CV 21; SG 58; MMCB I, 13. For the near certainty that the site was an early local *huaca* appreciably expanded by the imperial Inca rulers, see the figures cited in Chavez Ballón, *Alfarería*, cited above (i.e., of the decorated pottery found at Machu Picchu 12 per cent was early Inca, 35 per cent classical Inca, 41 per cent imperial Inca, 12 per cent foreign pottery of imperial period). Machu Picchu should not be mentioned without also mentioning Choqque Quirau, "Golden Cradle," a sister city on the opposite side of the Salcantay massif and even more remote and difficult of access.

For Choqque Quirau, "Informe del Senor Carlos A. Romero sobre las Ruinas de Choqquequirau," in *Revista Historica*, Tomo IV, Lima, 1909; Hiram Bingham, "Ruins of Choqquequirau," in *American Anthropologist*, Vol. 12, 1910; DSB 100–103. Some of my views of what Machu Picchu was have been suggested by a comparison of it with Choqque Quirau. It is quite possible—even probable—that Choqque Quirau was the site of the famous Apurimac oracle (BC XIII, 20; CL 28; CLPP 91; PPR 259f., 380); this possible identification has also helped me adjust my thoughts concerning Machu Picchu.

For *atitapia*, GHLQ 36, 88, 207, 245; JLD 962. The verb *tapiay* means "to foretell" from the song or action of birds, LDST 361. The *checollo* (translated as "nightingale" by the early dictionaries) was a bird of ill omen, GPF 281 f.; GHLQ 106, 663. It announced quarrels and altercations. It is the bird which gives advice to Chuqui Llantu in the story, MMCB, which is why I have introduced it here.

SECTION 8.

FOR THE TERM *hahua ricuysimi*, GHLQ 145. The word *acapana* in GPF 146 means swiftness or the like and is translated by him as "wind" (GPF 65) or as "whirlwind" (GHLQ 678). For its meaning as "scud" or flying cloud rock, GHLQ 12, 28; JLD 32. For *pumaranra*, "lion rocks," GHLQ 31, 295, 470, 662, 665; GPF 187. For the lion stalkers, LBVA II, 353. I have translated *titi camana* into Quechua *puma camayoc.* For Hahua Anti, GPF 269. The densest part of the jungle was called *pipu pipu hacha* (GHLQ 516) or *chuncu hacha* (GHLQ 121). For Anti Viracocha, MMCB III, 15. For getting lost in the montaña, *hacha hachapi pantacumuy*, GHLQ 278. For Pachacuti in the montaña, CL 52; CLPP 95. Another name for the dragon-serpent was *yahuirca*, SPYP 242.

The full title of the jaguar in the montaña was *achachi yaya*, GPF 269. Huaman Poma gives the story of Inca Roca and his son Apu Camac Inca who became jaguars in the montaña, GPF 103, 269, 156 (wrongly numbered); his identifications are garbled—he means Pachacuti and his son Otorongo Achachi who was Topa Inca's general in the montaña. For remarks on the Chunchos, GPF 322; ADS 47f. For gold dust from Opatari, SPYP 254. For the mother-eating star, GHLQ 242. For *pachap cuchun cuchun*, GHLQ 440. For Peñeca and Paititi, RGI IV, p. cxcviiiff.; MMCB III, 66. For Amazons see references in BE.

For the tale of the water-maiden in the sky, GVCR II, 27. For the sound of thunder, GHLQ 127, 130. For the crystal mirror tale, CM 17f. For the tale of Inca Roca and the spring, CL 35. For men turned into stone, GGO V, 7; JB 1; SG 6; ACCM II, 10; BC XII, 1. These early giants were the *Huaris*, ACCM II, 11; AEI 2. For the whale, *ura huaca*, LDST 223. For the worship of *mamacocha*, PO: Instr. I. For the dragon of Pachatusan, SPYP 242. For famine, eruptions, and earthquakes in the reign of Pachacuti, MMDN 11; GPF 286; SPYP 246f. I make the connection between the dragon and great disasters on the basis of SPYP 244f. For the *masaruna*, GHLQ 597. For *uma puric*, GHLQ 354, 516, 629.

For the *tutayapacha* and the specters that existed then, SPYP 210; GHLQ 516. For other references to bogeymen, GHLQ 88, 112, 207, 210f., 245. A nightmare or phantom was a *llapiy*, a "clutcher," GHLQ 210. For *chiquip muyoycuscan*, GHLQ 112. It was expected that Viracocha on his return would overturn the world, MMCB III, 57; IDI XXI, 152. For the worship of the Spaniards as foretold in old prophecies, GVHG I, 32. For Apurimac oracle, see notes to preceding section; the special oracle mentioned here is recorded in PPR 380. For *huatunasimi*, GHLQ 189.

Section 9.

For the retinues of the *pallas*, BLCL 24. For the *ñusta*, GHLQ 545; GVCR II, 27. The word *coya* (translated as "desired lady") is given in PPR 379 as a synonym of *palla*. This interpretation may well be accepted, but it was certainly in general restricted to the emperor's legitimate wife, probably meaning "the gracious one." For *pallas* going in hammocks, PPR 379. I arrive at the figure 400–500 for the Inca population of the Capac Ayllu from BLCL 12 (where he says "more than 300"). This figure roughly checks with the number of young knights yearly inducted into the caste, namely 800 (according to CM 70, where we must assume that the figure 800 includes both Capac and Hahua Incas with the latter in the majority). Cuzcoquiti had some 6,000 noble women which included wives of the *curacas* and ranking Hahua Incas (BLCL 24); again this figure is not out of line with 400–500 as the full complement of Capac Incas.

For the establishments of the *pallas*, CMS 163. For the rainbow-striped *lliclla*, GHLQ 566; GPF 130, 138. The girdle was the *ppichuc*, GHLQ 285. For the *ñañaca* or mantilla, GHLQ 276, 582 (in 368 it is given as *iñaca* which is a totally different word); RGI I, 208; LBVA I, 450. The *anaco*, "a woman's garment," is not the same word, LDST 69, 206, 222; VGD 45, 172, JLD 44. The coca bag was the *runcu*, GHLQ 321. Women generally painted with *paria*, ground vermilion (RGI I, 205f.), whence the verb "to rouge," *pariacuy*, GHLG 156. They could also use the juice of the red fruit, *ñuñunya*, GHLQ 263; LBVA II, 237. *Passicuy* and *hauicuy* were also used, the latter meaning specifically "to anoint or to oil with a black unguent," GHLQ 687; LDST 28; JLD 236. A number of other words could be employed, depending on the cosmetic used. *Hincuy* seems to have referred specifically to eye-painting, LDST 293. Huaman Poma mentions a certain kind of woman below the status of *palla* as *aui* meaning "painted one" (GPF 181; see *hawikk*, JLD 236). The reference may be to courtesans. For phrases describing a beautifully gotten-up woman, GHLQ 368, 471. For the equivalent in Aymara, LBVA II, 175. Quotation from Cieza, CLPP 40.

Description of a banquet based on BLCL 21; MMCB III, 6; BC XIII, 10; PPR 204, 264; PO: Fund. 123f. For meat-eating and the slaughterhouse, PPR 379. For *sancu*, GHLQ 583. Public eating for the Incas in the square was customary, ADS 32; GPF 66, 192. The evening meal was not large and was taken in private, PPR 227. For the variations on *llakhuay*, "to taste salt or hot peppers," GHLQ 208, 454. For the process of toasting, JB 18. For *muccu*, GHLQ 245, 248. For shell anklets worn by male dancers, MMCB I, 19; GPF 318. For the varieties of *taqui*, SPYP 227, 234. The verb *tusuy* means "to dance," GHLQ 348, 430, 471. *Taquiy* means "to sing and dance," GHLQ 338, 445. For the *pomatinya*, GPF 334. For the *huayñu*, JLD 1130f.; GHLQ 194, 430, 471. Among the Aymara the *huayñu* (meaning "friend" or "companion") was a circle of either men or women which enclosed a couple who danced to each other, LBVA II, 157.

For the *cachua*, BC XII, 14; XIV, 17. But note that the word *cachua* today means the dirge sung at an infant's burial, FQD 124. A woman addicted to the dance was a *huancar huayñu*, GHLQ 177. For sexual license at the banquets, BVP 177. There was a class of girls called *taqui acllas* who were professional entertainers, MMCB III, 39. It is probable that they were a courtesan class and may have been those called *(h)aui*, "painted," GPF above. For the tabu on the emperor's food, JB 8. For the *camchu*, GHLQ 61, 686. For the names of the clowns and *farceurs*, LDST 71, 112, 166, 298; SPYP 236, 251, 267; GHLQ 71, 156, 325; GPF 330. Devil dancing, i.e., in costume and mask, was a prominent feature of festivities also in Collao, LBVA I, 170, 189, 193, 226; II, 52. For the special ward where deformed people lived, GPF 337. For the *runatinya*, GPF 334; DTR 63; CV 23; SG 60.

SECTION 10.

FOR HOMOSEXUALISM among the Yauyos, MP 189. For such practices among Collas and Lupacas, LTOP 133, 140; ARGCS I, 20; LBVA II, 154. That adultery was a theft appears from the denomination for a child of adultery, "a stolen child," GHLQ 86. For words for adultery, GHLQ 41, 370. For the crippled child as probably the offspring of an illicit love affair, GHLQ 41. For the common practice of Incas on campaign to take *ñustas* with them, PPR 347f. In Quechua one had to use circumlocution for "virgin," phrases such as "a woman undamaged by a man" or "a girl not debauched by a man," etc., GHLQ 94, 493. But note that Garcilaso gives *tasqui* as "virgin," GVHG II, 25. For *sipas*, GHLQ 579, 594. For *coyay*, LDST 37, 72; GHLQ 73, 590.

For *mayhuay*, GHLQ 235f. For *munay*, GHLQ 249–51; LDST 41, 77. For *huaylluy*, GHLQ 192f. Note that these words for love also existed in Aymara (LBVA I, 43ff.) with approximately the same nuances. For examples in Quechua of love songs, GPF 17, 19; GVCR II, 27. For the orange *chinchercoma* flower, LBVA II, 83. For the initiation rites of young men and women coming together, GPF 257 and CM 60–77. The age of the girls at the ceremony is given in SPYP 221 as sixteen. The red and white *acsu* (CM 61, 66, 88) was a variety of *ancallu* (GHLQ 25; JLD 46; CM 88). *Ancallu* is probably connected in some way with the *anacu* (JLD 44), if we can judge from the fact that a part of the *quicuchicoy* was the *anacauiy* (obviously the putting on of a certain garment), GPF 257; see also remarks in notes to preceding section.

The scene of the girls' bathing is taken from GPF 316 which undoubtedly refers to the *quicuchicoy*, although it is not so explicitly stated. For words for "echo," GHLQ 25, 127, 361. For the *huarmihapiy pacha*, SPYP 222; PO: Inf. 139; ARGCS I, 24. There is a great amount of material on the *huacanqui*, see SPYP 222f., 230, 232; LDST 76; GHLQ 166; CV 12; MAH 20; MMCB III, 39, 47, 55, 58; GVCR II, 17; GPF 276; LBVA I, 255, 322; II, 80, 161. The word is said to be Aymara, BC IX, 4. For *causariy*, "to resuscitate, renew," GHLQ 52. Chuquillantu and her lover were changed into the twin spikes of Pitusiray, see GPF 268. For the love story of Efquem Pisan, CV 27.

SECTION 11.

FOR COLLCAMPATA as the site of Huascar's palace, CMS 175; SG

63. For the *carpahuasi* there, GVCR VII, 8. That the road from the fortress on Sacsahuaman came down obliquely, as described, into the heart of Cuzco can be plainly seen in Fig. 2 of JADG (see also page 9). For the *caumihua*, GHLQ 139, 536. For *chapa*, LDST 258; GHLQ 517. The word has, of course, military connotations basically (GHLQ 38, 96), and I have no reference to an actual police contingent called *chapacuna* in Cuzco. For the sheriff, GHLQ 186; GPF 344f.

For words for minions, GHLQ 202, 302, 642. For *quemikiru*, GHLQ 302. Why they should be called "wedge teeth" (JLD 405), I do not know. For the Equecos and Quillescachis, GHLQ 139, 308; GPF 306, 308, 363. For their destruction, MGP I, 1. On the *yanaconate* see FS 34, 36, 50; CL 18; VGD 21, 118, 438–41. For the role of the two *yanacona* in Pachacuti's *panaca*, JA VI, 21. For *pococ*, GHLQ 294. For *kallu*, GHLQ 132. For games played, LDST 162; GHLQ 196; GPF 243. For the fact that an emperor could and did give *acllas* to his trusted *yanaconas*, FS 34. For the right to the hammock, ADS 34. For the incident of the appointment of a certain Huayna Pari to a *curaca*-ship in Acora by an emperor who must have been Huascar, VGD 42.

SECTION 12.

FOR THE TERM *ramca ramca pacha*, GHLQ 311. I derive the existence of the conceit of a dancing star from its name, LDST 236; GHLQ 33; JLD 58. Another name of the morning star was Huarachasca. For the *puco puco*, GHLQ 293; LBVA I, 353; BC VIII, 1. For other expressions of dawn, LDST 37; GHLQ 266, 269, 279, 348. The word for "morning" is *paccarin*, GHLQ 266.

For *ticnu*, GHLQ 341. For *pirca llantuk pacha*, GHLQ 210. For the *chipa*, GHLQ 469. For *yanca yahuar*, GHLQ 364, 450. For *anta rupay*, GHLQ 28, 417, 645. Twilight was *sipi sipi pacha*, GHLQ 83, 115. For the *huaricolla*, LDST 41, 70; GHLQ 183. For *llipiyak tuta*, GHLQ 601; see also LDST 93, 276. For the Southern Cross, GHLQ 51, 465; ACCM II, 11. For *pacsa*, GHLQ 179, 271, 569f., 601; JLD 727. For the *Coya Pacsa*, CM 43.

SECTION 13.

THE MEANING of Situa is fairly clear. The word is given in JLD 923 as meaning "September sun," which he obviously connects with the verb *situy*, "to shine, to spread light" (see also GHLQ 85, 660 for this word). We know that the month preceding the *Capac Sithua* (GHLQ 394) or August was called sometimes the *Anta Sithua* (VRQ II, 39f.; GHLQ 551) which can mean either the "coppery" or "hot" sun, or the festival of that name as performed by the people of Anta. Thus Situa seems to refer to the end of the dry period made so menacing by the unrelieved sunshine. Modernly the word has the meaning of "spring," EQD 126. Whether the Aymara word *siythuu*, "well-tended, made much of, regaled" (LBVA II, 321), is in any way connected is moot.

SECTION 14.

THE TWO MAJOR SOURCES for the Situa are BC XIII, 28f.; CM 35–57. Far less detailed and useful is GVCR VII, 6f. There are corroboration and some additional facts in JA V, 28; JB 15; ARGCS I, 24. I have not bothered to ascribe minutely each fact concerning the Situa to one of the sources above, and only when a controversial matter or one of special interest is involved have I inserted notes and documentation.

SECTION 15.

THE MAKE-UP of the four ceremonial armies is from CM 38–40. Slight emendations have been made in accordance with material from SG 11 and BC XIII, 13–16. The only Inca family omitted from the four Situa armies is the half-*ayllus* of Ayavilla (SG 23; BC XIII, 15), probably because of its connection with Urcon, the proscribed coemperor whom Pachacuti displaced. In other words it was, as a family, not fully accepted in the Inca canon. The material on the special adjudication at the opening of the Situa is interesting. It comes from only two sources, IH 284; GGO IV, 16. Almost all the sources mention the *pancunco* with its great drama. The word is given in GHLQ 277 where it is applied to a disheveled and unruly head of hair, meaning simply "torch-head." We still only know that the torches themselves were called *pancunco* (or *mauro pancunco*, CM 41).

SECTION 16.

FOR THE WORD *achancara*, GHLQ 12f. For the statues of the Inca *ayllu* and the Palla *ayllu*, CM 31, 43; CV 18, 19. Prayers to Viracocha are to be read most accurately in RIP. The *coya* seemingly had produced two daughters for Huascar (ISP-VC 47f.) but no sons. Rowe translates *caylla* as "remote" (RIP), but inasmuch as its basic meaning seems to be "adjoining," I have translated it as "just beyond."

The name of the Incas' national dance has been seriously garbled in our sources. I have opted for *huayaya* on the authority of BC XIV, 17 (although BC XIII, 28 seems to make it Huayara). If the former is the proper spelling, then the word is amenable to dissection as *hua* and *yaya*, "hear!" or "have pity! O father." For other references on this dance, GVCR IX, 1; CM 33–35, 80. For the *muru urco*, CL 7, 49; CM 80; BC XIII, 26. The Spaniards never located this interesting object in Inca cult, and wild rumors had it thrown into lakes all over the sierra; see MMCB I, 13; SPYP 278; ACCM I, 17 (sequel).

SECTION 17.

NOTE THAT the *panaca* of Lloque Yupanqui, the third emperor, was charged with the responsibility of serving the *sancu*, JA V, 23. I do not know the reason.

PART IV

SECTION 1.

FOR HUASCAR's two demands that Atauhuallpa come to Cuzco to do homage, BC XIII, 18. The viceroy was the *capacpa ranti* (LDST 226) or *Incap ranti* (GPF 112) or *Apup ranti* (GHLQ 454). It may have been an honorary title with real power still in the hands of the governors. The Spaniards generally translated it as "second person" (VGD 107), it means literally "delegate, substitute." The office must be distinguished from the Inca's private secretary who passed on the royal commands and reported all matters back to him; this person was the *huchayachak*, "he who knows the matters," GHLQ 199; ISP-TY 60. Unfortunately, the Spaniards also translated this office as "second person," IH 280.

The fact that the office of "governor" of the Quito area also carried extraordinary viceregal powers with it is attested from the moment the province was first conquered by Topa Inca, CL 56f. For the provocative part played by the Cañar *curaca* in worsening relations between the two brothers, SPYP 268; CV 26. *Chasqui* time between Cuzco and Quito varied between eight days (CLPP 42) and five days (PPR 236). See also BC XII, 32; VEC 1148, 1578. For the *hatun chasqui*, GPF 350f. I follow CV 26 in the chronology of the two messages from the north. All that follows concerning the Quilaco embassy is based on CV 26f. which is the only source reporting it fully. Only material from other sources, therefore, will be noted here and in the following section.

Section 2.

The basic source on the Quilaco embassy is CV 26f. For the Huarupuncu bridge, BC XIII, 14. "Waru" is given in JLD 1113 as the bed or platform of a rope bridge, but it may be here simply a reference to the sacred community of Huaro farther down the road. For Pachatusan, SPYP 242; JLD 720. The name may be an abbreviation for [*Hanac*] *pachatusan*, "Pillar of the Sky." For Senca, GPF 316, 1051. The full name was Munay Senca, "Fine Ridge," LVCP 20. For Allpa Suntu, MMCB II, 3. The area is called Cantut Pata in GVCR VII, 8. I believe the obviously garbled word "Antuit Urco" in BC XIII, 14 is to be restored as "Cantut Urcu." This site, a fissure in the rocks, was connected with the Hualla Indians who are known to have lived here.

The summit of Senca was apparently known as Queancalla, TCYI 68; BC XIII, 13; GPF 316, 1051; on it stood the eastern sun pillars. The identification of Illacamarca with present-day Puca Pucara is mine. Illacarmarca was a "fortress" on the Yucay road, BC XIII, 13, and it was in a "valley" known as Yuncay Pampa (BC XIII, 14), both of which facts fit the present ruins. There is a general review of the Tambomachay area in PHA I, 161–70. For the two basins at Tambomachay

named Quinua Pucyo, BC XIII, 14. The hill Sapi was also called
Quisco (BC XIII, 13, 14) after a *huaca* worshiped on top of it, or
Chitacaca, MMCB II, 1.

The identification of the spring of Tambo Machay with the spring
of Pachacuti's vision is mine. The only other possibility is that it
existed over in the basin of Chita and since has been forgotten. For the
Viracocha Pucyo, BC XIII, 14. It was also called Susur Pucyo, BC XII,
12; SG 27 (it is spelled Corcor Pucyo in BC XIII, 13); CM 17. For
the magic mirror tale, BE 5. For *huaylla*, LDST 55, 62, 69; GHLQ
192, 428, 618, 639. For *chita*, JLD 132. For Lake Quihuipay (which
is present-day Coricocha), SPYP 42. For the *cuchuchu*-plant, BC IV,
21. For the villa of Pachacuti's queen at Pomamarca, BC XIII, 14.
For *puccochicuk*, GHLQ 294. For *huchacamayos*, CCDM 242. I
have translated this word as "inquisitor" to keep the word for an upright "judge" limited to *hucha patachac*, GHLQ 200, 280.

For the slaughter of the Chincha *curacas*, CCDM 242. For the
features of court etiquette, PO: Inf. 146; PPR 248; CL 13; BC XIII,
23. For the title "generous" given to the emperor, FS 46; LDST 138.
For title "unique," GHLQ 134, 500. For the veiling of the emperor, PPR 224f. For *Calca* meaning "a stony place," LDST 184,
348. I have taken the item about the *coya*'s coca-chewing and her love
of parrots from GPF 143.

SECTION 3.

THERE IS a general review of the remains of the greater Sacsahuaman
area in PHA I, 123–57. For Inca models of the fortress, PHA II, 511.
A splendid air view of the ruins of Sacsahuaman is found in GKA, Plate
164. The word *huaman* was used for any hawklike raptor. The great
royal eagle was the *anca* or the *sacsa huaman*, GHLQ 75. *Sacsa* here
means undoubtedly "speckled, variegated," JLD 870. Today it means,
specifically, "mottled brown and white," EQD 88. For *Intip llocsina*,
GHLQ 610, 616; LDST 177, 301. For the name of the fortress as
"House of the Sun," RGI II, 180; CL 51. Quotation from CL 51. For
numbers of men engaged in building the fortress, CL 51; NCC 64.
The number is given as 30,000 in BC XIV, 12. I am assuming that the

quarry used for the large blocks was the nearest one, the Huayrankallay or "Wind-stone," BC XIII, 13. The statement that Huascar built at Sacsahuaman (CL 51) is probably to be interpreted as referring to Collcampata. Building on it was certainly going on at the beginning of Huascar's reign, GVCR VII, 29. The information on Sacsahuaman taken from NCC 64f. is somewhat unreliable, but I have used the 1541 date for the *cabildo* ordinance against further demolition of the structure. For the triple circumvallation of the Peruvian fortress, CL 17. Only CL 50 gives the names of the three walls. For the name Chuquipampa, BC XIII, 13. For the spring Calispucyo, CM 75; BC XIII, 25 (see also OV XLVI, 17 and GPF 337 for garbled references to it). For Moyomarca, GVCR VII, 29; VEC 1532. Both CL 51 and PPR 275 mention only the two military towers, which in VEC 1532 are called Paucar Marca and Sacsa Marca. For the contents of the storerooms here, PPR 275f. For the underground galleries connecting the towers, GVCR VII, 29. For the water supply, GVCR VII, 29. For *sayapayak*, GPF 339; GHLQ 38. Other titles like *pucara camayoc* were also used. For the figure of 100,000 inhabitants, PPR 275. For *Suchona*, GPF 1051; JLD 931. I am unable to suggest a meaning for Sabacurinca (BC XIII, 13). Not everyone will accept my identification of this term with the so-called throne of the Inca on the Rodadero. For the names of the four architects, GVCR VII, 27. The precise location of the mountain Sapi is uncertain, but from the facts that Cobo puts it in the Chinchaysuyo sector (BC XIII, 13) and that it was also called Chita Caca (MMCB II, I), I have opted to put it somewhere back of Sacsahuaman. For Quisco as the ancestor of the Antasayas, LTOP 185; ISP-VT 134f. I suspect that punning upon Quisco and Cuzco helped to identify the Antasaya *huaca* with the "origin" of Cuzco or the Sapi.

SECTION 4.

THE WORD "war" is *auccay* ("fighting") or *auccanacuy* ("fighting with each other"), GHLQ 37. The verb *pucllay* means "to fight" and "to have fun, to play games," JLD 763; GHLQ 37f., 293; LDST 57. For quotation, ILPO 143. For the *puruchuco* or "feathered headdress," CL 7. For uses of the word *suyu*, as "army," LDST 71, 354; GHLQ

334, 397f. For Quechua as the language of the camp, CL 23. For the *aucacunap apu*, GHLQ 38. I have no direct evidence for my identification of the Lower Cuzco general with the "camp master" or *aucacta yachachik apu*, GHLQ 38, 577. I have merely looked for what might have been the office next in responsibility to that of the commander-in-chief and have arbitrarily assigned it to the Lower Cuzco general. In fact my whole view of the organization of officers in the Inca army comes from GHLQ and LDST which, being vocabularies only, are not the best sources for this kind of knowledge.

The only fact attested in our sources concerning the army organization is the dual command at the top. From this basic fact I have derived a number of other suppositions. For the "colonels," GHLQ 175. For the office of "sergeant major," GHLQ 38. To muster the army daily by its divisions was expressed by the verb *suyuchay* (GHLQ 398) or *suyuchapayay*, GHLQ 334. *Sericac* (LDST 352) comes from *ciriy*, "to recline, to stop to rest," GHLQ 84. For words for "captain," GHLQ 38, 175, 447. For *chapatiyac*, GHLQ 38, 96, 517; LDST 258. Fortified Inca garrisons on the frontiers were called *michucruna* (corrected from *michucrima*, SG 39) or *harccak*, GHLQ 38. The commander of the presidio was a *sayapayac*, GHLQ 38 (see also GPF 339). The large shield carried by a captain was a *marca querar*, GHLQ 232. I have no evidence for my statements on promotion to the rank of captain—it is suppositious only. For the role of the captain in training levies of colonials, BC XIV, 9. For the *caparisca*, LDST 42, 248.

For the review of troops, GHLQ 38; 397f.; LDST 354. For *huaminca*, GHLQ 536. Inca weaponry has been well covered in many secondary sources, so nothing exhaustive is intended here. For shields, GHLQ 294, 388. For helmets, LDST 91. The illustrations in GPF as well as JADG 10–19 and Figs. 1 and 6 are very useful here. The word *yauri* today means "a large needle," EQD 90. For war paint, BLCL 18. For *huallparicusca*, GHLQ 174. The golden medals were *pura pura*, RFC 258; SPYP 235, 266; GHLQ 297. For "hawk-companion," LDST 80. For "hawk-club," GHLQ 93, 175. For *pahuapuy*, GHLQ 273. For *aucay intuy*, GHLQ 38. For the battle cry, *chaya chaya*, JB 9; GHLQ 101; SPYP 274. For *cumpa*, GHLQ 54, 531.

For *haylli*, GHLQ 157 (for a variant, GHLQ 38). For *maruy*, GHLQ 232. For another verb meaning "to crush the enemy," GHLQ 276. For *atircuy*, GHLQ 37. For *chiñik purum*, GHLQ 111. For *hayllircoy*, GHLQ 157.

SECTION 5.

MY STATEMENT of the hostility between Upper and Lower Cuzco rests on SG and CV. Particularly revealing is Huascar's specific attempt to deny it in SG 66. For Misi as belonging to Lower Cuzco, SG 60. For the incident of the mutiny under Misi, BE 12. The name of this commander is consistently spelled *Mihi* in CV 22, which makes it probable that it is to be translated as "cat" (JLD 648; GHLQ 238, 532) rather than "shepherd" or "governor," GHLQ 237. For Huascar's hatred of the royal mummies, BC XII, 18. For the presence of sycophants in Huascar's court, PPR 237. For Huascar's general summons of all the *curacas*, CV 27.

Urco Colla is made out as one of the prime instigators of the war between the two brothers, CV 31. For Huayna Capac's dying prophecy regarding the Spaniards, ISP-VC 22; GVHG I, 32; GPF 378; ACCM I, 16. For Huascar's fury on receiving news of Atauhuallpa's coronation, CV 27. For his use of the prisons previously, SPYP 267. For statement that at hearing the news from the north Huascar almost had his mother and *coya* executed, CV 27. For the pressure on Huascar from his sycophants, PPR 237. For the name Huaminca Atoc, SPYP 268. For the name Hancu, LDST 87, 114, 174, 193; GHLQ 465; JLD 216. For the false story given out as to the mission of Atoc and Hancu, SG 63.

SECTION 6.

THE COMMON CONFUSION between Atauhuallpa's name and that which the Peruvians gave to the Spanish barnyard fowl is mentioned in BC X, 11. For Atauhuallpa's full name, SPYP 268. For sources on Atauhuallpa's parentage and affiliations, SG 63; CL 62, 69; SPYP 259. For Ticci Capac, CV 31; SG 65; ISP-VC 4. Atauhuallpa definitely had the concept of himself as the originator of a new aeon, ISP-VC 4. Ticci

418

Capac is translated as "Lord of the Whole World," SG 65; CV 31. The statement that Challcochima and Quizquiz represented, respectively, Upper and Lower moieties is mine alone and is purely inferential. No explicit statement backs it up.

SECTION 7.

FOR THE DATE 1530 as the commencement of hostilities, see SG 69. The order of events at the beginning of the war is difficult to reconstruct, especially from SG 63. I have assumed that Huanca Auqui was moved from the Pacamoro command to Tumibamba. Only as much of the war as is necessary for clarity is told here, as it has been done at more length in BE 13.

The captains under Huanca Auqui are listed as Hahuapanti and Paca Mayta in SG 64 (less correctly Yahuapanti and Huaca Mayta in CV 28). The name Hahuapanti may contain the Quechua name for the cosmos flower *panti* (*Revista Universitaria de Cuzco*, 1961, p. 41) which also gives its name to the color orange, GHLQ 210; RGH 262. That it was an accepted name is seen from BVP 138 where it is the name of one of Viracocha's archangels, spelled Hayhuaypanti.

SECTION 8.

It is known that Pachacamac gave a favorable oracle to Huascar, PPR 242; SPYP 271. The oracle of Catequilla was also favorable to Huascar which is why Atauhuallpa destroyed it, RHA 23f.; SG 64; AEI 2 (this last source has Huascar confused with Atauhuallpa). For Vilca Cutipa and his levies, VGD 105f. Viracocha's angelic helpers were called, according to BVP 138, "the beautiful warriors," *huaminca hayuaypanti*; this is the only source that gives a translation of *hayhuaypanti*.

Huascar's embassy to Pizarro is well attested. It seems to have occurred about the time of the founding of San Miguel, FMA 72; AZH II, 3; ACCM I, 17; GHV 327; PRN 241; VRQ II, 86f. I have decided to accept the facts about the embassy claimed by GPF 375f., although its accuracy is open to real doubt. For the calling together of the oracles after Yanamarca, CV 30; SPYP 271f.; SG 64. I assume that the convocation of *huacas* took place at the usual spot (Villcacona, BC XIII, 14) in the square where the Collasuyo road left the city (referred to as Hurin Haucaypata, BC XIII, 32). My picture of Huascar addressing the circle of *huacas* is based on GPF 261.

Huascar's full tirade against the *huacas* is given in Quechua in SPYP 272. For Huanca Auqui's retreat from Vilcas, SPYP 272f. For Huascar's appeal to Huanacauri, CV 31. The last reserves called up, according to SPYP 272, came from south of Collao and from the montaña, contradicting CV 31 who includes both Collas and Lupacas in the levy. I believe SPYP is more nearly correct here.

SECTION 9.

FOR HUANCA AUQUI's restoration to favor at court, SPYP 273. Cabello Valboa says the review was held in the valley of Sacsahuana, CV 31. Utcupampa, says SPYP 273. *Utcu* means either "cotton" or "hole," JLD 1061. For Quihuipay as meaning "the Bend," JLD 414. I am assuming from their prominence in the ensuing action that Titu Atauchi and Topa Atau represented the traditional dual command of the Inca regiments, but I have no specific statement to that effect.

For the part taken by the Hahua Incas in the array, SPYP 273. For the position of the Cañars in the order of march, SPYP 273. For Churuncana, BC XIII, 13. Churuncana may have been the top of present-day Huayna Corcor, but this assertion is not susceptible of proof. For the method of sacrificing children, BC XIII, 21. For the *capac hucha*, see Notes, Part II, sec. 12.

SECTION 10.

FOR THE SHRINE where the imperial weapons were kept, MMCB I, 22. Another possibility is that this chapel was a part of the *capac marca* (MMCB III, 5) in the palace. For *racay racay*, GHLQ 311; LDST 345. For the greeting *ña, ña*, GHLQ 546; 608. For *achallay*, GHLQ 12. For the events of the last battle, see BE 13. For *huay!* GHLQ 191. For *anay*, GHLQ 25, 426. For *Ticci camallipi*, LDST 276. For *anta rupay*, GHLQ 28, 417, 645 (see also 604). For the "starry night,"

GHLQ 83; LDST 93, 276. For *pacha yuracyan*, GHLQ 266, 269, 372.

SECTION 11.

FOR THE FINAL EVENTS of the war, BE 13. For the message from Atauhuallpa's forces and the Inca's debate over the terms of surrender, SG 65; CV 31. There is no evidence that the *coya* and her mother were present at the last council of the Cuzco Incas; I have assumed it as probable, inasmuch as they were the only legitimate rulers left in the city.

SECTION 12.

AGAIN FOR THE EVENTS of Quihuipay and the following terror, BE 13. For the insults offered to Huascar, SPYP 276; JLD 290. Rahua Ocllo's speech to her son, as I report it here, is a compendium of her remarks quoted in CV 31 and SG 65f. For the punishment of dropping a massive rock, *hihuaya* (GHLQ 158, 631) on the back, GPF 188, 313. *Subaya* in SPYP 257 is probably in error for this practice. For the Incas' invocation to the Creator on leaving Quihuipay, SG 66. For the slaughter of Urco Colla, the Cañars, and Chachapoyas, SG 67; CV 31. There is no statement in the sources that the major-domo of the Capac Ayllu *panaca* was killed, but it seems a justified assumption.

For Topa Inca's *huaoqui*, SG 54. For the 1,000 members of the *panaca* of Topa Inca, CV 31. For Topa Inca's *panaca* as being of the Huascar faction, SG 67. For the continuation of the cult of the Capac Ayllu *panaca*, SG 54. For the destruction of the *quipucamayocs* and the burning of their *quipus*, ISP-VC, 3–5. The nearly complete blank we draw on the events of the seven-year rule of Huascar is eloquent testimony to the thoroughness with which Atauhuallpa destroyed Huascar's personal historians. For Huascar's last statement, SG 67.

SECTION 13.

LADRÓN DE GUEVARA (in *Actos y trabajos del segundo Congreso Nacionál del Perú*, Vol. I, p. 249) believes the full name of such an establishment of women, as it existed in Tarma, was *acllana huarmi huasi*, "house of women for selection," with *acllana* a future participle; in the Quechua of the Incas, *acllana* would be *acllancca*. It is certainly quite possible that this name is proper for the provincial establishments from which selection of the women was to be made. There is no evidence to justify applying this name, however, to the Cuzco *aclla huasi*, in which *aclla* is an understood plural (more fully *acllacuna*) and means "those [already] selected."

The inner arrangements of the *acllahuasi* are described in GVCR IV, 2; GVHG II, 24; VEC 1523f. We can clearly see this split in the typical *acllahuasi* between the religiously devoted and the unassigned girls belonging to the emperor in FSP 63; BCP 55 (p. 81); ISP-HP 175; OV XLVI, 15. For its location in relationship to other *canchas*, VEC 1520. The statement that Huascar's women were kept in Pucamarca (SPYP 277) is probably a reference to Huascar's close connections with the Capac Ayllu *panaca*, and not to the situation of the *acllahuasi* as being a part of the Pucamarca complex. For the *cancha* of religious women between the *acllahuasi* proper and Coricancha, VEC 1521; it was probably referred to as Cusicancha, BC XIII, 13. I am under the impression that *cusicancha* is the Inca word for "harem"; see its appearance in the list of palace areas, GPF 338.

The plaza of Choqquepampa ("the Field of Gold," BC XIII, 13) is referred to also as Intipampa, GVCR VII, 9. For the *Intip huarmi* as *pallas*, MM-DN 60. For the name *Intip huarmi*, FS 34. For the figure of 3,000 *acllas*, BVP 169. For the delivery of the provincial *acllas* to Cuzco every February, PO: Fund. 91. This one is the same month as when tribute was brought in for storage. PO: Fund. 95. It is also the same month as the annual display of nubile girls, ARG I, 24. For a description of the mother superior role, BC XIII, 37. For the marriage rites of the *mamaconas* assigned as wives of Inti, BC XIII, 37. The distinction between *acllas* and *Intip huarmi* is clear, ISP-HP 175; OV XLVI, 15; FSP 63; BCP 55. For Inti's harem broken up into "wives," *Intip huarmi*, and "concubines," *Intip chinan*, BLCL 7; BVP 167–70.

There is no doubt that some, at least, of the *acllas* were used for general sexual purposes and for entertainment, GHV 233; ISP-HP 175; OV XLVI, 15; MMCB III, 36; BCP 55; GPF 299f. For the term *taqui aclla*, MMCB III, 39. For *sayapayak*, GHLQ 324; CV 19. For the *uiñachicoc acllas*, GPF 300; MMCB III, 40. For the classifications of red, white, and fair, SPYP 224; ARGCS I, 18; MMCB III, 38; CV 19; GPF 192, 253; LBVA I, 318; II, 157, 242. For the *wayruro* fruit, JLD 1133; EQD 10; RGH 138; BC VI, 91 (whether there is any connection here with the game of *huayru*, GHLQ 196, I do not know). For the execution of a delinquent *aclla*, GPF 308; ADS 32f. For Paullo's seduction of one of Huascar's women, SG 67.

PART V

SECTION 1.

THE REMARKS made in this section on the Quechua language are impressionistic only—because I lack a true linguistic competence. Essays on the Quechua language can be found in BC XIV, 1; GHLQ (Prólogo); GVCR (Advertencias); E. M. Middendorf, *La Lengua Keshua* in *Las Lenguas Aborígenes del Perú*, Lima, 1959. Its classification is discussed by J. A. Mason in HSAI VI, 196–200. For the most recent material on the history of Quechua dialects, see G. J. Parker, *La Clasificación genética de los dialectos quechuas*, in *Revista del Museo Nacional*, Lima, 1965. For the courtly dialect of Quechua, BC XII, 3; RGI II, 7. The identification of *topa simi* with the courtly dialect is mine; there is no textual support for it.

For *camac* and *camay*, GHLQ 47. For *churak* and *churay*, GHLQ 122. For *huayra huayralla*, GHLQ 675. For a "wind-like traveler," GHLQ 195. For different words for washing, LDST 157. For *ñuñu*, GHLQ 561; JLD 709; LDST 157, 164, 184, 222, 328. For *pacha*, JLD 719f.; GHLQ 268f.; EQD 46. For *cocha*, JLD 457; GHLQ 64. For *simi*, GHLQ 57, 326–28, 399, 564, 630, 643. For *ñaui*, JLD 705; GHLQ 528, 607f. Lack of preciseness can be seen also in modern Quechua—note the words which today can be translated as "plateau," *kata*, *puna*, *pata*, *urku*, *wayku*, *sallca* (Ayacucho dialect), all of which words we would prefer to keep for more specific meanings, EQD 100.

For "bad," GHLQ 578. For "vast," GHLQ 347f., 553. For "cruel," GHLQ 557.

For the category designations derived from specifics, GHLQ 260, 294, 599. True category words, such as those for "fish" and "birds," did of course exist, GHLQ 408. *Mallqui* is "fruit tree" or a tree artificially planted, GHLQ 224. *Hachha* is a wild tree of the forest, GHLQ 143, 415f. For *apup simin*, GHLQ 564; BE XI, 4; Middendorf, *op. cit.*, 35. For *hatun simi*, GHLQ 132. For *topa simi*, GHLQ 347. For the terms for elegance in speaking, GHLQ 63, 95, 393, 431, 462f., 498, 635. For the styles of greeting, GDST 153f. For *mirccasimicta rimac*, GHLQ 242. For other terms referring to common or vulgar ways of talking, GHLQ 93, 132, 233. For *chiwiwiwiñichiy*, GHLQ 115. For *runachay*, GHLQ 492. For *michiy runacta*, GHLQ 237.

On personal names, GDST 156f.; BV XIV, 6. One of the real hazards of writing Inca history is the temptation to double an event; this inclination is the result of the Inca system of naming boys after uncles or grandfathers. For the three names of an Inca, RZ III, 13; CM 87; BLCL 5. For the naming of a newborn child for some event or situation at the time, GVHG II, 13. *Yupanqui* certainly appears to be second person singular present indicative of *yupay*—if so, it must mean "You are esteemed, you count for something." The noun *yupa* means "that which or he who counts as . . .," GHLQ 371f. For instance, *apu yupa* means "a person of authority" or "he who counts as a leader," GHLQ 31; LBVA I, 146; II, 397.

Both JB 17 and MMCB I, 11 affirm that Yupanqui was the name of the Inca family descended from Manco Capac. The translation of the word which the Spaniards spelled *lloque* is uncertain; it can mean "dagger" (LDST 311), "sharp" (JLD 589), a "mountain mass" (SPYP 231), "a tree whose hard wood was used for making spears" (GHLQ 216), or, finally, the direction "left" or "left-hand" (GHLQ 215). For *titu* as meaning "liberal," GHLQ 344; GVCR V, 12. *Roca* may mean "finger," EQD 53; JLD 852. More probably it meant "magnanimous," RGH 317. For the taking by an Inca boy of the

name of the great person when he served as a page, PPR 267. For
Titu Cusi Huallpa as the knight's name of Yahuar Huacac (SG 23) and
of Huayna Capac, SG 56.

Choque can be translated as "gold," "parakeet," or "dancer," JLD
135; RGH 90. It was probably an Aymara word originally and seems
to have had the derived sense of "darling," LBVA II, 89. For *wipay*
as meaning "joy," JLD 1159. The word written *tocto* by the Spaniards
had a variety of meanings—"shoot, sprout" (LDST 62, 364); "flower"
(in general) and "maize flower" (in particular), RGH 365; feathers
used in the homage ceremony (BC XIII, 36); a bird with white feathers (CM 81); and "bee," or "honey," TRA 173. Each of these words
may have been a unique term and uniquely pronounced. This possibility can be seen from RGH 365, 375. For additional remarks on
tocto, see Notes, Part II, sec. 13.

SECTION 2.

THIS SECTION RESTS in great part on use of the early dictionaries. I
am aware that the friar's notions of the Christian concept of man must
be present in the Quechua words on which I have selected to build
my interpretation. Because the material which I have dug out, however,
is quite consistent with what I know or imply from other sources,
I have used it freely and without attempting a rigorous exegesis of
the Christian contamination—for which scrutiny indeed I am not
equipped. It is obvious, for instance, that the distinction between "inner"
and "outer" man (GHLQ 553) is one made by the friars. For an
essay on the Inca concept of man, GVCR II, 7. For *causay*, "life" or
"sustenance," GHLQ 51f.; LDST 226.

For the fact that "trees" constitute a species or *ayllu*, GHLQ 39.
For the subjects of the empire as belonging to a *hatun ayllu*, GHLQ
155. For *llamacayñin*, GHLQ 599. For all animals as classed in the
category *tahuachaquiyoccuna* "those who are four-footed," GHLQ
208. The brutal nature of animals can be seen not only in their four-
footedness but in their lack of *sonco*, GHLQ 438. *Sonco* means heart,
stomach, reason, intelligence, ability, skill, and soul. For the *uparuna*,

GHLQ 356. "Wilderness people," *purumruna*, lived without kings or laws (GHLQ 143, 428); they were thus scarcely human. They were "fools and dolts," *caeca*, LDST 58, 62f., 123; GHLQ 139.

For *paccariy*, GHLQ 266. With the same meaning, *pacarinin*, LDST 174; GHLQ 599. For *pacarisca*, GHLQ 557, 599. For *yuyay, yuyana*, and *yuyayruna*, GHLQ 372 f., 408; LDST 303. Today *yuyay* means "conscience," EQD 29. For *allpa camasca*, GVCR II, 7. For the need to retain the parts of one's earthly body, GVCR II, 7; FSP 61; BVP 148; OV XLVI, 17. For a person's "stature," GHLQ 325. *Tiascancay* (derived from *tiay*, "to sit; to exist in oneself") appears to be a synonym of *samay*, GHLQ 627. For *samay*, GHLQ 77, 401, 659; LDST 35, 40, 133, 246. For *soncoyoc*, GHLQ 408.

In the year 1532 it was still believed by the Incas that Huayna Capac would return to his mummy to reinstitute his rule, GBH 184. For *mana huañukcay*, GHLQ 553. For the return of the dead, FSP 61; BVP 148. For concepts of the afterlife, BC XIII, 3; LTOP 127; CM 79; FS 32; ACCM II, 12; CL 3; AEI 7. For the *illapas*, BLCL 25; GVCR I, 22; II, 8; IDI XXI, 209; CL 30. The early friars gave the word *hucha* its Christian connotation. That it meant "evil" can be seen from the word *huchacay*, GHLQ 578, where it is synonymous with *mana allicuy*, the opposite of goodness. For *huchallicuy*, GHLQ 200, 620. My statement about the overtones of the word rests upon the fact that the two entirely unrelated nouns, *cama* and *hucha*, both carry not only the meaning of "evil" but also of "business, matter, affair," GHLQ 600. For calamities as the result of *hucha*, MMCB III, 61; FSP 33, 62; BC XIII, 24; PO: Error. 5. Confession was *ichuco*, CM 103. The statement that the Incas did not confess at all (ILPO 195; FS 33) confutes BC XIII, 24; JA V, 25; BVP 159; CM 23; PO: Error. 5, where the opposite view is maintained. For the Huaro priests, CM 23. For "the ends of the earth," GHLQ 53, 64, 139f., 440.

SECTION 3.

FOR THE SLAUGHTER of retainers in Cuzcoquiti, GVCR IX, 39. For Quizquiz' rule of terror in Cuzco, BC XII, 19; FS 335; PPR 243.

For Quizquiz' use of the litter, OV XLVI, 9. For the orders to bring Huascar north, SG 68. I make the assumption that Quizquiz had his headquarters in the fortress. For the angels of Viracocha as *huaminca*, BVP 138.

For the word *pururauca*, JLD 816; GHLQ 298 (the common name in Quechua for these stones thrown down at a besieging army was *cumpa*, GHLQ 54, 531). The meaning of the word *pururauca* is debatable. If *purur* is the same as *puru*, then the word would mean literally "feather warriors," perhaps with reference to their lightness or agility. For the story of Pachacuti and the *pururaucas*, BC XII, 10; XIII, 8; JA VI, 21; PO: Fund. 54f. For the bringing of many of the *pururaucas* into Cuzco, BC XIII, 15f. The *pururaucas* were one of the bases of Inca power, PO: 1. 50.

For the worship of the Spaniards as Viracochas, GVHG I, 32. For the belief held in Cuzco that the Spaniards were Viracochas, PO: Inf. 154; CLTP May 1957, p. 259. On the Allcaviza matter, BE. The best accounts of Moguer and Bueno in Cuzco are in CLTP May 1957, pp. 263, 266; RGI I, 80; CA 254; AZH II, 6; FJ 343. For the two Spaniards in the Tumipampa *panaca*, CA 256–58. The question of whether there was a third Spaniard in Cuzco at this time is still open. There is a statement by Porras Barrenechea (*Nuevas estudios sobre el Inca Garcilaso de la Vega*, Lima, 1955, p 183) mentioning the existence in the Archives of the Indies of an account by Martín Bueno who says he was one of "three" who first saw Cuzco. When this document is published, it should settle the matter. That they arrived in May is evident from FJ 343.

Section 4.

FOR THE THREADING of Huascar's shoulders, PPR 231. The list of those killed at Antamarca is made up from BC XII, 19; CV 31. For Huascar's dying curse as predicting the Spaniards would soon kill Atauhuallpa, GHV 230.

Section 5.

FOR RUMIÑAUI'S PRESENCE at the battle of Cotapampa, CV 31. He is said to have been a trusted and intimate councilor of Atauhuallpa, and before that period he was Huayna Capac's chamberlain, BSC I, 6f. For material on his later career, GHV 234f.; OV XLVI 17, 19; AZH II, 5, 8f.; VRQ II, 111f., 120f.; MM II, 14. For the mountain's bearing his name, VRQ I, 9. For the sources on Topa Huallpa, VRQ II, 22, 107; PPR 252, 345; BC XII, 20; FJ 345; CA 274; ISP-VC 32. For the sources on Challco Chima, CA 266, 268; PPR 241, 248, 252–62; VRQ II, 12, 22; OV XLVI, 20; ISP-VC 32f.; Miguel Estete quoted in FJ 338–43. *Challcochima* as the name of a gambling game is quite erroneously given in GPF 243. It is an error for *cullu chuncana*, GHLQ 71.

For Yucra Huallpa and Quizquiz at Vilcaconga, ISP-VC 33; PPR 262f. For Manco Inca's meeting the Spaniards near the Apurimac, TCYI 23f.; CMS 156. The treaty which Titu Atauchi made with Francisco de Chaves had certainly a quasi legality, for its terms were discussed by Francisco Pizarro, and while the Spaniards in no sense formally ratified them, they did not openly denounce them. The party of Manco Inca believed the treaty was valid. See GVHG II, 5–7, 9, 22f. Note that this Titu Atauchi is not the man of the same name who was one of Huascar's councilors. He is undoubtedly the Don Alonso Titu Atauchi Inca who in 1544 succeeded in having his many children legitimized, SMN 306–308. It is known that Quizquiz was near Anta when the Spaniards burned Challco Chima, SPYP 280. For his death, PPR 262. Challco Chima is said to have been a Quito Indian, CA 268; VRQ II, 12.

Quizquiz is called a son of Huayna Capac in IDI XXI, 178, and a nephew, OV XLVI, 20. The name Quizquiz may be that of a little bird, GHLQ 310 (if related to *quisquisca*, LDST 135?), but more probably means "locust," BC IX, 8. I do not understand the statement in CA 256 that the name Quizquiz means "barber"; the word for barber is *rutuy camayoc*, GHLQ 323; LDST 56. For material on Quizquiz, OV XLVI, 17, 20; GHV 233, 236; VRQ II, 71, 127; PPR 262–64, 278; AZH II, 12; CV 31. For Huaypallca and the murder of Quizquiz, GVHG II, 14, 18. For the entry of the Spaniards and the smoke signals, SPYP 280; GHV 233; GBH 184; BCP 86.

SECTION 6.

FOR THE DATE of the Spanish entry into Cuzco, BCP 86; FMA 78. The figure of four months comes also from BCP 86. For the installation of Manco Inca as emperor, CL 11. For the date of the founding, NCC 96, 98; FEC 10f. The date is wrongly given in AC 123 as that of the Spaniards' entry. October is given as the month of the founding in CLPP 92, but this reference is probably to the *cabildo* of October 29 when the decision was taken concerning the size and assignment of the city lots, FMA 83; FEC 35f. For the ceremony wherein Pizarro founded the *cabildo*, FEC 11. The city was perhaps named Santiago del Cuzco, as asserted in GPF 1042. It was at least dedicated to that saint, GVHG II, 25.

For the Pachacutean concept of the city as a "lion-body," JB 17 ("lion-city," SG 53). For the size of the lots, FEC 36, 45f.; FMA 83. The only record of the first assignments is in FEC 36–45, but this information is not entirely trustworthy. Hernando Pizarro (at the time in Spain) received no lots at this time but later resided in Amaru Cancha, probably in De Soto's original allotment, GVCR VII, 10; GVHG V, 9; PPR 317; RSC 111. The original location to be used by the *cabildo* itself was on the square between the *acllahuasi* and Amaru Cancha, NCC 99. After Gonzalo Pizarro's execution, his townsite (Coracora) was assigned to the *cabildo*, BC XIII, 13. The site of the church (later cathedral) was subsequently moved to a site on the line of the Sapi between Casana and Amaru Cancha but then in 1540 returned to the original site, NCC 122f., 145, 161.

For the removal of Viracocha's statue, BVP 144. The best account of Manco Inca's career is G. Kubler: "A Peruvian Chief of State: Manco Inca," *Hispanic American Historic Review*, Vol. 24, 1944. For Manco Inca's age as sixteen years when he met Pizarro (CMS 156); all sources agree, however, that he was born during his father's residence in Callao (BC XIII, 19; CLPP 105), which could not have been later than 1511 or 1512, thus making Manco Inca twenty or twenty-one at the time of his coronation. His mother's name is given as Sihui Chimpu Rontocay in SPYP 260 but as simply Runtu in VRQ II, 19, 62f.; DF 5.

For Manco Inca's flight into the Andes of Hualla, ISP-VC 27. For Paullu's flight to Titicaca, ISP-VC 27, 33. His mother was Añas Collque, ISP-VC 23f., 32; VEC 1589. For his marriage to his sister, VEC, 1589, 1591; ARG I, 31; ISP-VC 45; SG 67. For Paullu's later career, ISP-VC 33–35, 45–47.

For the two brothers killed by Manco Inca, PPR 274. (BC XII, 20, however, has Atoc Supa alive and trusted by Manco Inca, even on his deathbed. This assertion is a total contradiction.) Undoubtedly the other brother was Pascac who is referred to in TCYI 59f., 77. For Manco Inca's attempts to capture Quizquiz, TCYI 25–28. For Paullu in the south with Almagro, ISP-VC 34f.; NCC 104. The famous golden cable, the *muru urco*, bedeviled the Spaniards for many years into fruitless treasure hunts. For its use in Inca cult, GVCR IX, 1; CL 7, 49; CM 80; BC XIII, 26. For rumors of its hiding place, ACCM I, 17 (sequel); MMCB I, 13.

For burning Indians in their houses, GPF 396. For Manco Inca's imprisonment, NCC 105. For Marca Chimpu, CMS 162f.; ABC 82; BC XII, 20 (where she is identified as the future mother of a Villacastín). For the tales of Spanish atrocities against Manco Inca, BCP 217; OV XLVI, 21; TCYI 54ff. For Cori Ocllo as the name of Manco's *coya*, TCYI 31, 89.

SECTION 7.

FOR THE TERM *auccay intuy*, "the circle of war" or "siege," GHLQ 38. Vilauma is said in ISP-VC 35 to have accompanied Paullu and Almagro south. He early escaped from that expedition, for we find him in Cuzco for the beginning of the siege. His flight from the expedition is mentioned in VEC 1592. Our sources agree that he was the effective leader of the uprising, ISP-VC 52; AZH III, 1. I have with hesitation accepted the fact of his mission to Chinchaysuyo (TCYI 62); TCYI is an unreliable source but yet essential for the period. For other remarks on Vilauma, see Notes, Part II, sec. 13. My statement that Inca governors were being appointed under Manco Inca is based on presence of a certain Cayo Topa who was governing the province of Chachapoyas at the time of the rebellion, RGI IV, p. xiiiff. The Chachapoyas in part supported the Spanish, RGI IV, p. xv. For the Cañars who supported the Spanish in Cuzco, PPR 291.

For the charge of *auca* against Inca defectors, BLCL 21. For the Inca magnates who went over to the Spaniards, TCYI 70; ISP-VC 36–42. For Manco Inca's release and actions in the Yucay valley, NCC 105f.; TCYI 62–65; ISP-VC 36–40. The date of the opening of the attack (May 3) is from ISP 36–42. Kubler, *op. cit.*, gives the date as April 18. For *tutapacuspa auccaycuy*, GHLQ 38, 349. The number of besieging Indians around Cuzco was surely not 200,000, as reported in PPR 289; SMN 342, I have arbitrarily cut the figure in half. The figures for the Spanish forces are quite accurate: 200 whites in OV XLVI, 21 and 80 horses. Note that PPR 291 gives the number of Cañars with the Spaniards in Cuzco as 50 or 60. Almost surely there were more.

I have assumed (following GBH 189; GHV 239; AZH III, 5, 7) that it was Tisoc Yupanqui who replaced the fallen commander in the siege of Lima—thus identifying the fallen commander as Quiso Yupanqui, TCYI 62; GPF 392; FMA 91. We know that Tisoc was alive after the collapse of the siege, BCP 214; TCYI 90. Garcilaso insists that Tizo is really Titu, GVHG II, 28. We know that Manco Inca sent a certain Huallpa Roca to Lima during the siege (PPR 301), but we also know this person as one who defected to the Spaniards, ISP-VC 36–42. The reader should be warned that my reconstruction of the events concerning Tisoc, Quiso Yupanqui, and Huallpa Roca rests on most uncertain ground; our sources are poor, contradictory, and scattered. For the tale of the *asarpay* garroted by Doña Inez, PPR 345f.

For the orderliness of the Inca siege army, ISP-VC 36–42. For one of the missed opportunities, TCYI 66. For the story of the storming of Intihuasi, PPR 291–97. The figure of 15,000 inside the fortress comes from SMN 342f. The most accurate pictorial representations of the siege are JADG, Fig. 6; Pal Keleman, *Baroque and Rococo in Latin America*, 1951, New York, Plate 149b. For the cutting of the Chincheros aquaduct supplying Cuzco, GVHG II, 27. Quotation on Mary from BSC I, 7.

Accounts of the Miracle of the Matriz are many, each with different details, ACCM I, 17 (second one); AC 113f., 168; GSC III, 63; PPR 301; JADG 7; GVHG II, 25. For the texts on the church of the Triunfo today which relate to the miracles, HV 46f. In the Miracle of the Matriz, one of the basic confusions is the identification of the *sunturhuasi* with *Quishuarcancha*. For the date of May 21, AC 168. For Santiago's hurling thunderbolts, ACCM I, 17 (second); GVHG II, 24. For the strengthening of Ollantaytambo, TCYI 73f. For Manco Inca's being in Ollantaytambo more than two years, ISP-VC 35.

For the quotation on the four years of Spanish depredations, PO: Fund. 103. For Contisuyo in rebellion for five additional years, ISP-VC 50–52. For the capture of Vilauma in Contisuyo, BCP 233. For over 20,000 deaths in the siege of Cuzco, BCP 215. For the famine in Peru, ISP-VC 52. For the assumption of power by the *curacas*, FS 58. For the coat of arms of the city of Cuzco, NCC 121, 133f.; RGEP 162; SMN 342f.

Section 8.

For Manco Inca's initial possession of Huanacauri and mummies, TCYI 82. The mummies however could not have been those of the great Inca emperors. For Cusi Rimachi, the captain general, said to be Manco Inca's brother, BCP 233; TCYI 90. For the fruitless Spanish attack on Ollantaytambo, PPR 306. For the battles around Pachar, TCYI 75. For Paullo's taking the fringe, BC XII, 20; VEC 1592.

The date of Manco Inca's retirement into the montaña is given as thirty-four years before the death of Tupac Amaru (i.e., 1538), BC XII, 20. We know that relatively few followed Manco Inca into the Andes, BCP 215. The number of fighting men is put at 3,000 by ISP-VC 45, and at 10,000 by OV XLVI, 9. For Manco Inca's raids on the Jauja area, TCYI 86–88. The list of montaña provinces from which Manco Inca drew tribute (given in MGP II, 18) is of interest but at present not susceptible of proof, although ACCM IV, 2 says his power extended six hundred miles to the east. For the expedition under Gonzalo Pizarro, TCYI 82f., 88–91; ISP-VC 42–45; OV XLVII, 9; BCP 233.

The attempted rape of Cori Ocllo took place in Pampaconac (TCYI 90); if this place is to be connected with the Pampacahuana River which enters the Urubamba at Quenti (just above Torontoy), this link would make it absolutely certain that the Spaniards knew the route to Machu Picchu and perhaps had even passed that way. Quotation from CL 22. For Santillán's estimate of the destruction of three-fourths of the Indian population, FS 53 (see also 60). For the date of Santillán's quotation, CP 258.

SECTION 9.

FOR QUOTATION from Valverde, BCP 215. It was reported that Paullu secreted Huanacauri at Collcampata (BC XIII, 15), but Manco Inca seems to have had it with him in the montaña. What Paullo may have had was a substitute *huaca*. For Paullu's claim in 1539 to be emperor after Manco Inca, BCP 215. Paullu and his family were already studying to be Christians at the end of November, 1542; see BCP 324. One of the Incas who became a Christian at this time along with his many children was Alonso Titu Atauchi Inca, undoubtedly the author of the disregarded treaty, SMN 306–308. The Incas continued the *huarachicoy* up to around 1553; see SG 12. For the invention of substitute rites, PO: Fund. 200.

For Paullu Inca's coat of arms, SMN 300, 381, BC XII, 20. For the festival for a ruler who has been dead a year, VEC 1573; PPR 254f. For the congregation of Inca warriors at the scene of Paullo's death, CMS 158f. For his rites at the end of the year, CL 32. Mary's first church was called Nuestra Señora del Rosario, BCP 215. For the changes in site up to 1552 when the present location was finally settled on, NCC 122f., 145. For the early history of the cathedral, HV 14–16. For the fortress as the quarry for the building of the cathedral, NCC 193, 196. It was Polo de Ondegardo who ordered the digging up of the sand in Haucaypata, PO: Fund. 110f.

For the early Spanish remodeling of the Cusipata area, see the important article by E. Harth-Terré, "Los Ultimos Canteros Incaicos," in *Actos y Trabajos del II Congreso Nacional de Historia del Peru*,

Vol. II, Lima, 1962. For oxen plowing in 1550 the lands where San Francisco is today, NCC 156. For the rubbish in the bed of the Huatanay, CL 35. Zárate describes the Spaniards as still living in only slightly altered Inca buildings at the time he left Cuzco in 1545; see AZH I, 9. Certainly by 1558 (the date of Sayri Tupac's entry into Cuzco) most of Inca Cuzco was unrecognizable, GVHG VIII, 11. For the early Spanish residences I have used DSB 63; in this source De Sartiges apparently is reporting simply local information at a very late date in Cuzco, and therefore the information cannot be properly checked. I have used it, however, because it in no place contradicts the little firm information we do have. Even in Cieza's day (1550) most of the Intihuasi had been destroyed, CLPP 92.

For the use of Cañars and Chachapoyas as police to keep the Incas of Cuzco submissive, RGEP 141; CL 22; RGI II, Appendix p. 10. For the hiding and later destruction of the stone statue of Viracocha, BVP 144. The fact that Paullu's Christian sons were assigned to the Tumipampa *panaca* (SG 62) proves that the institution continued to have a certain meaning. For the relegation of most of the Incas to Cayaocachi (Belém), SG 11. For the making of Paullu's *huaoqui*, BC XII, 20. For the quotation on the Incas as unprovided for, BCP 214. For their status in 1539 as virtually slavery, BCP 215. For the freedom from tribute of the Incas and the continued residence of a few in Cuzco, ILPO 147.

For Gonzalo Pizarro's burning of the mummy of Viracocha Inca, BC XII, 11. For the worship of the ashes of Topa Inca's mummy, SG 54. For the finding of the mummies, VEC 1512; JA V, 6; BC XII, 4, 11. For the finding of Huayna Capac's mummy, BC XII, 17; SG 62. For Pachacuti's mummy and the Chanca *huaca*, PO: Fund. 97. The mummies burned later by Toledo were those of the Vilcabamba Incas, ARGCS I, 22. For removal to Hospital of St. Andrew, ACCM I, 15. As late as 1610, Cobo saw a *purucaya* procession of the eleven *panacas*, BC XII, 2. For *cipi pacha*, GHLG 83. For *llipiyak*, GHLQ 214. For the reduction of the Cuzco Indians into four parishes, NCC 192, 194; CP 267. For the bastard sons of *ñustas* and *pallas* considered to be Incas with caste, GVHG I, 40; GVCR IX, 40.

SECTION 10.

THE IMPORTANT EVENTS of the latter part of the reign of Titu Cusi Yupanqui and that of Tupac Amaru—from the Spanish point of view—are summed up in A. F. Zimmerman, *Francisco de Toledo, Fifth Viceroy of Peru, 1569–1581*, Caldwell, Idaho, 1938, chap. V. The work, however, is sketchy and careless with the facts and should be used only as a general survey. Much more authoritative is Ruben Vargas Ugarte, *Historia del Peru*, Vol. I, 1949, Lima, chap. XII. An account adds to the list of Manco Inca's sons another who was to die in Lima, Don Felipe Huallpa Titu, ISP-VC 48, but it is probably a confused reduplication of Titu Cusi Yupanqui, see MMCB II, 16.

For Cusi Huarcay as only two years old at her father's death, ISP-VC 23. Paullu died as he was attempting to entice Sayri Topa out of the Vilcabamba country, BC XII, 21. Sayri Topa was baptized in October, 1558, see NCC 190. Sayri Topa is said to have died thirty days after his Christian wedding, ISP-VC 48. Garcilaso says three years, GVHG VIII, 11. For the marriage, MMCB II, 16. For Sayri's daughter, GVHG VIII, 20.

For the conversion of Titu Cusi Yupanqui to Christianity, NCC 206. The description of Titu Cusi Yupanqui is from *Relación de don Rodriguez de Figueroa*, 102f. For the name of the *coya*, NCC 206; ACCM IV, 2–6. Fray Diego Ortiz' story is told in ACCM IV, 2–6. For the dance sickness, CM 96–103; see also J. H. Rowe, "The Incas Under Spanish Colonial Institutions," *Hispanic American Historical Review*, XXXVII, #2 (May, 1957). I have no idea what the *taqui oncoy* or "dance sickness" was. It was one of the more common ailments known to the Incas (GPF 280) and was expelled from their presence in the Situa, GPF 253. It was also called the "corn disease," *sara oncoy*, PO: Fund. 196. The great mountain *huacas* of the Pariacaca range were involved in the heavenly warfare, MP 187f. For *lloclla unu pachacuti*, GHLG 270.

SECTION 11.

A SUMMARY ACCOUNT of the murder of Anaya, Toledo's envoy, is in BC XII, 21. For the offer of the Cañars to track down Tupac Amaru,

435

NCC 214. For their undying enmity toward Incas, GVHG II, 25; VIII 1. For García de Loyola's marriage to Doña Beatriz Clara Coya, the legitimate daughter of Sayri Topa, BCXII, 21; ISP-VC 48. She was the wife of Don Felipe Quispi Titu and was captured in Arbieto's raid, GOR 72f. The mummies burned were those of Manco Inca and Titu Cusi Yupanqui, ARGCS I, 22.

The execution of Tupac Amaru is an event famous in Peruvian history, and there are, consequently, several reports on it. They differ in some details but in general agree remarkably. My account uses all of them. They are GVHG VIII, 19; BC XII, 21; ACCM IV, 8; BOD; GOR; Antonio de Vega: an unedited history of the Colegio del Cusco quoted in Vargas Ugarte; *Historia del Peru*, I, 256–58, 262. Tupac Amaru's baptismal name is given as Pablo in GOR which I consider definitive for this information. Tupac Amaru may well have been buried in the Dominican monastery in Cuzco. There apparently was a grave so marked (see Plan #3 in R. P. Zárate, *El Cusco y sus monumentos*, 2d ed., Lima, 1940), although there is no trace of it at present. There is a curious statement in GVHG VIII, 11 that Manco Inca was buried in San Domingo.

I take the fact of the assignment of Collcampata to the Cañars from Vargas Ugarte, *op. cit.*, but I have not identified his source for the statement. The figure of thirty-six Capac Incas exiled from Cuzco is given in NCC 218f. See also Vargas Ugarte, *op. cit.*, 263 for these decisions of Toledo. For the inclusion of Tupac Amaru's children among the exiles, NCC 218f. Included in the group of exiles were Don Felipe Quispi Titu, the eighteen-year-old son of Titu Cusi Yupanqui who had been taken in Arbieto's foray; while he was exiled his young Inca wife, Doña Beatriz Coya, was given to Loyola, GOR 72f.

For the exile of most of the mestizos of Cuzco, GVHG VIII, 17. The number of male Capac Incas exiled was thirty-six, according to GVHG VIII, 18. One of the exiles was a certain Titu Atauchi Inca, a person of high standing. After two years in Lima, his sentence being reversed, he returned to Cuzco where he shortly died of fevers. He was reputed to be the last of the Capac Incas, GOR 72f.; MMCB II, 15.

436

He may have been a son of that Titu Atauchi who conceived the treaty between Manco Inca and Pizarro, VMP 34; GVHG II, 23.

Morúa (MMCB II, 15) lists as one of the exiles Don Carlos Inca; he probably meant the son of Paullo. Don Carlos was apparently removed partly to obtain the three encomiendas he still held, GOR 72f. But in any case these last notices are very uncertain, as witness the reference in VEC 1589 to a "legitimate" son of Huayna Capac named Titu Inca Yupanqui still living in 1594. By that time Inca legitimacy was a thing of the past. For the 567 bastard members of the *panacas* in 1603, see GVCR IX, 40. For the end of Paullo's line, GVHG VIII, 18; GVCR IX, 40. For charges of conspiracy against mestizos, GVHG VIII, 17.

Index

438

Huayna Corcor (mountain): 420
Huayna Pallca: 124
Huayna Pari: 194
Huayna Picchu: 171
Huayñu: 185, 409
Huaypallca: 286
Huaypar: 391
Huaypu, Lake: 110
Huayrancallay: 221, 416
Huayru: 259, 423
Hucha: 271–72, 426
Hucha camayoc: 201, 218
Huchallicuy: 272
Huchayachac: 414
Huilcarpay: 18
Huipay: 389
Huitcos: 299, 311
Hummingbird: 190
Huncolpi: 379
Hunu: 3; *see* council
Hurin Haucaypata: 420
Hurinchacan: 89
Hurtado de Arbieto, Martín: 340

Ichu: 88, 191, 202, 245, 296, 329
Ichuco: 426
Ichupampa: 109, 249
Ichuri: 88
Idol: *see villca*
Illacamarca: 216–17
Illapa: 42–43, 192, 271, 326
Illapa: *see* Chuqui Illa and God of Storm
Illapa Cancha: 96
Illegitimacy: 182
Illescas: 124, 281–82, 339
Imagination: 270
Immortality: 50, 271
Iñaca: 29
Iñaca Panaca: 39, 47, 79, 96, 99, 106, 121, 138, 193, 199, 234
Incas: basic characteristics, ix, 6–7, 17–18, 30–31, 52, 111–13, 176, 180, 187, 206, 237, 256, 267–68, 292; origin and descent, 4–6, 29, 31, 35–37, 205–206; early history, 5, 20, 32–33, 36;

weakening, 6, 58, 231, 277; *huacas* of, 18, 83, 129, 144, 151, 330–31 *(see also* Huanacauri [*huaca*]); as warriors, 30, 226–30; legitimacy 31, 153; names 31, 189, 226, 266, 268–69, 424–25; relationship with Cuzco, 31, 150–51, 302; religion, 33, 145, 152, 155, 159, 312; clientage, 34; *pacarina,* 35–36, 98, 113, 384; *ayllus,* 36–37, 201, 251, 412; factions, 51, 276–77, 283–84; moieties, 62, 137–138, 201, 218, 324, 337 *(see also* moiety); as hydraulic engineers, 88–89; intellectual life, 112–17; persecute foreign *huacas,* 159, 241, 300; prayers, 197–98, 252, 272; in Ecuador, 230–31, 235; defeat and degeneration, 237, 248–51, 192–93, 313; dialect, 263; religion under Spaniards, 284, 289, 303–304, 308, 316–17; besiege Cuzco, 293–97; end under Spaniards, 307–309, 318–19; see also *huaccha concha, palla, ñusta,* Capac Incas, *and* Hahua Incas
Inca Ayllu: 129, 206
Inca Pascac: 123
Inca Roca (emperor): 38, 40, 42–43, 51, 74, 89, 138, 179, 308, 334
Inca Roca (brother of Huascar): 100, 123, 233, 243, 279
Inca Yupanqui: 364
Incap ranti: 213
Incap michuscan runa: 97; *see also mitmacs*
Initiation rites: 19, 34, 91–92, 128, 243, 335; *see also huarachicoy and quicuchicoy*
Inquil: 268
Inquil Topa: 123
Inti: 29, 58–59, 69, 74, 78, 83, 93–94, 129, 132, 143, 154–55, 199, 233, 257, 315–16, 330, 340; *see also* Punchao
Inti Huasi: 12, 89, 97, 221–25, 246, 249–50, 252, 256, 274, 291, 294–95, 297–98, 306
Inti Illapa: 51, 78, 96, 120, 199, 375

Titu Atauchi Inca (last of the Capac
 Incas): 436
Titu Conti Mayta: 100
Titu Cusi Yupanqui: 301, 309–11,
 313–16
Toasts: 133, 184, 326, 332; see also
 drinking
Tocapu: 46, 137, 162, 335
Tocay Capac: 19, 25
Tocto: 389–90, 425
Tocto Coca: 121
Tocto Usica: 125, 269, 288
Toledo, Francisco de: 313–15, 317
Tomay: 268
Tomay Rimac: 247
Tomb: 326
Tonapa Viracocha: 401
Topa: 268, 400
Topa Atau: 100, 123, 233, 243–44, 248,
 279
Topa Atauchi: 233
Topa Cusi Huallpa: see Huascar
Topa Huallpa Inca: 121, 125, 282–83
Topa Inca: 44, 51, 75, 78, 143, 165–66,
 171–72, 254, 276, 308, 341
Topa simi: 263, 266
Topa yauri: 45, 246, 326
Topa Yupanqui: 214
Topo: 337
Torontoy: 168
Torture: 254
Totocachi: see San Blas
Totora: 21
Towers: 222–23
Traitors: 293
Treaty of Titu Atauchi: 284–85, 287,
 293
Tribute: 53, 133–34, 256, 258
Trinity: 199
Triunfo (church): 75, 296, 303–304,
 317, 433; see also cathedral
Triunfo (street): 79
Trumpet: 213, 328
Truth: 113–14
Tullu river: 86, 89, 215

Tumi: 339
Tumibamba: 213, 232, 235–36
Tumibamba Panaca: 39, 47, 99–100, 152,
 154, 165–66, 278, 308, 434
Tupac Amaru: 309, 314–18, 340
Tupu: 183, 204, 335
Turkey: 371
Tusuy: 409
Tutapacuspa aucaycuy: 293
Tutayapacha: 180
Tuya: 163

Uchu: 12, 184, 247
Uchulla llacta: 353
Ucumari: 234
Uimpilla: 16
Uimpillapayay: 355
Uiñaychicuc: 259
Uincha: see headband
Uiroy Paccha: 90, 323
Ullco colla: 379
Uma puric: 180
Umamaytucuna: 353
Umu: 156–58
Una Chullo: 234
Unacaucho Inca: 337
Unancha: 131
Uncu: 162; See also ahuaqui uncu,
 casana uncu, and cuchu uncu
Unu Huallpa: 129
Upa: 269
Upacuna: 87–88
Uparuna: 269
Upiachic: 330
Ura huaca: 407
Urcos Calla: 97, 111
Urco Colla: 232, 253
Urco Huaranka: 100, 233, 243, 279
Urcochillay: see Southern Cross
Urcon: 164, 215, 412
Urcos: 15, 24–25, 28
Urquillos Valley: 165–66
Uru Ayllu: 37
Urubamba River: 170, 300, 314; see
 Vilcañota River

Yahuira: 97, 243
Yahuirca: 407
Yanacona: 42, 49, 162–64, 182, 193
Yanamarca: 123, 239
Yanapac: 156
Yanca ayllu: 11, 30; see also yanca yahuar
Yanca yahuar: 196
Yapa: 55
Yapac: 196, 331
Yarampuy Cancha: 378
Yasca: 64–65
Yatiri: 58
Yaurana: see Raurana
Yauri: 206, 229
Yauriratha: 384
Yaurisque: 98, 203, 384
Yauyo Indians: 187
Year, the new: 130, 137, 197–98

Ylla: 365
Yllapa: see illapa
Yucay: 81, 162, 164, 166, 190, 214, 216, 293, 298, 300–301, 334
Yucra Huallpa: 283
Yuncaypampa: 216
Yupa: 269
Yupanqui: 31, 268–69, 424
Yupay: 268
Yuptiracuy: 229
Yurac: 259
Yuyana: 270
Yuyay: 270
Yuyaycucuy: 46
Yuyayruna: 270

Zárate: 278
Zenith: see ticnu